Singapore in a Post-Kyoto World

The **Institute of Southeast Asian Studies (ISEAS)** was established as an autonomous organization in 1968. It is a regional centre dedicated to the study of socio-political, security and economic trends and developments in Southeast Asia and its wider geostrategic and economic environment. The Institute's research programmes are the Regional Economic Studies (RES, including ASEAN and APEC), Regional Strategic and Political Studies (RSPS), and Regional Social and Cultural Studies (RSCS).

ISEAS Publishing, an established academic press, has issued more than 2,000 books and journals. It is the largest scholarly publisher of research about Southeast Asia from within the region. ISEAS Publishing works with many other academic and trade publishers and distributors to disseminate important research and analyses from and about Southeast Asia to the rest of the world.

Singapore in a Post-Kyoto World

Energy, Environment and the Economy

TILAK K. DOSHI

LSEAS

INSTITUTE OF SOUTHEAST ASIAN STUDIES

Singapore

First published in Singapore in 2015 by
ISEAS Publishing
Institute of Southeast Asian Studies
30 Heng Mui Keng Terrace
Pasir Panjang
Singapore 119614

E-mail: publish@iseas.edu.sg
Website: <http://bookshop.iseas.edu.sg>

The responsibility for facts and opinions in this publication rests exclusively with the author and his interpretations do not necessarily reflect the views or the policy of the publishers or their supporters.

ISEAS Library Cataloguing-in-Publication Data

Doshi, Tilak.
   Singapore in a Post-Kyoto World : Energy, Environment and the Economy.
   (ISEAS Energy Series)
   1. Energy policy—Singapore.
   2. Energy development--Environmental aspects—Singapore.
   3. Power resources—Economic aspects—Singapore.
   I. Title.
HD9502 S62D72   2015

ISBN 978-981-4620-39-0 (soft cover)
ISBN 978-981-4620-67-3 (e-book, PDF)

Typeset by Superskill Graphics Pte Ltd
Printed in Singapore by Markono Print Media Pte Ltd

To my late father, who made it all possible,
and to my mother, the most courageous person I know.

CONTENTS

TABLES AND FIGURES

FIGURES

PREFACE

Twenty-five years ago, the publicly accessible literature of what can be broadly termed the "energy economics" of Singapore was practically non-existent. Outside of specialized trade publications, proprietary consultant reports and periodic assessments by government agencies often for an internal civil service and ministerial audience, there was little by way of information about how energy issues, at global, regional and domestic levels, were affecting Singaporeans. To be sure, it is also true that the demand for such information primarily emanated from those relative few who "did" energy, that is, those who were in the energy industry as businessmen, academics, or civil servants responsible for some area of activity in the industry.

Energy issues occupied policymakers whose bailiwick include aspects of the energy sector, ranging from managing state-owned power utilities and attracting foreign direct investments in the export-oriented oil refining and petrochemical industry to setting up competitive domestic markets for petrol and diesel. But outside of these government responsibilities, the energy scene in the first decades of independence was primarily a private sector one, revolving around oil. Coal, natural gas, and other primary fuels had little or no role to play in the early years of the city-state. Post-independence government policy with respect to energy sector issues, wrought in an environment which saw the loss of its Malayan hinterland in the Malaysian Federation in 1965, was essentially one of properly managing public utilities, providing a hospitable investment climate for large investments in an export-oriented downstream oil sector, and ensuring a competitive domestic retail market for transport fuels.

Singapore had, by the 1980s, emerged as one of the world's great oil refining and trading centres, with the "East of Suez" region within its sphere of influence. Yet, little systematic work was done on the country's role in energy affairs, unique among its developing country counterparts in Asia, Africa, and elsewhere. The city-state's policymaking went against the grain in much of its practice of economic development. It ensured that energy products were bought and sold in the domestic market at essentially global prices (adjusted for indirect taxes), in contrast to the common practice in developing countries of subsidizing energy fuels for social equity. Without a drop of oil of its own, Singapore also managed to attract large foreign investments in the capital-intensive oil refining and petrochemical manufacturing sectors in an export-oriented strategy. This was at a time when governments of most newly independent countries were busy trying to promote heavy industry by protectionist trade policies and import-substituting industrialization.[1]

The first publicly available report covering Singapore's petroleum industry and ancillary activities such as oil trading and ship bunkering was only published in 1989.[2] It was not until 1997, with the publication of Paul Horsnell's book *Oil in Asia*,[3] that the full range of the city-state's role in the global oil industry was assessed in a focused, analytical manner. In the past decade and a half since Horsnell's book, popular interest in, and concern with, energy affairs, has risen dramatically.

The rise of resource nationalism and the ensuing oil shocks emanating from the Middle East in the 1970s have long been factors of critical concern in energy policy circles. It is only more recently that the environmental impacts of energy use on regional and global climate systems have become of interest to wider sections of a richer and more educated population, both in Singapore and in other countries around the world. For Singapore, the traditional policy focus on "keeping the lights on" and in encouraging manufactured exports in high-value-added sectors (such as petrochemicals) has been expanded to include a myriad of energy-related initiatives that aim to meet the perceived needs of energy security and environmental sustainability while ensuring continued economic growth.

The purpose of this book is twofold. It is intended to introduce a host of energy-related discussions relevant to a wider group of readers who do not "do energy" for a living, yet are keenly interested in understanding the many complexities of modern industrial societies which need to balance economic, environmental, and security priorities of ordinary citizens. It aims to bring to the fore the many aspects of energy choices, in terms of both private behaviour and public policy, affecting Singapore. Comparative examples of energy issues and policy choices in other countries are discussed to set the context for the many similar challenges facing Singapore.

This book is also meant to serve as an introductory assessment of key energy-related issues for those who are planning to enrol in undergraduate courses in energy economics and energy policy studies, with a particular relevance for small advanced countries such as Singapore. The diverse issues affecting Singaporean consumers and businesses in making choices over energy-related economic activity and the role of government in setting an appropriate policy context are brought together within the covers of a single book. Hopefully, the interested general reader need not track down the many specialist journals and reports that focus on narrower aspects of this broad topic. If this book serves as the springboard for informed debate about key energy issues affecting Singapore and its surrounding region, it would have served its purpose.

Detailed notes and references are included for the interested reader to follow up on particular threads of argument. As many of the sections and chapters are based on reports and studies published at different times over the past few years by the ESI Economics Division, some of the data presented in tables and charts are outdated. However, rather than take more time to complete this book, the more urgent need was to have an earlier release. As much of the book is concerned with fast-evolving current affairs in the various areas of energy policy and international negotiations, it is hoped that the issues covered still offer a good guide to the reader interested in contemporary debates in the areas of energy and the environment. The emphasis throughout the book is on the underlying arguments and counterarguments about key issues raised by energy choices facing individuals and governments rather than on the contemporaneity of the data. In those areas of the energy industry which have undergone profound evolution over the past three to five years, the data available are primarily in scattered and varied formats in industry journals. Examples would include the global Liquefied Natural Gas (LNG) and solar photovoltaic (PV) industries. In such cases, much of the discussion is based on the latest data available in current news media and industry reports.

Notes

1. For an assessment of the city-state's development policies during the tenure of Goh Keng Swee, Singapore's founding "economic architect", see Tilak K. Doshi and Peter A. Coclanis, "The Economic Architect: Goh Keng Swee", in Lam Peng Er and Kevin Tan, eds., *Lee's Lieutenants: Singapore's Oil Guard* (NSW:

Allen & Unwin, 1999). See also Tilak Doshi and Peter Coclanis, "Goh Keng Swee: the Practicing Economist", *Business Times*, 16 June 2010, p. 20 <http://www.esi.nus.edu.sg/docs/default-document-library/2010jun16-bt-goh-keng-swee-the-practising-economist.pdf>.

2. Tilak K. Doshi, *Houston of Asia: The Singapore Petroleum Industry* (Singapore: Institute of Southeast Asian Studies, 1989). Other early studies include Shanker Sharma, "The Changing Structure of the Oil Market and Its Implications for Singapore's Oil Industry", *ASEAN Economic Bulletin* 4, no. 3 (1988): 271–86; Tilak Doshi, "The Energy Economy of a City State: Singapore", in *Energy Market and Policies in Asean*, edited by Shankar Sharma and Fereidun Fesharaki (Singapore: Institute of Southeast Asian Studies, 1991).

3. Paul Horsnell, *Oil in Asia: Markets, Trading, Refining and Deregulation* (Oxford: Oxford University Press, 1997).

ACKNOWLEDGEMENTS

This book would not have been possible without the contributions of an enthusiastic team of young analysts at the Economics Division of the Energy Studies Institute (ESI) at the National University of Singapore (NUS). The team included Neil D'Souza, Wu Fulan, Nahim bin Zahur, Lin Fangjun, Nguyen Linh, Belinda Salim, Oliver Yuen, Allan Loi, Alvin Chew, Teo Han Guan, Dickson Yeo and Andre Lambine. Indeed, working with the team — mainly graduates or post-graduate economists and engineers out of NUS or Nanyang Technological University (NTU), hailing from all corners of Asia, including Bangladesh, China, India, Indonesia, and Vietnam as well as home-grown Singaporeans — had been the best part of my duties as Chief Economist. It has been as much a learning experience for me, as it has been, I hope, for the team I have had the pleasure of working with. Various chapters or sections of chapters in this book have drawn on a range of economic analysis conducted over the past four years or so at the institute.

I have also been privileged during the past few years to have discussed some of the issues and arguments raised in this book with a range of dedicated professionals, which include Alan Bollard, S.K. Chou, Peter Coclanis, Peter Hartley, William Hogan, Michael Lynch, K.U. Menon, Eduardo Pedrosa, Michael Quah, Euston Quah, Robert Stavins, Jim Sweeney, and Eric Yep.

I am deeply grateful to Ambassador K. Kesavapany, previous Director of the Institute of Southeast Asian Studies (ISEAS). This book would not have been written without his encouragement and advice. I would also like to thank Khoo Chin Hean, previous Executive Director of the ESI, who also kindly encouraged me to write this book once it was proposed. My gratitude also goes to the late Kernial Singh Sandhu, a previous Director of ISEAS and Fereidun Fesharaki, both of whom, by founding an energy research programme in ISEAS, set me on track for a career in the oil and gas industry, supporting my postgraduate studies at the East-West Center in Honolulu, Hawaii, followed by an appointment at ISEAS as Head of its then newly established Energy Programme.

The views and opinions expressed in this book are not to be attributed to ESI, ISEAS or any other institutions or companies I was, or am, affiliated with. Mistakes and shortcomings in this book are, of course, mine alone.

ABBREVIATIONS

A*STAR	Agency for Science, Technology, and Research (Singapore)
ADB	Asian Development Bank
AEA	Association of European Airlines
AGD	Aviation Global Deal
AGF	Advisory Group on Climate Change Financing
AOSIS	Alliance of Small Island States
APAEC	ASEAN Plan of Action for Energy Cooperation
APEC	Asia-Pacific Economic Cooperation
APG	ASEAN Power Grid
ARA	Amsterdam-Rotterdam-Antwerp conurbation
ARs	IPCC's Assessment Reports
ASCOPE	ASEAN Council on Petroleum
ASEAN	Association of Southeast Asian Nations
B&L	borrowing and lending
BAU	business-as-usual
BCA	Building and Construction Authority (Singapore)
Bcf/d	billion cubic feet per day
BGSGM	BG Singapore Gas Management
bpd	barrels per day
CAAS	Civil Aviation Authority of Singapore
CAEP	Committee on Aviation Environmental Protection
CAFE	Corporate Average Fuel Economy standards
CAGR	compound annual growth rate
CBA	cost-benefit analysis
CCC	Committee on Climate Change (UK)
CCGTs	combined cycle gas turbines
CCS	carbon capture and sequestration
CDM	Clean Development Mechanism

CEPO	Clean Energy Programme Office (Singapore)
CER	certified emission reductions
CERP	Clean Energy Research Programme (Singapore)
CERT	Clean Energy Research and Testbedding Programme (Singapore)
CHP	combined heat and power
CNG	compressed natural gas
CO_2	carbon dioxide
CO_2e	carbon dioxide equivalent
COE	certificate of entitlement (Singapore)
COP	Conference of the Parties (UNFCCC)
DES	delivered ex ship
E_2PO	Energy Efficiency Programme Office (Singapore)
EAS	East Asia Summit
EASe	Energy Efficiency Improvement Assistance Scheme (Singapore)
EC	European Commission
EDB	Economic Development Board (Singapore)
EEDI	Energy Efficiency Design Index (IMO)
EENP	Energy Efficiency National Partnership (Singapore)
EEOI	Energy Efficiency Operational Indicator (IMO)
EIA	Energy Information Administration (US)
EIPO	Energy Innovation Programme Office (Singapore)
EITs	economies-in-transition
EMA	Energy Market Authority (Singapore)
EPA	Environmental Protection Agency (US)
EPG	Energy Policy Group (Singapore)
EPMA	Environmental Protection and Management Act (Singapore)
ERC	Energy Research Centre (South Africa)
ERI@N	Energy Research Institute @ Nanyang Technological University (Singapore)
ESCAP	Economic and Social Commission for Asia and the Pacific
ESU	Energy Sustainability Unit (National University of Singapore)
ETS	EU Emission Trading System
EU	European Union
EVs	electric vehicles

EVS	electricity vending system
FITs	feed-in tariffs
G-77	Group of Seventy-seven developing countries
G-8	Group of Eight
GATT	General Agreement on Tariffs and Trade
GCF	Green Climate Fund
GDP	gross domestic product
GFA	gross floor area
GHG	greenhouse gas
GIACC	Group on International Aviation and Climate Change
GMS	Greater Mekong Subregion
GNI	gross national income
GREET	Grant for Energy Efficient Technologies (Singapore)
GSA	gas sales agreement
$GtCO_2e$	gigatonnes of carbon dioxide equivalent
GTP	Global Trader Programme
GWh	gigawatt-hour
HDB	Housing Development Board (Singapore)
HDI	Human Development Index
HHI	Herfindahl-Hirschmann Index
IA	Investment Allowance Scheme (Singapore)
IATA	International Air Transport Association
ICAO	International Civil Aviation Organization
ICE	Intercontinental Exchange
IE	International Enterprise (Singapore)
IEA	International Energy Agency
IMCSD	Inter-Ministerial Committee for Sustainable Development (Singapore)
IMF	International Monetary Fund
IMO	International Maritime Organization
IPCC	Intergovernmental Panel on Climate Change
IPPR	Institute for Public Policy Research (UK)
IPP	independent power producer
JKM™	Japan Korea Marker
JTC	Jurong Town Corporation
LCOE	levelized cost of electricity
LNG	liquefied natural gas
LPG	liquefied petroleum gas

LTA	Land Transport Authority (Singapore)
MBI	market-based instrument
MEPS	Minimum Energy Performance Standards (Singapore)
METI	Ministry of Economy, Trade and Industry (Japan)
MEWR	Ministry of the Environment and Water Resources (Singapore)
MFA	Ministry of Foreign Affairs (Singapore)
MITI	Ministry of International Trade and Industry (Japan)
MLA	multilateral agencies
mmcf/d	million cubic feet per day
MOF	Ministry of Finance (Singapore)
MOT	Ministry of Transport (Singapore)
MPA	Maritime and Port Authority of Singapore
MRT	mass rapid transit (Singapore)
MRV	measurement, reporting and verification
MTI	Ministry of Trade and Industry (Singapore)
Mtoe	million tonnes of oil equivalent
Mtpa	million tonnes per annum
MW	megawatt
MWp	megawatt-peak
NAMA	Nationally Appropriate Mitigation Actions
NATO	North Atlantic Treaty Organization
NBP	National Balancing Point (UK)
NCCS	National Climate Change Secretariat (Singapore)
NEA	National Environment Agency (Singapore)
NEMS	National Energy Market of Singapore
NGO	non-governmental organization
NHTSA	National Highway Traffic Safety Administration (US)
NICs	newly industrializing countries
NOC	national oil company
NPRA	National Petrochemical and Refiners Association (US)
NPV	net present value
NRF	National Research Foundation (Singapore)
OCIMF	Oil Companies International Marine Forum
ODA	official development assistance
OECD	Organisation for Economic Co-operation and Development
OPEC	Organization of the Petroleum Exporting Countries
OTC	over-the-counter

PAP	People's Action Party (Singapore)
PNG	piped natural gas
ppm	parts per million
PRD	Parks and Recreation Department (Singapore)
PV	photovoltaic
R&D	research and development
REDD	Reduced Emissions from Deforestation and Forest Degradation programme (UN)
RFP	request for proposal
RPS	Renewable Portfolio Standards
SCS	Solar Capability Scheme (Singapore)
SERIS	Solar Research Institute of Singapore
SINERGY	Singapore Initiative in New Energy Technologies
SLNG	Singapore LNG Corporation
SO_2	sulphur dioxide
SOE	state-owned enterprise
SOMS	Straits of Malacca and Singapore
SPC	Singapore Petroleum Company
SSA	Singapore Shipping Association
SWF	sovereign wealth fund
TAGP	Trans-ASEAN Gas Pipeline
TEU	twenty-foot equivalent unit
TTF	Title Transfer Facility (Netherlands)
TUA	terminal user agreement
TWh	terawatt hours
UAE	United Arab Emirates
UN	United Nations
UNEP	United Nations Environmental Programme
UNFCCC	United Nations Framework Convention on Climate Change
VLFS	very large floating structure
VQS	Vehicle Quota System (Singapore)
WEC	World Energy Council
Wp	watt peak
WTO	World Trade Organization

INTRODUCTION

The curious task of economics is to demonstrate to men how little they really know about what they imagine they can design.

Friedrich August von Hayek

Policymakers in Singapore, like their counterparts elsewhere, are faced with balancing priorities in meeting the simultaneous requirements of economic growth, energy security and environmental sustainability. To be sure, each of these broad societal objectives can mean radically different things to different constituencies of the population. Academics, businessmen, and career civil servants, along with the ordinary man on the street, would naturally have their own perspectives and questions on what each of these objectives entail. How are such objectives ranked? What do they mean in terms of concrete policy initiatives and regulatory action on the part of government and how would such governmental action affect the daily lives of consumers and businesses? How are trade-offs (if they do occur) between one policy objective (say energy security) and another (say economic competitiveness) weighed and debated in public?

Policy challenges related to energy sector issues facing Singapore can be grouped into four broad areas. The first policy challenge, on the domestic front, is the perceived need to promote energy efficiency and 'renewable' energy initiatives among local households and businesses sensitive to new cost burdens on existing financial budgets and bottom lines. The potential for improving energy efficiency and adopting new energy technologies in cost-efficient ways has attracted the keen attention of policymakers. Can we reduce energy use and emissions while at the same time reducing consumer or production costs? Are there barriers to households or businessmen from discovering cheaper ways of using energy or reducing pollutants and carbon emissions? What can governments do to help overcome these barriers?

Policy attention in the international arena covers three concerns. The first lies in the need to participate in international and regional forums in a way which balances the need to commit to reasonable national targets in energy intensity and emissions reduction metrics while ensuring that the country's economic competitiveness and growth prospects are not compromised by inefficient or defective multilateral agreements. How would the financial costs of such agreements be allocated among the parties to such agreements? Who are the likely net donors and net recipients in possible future international or regional climate change agreements?

The second policy challenge on the international front concerns the means of handling the impacts of possible carbon emission mitigation measures, adopted voluntarily or as part of some future international treaty obligations, on Singapore's key export industries. As an extremely open, trade-oriented economy, the competitiveness of Singapore's export industries, some of which are energy intensive, is crucial to its economic growth prospects. Can Singapore-based oil refiners, petrochemical producers, and civil aviation and shipping companies be subject to international emission mitigation agreements while still keeping their competitive positions? What of those countries that are not party to such conventions or those which sign up but fail to implement measurement, reporting, and verification procedures? Are market-based incentives such as carbon taxes or carbon trading regimes the way to go in meeting international obligations or should governments have specific mandates to determine technology choices and consumer behaviour?

The third policy challenge in the international arena lies in the perennial concerns about enhancing energy security in the context of a small island-state importing all its energy needs. What steps should small countries like Singapore take to minimize vulnerabilities to energy supply disruptions? In the wake of 9/11 and the Arab Spring, this question has taken on an urgency not seen since the oil price shocks and the emergence of resource nationalism in the Middle East during the 1970s. The term has taken on a further dimension as climate change mitigation and adaptation measures begin to take higher billing in the policymakers' portfolio of "pressing security issues to deal with".

It is commonly observed that as a small "alternative energy disadvantaged" city-state without access to a number of low or zero emission energy technologies such as hydroelectric, wind, geothermal or nuclear power, Singapore's options are limited. Singapore's pattern of energy use and carbon dioxide (CO_2) emissions is examined in Chapter 1 with a view to describing the broad features of this "alternative energy disadvantage".

Chapter 2 sets the climate change negotiations from Copenhagen to Durban in context. It examines the economic and environmental criteria that have been raised by various academic, non-governmental and government analysts in climate change debates. The focus is on how to "widen" and "deepen" international participation, including non-OECD (Organisation for Economic Co-operation and Development) countries, in emission mitigation and climate change adaptation efforts. The chapter notes the implications for Singapore, a high per capita income non-OECD city-state.

The highly contested issue of "who pays?" and "who receives?" in climate change finance is the subject of Chapter 3. The transfer of financial resources and the distribution of the financial burden of emission mitigation and adaptation efforts are key areas of contention in climate change negotiations. The criteria which will qualify United Nation (UN) members as either donors or recipients as promulgated by different multilateral institutions, non-governmental organizations (NGOs), academics and government negotiators are discussed in the chapter.

Chapter 4 examines the likely impact of possible future international climate change agreements on Singapore's role as a regional and global hub for shipping and fuel bunkering, oil refining and petrochemicals, and civil aviation. As the world's most trade-oriented country, the impact of possible future international emission mitigation regulations on these export-oriented industries would have profound and far-reaching impacts on Singapore.

In Chapter 5, attention is turned to the government's five-pronged energy-policy framework meant to (i) promote competitive energy markets; (ii) diversify energy sources; (iii) enhance energy efficiency; (iv) develop Singapore's energy industries and invest in energy R&D; and (v) step up international and regional cooperation on energy security issues.

The final chapter draws conclusions on the need to balance competing policy objectives in meeting societal goals of economic development, energy security and environmental sustainability. Rigorous definitions of these oft-proclaimed goals form a critical first step towards understanding their implications for societal choice and policymaking. It is the contention of the book that poor understanding of key terms such as "energy security" and "environmental sustainability" often gets in the way of an informed policy debate on the many issues involved. Clarity of policy objectives is not just a matter of "good science", though this is a requirement. Good economics is critical — policy formulation and implementation require an informed way of valuing costs and benefits in the context of market-based economies and open societies where consumer choice and competitive politics matter.

1

ECONOMY, ENERGY, AND EMISSIONS

Singapore is among the most affluent and urbanized countries in the world. It rapidly grew from a colonial island-entrepôt with a gross domestic product (GDP) per capita of US$428 in 1960 to a vibrant global city-state with a GDP per capita of US$55,183 in 2013 at market prices.[1] Reclamation of land has resulted in the expansion of Singapore's land area to approximately 710.3 km² in 2009 from 581.5 km² in the 1960s. With an estimated population of 5.08 million in 2009, Singapore's population density stands at 7,100/km². This makes it one of the most densely populated countries in the world.[2]

In international rankings of per capita carbon dioxide (CO_2) emissions (as in Table 1.1 below), Singapore is comparable to such developed Asian industrial economies as South Korea and Japan, significantly lower than resource-rich Organisation for Economic Co-operation and Development (OECD) economies such as Australia and the United States, and much lower than the rich, small petroleum-based states such as Qatar and the United Arab Emirates (UAE). As an affluent city-state, Singapore's per capita emissions are significantly higher than the more populous,

Table 1.1
International Rankings of Per Capita CO_2 Emissions, 2010

Country	(tonnnes)
Qatar	48.3
UAE	26.0
Brunei	15.1
Australia	19.0
USA	19.0
Taiwan*	11.9
South Korea	9.9
Singapore	9.6
Japan	9.5
Israel	8.9
Hong Kong	6.1
Thailand	3.4
Malaysia	5.9
China	4.3
Brazil	1.8
India	1.1
World	4.3

*Data for Taiwan is for 2009.
Sources: International Energy Agency "CO_2 Emissions from Fuel Combustion" 2011. CIA World Factbook 2009 (for Taiwan).

middle-income developing countries such as its neighbours Malaysia and Thailand, and much higher than China and India with their huge populations and lower per capita incomes.

The key attribute of Singapore's uniqueness in terms of energy and emissions is that it is a city-state, in a world of generally larger, less-urbanized countries. This fact of high population density and urbanization skews per capita indicators of wealth, energy use, and CO_2 emissions. In any consistent ranking, Singapore would need to be appropriately compared to other global cities and their immediate suburban environs such as Hong Kong, Dubai, London, Houston, or Sydney. And even when such comparisons are made, allowances are required for the fact that for most of these cities, actual emissions caused by households and businesses in the cities are associated with electricity which is usually generated *outside* city limits.[3]

In Table 1.2, this is adjusted for by taking into account emissions from end-use rather than primary fuel combustion. This considers all emissions accounted for by city dwellers, even when the actual location of emissions caused might be outside city limits. While the study cited does not include Singapore in its sample, a simple ranking of cities by end-use emissions is given in the table, with Singapore's *national* per capita emissions incorporated as a memo item.[4] Singapore, along with London, causes the lowest emissions in per capita terms, in comparison to all the other cities in the sample. Developing country cities like Bangkok and Cape Town, as well as New York and Toronto, are higher, at between 10.5 and 11.6 tonnes. In general, only Denver is an outlier,[5] as all other cities fall quite close around the 10 tonnes per capita level. Singapore is not inordinately out of range of this sample.

As importantly, Singapore is the only city-state in the sample, and hence is disadvantaged from being able to consider alternative sources of energy which require a large hinterland for location and siting purposes such as hydroelectric, wind, or nuclear power. Chew Tai Soo, previously Singapore's chief negotiator on climate change issues, states it as follows: "Small countries like Singapore or the Bahamas lack the alternative energy potential, or as I would call it, [are] alternative energy disadvantaged....

Table 1.2
Ranking by End-use Emissions within Cities, 2005–6

	CO_2/capita (tonnes)
Bangkok	10.7
Cape Town	11.6
Denver	21.5
London	9.6
New York	10.5
Toronto	11.6
memo:	
Singapore	9.6

Sources: IEA, "CO_2 Emissions from Fuel Combustion", 2008; Kennedy, C., et al., "Greenhouse Gas Emissions from Global Cities", *Environmental Science and Technology* 43, no. 19 (2009).

The potential for further reductions [of carbon emissions] in Singapore is less than a country, say South Korea which has space enough for 50 per cent of its power to be generated by nuclear or renewable energy sources."[6]

Figure 1.1 shows the energy consumption of the end-use sectors for 1990 and 2010 in million tonnes of oil equivalent (Mtoe). Final energy consumption went up from 5 Mtoe to 13.2 Mtoe, growing at a compound annual growth rate (CAGR) of 5 per cent. This is somewhat more than half of the annual 9.2 per cent growth rate of total GDP over the same period, from US$38.8 billion to US$227.4 billion. At 7.6 Mtoe, "non-energy use" accounts for well over half of total energy end-use in 2010, primarily due to the large export-oriented petrochemical sector using naphtha as a feedstock. Other non-energy use products include bitumen and lubricants. Transport is the next-largest end-use sector in Singapore, followed by "others" (which includes residential, commercial, and public services) and industry.

Figure 1.1
Energy Consumption in End-use Sectors

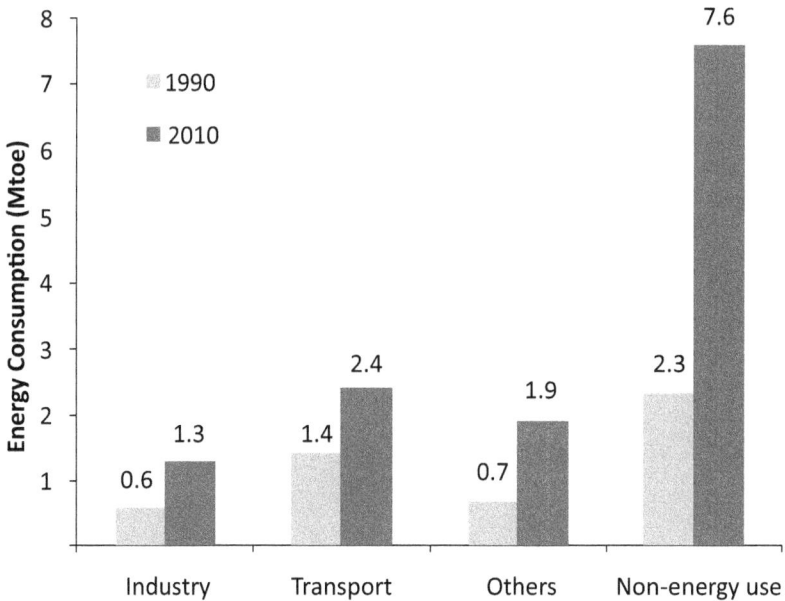

Source: IEA Energy Balances of Non-OECD Countries (2011).

The increase in energy consumption has been accompanied by greater CO_2 emissions. However, on a per capita basis, CO_2 emissions reached some levelling off since the mid-1990s, keeping mainly just below the 12 tonne level (see Fig 1.2). There has been a decline since 2006–7, reaching to just over 11 tonnes, a level not much higher than that reached in the early 1990s. The most recent data sourced from the International Energy Agency (IEA) shows a sharp upturn since 2009, probably due to a range of reasons such as the upturn in economic activity after the worst of the financial crisis was over, a recent spate of energy-intensive petrochemical investments, and the decline in the rate of inward labour migration.

A COMPARISON OF EMISSIONS BY ECONOMIC SECTORS

Table 1.3 below shows sectoral contributions to CO_2 emissions for the four Asian economies — the city-states Hong Kong and Singapore, along with Taiwan and South Korea — which have commonly been referred

Figure 1.2
CO_2 Emissions Per Capita (tCO_2)

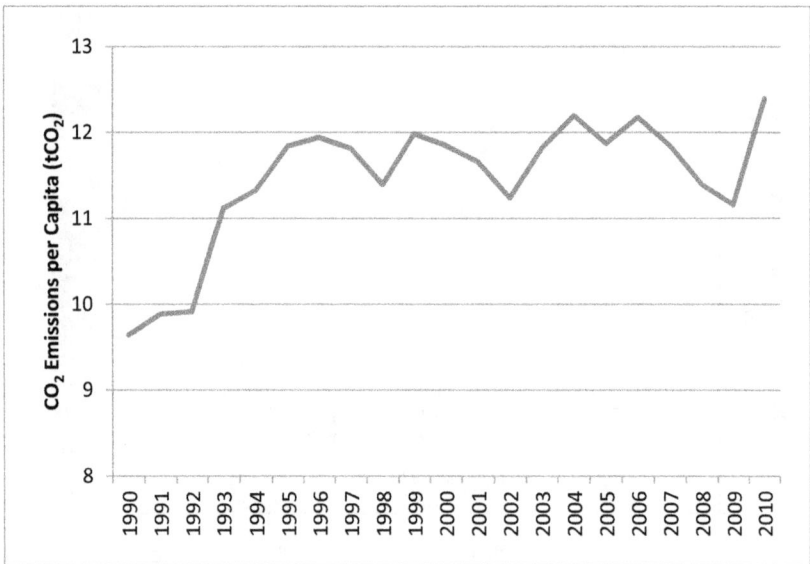

Source: International Energy Agency, "CO_2 Emissions from Fuel Combustion", 2012.

Table 1.3

CO_2 Emissions by Sector, Select Countries

	CO_2 emissions by sector (2010) (million tonnes)				
	Singapore	Taiwan	South Korea	Hong Kong	UAE
Total (a)	62.9	270.2	563.1	41.5	154.0
Percentage composition					
Electricity and Heat Production (b)	36%	56%	50%	67%	38%
Other Energy Industries (c)	10%	5%	6%	0%	1%
Manufacturing Industries and Construction (d)	41%	22%	18%	14%	44%
Transport (e)	13%	13%	15%	13%	17%
Road Transport	13%	13%	15%	13%	17%
Residential, Commercial and Public Services (f)	1%	4%	11%	6%	0%
Others	0%	2%	6%	2%	0%
Memo Items (million tonnes):					
International Marine Bunkers (g)	125.9	5.5	28.7	38.6	41.4
International Aviation (h)	17.0	6.3	11.9	16.2	12.4

Notes:

(a) Emissions calculated using a Sectoral Approach include emissions only when the fuel is actually combusted in the sector.

(b) Main Activity Producer Electricity and Heat contains the sum of emissions from main activity producer electricity generation, combined heat and power generation, and heat plants. Main activity producers (formerly known as public utilities) are defined as those undertakings whose primary activity is to supply the public. They may be publicly or privately owned. Emissions from own on-site use of fuel are included.

(c) Other Energy Industries contains emissions from fuel combusted in petroleum refineries, for the manufacture of solid fuels, coal mining, oil and gas extraction and other energy-producing industries.

(d) Manufacturing Industries and Construction contains the emissions from combustion of fuels in industry. This segment includes Iron and Steel, Chemical and Petrochemical, Non-Ferrous Metals, Non-Metallic Minerals, Transport Equipment, Machinery, Mining and Quarrying, Food and Tobacco, Paper, Pulp and Printing, Wood and Wood Products, Construction, Textile and Leather, Non-specified Industry and Non-Energy Use.

(e) Transport contains emissions from the combustion of fuel for all transport activity, regardless of the sector, except for international marine bunkers and international aviation. This includes domestic aviation, domestic navigation, road, rail and pipeline transport.

(f) Other Sectors contains the emissions from commercial/institutional activities, residential, agriculture/forestry, fishing and other emissions not specified elsewhere.

(g) International Marine Bunkers contains emissions from fuels burned by ships of all flags that are engaged in international navigation. The international navigation may take place at sea, on inland lakes and waterways, and in coastal waters. Consumption by ships engaged in domestic navigation is excluded.

(h) International Aviation contains emissions from fuels used by aircraft for international aviation. Fuels used by airlines for their road vehicles are excluded. Emissions from international aviation should be excluded from the national totals.

Source: IEA CO_2 Emissions from Fuel Combustion — Highlights 2012 (<http://www.iea.org/media/freepublications/2012/CO2Highlights2012.xls>).

to by economists as "newly industrializing countries" (NICs) as well as the UAE. The UAE is included as it shares some key characteristics with Singapore.[7] For Taiwan, South Korea, and Hong Kong, power generation is the major contributor to carbon emissions, accounting for at least half of the total. For Hong Kong, it accounts for two-thirds of all emissions, reflecting the service-intensive nature of the city. At the lower end, power generation accounts for 36 and 38 per cent of total carbon emissions in Singapore and the UAE respectively.

At first sight, the high share of manufacturing and construction sectors in total CO_2 emission in both the UAE and Singapore (41 and 44 per cent of total emissions respectively) is contrary to expectations. Both countries are not known as manufacturing-based economies in the sense that South Korea and Taiwan are. However, the very significant petrochemical investments (included in the manufacturing sector) in Singapore in recent years explain the very high share of the manufacturing sector in total emissions.[8] For the UAE, energy-intensive installations such as aluminium smelting and water desalination, explain the high contribution of the manufacturing sector. And both economies have had major construction sector activity in the past decade, particularly in Dubai where, until the financial crisis led to a dramatic fall in property values in 2009, the scale of residential and commercial property construction was unprecedented by regional standards.

Singapore also stands out among the sample of countries in the relative size of CO_2 emissions in the "Other Energy Industries" category. This category contains emissions from fuel combusted in oil refineries and petrochemical plants, as well as other energy-extractive industries such as coal mining, oil and gas extraction, etc. As a country with no mineral resources, Singapore of course does not have energy-extractive industries. While this category accounts for between 0 and 6 per cent of total CO_2 emission for the other countries in the sample, it accounts for 10 per cent of all carbon emissions in Singapore. This reflects Singapore's role as one of the world's largest conurbations of export-oriented petroleum refining and petrochemicals, far in excess of Singapore's domestic requirements for oil and chemical products.

It should be noted here that CO_2 emissions reported in the table are on the basis of where primary fuels are actually combusted, the "sectoral approach".[9] Households or businesses are therefore not accounted for as sources of emissions for their use of electricity, a secondary energy fuel, as combustion of fuel is accounted for in the power generation sector. So, for example, efficiency improvements in the household or commercial sector gained by better household appliances or better air-conditioning systems cannot be measured directly; such efficiency improvements need to be estimated as potential decreases in future demand for electricity relative to the projected demand under a "business-as-usual" (BAU) scenario. Its emission reduction impact can then be estimated on the basis of reduced need for electricity (which gives rise to emissions) compared to the BAU baseline.

Table 1.4 below illustrates a hypothetical 10 per cent efficiency improvement in terms of emission reduction in each sector. Given the large contribution of the power generation and manufacturing sectors to total emissions, a 10 per cent cut leads to between 2.3 and 2.6 million tonnes of reduced emissions. In contrast, a 10 per cent cut in the transport or the

Table 1.4
Hypothetical Emission Reduction Impacts by Sector

		10% efficiency improvement (mn tonnes CO_2)
Total emissions (mn tonnes CO_2)	62.9	6.3
Electricity and Heat Production[b]	36%	2.3
Other Energy Industries[c]	10%	0.6
Manufacturing Industries and Construction[d]	41%	2.6
Transport[e]	13%	0.8
Road	13%	0.8
Residential, Commercial and Public Services[f]	1%	0.1
Others	0%	
Memo Items:		
International Marine Bunkers[g]	125.9%	12.60
International Aviation[h]	17.0	1.70
CO_2 emissions with electricity and heat allocated to consuming sectors		
Residential	6.4%	0.40
Commercial/public	16.5%	1.04
Industry	53.4%	3.36

Source and Notes: See Table 1.3.

residential, commercial or public services sectors leads only to between 0.1 and 0.8 million tonnes. Under the "memo items", the enormous impact of emission cuts in shipping stands out, since marine bunkers sold in the Singapore market have a carbon emitting content (though not emitted within Singaporean territory) that is double (126 million tonnes) that of the country's entire CO_2 emissions (62.9 million tonnes). It should be noted however that emissions from marine bunkers happen outside Singapore's jurisdiction and so are not counted as part of the country's national emissions.

Emissions by sector which include not only direct combustion of fuels but also the use of electricity and heat (as secondary energy) are given in the bottom three rows of the table. A 10 per cent efficiency improvement in the manufacturing and construction sector, including the use of electricity and heat, leads to a reduction of 3.4 million tonnes in emissions. For the residential sector, a 10 per cent emissions reduction amounts to only 0.4 million tonnes, even when use of electricity is included. The 10 per cent cuts in the table are purely illustrative of relative carbon-intensities of various sectors, whether measuring direct (or "primary") combustion only or including the use of electricity (or "secondary" use of energy). It would not make sense to try to cut emissions equally across all sectors. Efficient, least-cost paths through emission reduction trajectories for the economy would require different levels of emission reduction rates across different sectors, depending on where it would be most effective to cut emissions at least cost.[10]

Accounting for about 41 per cent of total CO_2 emissions in Singapore, the manufacturing and construction sector is the largest contributor of CO_2 emissions after electricity and heat production. According to IEA classification, manufacturing industries and construction emissions include those from "Iron and Steel, Chemical and Petrochemical, Non-Ferrous Metals, Non-Metallic Minerals, Transport Equipment, Machinery, Mining and Quarrying, Food and Tobacco, Paper, Pulp and Printing, Wood and Wood Products, Construction, Textile and Leather, Non-specified Industry and Non-Energy Use". Given the range of distinct manufacturing industries in the sector, some energy-intensive and some not, it is difficult to make generalizations about efficiency improvement or emission reduction programmes for the sector as a whole. Nevertheless, it is clear that Singapore's petrochemical sector, which includes some of the world's largest export-oriented integrated plants, is a major source of the emissions attributed to the manufacturing and construction sector.

The other industries included in the IEA definition of manufacturing and construction play a minor, if any, role in Singapore's economy.

Singapore's sole source of primary energy in 1990 was oil. Oil consumption increased rapidly from 11.4 Mtoe in 1990 to 21.8 Mtoe in 2005 at an annual growth rate of 4.4 per cent. Singapore's power sector has substituted fuel oil with natural gas substantially since 1990. Natural gas's share grew after the construction of pipelines to fuel natural gas–fired power plants. The first of pipeline-sourced gas from Malaysia in 1991 was followed by two more pipelines from Indonesia. Consumption of natural gas increased from 0.4 Mtoe in 1992 to 5.9 Mtoe in 2007 at a growth rate of 20.7 per cent per annum. Natural gas, which accounted for 28 per cent of electricity generation in Singapore in 2001, grew rapidly to supply almost three-quarters of Singapore's electricity by 2005.[11]

Figure 1.3 below shows the percentage distribution of power generation by fuel source (natural gas and fuel oil measured on a tonnes of oil equivalent basis). Natural gas has grown from accounting for 15 per cent of power generation in 2000 to over 70 per cent by 2005. According to the Energy Market Authority, 79 per cent of electricity was generated from natural

Figure 1.3
Power Generation by Fuel Source

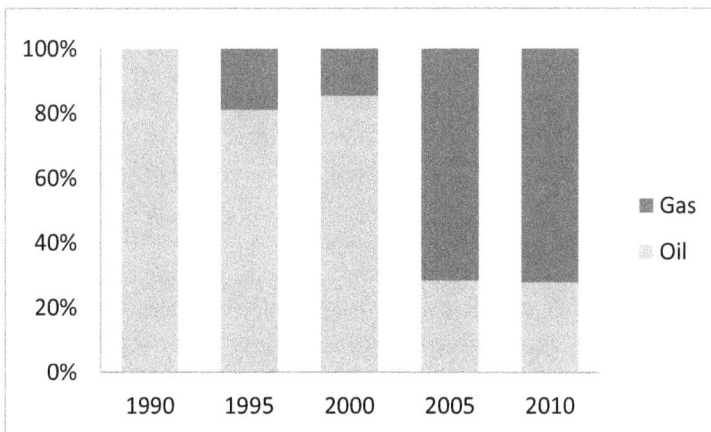

Source: IEA, "Energy Statistics of Non-OECD Countries", 2012.

gas in 2007, 18 per cent from fuel oil and the remaining 3 per cent from refuse generation and some diesel use.[12] With respect to improving (i.e., lowering) the carbon intensity of power generation in Singapore, most of the efficiency gains have already been achieved by the rapid switch to natural gas from oil. Further reducing the rate of CO_2 emissions appreciably from power generation can only occur with further substitution of fuel oil with natural gas. As natural gas is already supplying over 85–90 per cent of total fuel used (on a tonnes of oil equivalent basis) in the sector, future emissions reduction from the power sector by fuel switching will consequently be limited in scope.[13]

After "manufacturing and construction" and the "power generation and heat production" sectors, the "road transport" sector accounts for the largest amount of CO_2 emissions, at 13 per cent of total CO_2 emissions. The lack of competitive alternatives to fossil fuel use in the transportation sector is an established feature of the technologies currently available. The conversion of vehicles to the use of compressed natural gas (CNG), use of "bio-fuels" such as ethanol, hybrid electric-gasoline, and electricity are some of the methods being implemented in different countries around the world, but the make-over of existing fleets of vehicles everywhere will be relatively slow, and emission-reduction programmes in the transportation sector are inherently long term with significant uncertainties in technological trajectories in the sector. As a densely populated city-state, Singapore does have advantages in improving the energy efficiencies of various public transport modes. Singapore's (primarily gas-fuelled) electricity-powered mass rapid transit (MRT) system, for example, would be relatively efficient in terms of passenger-miles travelled.

The "Other Energy Industries" category contains emissions from fuel combusted in petroleum refineries, accounting for 10 per cent of total emissions in 2010. The use of petroleum in the form of by-products such as waste gas or "refinery gas" and petroleum coke accounts for a significant portion of the CO_2 emissions in this sector. As an energy-intensive sector, the petroleum refining sector also emits greenhouse gases (GHG) in using both electricity and gas for its power and heating needs.

In summary, Singapore's energy economy can be characterized as one of complete dependence on oil and gas imports, both for its domestic energy consumption and for its very large export-oriented oil refineries and petrochemical industry. While it shares some characteristics of a less energy-intensive, services-oriented economy like that of Hong Kong, the large role played by the oil refining and petrochemicals complex in Singapore's economy accounts for a large proportion of the country's "carbon footprint". Despite the lack of an energy-intensive heavy industrial sector (producing industrial commodities such as cement, steel, aluminium, glass, and paper and pulp), Singapore's regional export role as a pre-eminent oil refiner and petrochemical producer raises its per capita emissions to relatively high levels, comparable to major industrial countries such as South Korea and Japan.

Notes

1. Department of Statistics Singapore, "Statistics" <http://www.singstat.gov.sg/statistics/>.
2. Ibid.
3. See, for instance, Christopher Kennedy et al., "Greenhouse Gas Emissions from Global Cities", *Environmental Science and Technology* 43, no. 19 (2009).
4. Singapore's *national* per capita emission is, by definition, the same as the *city* per capita emission numbers listed in the table to the extent that Singapore is a city-state with characteristics akin to a large city and suburban environs. The study refers to GHG emissions, while the Singapore measure is of CO_2 emissions from the IEA database. However, as CO_2 constitutes the dominating share of GHG emissions, this difference does not detract from the illustrative value of the comparison made in the table.
5. See Christopher Kennedy et al., "Greenhouse Gas Emissions from Global Cities", *Environmental Science and Technology* 43, no. 19 (2009) for some of the reasons underlying Denver's high carbon footprint.
6. See David Fogarty, "Singapore Says to curb CO_2, Steps Depend on UN Pact", Reuters, 8 September 2009 <http://uk.reuters.com/article/2009/09/08/us-summit-singapore-idUSTRE5871NV20090908>. Singapore Prime Minister Lee Hsien Loong also spoke of being "alternative-energy disadvantaged". See the transcript of PM Lee's speech at the launch of "Clean and Green Singapore 20" held on 30 October 2009, available at <http://www.pmo.gov.sg/mediacentre/speech-mr-lee-hsien-loong-prime-minister-launch-clean-and-green-singapore-2010-30>.
7. Dubai, an emirate within the UAE, is a regional entrepôt like Hong Kong and Singapore, while Fujairah, another UAE emirate, is a major ship-bunkering centre like Singapore.
8. See Tony Chua, "Singapore Houses Shell's Largest Petrochemical Project", *Singapore Business Review*, 6 May 2010 <http://sbr.com.sg/energy-offshore/news/singapore-houses-shell%E2%80%99s-largest-petrochemical-project>.

See also ExxonMobil, "ExxonMobil Commissions Singapore Petrochemical Plant Expansion", news release, 29 December 2012 <http://www.exxonmobil.com.sg/AP-English/news_releases_20130103.aspx>. In 2006, for instance, manufacturing and construction accounted for less than 12 per cent of total emissions in Singapore. See International Energy Agency, CO_2 *Emissions from Fuel Combustion: Highlights, 2008 Edition* (Paris: OECD/IEA, 2008).

9. The sectoral approach is in contrast to the "reference approach". The reference method estimates fossil fuel consumption by adjusting national aggregate fuel production data for imports, exports, and stock changes rather than relying on end-user consumption surveys. "The basic principle is that once carbon-based fuels are brought into a national economy, they are either saved in some way (e.g., stored in products, kept in fuel stocks) or combusted, and therefore the carbon in them is oxidized and released into the atmosphere". See "Annex 4 IPCC Reference Approach for Estimating CO_2 Emissions from Fossil Fuel Combustion", available at <http://www.epa.gov/climatechange/Downloads/ghgemissions/US-GHG-Inventory-2013-Annex-4-Reference-Approach.pdf>.

10. In economic terms, optimal investments in CO_2 emission reductions across sectors would be allocated such that the marginal benefits equal the marginal costs of CO_2 abatement in each sector.

11. International Energy Agency, *Energy Statistics of Non-OECD Countries* (Paris: OECD/IEA, 2009).

12. See Energy Market Authority, "Statement of Opportunities for Electricity Industry 2008", n.d.

13. Local press reports have noted plans for a "clean coal" power plant but it is not clear what the impact would be on carbon emission rates. See, for instance, Clarissa Oon, "Singapore's First 'Clean Coal' Power Plant to be Built", *Straits Times*, 26 September 2008.

2

CLIMATE CHANGE NEGOTIATIONS:
From Copenhagen to Durban
via Cancun

Each country's specific evolving pattern of energy-economy interactions will determine how various proposals on greenhouse gas (GHG) emission reductions will impact the economy. In preparing their negotiating positions, governments need to be informed of quantitative impacts on costs, prices, and export competitiveness, both at the sectoral and national levels. Planning agencies typically implement computable energy-economy models to deliver informed assessments of the probable impacts of various policies on emission mitigation and energy technology choices.

While quantitative estimates of various energy-economy models set a "baseline" of expected impacts that planning agencies need to know, negotiations in a *strategic* context, where one party's optimal choice is a function of the choice of other parties, are the focus of games-theoretic models in economics. Climate change is posed in these models as the ultimate global commons problem, with damages imposed on life and property globally being independent of the actual location of GHG emissions anywhere on the planet. Strategic behaviour is inherently hard to model, however, and game theory models are often highly abstract.[1] However, a summary of the main results of the literature is useful in framing the overall context of United Nations Framework Convention on Climate Change (UNFCCC) negotiations.

Given that participants to an international environmental treaty are sovereign nation-states in the United Nations (UN) system, and given the absence of a supranational judicial institution with enforcement powers, the incentives to free ride would be strong for all participants.[2] Given free ride incentives, countries will see advantages in being the last to commit to policy targets, hence risking coordination failure in negotiating agreements.[3] In a large group (such as the UN), the incentives to free ride make the existence of a universal agreement, of net benefit to all countries and in stable equilibrium, highly unlikely. It is more likely that self-enforcing agreements emerge among limited groups of countries within different coalitions of different sizes. Since a global binding agreement is unlikely to be signed by all countries, a more credible scenario is that several parallel agreements emerge over time, much like the case in current international trade and economic cooperation negotiations. The failure in concluding World Trade Organization (WTO) agreements over a range of issues has led to continuous multilateral summits and negotiations for regional economic integration and a multiplicity of investment and trading agreements and blocs.[4] The potential emergence of parallel "climate blocs", based on regional and other common interests, has been posed by some observers. David Victor calls this outcome the "variable geometry of participation and effort" where the most serious negotiation efforts concentrate on the countries whose participation matters most. He cites the examples of the General Agreement on Tariffs and Trade (GATT), the EU, and the North Atlantic Treaty Organization (NATO) as examples of viable and self-enforcing international agreements.[5] Hence the necessity to design negotiation mechanisms leading to self-enforcing agreements, i.e., agreements to control climate change voluntarily signed by a group of countries that will credibly commit to keep climate change under control.

At the national level, practical political considerations, especially those involving political lobbies and domestic special interest groups, play a critical role in dictating actions governments are willing to undertake. Ultimately, the interplay of domestic interest groups and policy compromises among competing claims in the national capitals of the largest GHG-emitting countries will set the parameters for climate change negotiations. When looking at negotiating positions of specific countries, the political limits to government autonomy in making policy commitments set by domestic constituencies and vested interests needs to be part of the analysis.

The developed and developing countries hold widely divergent views and negotiating positions over a range of unresolved issues related to global climate change. Each country will have its own specific pattern of energy-economy interactions. This will determine how proposed GHG emission constraints will affect the competitiveness of different industry sectors and the welfare of different constituencies. Estimates of economy-wide impacts of specific emission mitigation policies on costs, prices, and export competitiveness can then guide each government's policy response to various emission mitigation and adaptation proposals being negotiated. At the extreme, small island nations, for example, might find the prospects of rising sea levels to be of overriding importance in their approach to global climate change negotiations. An appropriate government policy response also requires an assessment of the wider context of international and regional negotiating positions of the various constituencies being represented, including not only national governments but also non-governmental organizations (NGO) and business groups representing an array of interests.

Among the many questions in climate change negotiations that Singapore policymakers face, the following are only the most obvious: what are the different negotiating positions of various developed and developing countries that will play a key role in climate change negotiations? What are the economic, social, and environmental indicators that are used by multilateral agencies, research institutions, and national authorities to group countries and proposed levels of participation in a post-Kyoto global climate policy regime? Will Singapore's uniqueness in terms of its key environmental and economic attributes support any particular policy position on various core issues? What is Singapore's optimal position in climate change negotiations, given its membership of various regional groups and multilateral institutions and its congruence of interests (or lack thereof) with various interest groups and country blocs? How might participation in a post-Kyoto global climate change policy regime benefit Singapore, and what modes of participation will be most advantageous to Singapore's interests?

2.1 IPCC, UNFCCC AND THE KYOTO PROTOCOL

The Intergovernmental Panel on Climate Change (IPCC) was established by the World Meteorological Organization and the United Nations Environmental Programme (UNEP) in 1988. The IPCC convenes thousands of natural and social scientists periodically to review evidence on global climate change. It has issued five major Assessment Reports (ARs), with each review finding stronger evidence of human impact on the global climate. According to its Fourth AR, the IPCC stated that the "warming of the climate system is unequivocal, and is now evident from observations of global average air and ocean temperatures, widespread melting of snow and ice, and rising global mean sea level".[6] With 90 per cent confidence, the IPCC attributed most of the warming of the past half century to increasing anthropogenic GHG emissions.

In the "Summary for Policymakers" of the Fifth AR released in September 2013, the IPCC maintained its central message communicated in its previous AR issued in 2007:

> It is extremely likely that human influence has been the dominant cause of the observed warming since the mid-20th century. The evidence for this has grown, thanks to more and better observations, an improved understanding of the climate system response, and improved climate models.[7]

According to media reports, the tone of AR5's first Working Group Report is considerably stronger than its predecessors. Reuters called it the "strongest warning yet", while the *Financial Times* found it "a departure from the more cautiously worded findings in its past reports". Between AR4 and AR5, however, there were a number of scandals that undermined the authority and validity of some of the more alarmist IPCC pronouncements. The "near-unanimity" of scientific opinion as represented by the ARs regarding the risk of irreversible climate change and the scale of potential costs involved has been subject to increasing scrutiny and scepticism among climate scientists.[8]

For instance, AR4 warned that the Himalayan glaciers would disappear by 2035, which sparked a furore among environmental scientists.[9] In 2009, an email chain between IPCC researchers was leaked, suggesting that scientific data was manipulated and figures compromised for the sake of producing a coherent report. Critics accused the IPCC of "evasion of freedom of information law, secret deals done during the writing of reports ... a cover-up of uncertainties in the key research findings and the misuse of scientific peer review to silence critics".[10]

IPCC Fourth Assessment Report

The broad long-term goal of capping global average temperatures to an increase of no more than 2°C is underpinned by IPCC's Fourth Assessment Report. According to the models employed by the report's authors, this would require a global steady-state limit of 450 parts per million (ppm) of carbon dioxide (CO_2) emissions.[11] According to AR4, given emission reductions in industrialized countries of at least 80 per cent by 2050, the developing countries would need to achieve a "substantial deviation from baseline emissions" by 2020, amounting to a 15 to 30 per cent reduction below projected business-as-usual (BAU) level of emissions.[12]

Table 2.1 below shows the estimated emission cuts required from industrialized countries, relative to their 1990 emission levels, and from developing countries relative to the BAU levels, consistent with a steady state 450 ppm GHG concentration level.

Despite very low levels of *per capita* emissions, the developing countries will account for over half of global CO_2 emissions by 2020 if not before.[13] According to the United States Energy Information Administration (U.S. EIA), non-OECD (Organisation for Economic Co-operation and Development) countries will account for more than 60 per cent of energy-related global CO_2 emissions by 2020, from 53 per cent in 2006.[14] Some of the world's largest and most rapidly growing economies, including China, India, Brazil, South Africa, Indonesia, South Korea, and Mexico,

Table 2.1
Emission Cuts and Equilibrium

| | Emission cuts required, 450 ppm steady state equilibrium | | |
	2020	2050	baseline for cuts
Annex-I	25–40%	80–90%	1990 emission levels
non Annex-I	15–30%	50–60%	deviation from BAU levels

Source: den Helzen, M. and N. Hoehne (2008), "Reductions of GHG Emissions in Annex 1 and Non-Annex 1 Countries for Meeting Concentration Stabilization Targets", Climate Change 91, pp. 249–74, December 2008.

have no obligations to reduce emissions under the Kyoto Protocol. China overtook the United States as the world's largest emitter of CO_2 in 2006, with each country accounting for about one fifth of global emissions. The rate of growth of China's emissions is of special concern: from 8 per cent of global CO_2 in 1981, it accounted for 14 per cent in 2002, 21 per cent by 2008, and 24 per cent in 2010.[15]

The Kyoto Protocol

In 1990, based on IPCC's first assessment, the United Nations (UN) General Assembly initiated negotiations for a multilateral framework to address global climate change issues, resulting in the establishment of the UNFCCC in 1992. The Kyoto Protocol was negotiated in December 1997 in Kyoto with the goal of achieving "stabilization of greenhouse gas concentrations in the atmosphere at a level that would prevent dangerous anthropogenic interference with the climate system". In full, Article 2 of the UNFCCC states:

> The ultimate objective of this Convention and any related legal instruments that the Conference of the Parties may adopt is to achieve, in accordance with the relevant provisions of the Convention, stabilization of greenhouse gas concentrations in the atmosphere at a level that would prevent dangerous anthropogenic interference with the climate system. Such a level should be achieved within a time-frame sufficient to allow ecosystems to adapt naturally to climate change, to ensure that food production is not threatened and to enable economic development to proceed in a sustainable manner.[16]

The Kyoto Protocol only entered into force in February 2005, partly due to the inordinately long negotiations associated with Russia's accession.[17] The Kyoto Protocol and the UNFCCC, within which the former is placed, constitute the only existing international treaty and multilateral framework to tackle global climate change. The UNFCCC created a global policy architecture with four key elements.

Equity

With regard to concerns for equitable burden sharing, Yvo de Boer, Executive Secretary of the UNFCCC, stated at the 2007 Bali meeting that the principle of "common but differentiated responsibilities" is "the cornerstone of the UNFCCC and it will play an important role at the Bali meeting".[18] This translates into a clear policy dichotomy between the industrialized and the developing countries. The former constitute the Annex I countries which are committed to specified quantitative emission targets for the first commitment period (2008–12) and have financial and technology transfer obligations to the developing countries. The latter have neither policy obligations nor quantitative emission targets under the Kyoto Protocol.

Efficiency

For efficiency requirements, the Kyoto Protocol established project-based international emissions trading via the Clean Development Mechanism (CDM). The CDM-based international trade in emissions uses market-based incentives to implement least-cost GHG emission abatement opportunities in the developing countries. The rationale for CDM was that the joint implementation of projects between industrialized and developing countries would not only offer the benefits of lowering costs of emission reduction (since it would typically be cheaper to curb emissions in the developing countries than in the developed countries), but would also lead to technology transfer and financing opportunities for the non–Annex I developing countries. While non–Annex I countries do not have GHG emission restrictions, they would have financial incentives to participate via CDM in promoting GHG emission reduction projects in their countries (against agreed BAU projections) which can qualify for UN-certified "carbon credits" and which can then be ultimately sold to Annex I buyers who exceed their allowances.

A Long-term Environmental Goal

Under the long-term goal, with a target date of 2050, there is a widening consensus that the rise in global average surface temperature be limited to an increase of no more than 2°C. According to the Stern Review, staying within this limit would require a reduction in global greenhouse gas emissions of at least 50 per cent below the 1990 level by 2050, equating to a maximum steady-state GHG concentration of 450–550 ppm of CO_2 equivalent (CO_2e) in the atmosphere.[19] At the Group of 8 (G-8) meeting in L'Aquila, the leaders of the group proposed a "vision" in which the industrialized countries would cut their GHG emissions by 80 per cent by 2050 (though the base year was not indicated) in order to cap the rise in global mean temperature at 2°C.[20]

A Medium-term Emissions Strategy

Under the medium-term goal, the Kyoto Protocol Annex I countries agreed to reduce their collective GHG emissions by 5.2 per cent by 2020 from 1990 levels.[21] National limitations for the Annex I countries range from a reduction of 8 per cent for the EU, 6 per cent for Japan, and 0 per cent for Russia to allowed increases of 8 per cent for Australia and 10 per cent for Iceland. Stipulated emission reductions are legally binding under the Kyoto Protocol, and if emissions exceed the target to be achieved over the first commitment period (2008–12), the Annex I country concerned is obligated to "repay" the tonnage exceeded together with a 30 per cent penalty during the second commitment period (yet undefined). However, the incentives for compliance are weak, and the agreement allows countries to withdraw from the treaty after a notice period of one year. In effect, the legally binding nature of the Kyoto Protocol commitments for Annex I countries is undercut by the lack of effective sanctions under the treaty.

2.2 NEGOTIATING POSITIONS *CIRCA* 2010

Key Countries and Coalitions

Table 2.2 below gives the global share of CO_2 emissions of ten countries and one region (EU) which were among the largest emitters in 2010 and which will play a determining role in the global climate change negotiations.[22] The top ten account for over three-quarters of global CO_2 emissions, with China, the United States, and the EU accounting for over half of such emissions.

Fig 2.1 below shows the largest GHG emitters within the various groups in the Annex I and non–Annex I countries. Within the Annex I group, the EU (which has a common position on global climate change) and Japan are the two most important players by virtue of the size of their economies and their total emissions. Together, the EU and Japan accounted for just under 16 per cent of CO_2 emissions in 2010 and are the most important constituents of the Annex I group.

Within the non–Annex I group, the key players are China, India, South Africa, Indonesia, and Brazil. These five countries constitute the largest developing country CO_2 emitters, together accounting for almost a third

Table 2.2
The Largest CO_2 Emitters, 2010

	Million tonnes of CO_2	% of Global CO_2
China	7,259	24.0%
USA	5,369	17.7%
EU	3,660	12.1%
India	1,626	5.4%
Russia	1,581	5.2%
Japan	1,143	3.8%
Germany	762	2.5%
Korea	563	1.9%
Canada	537	1.8%
Iran	509	1.7%
United Kingdom	484	1.6%
Saudi Arabia	446	1.5%
World	30,276	100.0%
Memo		
OECD	12,440	41.1%
Non-OECD	16,737	55.3%

Note: Total world includes non-OECD and OECD totals and marine bunkers and international aviation bunkers using the "sectoral approach" to calculating emissions.
Source: International Energy Agency "CO_2 Emissions from Fuel Combustion" 2012.

Figure 2.1
Top GHG Emitters and Blocs

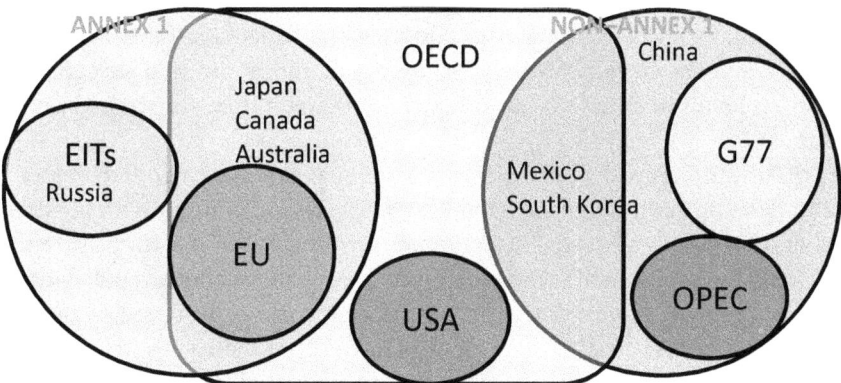

of global emissions. China alone is responsible for 24 per cent, the largest single global emitter of CO_2. These countries have emerged as the leading representatives of the Group of 77 (G-77) developing country bloc. The G-77, now comprising 130 countries, is

> the largest intergovernmental organization of developing states in the United Nations, which provides the means for the countries of the South to articulate and promote their collective economic interests and enhance their joint negotiating capacity on all major international economic issues within the UN system...[23]

Although the group excludes China, a joint statement was made on behalf of G-77 and China at the Bonn meeting on 12 June 2009 at the "Closing Plenary of the 8th Session of the Ad Hoc Working Group under the Kyoto Protocol",[24] reflecting the broad congruence between China and the G-77 on core issues.

The United States ranks as the world's second-largest emitter after China, accounting for almost a fifth (18 per cent) of global CO_2 emissions. The United States remains the sole OECD large emitter that has not ratified the Kyoto Protocol. Australia ratified the Protocol only on 30 September 2008 with the election of Prime Minister Kevin Rudd's new government. Both Australia and Canada, as large energy exporters with ramped up production of coal, natural gas, and tar-sands oil, are among those with the largest increase in GHG emissions in the OECD group since the Kyoto Protocol was agreed upon in 1997.

South Korea and Mexico occupy a unique position of being (relatively recent) OECD members without being subject to Annex I obligations of the Kyoto Protocol. Many of the Economies-In-Transition (EITs), including Russia and the Ukraine, have GHG emission allocations that exceed their current levels of emissions, and hence have no binding constraints under Annex I.

The publicly articulated positions of key players from both developed and developing countries are widely divergent and fraught with tensions over a host of basic issues that remain unresolved. In the lead up to the Copenhagen summit, there was increasing scepticism about any substantive universal agreement coming out of the negotiations designed to replace the expiring first commitment phase (2008–12) of the Kyoto Protocol.

The classifications of countries according to their development status by multilateral agencies (MLA), at the broadest level (i.e., "developed" and "developing"), were explicitly recognized in the Kyoto Protocol treaty obligations which were adopted in December 1997 and finally entered into force in February 2005. The key element of the Kyoto Protocol was presaged by text of the UNFCCC which set negotiations on national targets and timetables locked into a two-track system of negotiations with a clear distinction in expectations of Annex I (mainly OECD countries, with the significant exclusion of the United States) and non-Annex I (mainly developing) countries. Under article 3.1, the UNFCCC unambiguously recognized the principal of "common but differentiated responsibilities", with no binding emission commitments to be introduced for non–Annex I parties.

The major developing countries with large GHG emissions will play a critical role in negotiating a post-Kyoto climate change agreement. China, India, and Brazil, among the largest developing country CO_2 emitters, have played a lead role in establishing the "developing country" position adopted through the series of Kyoto negotiations. As articulated not only by the three countries but also by the G-77, the largest developing country bloc within the UN system, the developing country position seeks steep and binding GHG emission cuts from the developed Annex I countries; it also expects strong technical and financial support from Annex I countries to assist non–Annex I developing countries to adapt to the adverse consequences of global warming and to voluntarily mitigate GHG emissions under Nationally Appropriate Mitigation Actions (NAMAs). At the Bangkok UNFCCC meeting in 2009, the G-77 and China bloc reiterated their opposition to any binding commitments to reduce GHG emissions from developing countries and EITs.

Among the developed countries, the United States remains the single most important GHG emitter. The United States, while a signatory to the Kyoto Protocol, has not ratified nor withdrawn from the treaty. The Clinton Administration, which signed the treaty, declined to submit it to the Senate for ratification until "meaningful" participation by large developing country emitters was attained. In July 1997, before the treaty was adopted by its signatories (in December 1997), the U.S. Senate unanimously passed the Byrd-Hagel Resolution which stated that the United States should not participate in any international agreement which did not include binding targets and timelines for key developing countries as well since it "would result in serious harm to the economy of the United States".[25]

Much depends on U.S. leadership for the success of global efforts at mitigating climate change. More specifically, the outcome of the

Copenhagen summit was critically a result of the U.S. negotiating position which called for "meaningful" participation in quantified emission targets by the large developing countries *and* the response of the key developing countries such as China, India, and Brazil to such calls. The response of the EU and Japan, as the largest Annex I participants in the Kyoto Protocol, as well as other large GHG emitters, namely South Korea, Mexico, Indonesia, Canada, and Australia, will set the larger context for a post-Kyoto global policy architecture.

Neither the developed nor the developing countries constitute monolithic blocs with respect to negotiating postures and policy preferences. For example, in the run-up to the Copenhagen negotiation in 2009, South Korea and Mexico, both OECD member countries which currently do not have obligations under the Kyoto Protocol to curb emissions, announced substantial emission reduction targets. Even China and India have recently adopted more nuanced positions regarding their approach to climate change negotiations.

Positions and Views on Emission-Reduction Targets

Developing Countries

The bigger developing countries such as China or India have not asserted any views on long-term targets in their UNFCCC submissions. China's position is that it would not be meaningful to talk about long-term targets without credible medium-term targets of the industrialized countries being clearly determined.[26] However, some of the smaller countries as well as the Alliance of Small Island States (AOSIS) — of which Singapore is a member[27] — have called for lower levels, at below 350 ppm citing excessive risks faced by low-lying islands from global warming and the associated rise in mean sea levels.[28]

In the medium term, the developing countries expect Annex I countries to be consistent with the IPCC's recommended path to the 450 ppm CO_2e equilibrium level, cutting emissions in aggregate by 25 to 40 per cent from 1990 levels. According to the draft amendment proposed by Brazil, China, India, Indonesia, and South Africa among other developing countries, the industrialized countries "shall reduce their aggregate emissions by at least 40 per cent below 1990 levels in 2020", asserting that "individual quantitative emission reduction commitments … are determined by applying the principle of historical responsibility from 1850–2005".[29]

The rationale behind this developing country position is based on the grounds of equity and historical responsibility: since the major portion of the *stock* of man-made CO_2 in the earth's atmosphere is accounted for by the industrialized West, the developed countries should launch serious efforts to reduce their own emissions before calling upon the developing countries to begin contributing to such efforts.

The developing countries stress the primacy of economic development and the alleviation of poverty, insisting upon the distinction between the voluntary and non-binding nature of developing country actions in emission reductions against the mandatory and binding cuts expected of the industrialized countries under the Kyoto Protocol and UNFCCC agreements.

In the Bali Action Plan, the developing countries pledged to implement NAMAs. The developing countries view NAMAs as country-initiated plans for reducing emissions within the primary goal of economic growth. These plans are implemented in lieu of the mandatory quantified emission reduction targets, in favour of reducing BAU emissions but against imposed caps on economy-wide emissions. Emission caps present constraints on economic growth, and hence are rejected, however generous the proposed emission targets are.

Developing countries such as China want measurement, reporting and verification (MRV) to be implemented by country authorities in cases where NAMAs do not receive international financial support.[30] India's position is similar, stating that only in cases where projects receive international public funding, then an MRV regime may be implemented by UNFCCC or by bodies directed by the UNFCCC's Conference of Parties (COP), its decision-making body.

Among the large developing countries, Brazil, China, and India have adopted what may be considered as the "maximalist" position, seeking steep emission cuts in the medium- and long-terms by the Annex I countries, as well as substantial financial aid and technology transfers to the developing countries, to help the latter voluntarily mitigate GHG emissions and to adapt to the adverse impacts of global warming.[31]

United States

The United States will be unlikely to ratify any successor treaty to the Kyoto Protocol unless key developing countries agree to take on meaningful and binding emission-reduction agreements or agree to graduate towards such obligations. In its recent negotiation text, the United States states that "developing country Parties whose national circumstances reflect greater responsibility or capability" should submit NAMAs in the 2020 time frame with quantified emission reductions from BAU levels, as well as specify dates by which the developing country parties will take on binding quantitative commitments equivalent in nature to those made by developed countries.[32]

The United States and several industrialized countries argue that the rapid increase in the *flow* of emissions from the large and rapidly growing economies of China and India make it imperative that they and other large developing countries participate meaningfully in global efforts to mitigate carbon emissions, at least in the medium to long term (possibly post-2020). Under projected growth paths of emissions of various countries, the IPCC's recommended steady state 450 ppm of GHG concentration by 2050 would not be feasible even if all Annex I countries and the United States were to reduce their CO_2 emissions to zero by 2020–30.[33]

The U.S. House of Representatives passed its version of a "cap-and-trade" climate change bill in June 2009.[34] The bill envisions modest emission cuts of 17 per cent by 2020, relative to 2005 levels. The cuts get steeper in the long term, with cuts by 2050 amounting to 83 per cent. The medium-term cuts proposed by the House bill translate to only about 3 per cent by 2020, relative to 1990 levels,[35] compared to the 20 per cent committed to by the EU as a whole under the Kyoto Protocol, for example.

The bill, however, was opposed by most Republicans, and is much compromised by a series of exemptions, exceptions, and pay-offs to special interest groups. About 85 per cent of the permits conferring the right to emit GHG will be given away, with only the remaining 15 per cent to be sold to the highest bidders. Among the sectors most favoured by the bill is agriculture, a sector which will likely be given even more consideration when the Senate considers the bill, given that agricultural states have a greater representation in the Senate. However, in July 2010 it was reported that the Senate would not consider climate change legislation before the end of the legislative term.[36]

EU

The EU has been the most vocal regional organization in support of the Kyoto Protocol and its continuation under a second commitment period, and beyond. The EU's announced plans in 2007 for the regional group to commit to reduce emissions by 20 per cent by 2020 from 1990 levels, and pledged to cut by 30 per cent if there is an international agreement at Copenhagen.[37] In the lead up to the Fifteenth session of the Conference of the Parties (COP15), the EU has called for stronger commitments from OECD members, including newer members South Korea, Mexico, and Turkey, none of which now have binding targets under the Kyoto Protocol. In the EU's view, plans for emission reduction targets should include countries such as Chile, which is an official candidate for OECD membership, as well as other countries "with enhanced engagement [with the OECD] with a view to possible membership" such as Brazil, China, India, and South Africa.[38]

Japan

While Japan has also been one of the most ardent supporters of the Kyoto Protocol, its emission reduction plans under the previous administration were widely considered feeble. Compared to the EU's commitments of 20 per cent cuts, the Japanese administration of Prime Minister Taro Aso announced in June 2009 emission cuts of 8 per cent by 2020, a slightly higher level than the 6 per cent cut agreed to under the Kyoto Protocol.[39] After winning the elections in August 2009, the incoming Prime Minister Yukio Hatoyama announced in September a significantly more aggressive 25 per cent cut target by 2020.[40] The Prime Minister said that the plan was dependent on other nations agreeing to substantive targets at COP15. Japan, like the United States and the EU, supports greater participation by advanced developing countries "which have a substantial contribution to global climate emissions of GHG and have appropriate response capabilities"; it sees such countries as being obliged to set economy-wide and sectoral intensity targets.[41]

Australia and Canada

Canada and Australia, both large energy producers, have difficult domestic balancing of interests to contend with, and their governments have had significant domestic opposition, especially from the large firms in the oil, gas, and coal industries, to plans for aggressive targets for GHG emission reductions.

The new government of Prime Minister Kevin Rudd of Australia ratified the Kyoto Protocol immediately upon taking office in December 2007, which took effect in March 2008.[42] The previous administration refused to ratify the treaty on the same grounds as the United States, citing high costs and the lack of participation by large developing country emitters. Subject to international agreement, Australia would commit to a reduction of 25 per cent from the 2000 level. In August 2009, the Australian Senate rejected the landmark climate change bill pledged by the government. Australia is the biggest per capita emitter of CO_2 among the developed countries, primarily because of the country's heavy reliance on coal-generated electricity and the export-oriented mining industry.

Canada ratified the treaty in February 2005, requiring it to reduce emissions by 6 per cent below 1990 levels during the first commitment period of 2008–12. Despite strong support from the public, the government faced stiff opposition from business groups, particularly energy firms based in Alberta, Canada's primary energy-producing province. Canada was the first country in the world to renounce its climate change commitments under the Kyoto Protocol. The conservative minority government under Prime Minister Stephen Harper which was elected in January 2006 announced that Canada had no possibility of meeting its Kyoto Protocol targets.[43]

South Korea and Mexico

South Korea and Mexico share a number of traits that make them important players at UNFCC forums. Both are large industrial economies and are among the largest dozen CO_2 emitters. Both are also members of the OECD but are not in the Annex I group of countries which face binding emission reduction targets. In contrast to the developing country position as articulated in UNFCCC submissions and public statements by Brazil, China, India, and more broadly the G77, Mexico and South Korea hold intermediate positions between the developing country position and the views of OECD countries such as the United States. Partly as a result of their shared traits, they have recently announced substantial emission reduction targets to be achieved by 2020. Observers of climate change negotiations have perceived these announcements as positive signs that "will push developing countries like China and India to set their own goals to curb emissions".[44]

In August 2009, South Korea unilaterally pledged for the first time to set 2020 emission reduction targets, thereby voluntarily indicating that it is prepared to join the group of countries currently under Annex I emission reduction obligations.[45] It committed to one of three options to be achieved by 2020, all of which are relatively modest compared to other OECD countries in the Annex I group: an 8 per cent increase from 2005 levels; no increase from 2005 levels; or a 4 per cent decrease below 2005 levels.

According to the chief of the Inter-American Development Bank's Sustainable Energy and Climate Change Unit, "Mexico is one of the very few developing economies that are adopting emission reduction targets in advance of the UN's Copenhagen conference on climate change in December.[46] The Mexican government set targets that could lead to an 18 per cent drop in emissions by 2012, "putting Mexico at the vanguard of the global movement to curb emissions."[47] At the December 2008 UN climate change talks at Poznan, Mexico became the first developing country to set a specific carbon reduction target, with a pledge to halve GHG emissions by 2050, relative to 2002 levels. Mexico intends to put in a detailed offer to cut GHG emissions at the negotiations in Copenhagen; according to the President of the National Ecology Institute, Mexico will "set a positive precedent for the other big emerging economies".[48]

ASEAN Member States

The ASEAN (Association of Southeast Asian Nations) view conforms to the broad negotiating position of the developing country bloc, as expressed by the G-77 plus China for example.[49] At the Bali conference in December 2007, ASEAN leaders "resolved to work closely to pave the way for establishing an effective, fair, flexible, and comprehensive multilateral arrangement, in addressing climate change beyond 2012 taking into account common but differentiated responsibilities."[50]

According to one observer from a Singapore-based research institute, "ASEAN countries have a much better chance of addressing climate change collectively rather than individually."[51] This view of a common ASEAN view is challenged by a senior Indonesian spokesman, Agus Purnomo. As head of Indonesia's national climate change committee, Purnomo said that such a stance was hard to achieve: "A united ASEAN position would be difficult. It's not completely closed off but there have been no agreements because all the countries are very different."[52]

Indonesia, Southeast Asia's largest and most populous country by far, and among the largest GHG emitters in the world, has played an important role in climate change negotiations. In a speech at the G-20 summit in

Pittsburgh in September 2009, President Susilo Yudhoyono announced a national climate change plan "that will reduce [Indonesia's] emissions by 26 per cent by 2020 from BAU"; although this announcement is not legally binding, it is seen as a statement of voluntary commitment "as good citizens of the world", as stated by one senior Indonesian delegate.[53] Indonesia was the first ASEAN country to have announced a national emission reduction plan with quantitative targets, promoting forestry conservation and re-forestation as the main contributor to emission reductions. In March 2009, the Thailand government was reportedly drafting a plan which would "require major industrial companies to cut CO_2 emissions by 15 to 20 per cent", although there were no firm timelines for implementation.[54] In December 2009, Singapore announced its first ever emission reduction target, pledging to cut emissions by 16 per cent below "business-as-usual" levels by 2020 provided there was a legally binding global agreement.[55]

In a number of recent statements by government ministers, diplomats, and the Prime Minister, Singapore has articulated its approach to carbon emission reduction policies. According to Chew Tai Soo, the chief climate negotiator for Singapore, "We will have a plan to put on the table if there's a global agreement [on climate change]. When there's an agreement, Singapore will be part of that agreement."[56] At the 11th ASEAN Ministerial Meeting on the Environment, the Minister for the Environment and Water Resources (MEWR), Yaacob Ibrahim, said that "whatever we do, we cannot compromise our ability to grow. So how we find a balance will be a continuous process."[57] This view reflects closely that expressed by Minister Mentor Lee Kuan Yew, who said that imposing emission targets on Singapore would constrain economic growth.[58] At the December 2007 UNFCCC Bali Conference, Prime Minister Lee Hsien Loong stated:

> Given this wide range of situations of different countries, the post-2012 framework cannot use a one-size-fits-all approach. An equitable solution must take into account diverse national circumstances. The smaller and more vulnerable countries in particular will need technical assistance to put in place effective adaptation measures.[59]

In a later speech, Prime Minister Lee said "we are a responsible member of the international community and we have to bear the fair share of the collective global effort to reduce carbon emissions. Therefore, provided other countries also commit to do their part in a global deal, we will reduce emissions from BAU levels and do what we need to do, together with other countries, to reduce human-kind CO_2 emissions."[60] This view — that governments can support an agreement provided it is equitable and does not impose an unnecessary burden on economic growth — is shared in general by the ASEAN countries.

2.3 POST-COPENHAGEN: DURBAN AND BEYOND

As has already been noted, a major source of debate in climate change policy circles has been the integration of non–Annex I countries into a post-Kyoto climate policy architecture. With the Kyoto Protocol having expired at the end of 2012, international negotiation efforts in recent years have focused on establishing a successor to the treaty. However, the end-goal of such efforts, a binding international treaty, specifying in detail obligations for both Annex I and non–Annex I countries, has yet to materialize. Instead, at COP15 held in Copenhagen in December 2009, a non-binding agreement called the Copenhagen Accord emerged. Annex I countries were asked to submit their proposed economy-wide, quantified emissions reduction targets to be included in Appendix I of the Accord, while non–Annex I countries were asked to submit NAMAs to be included in Appendix II of the Accord.[61] Since the targets specified by countries in the Copenhagen Accord are voluntary, not the product of negotiations, and in any case are non-binding, we may regard the Copenhagen Accord as the preliminary step towards a more comprehensive future agreement, as opposed to being a complete climate policy architecture in its own right.

Unlike the earlier negotiations leading up to the Kyoto Protocol which focused entirely on emission mitigation targets for the developed countries, UNFCCC summits since then have increasingly focused on mitigation actions among non–Annex I countries without which, it became increasingly evident, there would be no viable solution to global warming. The question of "deepening and widening" participation in an extended Kyoto Protocol, covering large developing country emitters along with the Annex I countries, became a central focus of UNFCCC negotiations. In the 2007 Bali conference, parties to the UNFCCC established a parallel negotiating track involving other big emitters such as China, India, and the United States to consider long-term cooperative action under the convention in order to achieve comprehensive agreement for mitigation, adaptation, finance, and technology.[62]

COP15 of the UNFCCC commenced on 7 December 2009 and adjourned some two weeks later, issuing the Copenhagen Accord, a political agreement negotiated by leaders of over twenty-five large emitting countries from both the OECD and developing country blocs. While the Accord did not result in any new legally binding agreement to extend or replace the Kyoto Protocol, it did address all the key components under protracted negotiations, including emission mitigation and adaptation, finance, technology transfer, the forestry sector, and MRV.

Among its key elements, the Accord set an "aspirational" goal of a global temperature increase of no more than 2°C above pre-industrial levels, established a process for recording national emission targets and policy actions for both industrialized and developing countries, pledged significant financial resources to assist poorer developing countries in climate change mitigation and adaptation, and provided for "international consultations and analysis" of developing country actions together with fuller MRV procedures for emission mitigating actions in developing countries which receive international funding.[63]

However, not only was the Accord not a legally binding agreement, but it was merely "taken note of" rather than "adopted" by the COP at the summit.[64] This weak outcome reflected the fact that COP15 was the first UNFCCC summit which directly addressed the issue of developing country mitigation actions as an integral part of climate change negotiations. The Accord, agreed to only after a contentious final all-night session among a small group of countries, was a culmination of several years of increasing insistence by the industrialized countries, including the EU and the United States, that "advanced" developing countries such as China, India, Brazil, and South Africa (i.e., the so-called "BASIC" group of countries) should be party to the necessary actions required to achieve global emission mitigation targets.[65]

Given the deeply ingrained dichotomy of expectations between Annex I and non–Annex I countries in the Kyoto Protocol, it was indeed no surprise that COP15 proved so difficult. In particular, the fundamental disagreement between the world's two largest emitters, China and the United States, meant that the Accord needed to bridge fundamentally opposed views of the legal architecture of the global climate change regime. The former was unwilling to agree to any binding legal constraint on emissions, regardless of how such constraints may differ in severity between industrialized and developing countries. The latter insisted that any future international agreement would need to be "symmetric" with both industrialized and developing countries subject to binding legal agreements, even if the stringency and content of required emission targets would be different between the two groups of countries. The Copenhagen Accord, although delaying the decision on the continuation and amendment of the Kyoto Protocol, achieved as much as could have been expected.[66]

Following the Copenhagen climate change talks, expectations for the following COP16 summit in Cancun were low. At the event, the Cancun Agreements reiterated the key components of the Copenhagen Accord and served to bring the details of the Accord into the UNFCCC process. The Agreements elaborated and made operational the three-page Accord into thirty pages of decision text which provided for a "Subsidiary Body on Implementation" for the "international consultations and analysis" process for developing country mitigation actions; established a board of twenty-four members split between developing and developed countries to manage the Green Climate Fund (GCF) which would be administered for the first three years by the World Bank; set up a Technology Mechanism for technology development and transfer; set provisions on climate change adaptation in the Cancun Adaptation Framework; and established a framework for emission mitigation from deforestation and forest degradation.[67]

The UNFCCC Durban summit (COP17) adjourned on 11 December 2011, two days after its scheduled close, issuing a two-page eight-paragraph statement known as the Durban Platform for Enhanced Action[68] with three major components. The delegates agreed to a second five-year extension of the Kyoto Protocol, a key outcome that avoided a complete collapse of the Durban talks. Although Japan, Russia, and Canada did not agree to sign up for the second commitment period of the Kyoto Protocol, and the United States retained its non-ratification status, the EU agreed to implement its emission mitigation targets for the extended period of the Protocol in return for a road map to a new international treaty requiring meaningful participation by all countries — which was the second element of the Durban Platform. The parties agreed to "launch a process to develop a protocol, another legal instrument or an agreed outcome with legal force under the UNFCCC applicable to all Parties".[69] The document states that this process should be completed by 2015, with resulting emission mitigation actions to begin by 2020.

The third element of the Platform comprised details of implementation of the various components of the Cancun Agreements, including enhanced transparency of national commitments through new procedures for international consultations to increase confidence in progress towards achieving those commitments; a governance structure for the new GCF; and a more fully specified Technology Mechanism to effect technology transfer. The Durban Platform also had delegates agree on procedures to handle carbon capture and sequestration as part of the Kyoto Protocol's CDM and to guide reduced deforestation projects.

The Durban Platform represented a continuation of the approach adopted by the previous Copenhagen and Cancun meetings by asserting that the outcome of climate change negotiations be "applicable to all parties". Delegates reached a non-binding decision to reach an agreement by 2015 that is meant to bring all countries under the same legal climate change regime by 2020. While this is little more than an agreement to talk about an agreement, it can be argued more positively that the Durban Platform has effectively obviated the dichotomous distinction enshrined in the Kyoto Protocol between Annex I developed countries and non–Annex I developing countries, an impasse which bedevilled all attempts at progress in climate change negotiations.[70] It would be overly optimistic to assume that large developing country emitters such as China and India would sign on to binding emission constraints come 2015, but the Durban Platform has institutionalized an approach to climate change negotiators that involves all parties by building on the progress made at the Cancun summit. As one well-known observer of the UNFCCC summits over the past several years put it, the Durban Platform "is a real departure from the past, and marks a significant advance along the treacherous uphill path of climate negotiations".[71]

Public concern in the OECD countries over climate change has declined dramatically since what has been termed the Great Recession of 2008–9. Social surveys in the United States and Western Europe suggest that the perceptions of economic insecurity amidst worsening labour market conditions brought on by the impact of the financial crisis and its economic aftermath since 2008 have led to a "crisis of confidence" in climate science and climate change concerns are far lower in the rank of major concerns of the public.[72] At the Warsaw COP19 meetings of the UNFCCC in November 2013, a more restrained tone was set by the EU compared to its previous leading role in championing aggressive climate change targets and deadlines.[73] While the EU is still the main group among the developed countries urging for a global climate agreement by 2015, it is clear that most countries, including large global emitters such as the

United States and China, have adopted restrained and modest ambitions in mitigating their forecast emission trajectories. In Europe itself, there are substantive divergences of opinion among national authorities. Poland, the host of the COP19 meetings, emphasized responsible global collective action rather than leadership by the EU in championing aggressive targets when Europe itself accounts for a relatively small proportion of global GHG emissions.[74]

2.4 COUNTRY CLASSIFICATIONS, INDICATORS AND COMPARISONS

The clear distinction between Annex I countries with legally binding emission mitigation responsibilities and non–Annex I countries with no mitigation responsibilities beyond purely voluntary policy actions in the Kyoto Protocol is derived from the simple demarcation of countries into that of "developing" and "developed". The classifications of countries according to their development status accorded by multilateral agencies (MLAs) such as the UN, the World Bank, the International Monetary Fund (IMF), the OECD at the broadest level (i.e., "developed" and "developing") were explicitly recognized in the Kyoto Protocol treaty obligations.

According to the UN Statistical Division, "there is no established convention for the designation of 'developed' or 'developing' countries"[75]. The UN lists Singapore within the Southeast Asia group as a geographical reference. It states that it adheres to "common practice" in treating Japan as the only Asian country included within the "developed regions or areas". Therefore, Singapore, like all other Asian countries ex Japan, is designated as a "developing" country. The UN also lists Singapore within the "small island developing states" group.

The World Bank reports for geographic regions are for low-income and middle-income economies only. In its description of country groups, the World Bank states that "low-income and middle-income economies are sometimes referred to as developing economies". All other countries are classified by income groups using the Gross National Income (GNI) per capita measure, although the World Bank also adds the proviso that classification by income "does not necessarily reflect development status."[76]

Income groups listed by the World Bank, according to 2008 GNI per capita, are:

1. low income, US$975 or less;
2. lower middle income, US$976–US$3,855;
3. upper middle income, US$3,856–US$11,905; and
4. high income, US$11,906 or more.

Accordingly, Singapore is listed under the "high-income" category, along with other countries in the OECD, as well as the smaller countries such as Bahrain, Brunei, Hong Kong, Israel, Oman, and Qatar.

On 1 January 1995, the OECD reclassified Singapore, together with Brunei, Bahamas, Kuwait, Qatar, and the United Arab Emirates (UAE), from the previous "developing country" status to "more advanced developing countries". This was preceded by its decision to remove these high *per capita* income countries from the list of countries eligible to receive aid drawn up by the body's Development Assistance Committee. The OECD considers all its members as "developed" countries, and the question as to whether Singapore could qualify as a developed country would only emerge if it considered applying for membership of the group.

In May 1997, the IMF reclassified Singapore, together with Israel, Hong Kong, South Korea, and Taiwan as within the group traditionally known as industrial countries but now listed simply as "advanced economies". It noted in its World Economic Outlook report of May 1997:

> Beginning with the current issue of the World Economic Outlook, a number of newly industrialized economies in Asia (Hong Kong, Korea, Singapore, and Taiwan Province of China), as well as Israel, are considered together with the group of countries traditionally known as industrial countries. The reclassification reflects the advanced stage of economic development these economies have now reached. In fact, they all now share a number of important industrial country characteristics, including per capita income levels well within the range indicated by the group of industrial countries, well-developed financial markets and high degrees of financial intermediation, and diversified economic structures with relatively large and rapidly growing service sectors. Rather than retaining the old industrial country label, the expanded group is labelled as the "advanced economies".

Following the reclassification of Singapore by the OECD, there was coverage of the issue in the local press.[77] According to the then Minister of Trade and Industry, Yeo Cheow Tong, Singapore "lacked the depth and breadth of the developed economies" and could only be considered an "advanced developing country", not a "developed country".[78]

Table 2.3 below shows economic and environmental indicators for selected countries. The Gulf states of Qatar and the UAE, as large gas and oil producers with small populations, are the largest per capita emitters. As a small Southeast Asian country with oil and gas exports, Brunei also falls within the same category as the Gulf state examples, although its carbon footprint, as measured by per capita CO_2 emissions, is relatively small. Following the Gulf states, the OECD countries the United States and Australia both have per capita emissions of 19 tonnes, significantly higher than the average for the high income OECD group which is at 12 tonnes.[79]

Singapore naturally belongs to the group of Asian countries with relatively high per capita incomes and high urbanization, relative to middle income and low income economies. Singapore, with per capita CO_2 emissions of nearly 10 tonnes, is among a group of Asian countries such as Japan, South Korea, and Taiwan, whose per capita CO_2 emissions lie between 9 and 12 tonnes. Israel also exhibits a similar carbon footprint as this group. Hong Kong's carbon footprint is notably lower, at just over 6 tonnes, reflecting the fact that the entrepôt lacks energy-intensive industries. Singapore, in contrast, has significant energy-intensive sectors such as refining and petrochemicals, despite also serving as a services-oriented entrepôt in the Southeast Asian region.

In "energy intensity" terms, measured as tonnes of CO_2 emitted per U.S. dollar gross domestic product (GDP),[80] it ranges from 0.34 and 0.35 tonnes respectively for Japan and Singapore, to Taiwan and South Korea at 0.69 and 0.71 tonnes. Hong Kong is once again an outlier, with a low 0.19 tonnes, reflecting its primary function as a service and trading centre with little energy-intensive manufacturing and power generation activities. Thailand, a lower middle income economy, and Malaysia, an upper middle income economy, emit 3.4 and 5.9 tonnes of CO_2 per capita respectively. Both are significantly more energy-intensive, at about 1.3 tonnes per U.S. dollar GDP, comparable to the oil producers like Qatar, UAE, and Brunei.

In the next group come the two largest Asian developing countries with low per capita incomes and significantly lower urbanization rates. Per capita emissions are below 5 tonnes for China and India. China, like the global average, emits just over 4 tonnes of CO_2 per capita, while India emits less, at 1.1 tonnes. China's higher per capita emissions is partly a reflection of that country's dependence on coal-based power generation for

Table 2.3
Economic and Emission Indicators for Select Countries

	Per Capita CO$_2$ emissions (2010)[1] (tonnes)	CO$_2$ per US$ GDP (2010)[1] (tonnes/US$ of GDP)	Per Capita GDP (2012)[2] (1000 US$)	Population (2010)[3] (millions)	Population Density (2010)[3] (pop per km²)	Urbanization (2010)[3] % of population in urban areas
Qatar	48.3	1.40	93,204	1.51	137	95.8
UAE	26.0	0.97	54,606	4.71	56	78.0
Brunei	15.1	1.15	37,053	0.41	71	75.7
Australia	19.0	0.82	47,400	21.50	3	88.7
USA	19.0	0.51	46,859	317.60	33	82.3
Taiwan[4]	11.9	0.69	31,900	22.97	1,849	75.0
South Korea	9.9	0.71	19,504	48.50	487	81.9
Singapore	9.6	0.35	38,972	4.83	7,082	100.0
Japan	9.5	0.34	38,559	127.00	336	66.8
Israel	8.9	0.47	24,700	7285.00	329	91.7
Hong Kong	6.1	0.19	30,755	7.07	6,433	100.0
Thailand	3.4	1.32	3,869	67.39	125	10.0
Malaysia	5.9	1.29	7,221	26.99	84	12.0
China	4.3	2.68	3,315	1354.15	141	44.9
Brazil	1.8	0.43	6,852	191.79	22.4	86.5
India	1.1	1.78	1,016	1214.46	369	30.1
World	4.3	0.74	7,995	6908.69	51	50.6

1 International Energy Agency "CO2 Emissions from Fuel Combustion 2010".
2 World Bank, World Development Indicators Database as of 1st July 2009.
3 Population Division, Department of Economic and Social Affairs, United Nations Secretariat.
4 CIA World Factbook 2009.

a major part of its electricity supply and partly its role as the "manufacturing workshop of the world". Despite low per capita emission rates (given their huge populations), their economies are energy, and hence carbon, intensive. China and India emit 2.7 and 1.8 tonnes per U.S. dollar GDP respectively, significantly higher than the newly industralized countries (NICs) (0.3–0.7 tonnes) and the two OECD countries (0.5–0.8 tonnes).

2.5 "WIDENING AND DEEPENING" INTERNATIONAL PARTICIPATION

What would a post-Kyoto climate policy architecture be like? In general, there are two major ways in which such an architecture would differ from the Kyoto Protocol. Unlike the Kyoto Protocol, which only involved participation from a limited number of countries in Annex I of the UNFCCC, a post-Kyoto architecture will require the participation of both Annex I and non–Annex I countries. Given the required participation of both developed and developing countries, such an architecture has to recognize the differential capabilities and responsibilities of developed and developing countries. This means, first of all, that developing country mitigation obligations will have to be differentiated from those of developed countries.

Another key feature of the architecture that needs to be specified is the *structure* of the architecture. Aldy and Stavins point out that three principal types of climate policy architecture may be identified.[81] The first is "targets and timetables", in which quantitative emission targets over a specified time frame are set for each country that is party to the agreement. This is the structure that has been adopted by the Kyoto Protocol. However, two other types of architecture have been proposed as well. "Harmonized domestic actions" recognize the limits of international institutions and the fact that sovereign countries cannot be forced to abide by binding targets and timetables. They adopt a more decentralized approach in which countries have greater flexibility and discretion in designing their climate policies, although these domestic actions are still "harmonized" with each other by means of a global agreement. Finally, "coordinated and unilateral policies" form the structure most divergent from the existing structure of targets and timetables. This approach does not require an international agreement at all, and would instead rely on individual countries to implement unilateral policies that are coordinated with one another.

Given the complexities of reaching an agreement under the existing structure of targets and timetables, it is possible that one of the alternative structures may be adopted in the future. Indeed, the Copenhagen Accord, the Cancun Agreements, and the Durban Platform may be regarded as an architecture of the third kind, since the targets or nationally appropriate mitigation actions specified by countries in these non-binding agreements are essentially "pledge and review" policies that are not the result of legally binding negotiations and treaty agreements (unlike the Kyoto Protocol).

A critical issue at the international level is the design of rules for accession and "graduated responsibilities" for developing countries that are widely perceived to be fair, while at the same time minimizing deviations from cost-effective emissions reduction paths to steady-state equilibrium in the 2030–50 time frame.[82] Some policy analysts have proposed a compromise between the developing country position that emphasizes concerns with equity (the responsibility that comes with the large stock of GHG emissions that developed nations have already emitted into the earth's atmosphere) and the industrialized country position that emphasizes the importance of efficiency (constraining the large and rapidly increasing flow of GHG emissions that non-OECD countries are now emitting). The compromise "graduation and deepening" scenarios propose phased integration of the developing countries into a credible post-Kyoto climate regime.[83] Expanding the group of countries with obligations could be achieved, for instance, by requiring countries to achieve emission targets once they reach the level of wealth and financial capability comparable to the developed countries that already have binding commitments under the existing Kyoto Protocol ("Annex I" countries).

Singapore's Ranking on Graduation Scenarios

In Fig 2.2, Singapore is located at the extreme northeast corner of the quadrant, reflecting both high per capita income and high per capita CO_2 emissions. Hong Kong is high on per capita income or GDP terms but lower on the per capita emissions criterion. Four lower-income EU countries which are subject to Annex I obligations are listed in the figure to compare with the NICs. South Korea and Taiwan are at the same level as Greece and Portugal in GDP per capita. The figure also explains why poorer countries such as Poland in the EU have made strong representations to the EU about their limited ability to contribute to adaptation and mitigation costs.

Figure 2.2
CO$_2$ Emissions Per Capita vs GDP Per Capita, 2008

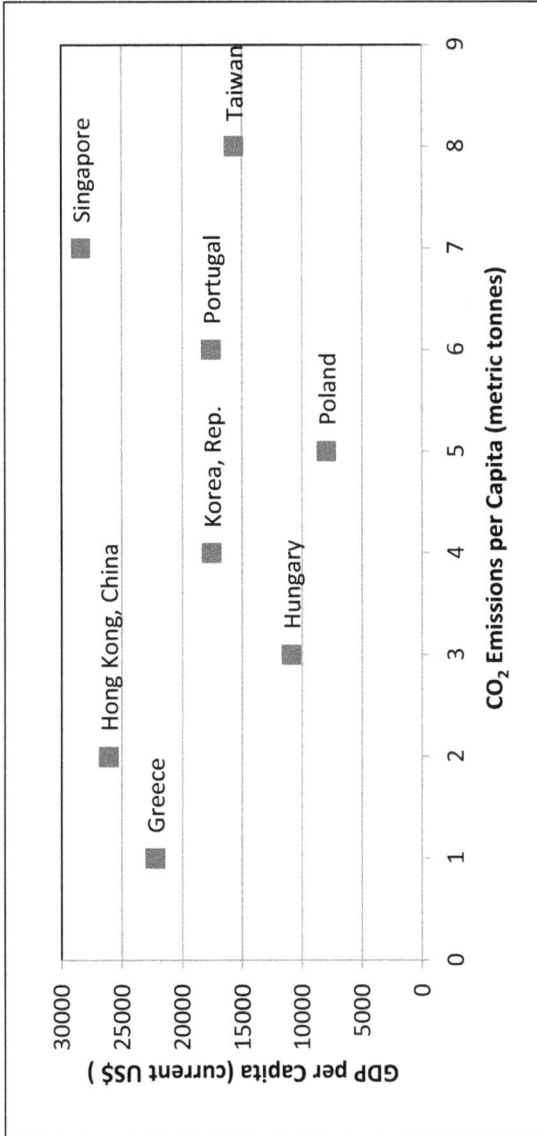

Source: World Bank, "World Development Indicators Database", 2008.

The various "graduation indices" that have been proposed are based on some combination of per capita income and emission thresholds, fulfilling both the "ability to pay" and the "polluter pays" principles. Under an equal weighting of both thresholds, for example, countries in Asia such as Brunei, Singapore, Taiwan, South Korea, and Hong Kong, and in the Middle East, the oil-states Qatar, the UAE, Kuwait, and Bahrain would be among the candidates to "graduate" to a higher level of responsibility in curbing GHG emissions.

Singapore ranks fairly high compared to a group of select countries and regions given in Table 2.4. The table shows CO_2 emissions per capita and GDP per capita weighed equally. With Singapore's index weighting normalized to 1, the poorer countries like China, the world average, and middle income countries such as Thailand and Malaysia all have lower ranks (index values ranging from 0.2 to 0.5) than richer more developed countries such as South Korea, Hong Kong, the EU, Taiwan, or the OECD

Table 2.4

Ranking of Countries and Regions by Per Capita GDP and Per Capita Emissions

$$\text{Index} = \sqrt{\left(\frac{CO_2/capita_{country}}{CO_2/capita_{Singapore}} * \frac{GDP/capita_{country}}{GDP/capita_{Singapore}} \right)}$$

Ranking by Equal Weight for Two variables

Thailand	0.18
China	0.21
Europe and Central Asia	0.26
World	0.31
Malaysia	0.34
EU-27	0.72
Korea, Rep.	0.79
Israel	0.86
Taiwan	0.87
Hong Kong, China	0.91
Singapore	*1.00*
High income: OECD	1.09
Brunei Darussalam	1.16
Australia	1.29
United States	1.55
United Arab Emirates	1.78

Source: Derived from IEA (2011) data. "Europe and Central Asia" as per the World Bank definition.

countries (index values ranging from 0.6 to 0.9). Singapore is, in its turn, lower in rank than high income oil states like Brunei and the UAE as well as OECD-members Australia and the United States (with index values ranging from 1.05 to 1.7).

If the index is widened to include three variables, GDP and CO_2 emissions per capita as well as CO_2 emissions per U.S. dollar GDP ("energy intensity"), all equally weighted, then Hong Kong's relative position changes radically, being credited for the very low energy-intensiveness of the Hong Kong economy (see Table 2.5). On the other hand, China goes up the ranking to just behind the United States once CO_2 emissions per U.S. dollar GDP is included as one of the variables in the ranking. This reflects China's very energy-intensive economy. Other countries which are ranked higher than Singapore include Brunei, Malaysia, Australia, and the UAE. In the case where all three variables are weighted equally,

Table 2.5
Ranking of Countries and Regions by Per Capita GDP,
Per Capita CO_2 Emissions and CO_2 Emissions per U.S. Dollar GDP

$$\text{Index} = \sqrt[3]{\left(\frac{CO_2/\text{capita}_{country}}{CO_2/\text{capita}_{Singapore}} * \frac{GDP/\text{capita}_{country}}{GDP/\text{capita}_{Singapore}} * \frac{CO_2/GDP_{country}}{CO_2/GDP_{Singapore}} \right)}$$

Ranking by Equal Weight for Three variables	
Thailand	0.52
World	0.61
China	0.69
Malaysia	0.76
Hong Kong, China	0.81
Europe and Central Asia	0.83
EU-27	0.86
Israel	0.98
Singapore	*1.00*
Korea, Rep.	1.11
Taiwan	1.14
High income: OECD	1.14
United States	1.52
Australia	1.58
Brunei Darussalam	1.72
United Arab Emirates	2.33

Source: Derived from IEA (2011) data.

Singapore's relative ranking improves because of its relatively less-intense use of energy in economic activity.

If the criteria were widened even further to include four equally weighted variables (see Table 2.6), namely per capita GDP and CO_2 emissions, CO_2 emissions per U.S. dollar GDP and *increase* in per capita emissions from 1990 to 2005, Singapore's relative position improves even more. The city-state's growth in per capita emissions over the past fifteen years has been alleviated by two major factors: the substitution of fuel oil with natural gas for power generation and the large increase in population via immigration. The relative positions of countries such as Australia, Thailand, China, South Korea, the UAE, and especially Malaysia are all worsened considerably by the addition of the fourth variable, reflecting the very large increase in CO_2 emissions these countries have produced with rapid, energy-intensive economic growth over 1990–2005.

Table 2.6
Ranking of Countries and Regions by Per Capita GDP,
Per Capita CO_2 Emissions, CO_2 Emissions per U.S. Dollar GDP, and
Growth in Per Capita CO_2 Emissions over 1990–2009

$$\text{Index} = \sqrt[4]{\left(\frac{CO_2/cap_{country}}{CO_2/cap_{Singapore}} * \frac{GDP/cap_{country}}{GDP/cap_{Singapore}} * \frac{CO_2/GDP_{country}}{CO_2/GDP_{Singapore}} * \frac{CO_2 \text{ per cap}[2009]/CO_2 \text{ per cap}[1990]_{country}}{CO_2 \text{ per cap}[2009]/CO_2 \text{ per cap}[1990]_{Singapore}} \right)}$$

Ranking by Equal Weight for Four variables	
World	0.71
Thailand	0.77
East Asia and Pacific	0.81
EU-27	0.86
Hong Kong, China	0.89
China	0.97
Singapore	*1.00*
Malaysia	1.01
Israel	1.05
High income: OECD	1.10
Korea, Rep.	1.30
Taiwan	1.31
United States	1.34
Australia	1.49
United Arab Emirates	1.98

Source: Derived from IEA (2011) data. "East Asia and Pacific" as per the World Bank definition.

The carbon intensity of imports and exports is an important factor in an open, trade-oriented country like Singapore. In one study, a trade-adjusted[84] account for emission measures for Singapore leads to somewhat higher measures of GHG emissions per capita. From an unadjusted estimated average level of 9.88 tonnes during 2000–2003, it increases to 15.88 tonnes.[85] It is clear that Singapore is both an importer and an exporter of a significant amount of carbon-intensive products — as a refining centre, it imports crude oil and natural gas and exports most of its refined oil products and petrochemicals. Adjusting for trade effects of embodied carbon increases Singapore's per capita emission estimates according to the study cited.

NICs and Graduation Scenarios

In general, taking these "graduation" scenarios into account, Singapore's high income per capita and relatively high per capita CO_2 emissions puts the city-state high on the list of potential candidates for "graduation" to emission reduction policies. The world's large emitters such as India and China are low on the list due to their relative poverty as measured by low per capita GDP. Once variables to measure the energy efficiency of the economy and the growth of per capita emissions over the past one and a half decade are taken into account, then Singapore's relative position improves on such "graduation" scenarios.

In the academic literature on the phenomenon of rapid East Asian economic growth, the term "newly industrializing countries" (NICs) has referred to countries formerly classified as less developed but which were becoming rapidly industrialized. The first wave of countries to be identified as "newly industrializing" included Hong Kong, South Korea, Singapore, and Taiwan. These countries underwent rapid industrial growth in the 1970s and 1980s and are now associated with finance, tourism, high-technology, and export-oriented manufacturing industries. More recently, within Asia, Thailand and Malaysia have also been classified as "second tier" NICs.[86]

In the context of heterogeneous national interests, the smaller NICs such as Singapore, Taiwan, and Hong Kong occupy an anomalous position. As affluent and highly urbanized countries with relatively high per capita emissions, the smaller NICs may find themselves under diplomatic pressure to accede to "more appropriate" and higher levels of responsibility for GHG mitigation efforts, even though their contribution to the global flow (and stock) of GHG emissions amount to very little in absolute terms.

In this group of NICs, there is another important anomaly: Hong Kong, as a Special Administrative Region, is not a sovereign entity and Taiwan is not a member of the UN and hence cannot be party to UNFCCC conventions. Among the Asian NICs, South Korea and Singapore are the remaining "high income/high emissions per capita" countries. South Korea's recent activist role in participating in binding emission targets, along with Mexico (as one of Latin America's NICs), has challenged the previous unity of the G-77 plus China bloc on climate negotiations.

According to one Reuters report on South Korea's newly announced emission targets, "wealthy developing states such as South Korea, Singapore, and Mexico have also come under pressure to announce emission curbs."[87] This is the only news report by a major press agency that the author is aware of to have specifically mentioned Singapore as one of the countries to have come under "pressure" to announce emission targets. The Reuters report does not attribute sources of this "pressure". In more specialized industry forums, however, Singapore has been specifically mentioned in the context of emissions in key industries such as shipping and petroleum refining.[88] In a dialogue with students at the National University of Singapore, Minister Mentor Lee Kuan Yew stated bluntly that "the Japanese and Australians want to upgrade us into Category One where we have to make firm commitments [to cut emissions]".[89]

Notes

1. Game theory was founded on the work of John von Neumann and Oskar Morgenstern, *Theory of Games and Economic Behavior* (New Jersey: Princeton University Press, 1953). For a summary of the literature on global climate change negotiations modelling, see Carlo Carraro, "Incentives and Institutions: A Bottom-up Approach to Climate Policy", in *Architectures for Agreement: Addressing Global Climate Change in the Post-Kyoto World*, edited by Joseph E. Aldy and Robert N. Stavins (Cambridge: Cambridge University Press, 2007).
2. The free rider problem is defined as the difficulty of undertaking group efforts in which all individuals (or individual nations) in the group share in the benefits from the effort regardless of how much (or little) each has contributed to it, because each selfishly rational individual in the group tends to refuse to contribute to the effort, and instead each tends to hope that others in the group will contribute to the effort.
3. Coordination failure in a game-theoretic context is a state of affairs in which agents's inability to coordinate their behaviour (choices) leads to an equilibrium

outcome that leaves all agents worse off than in an alternative situation that is also an equilibrium. This can occur due to lack of information, inefficiencies, or differing expectations.

4. One prominent example is the "Trans-Pacific Partnership" (TPP), a proposed trade agreement currently under negotiation by Australia, Brunei, Chile, Canada, Japan, Malaysia, Mexico, New Zealand, Peru, Singapore, the United States, and Vietnam. The TPP is claimed by its protagonists to be a "high-standard" agreement to resolve extant trade issues in the twenty-first century.

5. See David G. Victor, "Fragmented Carbon Markets and Reluctant Nations: Implications for the Design of Effective Architectures", in *Architectures for Agreement: Addressing Global Climate Change in the Post-Kyoto World*, edited by Joseph E. Aldy and Robert N. Stavins (Cambridge: Cambridge University Press, 2007).

6. Intergovernmental Panel on Climate Change, *Fourth Assessment Report* (Geneva: IPCC, 2007) <http://www.ipcc.ch/publications_and_data/publications_ipcc_fourth_assessment_report_synthesis_report.htm>.

7. Intergovernmental Panel on Climate Change, "Human Influence on Climate Clear, IPCC Report Says", press release, 27 September 2013 <http://www.ipcc.ch/news_and_events/docs/ar5/press_release_ar5_wgi_en.pdf>.

8. For one early example, see Richard S. Lindzen, "Global Warming: The Origin and Nature of the Alleged Scientific Consensus", *Regulation: Cato Review of Business and Government"*, Spring 1992, pp. 87–98. For a more recent example, see Richard McNider and John Christy, both climate scientists and one of whom was a member of the IPCC, "Why Kerry is Flat Wrong on Cimate Change", *Wall Street Journal*, 21–23 February 2014, p. 14.

9. F. William Engdahl, "Glacier Meltdown: Another Scientific Scandal Involving the IPCC Climate Research Group", *Global Research*, Centre for Global Research, 23 January 2010 <http://www.globalresearch.ca/glacier-meltdown-another-scientific-scandal-involving-the-ipcc-climate-research-group>.

10. Fred Pierce, "Battle Over Climate Data Turned into War between Scientists and Sceptics", *The Guardian*, 9 February 2010.

11. This is in contrast to the Stern Review which states that "the risks of the worst impacts of climate change can be substantially reduced if GHG levels in the atmosphere can be stabilized between 450–550 ppm CO_2e" (Nicholas Stern, *Stern Review on The Economics of Climate Change*, 2007, pp. xvi). The conductor of the review, Sir Nicholas Stern, is Advisor to the UK Government on the Economics of Climate Change and Development. Stern was former Chief Economist of the World Bank.

12. United Nations Framework Convention on Climate Change, "Ad Hoc Working Group on Long-term Cooperative Action: Fulfilment of the Bali Action Plan and Components of the Agreed Outcome [FCCC/AWGLCA/2009/4.II]" (New York: UNFCCC, 18 March 2009).

13. Nebojsa Nakicenovic and Rob Swart, eds., *Intergovernmental Panel on Climate Change Special Report on Emissions Scenarios* (Cambridge: Cambridge University Press, 2000).

14. U.S. Energy Information Administration, "International Energy Outlook 2009" (Washington DC: EIA, 2009).

15. Jay S. Gregg, Robert J. Andres and Gregg Marland, "China: Emissions Pattern of the World Leader in CO_2 Emissions from Fossil Fuel Consumption and Cement Production", *Geophysical Research Letters* 35, no. 8 (2007), as cited in Sheila M. Olmstead and Robert N. Stavins, *An Expanded Three-Part Architecture for Post-2012 International Climate Policy*, Harvard Kennedy School, The Harvard Project on International Climate Agreements, September 2009. See also International Energy Agency (IEA), "CO_2 emissions from Fuel Combustion 2012".

16. See United Nations Framework Convention on Climate Change, "Full Text of Convention Article 2" <http://unfccc.int/essential_background/convention/background/items/1353.php>.

17. Russia's emission limits were eased, and its accession to the WTO was endorsed by the EU before it ratified the Protocol in November 2004. See, for instance, Scott Barrett, "A Multitrack Climate Treaty System", in *Architectures for Agreement: Addressing Global Climate Change in the Post-Kyoto World*, edited by Joseph E. Aldy and Robert N. Stavins (Cambridge: Cambridge University Press, 2007), p. 240.

18. United Nations Framework Convention on Climate Change, "Welcome Speech to the UN Climate Change Conference in Bali" <http://unfccc.int/meetings/cop_13/items/4094.php>.

19. Nicholas Stern, *The Economics of Climate Change: The Stern Review* (Cambridge: Cambridge University Press, 2008).

20. See, for instance, "Wanted: Fresh Air", *The Economist*, 9 July 2009.

21. United Nations Environment Programme, "Industrialized countries to cut greenhouse gas emissions by 5.2%", press release, 11 December 1997 <http://unfccc.int/cop3/fccc/info/indust.htm>. Emissions exclude those from international aviation and shipping.

22. The EU holds a common representation for its members, and is listed as a party to the Kyoto Protocol, along with individual EU countries.

23. See The Group of 77 at the United Nations website <http://www.g77.org>.

24. See The Group of 77 at the United Nations, "Statements and Speeches", <http://www.g77.org/statement/>.

25. Byrd-Hagel Resolution <http://www.nationalcenter.org/KyotoSenate.html>.

26. United Nations Framework Convention on Climate Change, "Ad Hoc Working Group on Long-term Cooperative Action: Ideas and Proposals on the Elements Contained in Paragraph 1 of the Bali Action Plan [FCCC/AWGLCA/2009/MISC.1]" (New York: UNFCCC, 13 March 2009).

27. See AOSIS website for a list of member countries. <http://aosis.org/about/members/>.

28. See "Statement of by [*sic*] Mr. Selwin C. Hart, Barbados on Behalf of the Alliance of Small Island Developing States (AOSIS) to the Ad Hoc Working Group on Long term Cooperative Action (AWG-LGA) on 'Mitigation' 2 April 2008" <http://www.foreign.gov.bb/UserFiles/File/Mitigation.pdf>.

29. United Nations Framework Convention on Climate Change, "Conference of the Parties Serving as the Meeting of the Parties to the Kyoto Protocol [FCCC/KP/CMP/2009/7]" (New York: UNFCCC, 15 June 2009).

30. United Nations Framework Convention on Climate Change, "Ad Hoc Working Group on Long-term Cooperative Action: Ideas and Proposals on the Elements Contained in Paragraph 1 of the Bali Action Plan Part I [FCCC/AWGLCA/2009/MISC.4]" (New York: UNFCCC, 19 May 2009).

31. See, for instance, Jan von der Goltz, "High Stakes in a Complex Game: A Snapshot of the Climate Change Negotiating Positions of Major Developing Country Emitters", Center for Global Development Working Paper No. 177 (August 2009).

32. United Nations Framework Convention on Climate Change, "Ad Hoc Working Group on Long-term Cooperative Action: Ideas and Proposals on the Elements Contained in Paragraph 1 of the Bali Action Plan Part II [FCCC/AWGLCA/2009/MISC4.II]", (New York: UNFCCC, 19 May 2009).

33. Sheila M. Olmstead and Robert N. Stavins, "Three Pillars of Post-2012 International Climate Policy", Harvard Project on International Climate Agreements, Viewpoints, 2009, p. 2.

34. The "Waxman-Markey" bill was passed on 26 June 2009. See "America's Climate-change Bill: In Need of a Clean", *The Economist*, 27 June 2009.

35. von der Goltz, "High Stakes in a Complex Game", pp. 6–7.

36. Carl Hulse and David Herszenhorn, "Democrats Call Off Climate Bill Effort", *New York Times*, 22 July 2010.

37. European Union, "The Copenhagen Climate Change Negotiations: EU Position and State of Play", press release, 9 November 2009.

38. United Nations Framework Convention on Climate Change, "Ad Hoc Working Group on Long-term Cooperative Action: Ideas and Proposals on the Elements Contained in Paragraph 1 of the Bali Action Plan [FCCC/AWGLCA/2009/MISC.4]" (New York: UNFCCC, 19 May 2009).

39. Hiroki Tabuchi, "Japan Sets Emission Targets and No One Seems Pleased", *New York Times*, 11 June 2009.

40. "Japan Vows Big Climate Change Cut", *BBC News*, 7 September 2009.

41. United Nations Framework Convention on Climate Change, "Proposal from Japan for an Amendment to the Kyoto Protocol [FCCC/KP/CMP/2009/11]" (New York: UNFCCC, 17 June 2009).

42. United Nations Framework Convention on Climate Change, "Kyoto Protocol: Status of Ratification", 13 November 2009.

43. Les Whittington, "Liberals Knew Kyoto a Long Shot", *Toronto Star*, 23 February 2007.

44. See "South Korea, Mexico to Set CO2 Reduction Goals", *Environmental Leader*, 6 August 2009 <http://www.environmentalleader.com/2009/08/06/south-korea-mexico-to-set-co2-reduction-goals/>.

45. Cho Meeyoung, "South Korea Unveils CO_2 Target Plan", Reuters, 4 August 2009.

46. See Inter-American Development Bank, "IDB Supports Second Stage of Mexico's Climate Change Agenda", 17 September 2009 <http://www.iadb.org/en/news/news-releases/2009-09-17/idb-supports-second-stage-of-mexicos-climate-change-agenda,5656.html>.

47. Ibid.

48. Robert Campbell, "Mexico Aims to Bring CO_2 Cut Plan to Climate Talks", Reuters, 4 August 2009.

49. ASEAN Secretariat, "Singapore Declaration on Climate Change, Energy and the Environment", 21 November 2007 <http://www.asean.org/asean/external-relations/east-asia-summit-eas/item/singapore-declaration-on-climate-change-energy-and-the-environment>.

50. ASEAN, "ASEAN Declaration on the 13th Session of the Conference of Parties (COP) to the UN Framework Convention on Climate Change (UNFCCC) and the 3rd Session of the Conference of the Parties Serving as the Meeting of the Parties (CMP) to the Kyoto Protocol", 20 November 2007 <http://www.asean.org/news/item/asean-declaration-on-the-13th-session-of-the-conference-of-parties-cop-to-the-un-framework-convention-on-climate-change-unfccc-and-the-3rd-session-of-the-conference-of-the-parties-serving-as-the-meeting-of-the-parties-cmp-to-the-kyoto-protocol-singapore-2>.

51. Catherine Wong, "ASEAN Must Step Up and Act Without Delay", *Straits Times*, 14 September 2009, p. 23.

52. Danny Kemp, "SE Asia Gains Climate Clout After Storm", *China Post*, 2 October 2009.

53. *Straits Times*, "Indonesia to Cut Gas Emissions", 29 September 2009.

54. "Thailand: Government Planning to Cut CO_2 Emissions by 15–20 Percent", *IRIN*, 30 March 2008.

55. Jessica Cheam, "Singapore's Leaders Pledge Carbon Cut", *Straits Times*, 3 December 2009.

56. David Fogarty, "Singapore Says to Curb CO_2, Steps Depend on U.N. Pact", Reuters, 8 September 2009.

57. Amresh Gunasingham, "S'pore Rejects Emission Cuts", *Straits Times*, 30 October 2009.

58. Chew Xiang, "IP Rights, Rule of Law Our Competitive Edge: MM Lee — S'pore Will Resist Commitments to Firm Cuts in Emissions at Kyoto II", *Business Times*, 20 October 2009.

59. Lee Hsien Loong, "Speech Given at the UNFCCC Conference in Bali", 12 December 2007 <http://app.mewr.gov.sg/data/ImgCont/464/UNFCCC_CONFERENCE.pdf>.

60. Lee Hsien Loong, "Speech Given at Launch of Clean and Green Singapore 2010 at Hortpark", 30 October 2009 <http://www.pmo.gov.sg/mediacentre/speech-mr-lee-hsien-loong-prime-minister-launch-clean-and-green-singapore-2010-30>.

61. Robert N. Stavins and Robert C. Stowe, "What Hath Copenhagen Wrought? A Preliminary Assessment", *Environment*, May–June 2010 <http://www.environmentmagazine.org/Archives/Back%20Issues/May-June%202010/what-wrath-full.html>.

62. United Nations Framework Convention on Climate Change, "Bali Action Plan", 14 March 2008 <http://unfccc.int/resource/docs/2007/cop13/eng/06a01.pdf>.

63. See, for instance, Robert N. Stavins and Robert C. Stowe, "What Hath Copenhagen Wrought? A Preliminary Assessment", *Environment*, May–June 2010 <http://www.environmentmagazine.org/Archives/Back%20Issues/May-June%202010/what-wrath-full.html>.

64. See United Nations Framework Convention on Climate Change, "Copenhagen Accord", 18 December 2009 <http://unfccc.int/meetings/copenhagen_dec_2009/items/5262.php>.

65. See, for instance, Bryan Walsh, "Lessons From the Copenhagen Climate Talks", *Time Magazine*, 21 December 2009.

66. Among those who share this view are Daniel Bodansky, "The International Climate Change Regime: The Road from Copenhagen", Harvard Project on International Climate Agreements, Viewpoint, October 2010 <http://belfercenter.ksg.harvard.edu/files/Bodansky-VP-October-2010-3.pdf>.

67. See United Nations Framework Convention on Climate Change, "The Cancun Agreements: An Assessment by the Executive Secretary of the UNFCCC". <http://cancun.unfccc.int/>.

68. United Nations Framework Convention on Climate Change, "Establishment of an Ad Hoc Working Group on the Durban Platform for Enhanced Action", December 2011 <http://unfccc.int/files/meetings/durban_nov_2011/decisions/application/pdf/cop17_durbanplatform.pdf>.

69. Ibid.

70. See, for instance, Robert N. Stavins, "Assessing the Climate Talks — Did Durban Succeed?", 12 December 2011 <http://www.robertstavinsblog.org/2011/12/12/assessing-the-climate-talks-did-durban-succeed/>; Nathan

Hultman, "The Durban Platform", 12 December 2011 <http://www.brookings.edu/opinions/2011/1212_durban_platform_hultman.aspx>.

71. Robert N. Stavins, "Assessing the Climate Talks: Did Durban Succeed?", 12 December 2011 <http://www.robertstavinsblog.org/2011/12/12/assessing-the-climate-talks-did-durban-succeed/>.

72. See Lyle Scruggs and Salil Benegal, "Declining Public Concern about Climate Change: Can We Blame the Great Recession?", *Global Environmental Change* 22, no. 2 (2012): 505–15.

73. Barbara Lewis, "EU More Cautious as Nations Approach 2030 Climate Targets", Reuters, 8 November 2013.

74. Alister Doyle, "Talks Seek Modest U.N. Climate Deal for 2015, to Raise Aid", Reuters, 10 November 2013.

75. Under footnote (c) to the "Composition of macro geographical (continental) regions, geographical subregions, and selected economic and other groupings", see Standard Country and Area Codes Classification, United Nations Statistical Division <http://unstats.un.org/unsd/methods/m49/m49.htm>.

76. See The World Bank, "Data" <http://data.worldbank.org/>.

77. For instance, see Anna Teo, "OECD: Singapore Only a More Advanced Developing Country", *Business Times*, 17 January 1996.

78. Ibid.

79. All emission data, including group averages, is sourced from International Energy Agency, CO_2 *Emissions from Fuel Combustion: Highlights, 2008 Edition* (Paris: OECD/IEA, 2008).

80. This measure is also used as an indicator of energy efficiency, "how much CO_2 is emitted for every dollar of GPD being produced?"

81. Joseph E. Aldy and Robert N. Stavins, *Architectures for Agreement: Addressing Global Climate Change in the Post-Kyoto World* (Cambridge: Cambridge University Press, 2007), p. 17.

82. See, for instance, Joseph E. Aldy et al., "Designing Climate Mitigation Policy", *NBER Working Paper 15022*, June 2009.

83. See, for instance, Axel Michaelowa et al., "Graduation and Deepening: An Ambitious Post-2012 Cimate Policy Scenario", in Joseph E. Aldy and Robert N. Stavins, *Architectures for Agreement: Addressing Global Climate Change in the Post-Kyoto World* (Cambridge: Cambridge University Press, 2007).

84. That is, adding the emission caused elsewhere in producing carbon-intensive imports into the country on the input side, and subtracting carbon embodied in exports from the country on the output side of the economy.

85. See Niels B. Schulze, "Delving into the Carbon Footprints of Singapore — Comparing Direct and Indirect Greenhouse Gas Emissions for a Small and Open Economic System", *Energy Policy* 38, no. 9 (2010): 4848–55.

86. See, for example, World Bank, *The East Asian Miracle: Economic Growth and*

Public Policy (New York: Oxford University Press, 1993); Hans C. Blomqvist, *Economic Interdependence and Development in East Asia* (Westport: Praeger, 1997).

87. "Update 1 — S. Korea Says to Set 2020 Emissions Target", Reuters, 4 August 2009.

88. See the discussion in Chapter 4.

89. Chew Xiang, "IP Rights, Rule of Law Our Competitive Edge: MM Lee — S'pore Will Resist Commitments to Firm Cuts in Emissions at Kyoto II", *Business Times*, 20 October 2009.

3

CLIMATE CHANGE FINANCE:
Who Pays and Who Receives?

In the long climate change negotiation process since the Kyoto Protocol, which was adopted in 1997 and entered into force in 2005, the key areas of contention regard not only the apportionment of national responsibilities and obligations in emission reduction activity, but also the rules governing the raising and distribution of public and private finance.[1] At stake are not only questions on which country (or group of countries) does what in curbing emissions and preparing to adapt to climate change impacts, but also which countries are net recipients of climate finance and which are net contributors and by what amount. An agreement on climate change finance is now viewed as critical to the success of the ongoing United Nations Framework Convention on Climate Change (UNFCCC) negotiations that aim to reduce global greenhouse gas (GHG) emissions. However, it is only in the aftermath of the Fifteenth session of the Conference of Parties (COP15) that was held in Copenhagen in 2009, that climate change finance assumed a central role in the negotiations over climate change.

Climate change finance played a relatively peripheral role in the negotiations over the Kyoto Protocol. Although under the UNFCCC, Annex II countries (which include only the Organisation for Economic Co-operation and Development [OECD] members of Annex I) are required to provide climate-related finance to developing countries, this did not really become a pivotal issue since the developing countries had no emission reduction targets that required financial support. The only issue as far as finance was considered was how the Annex I mitigation targets could be achieved in a cost-effective manner. The Clean Development Mechanism (CDM), which allows Annex I countries to meet their mitigation obligations by financing emission reduction projects in developing countries, has been the main vehicle for financial flows to developing countries. Primary CDM flows peaked at US$6.5 billion in 2008, but have since declined to US$2.7 billion in 2009 and US$1.5 billion in 2010 as the Kyoto Protocol nears its expiry year of 2012.[2]

As subsequent negotiation efforts have started focusing on increased participation by large developing country emitters in any post-Kyoto international treaty on climate change, climate change finance began to assume greater importance in the negotiations and was highlighted as a priority area in the Bali Action Plan of 2007.[3] One reason for this is simply that with the threat of climate change looming nearer, developing countries most vulnerable to climate change (such as the least developed countries or LDCs and small island developing states or SIDS) have increasingly argued for developed countries to provide financial support for adaptation activities. But in addition, with developing countries set to contribute over half of global carbon dioxide (CO_2) emissions by 2020,[4] it is now recognized that to adequately combat climate change, not only all the developed countries (including those such as the United States that did not ratify the Kyoto Protocol), but major developing countries as well have to carry out emission reduction activities. Indeed, the steady state, recommended by the Intergovernmental Panel on Climate Change (IPCC), of 450 parts per million (ppm) of GHG concentration by 2050 would not be feasible even if all the Annex I countries were to reduce their CO_2 emissions to zero by 2020–30,[5] highlighting the imperative for including developing countries in future climate agreements.

This impasse in the climate change negotiations was starkly apparent during the Copenhagen and Cancun conferences in 2009 and 2010 respectively. The United States would only agree to binding medium-term emission reduction targets if "advanced" developing countries (such as China, Brazil, India, etc.) agreed to take on binding targets under a common legal regime, arguing that otherwise any reduction in emissions in developed countries would have little impact on global GHG emissions and might well be offset by increasing emissions in developing countries (i.e., emissions "leakage"). China, already the largest CO_2 emitter on the planet, argues on the basis of historical responsibility and equity that developed countries should agree to credible medium-term emission targets before developing countries commit to any legally binding obligations,[6] even as many of them have agreed to voluntary and non-binding curbs on their emissions under the Copenhagen Accord. This impasse was further deepened at Cancun when Japan, Russia, and Canada (who had accepted binding targets in the first Kyoto commitment period) made it clear that they would not accept binding targets in the second period without participation from all other major emitters, including the United States and China.[7]

Resolution over climate change finance would seem to be a prerequisite to overcoming the negotiations impasse between the classic "developed" versus "developing" country fault line. If the richer OECD group, for instance, agreed to finance mitigation and adaptation activities in the low income per capita countries, the relatively larger or "advanced" developing countries (viz. those in the "BASIC" group, comprising Brazil, South Africa, India, and China) may be more willing to take on binding emission targets in the medium term. Yet, choices in energy technology investments which will have to be made for any durable approach to mitigation and adaptation policies have to be made in a context of competing policy priorities. In the aftermath of the global financial crisis, with heightened risks of a global economy in the throes of the worst downturn since the Great Depression, climate change policies have reached stasis in the United States, while a holding pattern would be the default position of the European Union (EU), which is currently facing existential threats to its very foundations of monetary union. An agreement on climate finance, even at a modest scale relative to the US$100 billion by 2020 target, would make an overall agreement on climate change more feasible.

Climate change finance, going into the heart of questions of resource transfer in zero-sum outcomes, of course rapidly becomes a highly contested issue among countries, regional organizations, and myriad vested interests holding widely varying views. Transfers of financial resources from developed to developing countries raises issues of fairness and equity, and given the fungibility of international finance, become inextricably interlinked with developmental aid.

COP15 brought finance to the forefront of the negotiations, by stating that "scaled-up, new and additional, predictable and adequate funding" would be provided to developing countries, with the funding to come from "a wide variety of sources, public and private, bilateral and multilateral, including alternative sources of finance." A preliminary agreement on finance was reached, including a promise by developed countries to provide US\$30 billion of "fast-track" finance for the years 2010–12 and long-term finance of US\$100 billion annually by 2020.[8] Further progress was made on climate change finance at the sixteenth session of the Conference of Parties (COP16) in Cancun in 2010, where the agreement on finance reached at Copenhagen was formalized under the UNFCCC and a Green Climate Fund (GCF), the vehicle through which much of the climate finance will flow, was established.[9]

Perhaps the signal contribution of the three UNFCCC summits, from Copenhagen to Cancun and Durban, was the fracturing of the dichotomy between Annex I and non-Annex I countries institutionalized by the Kyoto Protocol. As Meija observes, though, there has been a growing fragmentation process within the "South", an extremely heterogenous group within itself, with the major or "advanced" developing countries (in particular, the BASIC group often taking quite different positions on climate change issues from other developing countries such as the LDCs and the small island states).[10] While India and China remain steadfastly opposed to any legal regime with monitoring, reporting, and verification (MRV) functions addressing emissions, other poorer developing countries as well as the small island states represented by the Alliance of Small Island States (AOSIS) support a new legal agreement that covers the major developing countries in addition to developed countries.[11] For the large-emitter developing countries, finance is largely for mitigation and a prerequisite before they agree to binding emission cuts, whereas for the less-developed countries, finance is largely for adaptation and functions as compensation for the damages that will incur due to climate change.

3.1 CLIMATE CHANGE FINANCE: HOW MUCH IS NEEDED?

According to the European Commission (EC), developing countries are likely to need €100 billion (US\$150 billion) a year by 2020 to limit their GHG emissions and adapt to the effects of climate change.[12] According to the International Energy Agency (IEA), which released its findings at the United Nations (UN) climate change talks in Bangkok, the costs of curbing climate change and transforming the energy sector via low carbon technologies would cost about US$10 trillion, or US$500 billion a year, between 2010 and 2030. Preliminary findings from a new more detailed and authoritative global study by the World Bank put estimated costs of adapting to impacts of climate change at US$75–100 billion per year from 2010.[13] This is roughly equivalent to existing levels of overseas aid (official development assistance, or ODA). Another recent report, issued by Deutsche Asset Management, estimates a funding requirement of almost US$3 trillion in additional investments by 2020 to meet emission reduction targets as set out in European and pending U.S. legislation.[14]

The developed countries are under pressure to agree to substantial funding to developing countries as the price of their participation in a global agreement to succeed the Kyoto Protocol when its provisions expire in 2012. The negotiating texts of the EU, Japan, and the United States all accept the principle of funding and technology transfer by the richer countries to assist the developing countries in mitigating emissions and adapting to the effects of climate change, although the quantum of funding and the treatment of intellectual property rights to proprietary technology remains open.

It is no surprise that in a context of rising public debt in the developed countries, as a result of the global financial crisis, few of the OECD countries have been willing to specify pledges of financial aid. The key governments and coalitions at COP15, from both developed and developing countries, view funding commitments as bargaining tools in the debate over participation and the sharing of the financial burden of mitigating and adapting to climate change.[15]

The Kyoto Protocol includes several important provisions for market-based approaches intended to improve the cost-effectiveness of the global climate change policy regime: emissions trading among Annex I countries; "joint implementation" which allows project-level trades in carbon credits among the Annex I countries; and the CDM which provides for project-level emission offsets created in non-Annex I countries to help meet the compliance obligations of firms in Annex I countries. The CDM lowers marginal and total global costs of climate change policies by allowing Annex I countries to invest in projects in the developing countries as an alternative to more expensive emission reductions in their own countries. The Kyoto Protocol created tradable emission allowances for the Annex I countries that would serve as the basis for an international emissions market.

The 2008 overall carbon market reached a total value transacted of about US$126 billion at the end of the year, which is approximately double its 2007 value.[16] Approximately US$92 billion of this overall value is accounted for by transactions of allowances and derivatives under the EU Emissions Trading Scheme (EU ETS). Project-based transactions in the primary CDM market went down in 2008 compared to 2007 with values of US$6.5 billion and US$7.4 million respectively.

Just over 5 per cent of the global carbon credits traded annually come from projects funded under the CDM. China and India are the largest generators of such credits (certified emission reduction or CER credits), as seen in Table 3.1. The current size of the CDM market, however, is very small relative to the needs of emission reduction in the developing countries, and it would need a massive scaling up if it were to provide a major source of finance for emission reduction efforts in the developing countries.

Table 3.2 illustrates estimates of the magnitude of climate change finance required annually by different organizations and countries. The figures refer to the total incremental costs required for mitigation and adaptation, not the amount of upfront investment. This is a necessary distinction because the cost-saving nature of many mitigation and adaptation projects means that the initial financing requirement for a given project will often exceed the incremental costs (which take into account any cost savings made). For instance, the World Bank estimates that while incremental mitigation costs in developing countries range between US$140 billion and US$175 billion annually, associated financing needs lie between US$265 billion and US$565 billion annually.[17] We report incremental costs since, according to article 4.3 of the UNFCCC, developed countries agree to fund "full incremental costs".[18] However, what this discussion implies is that even if developed

Table 3.1
CERs Issued by Country

Total CERs Issued by Host Party, 2009	
China	47.29%
India	20.49%
Republic of Korea	13.15%
Brazil	10.22%
Mexico	1.73%
Others	1.73%

Source: UNFCCC "CERs issued by host party" accessed 18 November 2009, http://cdm.unfccc.int/Statistics/Issuance/CERsIssuedByHostPartyPieChart.html

Table 3.2
Estimates of Annual Climate Finance Requirements

Organization	2010–12	2020	2030
Copenhagen/ Cancun Agreement	US$10 billion	$100 billion	
UNFCCC			US$138–177 billion
World Bank			US$170–275 billion
African Group		> US$267 billion	
European Commission	US$7–10 billion	US$146–165 billion	
G-77 and China	US$200–400 billion*		
India, South Africa	US$200 billion*		
Oxfam	US$150 billion (2013)	US$200 billion	
ActionAid and Eurodad		US$200 billion	
Project Catalyst	US$21–42 billion	US$126–203 billion^	

* long-term average
^ Average for 2015–20

Notes: (1) For the estimates by the European Commission and Project Catalyst, a conversion rate of €1 = US$1.4 is used. (2) The UNFCCC's 2007 estimate of annual mitigation costs in developing countries is US$64.7 billion, but global costs of mitigation estimated in 2008 were 170 per cent of the costs estimated in 2007. We assume that developing country mitigation costs are also higher by 70 per cent. (3) The African Group consists of all fifty-three African countries, while G-77 and China comprises all UN members except those that are also members of OECD, Council of Europe, and Commonwealth of Independent States. (4) Oxfam is a UK-based international confederation of fifteen NGOs, working on issues of poverty and injustice;[1] ActionAid is an international NGO based in Africa working on issues of poverty and injustice,[2] while Eurodad is a network of fifty-seven European NGOs working on debt, poverty reduction, and development finance.[3] (5) Project Catalyst is an initiative of the ClimateWorks Foundation, a non-profit philanthropic foundation, and was launched to provide analytical and policy support to the UNFCCC negotiations.[4]

Sources UNFCCC, Investment and Financial Flows to Address Climate Change: An Update (2008); World Bank, World Development Report 2010: Development and Climate Change (2010); Algeria, Key Elements of LCA Negotiating Text: Final Version (2009); European Commission, Stepping Up International Climate Finance (2009); Group of 77 and China, "Financial Mechanism for Meeting Financial Commitments Under the Convention" (2008); Government of India, Climate Change Negotiations: India's Submissions to the United Nations Framework Convention on Climate Change (Aug 2009); World Resources Institute, Summary of UNFCCC Submissions: August 2008 to October 29, 2009; Oxfam International, "Climate Finance Post-Copenhagen: The $100 bn questions" (2010); Eurodad and ActionAid, Climate Adaptation Funding: Lessons from Development Finance (2010); Project Catalyst, "Scaling up Climate Finance", Finance Briefing Paper (2009).

1 Oxfam International, "About Oxfam International", accessed 16 September 2011, http://www.oxfam.org/en/about.
2 ActionAid, "ActionAid — Who We Are", accessed 16 September 2011, http://www.actionaid.org/who-we-are.
3 Eurodad, "The European Network on Debt and Development: About Us", accessed 16 September 2011, http://www.eurodad.org/aboutus/index.aspx?id=86.
4 Project Catalyst, "Scaling up Climate Finance", Finance Briefing Paper (2009), http://www.climateworks.org/download/?id=46b5eacc-14a4-4682-9734-b016b4983129.

countries do provide funding equal to full incremental costs, developing countries will still have to provide the remainder of the funding initially required, although these costs are eventually recouped.

The one feature that stands out in this table is how much the estimates vary from one another. In the short run, for instance, EC's estimate of US$7–9 billion annually (for the period 2010–12) stands in stark contrast to Oxfam's estimate of US$150 billion (by the year 2013). Similarly, in the medium and long term, estimates of annual finance requirements range from as low as US$126 billion (Project Catalyst's estimate for the period 2015–20) to as high as US$400 billion annually (the upper range of estimates given by the Group of 77 [G-77] and China).

To some extent, such differences are explained by the fact that estimates of the costs of mitigation and adaptation (which in turn determine financing requirements) are based on differing methodologies and differing assumptions about future variables. Moreover, current estimates of future climate finance requirements are highly uncertain — a fact reflected in the lack of precision of the estimates, with most presented as very broad ranges of values — and thus should be only interpreted as roughly indicative of the actual amounts that will be needed.

The starkness of some of the differences, though, suggests that other factors are also at play here. In particular, differing estimates often seem to reflect diverging views on how much developed countries *should* contribute to climate change finance. Developed country estimates of the required quantum of climate change finance tend to be more conservative than those made by developing countries and development non-governmental organizations (NGO), with estimates by multilateral organizations (UNFCCC or the World Bank) lying roughly in the middle of the spectrum. The EC's estimate of US$130 billion of climate finance by 2020, for instance, is considerably lower than the estimate of US$200–400 billion (or 0.5–1 per cent of the gross national product [GNP] of developed countries) made by the G-77 and China negotiating group.

These figures also indicate the conundrum currently confronting negotiators on climate change finance. On the one hand, the target of US$100 billion of annual climate change finance by 2020 that was agreed to at the Copenhagen and Cancun conferences is considerably less than all medium-term and long-run estimates of the amount of finance that is actually required, including both developed and developing country estimates. At the same time, the US$100 billion figure is an ambitious target in itself, one that dwarfs existing climate finance flows (i.e., those promised before the Copenhagen conference) that amount to less than US$9 billion a year[19] and is comparable to current ODA flows that equalled US$141 billion in 2010.[20] Moreover, it is unclear whether the significant ramping up of climate change finance from US$10 billion a year now to US$100 billion a year by 2020 is politically credible, even if it is feasible. Developed country governments, whether now or ten years in the future, will have an incentive to deliver low levels of finance to avoid a domestic backlash while promising much larger amounts of finance in the future to mitigate international pressure to contribute to climate finance. Such considerations have become especially pertinent in the context of the weak macroeconomic climate prevailing in many developed countries that constrains the ability of governments to deliver on their climate change finance promises.

3.2 DIFFERING VIEWS ON CLIMATE FINANCE AND CARBON MARKETS

United States

As already stated, the United States recognizes the principle of funding mitigation programmes in poorer developing countries as part of the obligation of richer countries, akin to official development aid. Furthermore, the new U.S. administration of President Barack Obama reversed the earlier George W. Bush administration's dismissive predilections on both the findings of the IPCC Assessment Reports and participation in the Kyoto Protocol. Indeed, the Danish climate minister Connie Hedegaard said that, with the election of President Obama, U.S. emissions policy "had moved forward 35 years overnight".[21]

However, the onset of the financial crisis and urgent competing policy priorities of the Obama administration has led to a reassessment of earlier hopes of active and generous U.S. support for a global climate change agreement. The projected budget deficits of the United States, as a consequence of the financial crisis, will put a severe strain on its ability to raise public grants for contributions to climate change mitigation and adaptation costs in the developing countries. In budget legislation, the U.S. administration will find it difficult to convince Congress representatives that taxpayer dollars should fund huge transfers of wealth to rapidly growing Asian economies like China and India.

European Union

At the 2009 climate change talks held in London involving governments of seventeen of the world's largest emitters to discuss financial commitments by the developed countries, no firm offers were put on the table.[22] The EU's twenty-seven members remain undecided on whether to specify the amount of funds the group would be willing to pledge to help developing countries meet the costs of emission reductions and adapting to the consequences of climate change. Former prime minister of the United Kingdom, Gordon Brown, proposed setting up a US$100 billion fund for climate change adaptation finance. The U.S. special envoy for climate change, Todd Stern, declined to talk numbers, only that "more progress can be made".[23]

At a 2009 EU summit, the region's leaders declared that it was time to declare their "fair share" of climate finance.[24] The EC puts the EU's "fair share" at up to €15 billion per year by 2020.[25] However, while claiming that "the EU is at the forefront of efforts to fight climate change", there is no single position regarding the quantum of finance that countries within the EU are willing to commit to. Countries such as Poland, supported by other east and central European states, insist that questions regarding the sharing of the financial burden within the EU be resolved first, before financial commitments are made by the EU as a group.[26] Other EU countries such as the United Kingdom and Denmark were keen to name a figure to maintain the region's credibility at the COP15 talks. Sweden, occupying the EU presidency, wanted an agreement on "upfront financing" in the order of €5–7 billion annually beginning in 2010.

The EC envisages that at least half of the financing sums being discussed would come from private carbon markets. At a domestic level in some of the OECD countries, systems of tradable permits, or cap-and-trade, have already been used to achieve national targets at least cost. For example, a cap-and-trade system was used in the United States to eliminate leaded gasoline in the 1980s at savings of more than US$250 million a year, and the same mechanism was also used to cut sulphur dioxide (SO_2) emissions from power plants in the country by 50 per cent with estimated savings of US$1 billion per year.[27]

Developing Countries

In principle, the developing countries require industrialized countries to fully cover costs of adaptation to climate change and the incremental cost of Nationally Appropriate Mitigation Actions (NAMA) integrated with general development projects in the developing world. India mentioned funding requirements of "at least several tens of billions of dollars per year" for adaptation programmes, and "several hundreds of billions of dollars per year" for emission reduction activities.[28] South Africa has put on record that "by 2020, the scale of financial flows to support adaptation in developing countries to be at least US$67 billion per annum".[29] In other UNFCCC submissions, India puts assessed contributions by the industrialized countries, over and above total existing ODA, at "equal to at least 0.5 per cent of the gross domestic product (GDP) of the developed world".[30] China supports industrialized countries contributions at 0.5–1 per cent of GDP in addition to existing ODA.[31]

The appropriate role of markets as a source of finance has been an area of contention in the climate change negotiations process in the UNFCCC and Kyoto negotiations. Both India and China, and in general the G-77 bloc, see carbon markets only in a limited and subsidiary role as a source of finance, and see measured and stable public finance contributions by the industrialized countries as the cornerstone of any global agreement. China considers that "the private sector approach and market-based mechanisms can only play a complementary role" to public funding.[32] This position is in distinct contrast to policy analysts, academics, and key players from the corporate sector in the industrialized countries, who view carbon markets as integral to the question of financing of climate change mitigation efforts.

It should be noted, however, that China plans to include a pilot emissions trading system in its five-year plan for 2011–15, according to its Environment Ministry.[33] With 84 per cent of the global CDM market share, many Chinese companies have already participated in CDM projects, and the Tianjing Exchange announced in 2009 its plans to launch China's first carbon contracts in six to twelve months' time.[34] Large Indian banks such as ICICI, Industrial Development Bank of India, and the State Bank of India have opened desks for participating in carbon markets in alliance with the IFC (International Finance Corporation — the private sector arm of the World Bank), as part of the CDM, earning some US$500 million since 2005.

ASEAN Member States

The position of the Association of Southeast Asian Nations (ASEAN) on issues of finance and technology transfer reflects the broad position taken up by developing countries such as China and the G-77. However, on the question of carbon markets and a cap-and-trade system as the market mechanism to incentivize emission reductions, some ASEAN countries have taken on a more active role. For example, Thai business leaders have suggested the development of a voluntary emissions cap to help establish a local emissions trading scheme.[35] The Federation of Thai Industries supports the idea of setting up a carbon market like the one in Japan, and to allow trans-ASEAN trade in carbon credits along the lines of the CDM. A carbon market would increase the willingness of financial institutions to invest in emission reduction projects.

According to one official of the Asian Development Bank (ADB), carbon markets are expected to grow in the post-Kyoto environment, and CDM will continue to play a role in developing countries' transition to a low-carbon economy.[36] Singapore's mature capital markets, with the requisite expertise and exposure to carbon trading around the world, puts the country in a good position to establish itself as the region's carbon market. In an opening speech to the Carbon Asia Forum 2009, Senior Minister of State for Trade and Industry S. Iswaran stated that "while the CDM process may have its shortcomings, let us not lose sight of the fact that the carbon and CDM markets have been successful on many counts".[37] Describing Singapore's strengths as a financial centre, the minister went on to describe the logic of Singapore's role as an Asia-Pacific Carbon Hub.

3.3 DETERMINING INDIVIDUAL COUNTRY CONTRIBUTIONS TO CLIMATE FINANCE

While developed countries have *collectively* committed to contribute to climate finance for the mitigation and adaptation needs of developing countries, how much *individual* developed countries have to contribute (both to the US$30 billion of fast-start finance and to the US$100 billion of long-term finance per year) has not been specified in either the Copenhagen Accord or the agreement reached at Cancun. An individual country's contribution to climate finance is thus effectively voluntary as long as it is ensured that developed countries, as a group, can meet their financial commitments. For instance, though close to US$30 billion of fast-start finance has already been pledged by developed countries for the years 2010–12,[38] individual developed countries are not under any obligation to contribute a particular amount. As such, individual country contributions do not appear to follow a systematic pattern with regards to their income or emissions. Table 3.3 below illustrates, for instance, how Japan, with per capita GDP and per capita CO_2 emissions lower than that of the United States, has pledged considerably higher per-capita contributions to fast-start finance.

The current system of burden-sharing is clearly undesirable from a developing country perspective, since it can result in a lack of stability and predictability in the delivery of funds. A number of developing countries and developing country groups, including the African Group, AOSIS, the G-77 and China group, India, Mexico, and Saudi Arabia, have highlighted such concerns and advocated a more systematic method of burden-sharing, in which assessed contributions for each contributing country are determined in advance.[39] It is less clear whether the contributing countries lose out from the absence of a clearly defined burden-sharing mechanism — while the absence of binding, externally assessed financial targets is welcome at a time when the budgets of developed countries are squeezed, countries also have to bear the risk that the contribution they make will not be matched accordingly by other contributing countries. Partly for the latter reason, the EC has also been an advocate of systematic burden-sharing.[40] Although burden-sharing based on assessed contributions is yet to be officially incorporated into the UNFCCC framework as such, there are signs that future negotiations could move in that direction — assessed contributions are one of the ideas being considered by the Transitional Committee that has been tasked to design the GCF.[41]

Table 3.3
Pattern of Fast-start Pledges (as of 9 May 2011)

	Pledge (US$ billion)	Pledge/cap (US$)	Per capita CO_2 emissions in 2008 (metric tonnes)	Per capita GDP in 2008 (US$ thousand)
Japan	15	117.59	9.01	38.27
EU	10.3	20.66	7.75	36.84
US	1.7	5.54	18.38	47.21
Norway	1	207.17	7.89	94.57

Sources: Athena Ballesteros et al., *Summary of Developed Country Fast-Start Finance Pledges* (World Resources Institute, 20 May 2011); International Energy Agency, *CO_2 Emissions from Fuel Combustion: Highlights, 2010 Edition* (Paris: International Energy Agency, 2010); World Bank, *World Development Indicators 2011* (Washington DC: The World Bank, 2011).

Underlying much of the discussion on burden-sharing is the UNFCCC principle of common but differentiated responsibilities:[42] the idea that countries with a greater level of responsibility for the climate change problem and a greater ability to tackle the problem should contribute to a greater extent to climate change finance (just as they have to bear more stringent mitigation obligations under the Kyoto Protocol and most proposals for a post-Kyoto climate deal). Burden-sharing based on assessed contributions thus typically involves a two-stage approach. The first stage requires deciding which countries contribute at all to climate change finance. In the second stage, indicators of responsibility and/or capability are used to determine an individual country's level of contribution.

At the end of the spectrum of opinion on "who pays" is the maximalist G-77 plus China position where only the developed countries as institutionalized in the Kyoto Protocol (i.e., Annex I countries) have to contribute to climate change finance. [43] In this view, as held by most developing countries in their pre-Copenhagen position, economic capability and historical responsibilities made the developed countries, largely coterminous with the OECD group, obliged to cover the full incremental costs of mitigation and adaptation in developing countries. In contrast, the Unites States, EU, Canada, and Japan have signalled in the Copenhagen and the following UNFCCC summits that, with per capita income and emission levels in several "advanced" developing countries at comparable levels to those of developed countries, it would be inequitable to assign the entirety of climate finance obligations on the traditionally defined "developed country" group, despite the acceptance of this definition in the Kyoto regime.

At the other end of the spectrum, the proposal by Mexico is to have *all* countries contribute to climate change finance, thus circumventing the problem of dividing the world into countries which are "developed" and countries which are not.[44] Mexico has argued that such a framework conforms to the UNFCCC principles of "differentiated capability and responsibility", since richer countries with greater levels of responsibility for climate change would have to contribute a greater amount, while the LDCs, despite also making contributions, would end up as net recipients of climate change finance. As a variation on this theme, the United States and the EC have proposed that all countries should have to contribute, with only the LDCs, as defined by the UN, excluded.[45] In the case where all countries with the possible exception of the LDCs contribute, most non-OECD countries would be required to take on financial obligations.

Other proposals offer criteria to select non-Annex I countries that are deemed to have "graduated" to capability and responsibility levels comparable to those of developed countries. The OECD, for instance, divides countries into developing, more advanced developing and developed countries (this last of which are also OECD members).[46] The existing Annex I/non-Annex I classification institutionalized in the Kyoto Protocol has been outdated for some time, with non-Annex I countries such as Israel, Mexico, and South Korea already OECD members.[47] Singapore is classified by the OECD as a more advanced developing country.

The ADB categorizes developing countries into several groups based on gross national income (GNI) per capita (Atlas method) and creditworthiness. Singapore, together with Hong Kong, South Korea, and Taiwan, has already graduated from receiving ADB assistance.[48] Under the World Bank's classification of countries as low-income, lower middle income, upper middle income, and high income, Singapore is listed under the highest category as a high-income country.[49] Finally, the International Monetary Fund (IMF) classifies countries as "advanced economies" or "emerging and developing economies", and Singapore is categorized as an advanced economy.[50]

The adoption of any of these classification regimes as indicators of "graduation" for countries being required to contribute to climate change finance would obviously be highly contentious, revolving around precise economic and environmental measures used to rate "capability" and "responsibility" rankings among countries. Similarly, threshold-based methods for determining graduation, whereby countries that have crossed a certain threshold value of a selected metric will undertake financial obligations, would also be subject to debate and negotiation.

A simple example of such a method is a proposal by Australia.[51] Australia argued that countries with a GDP per capita greater than that of Portugal, which is chosen as the benchmark country because it has the lowest GDP per capita among Annex II countries, graduate and contribute to climate finance. With this graduation rule, fifteen traditionally defined developing countries (including Singapore as well as countries such as Israel, South Korea, Qatar, and Saudi Arabia) would graduate and therefore be required to make financial contributions.

Multilateral agency classifications, as well as the graduation rule proposed by Australia, focus on the capability dimension while ignoring the dimension of responsibility for emissions mitigation and adaptation. Other proposed graduation indices combine indicators of capability and responsibility to determine which countries graduate. Such indices have already been proposed in the climate change mitigation literature to determine which countries graduate and take on mitigation targets.

One academic proposal ranks countries based on the arithmetic mean of their per capita GDP and per capita CO_2 emissions, with the former as a reasonable proxy for capability and the latter for responsibility. Both variables are normalized by dividing with a selected benchmark value, and then several thresholds are constructed to divide countries into distinct graduation groups in order to determine the relative mitigation commitments of countries from each group.[52] A similar metric could theoretically be used to rank individual country contribution requirements for climate change finance. Table 3.4 below ranks countries based on a graduation index for climate change finance along a similar metric, but with the key difference being that the values of per capita GDP and per capita CO_2 (which are normalized by dividing them with the world average) are averaged using the geometric mean rather than the arithmetic mean.[53] The rankings suggest that countries such as China, India, and Brazil with relatively low per capita incomes are unlikely to graduate, whereas Singapore, Israel, and the oil-rich Middle Eastern countries are the most likely candidates for graduation.

If the threshold for graduation is chosen to be the lowest index value among Annex I countries (i.e., the index value of Ukraine), China, Malaysia, as well as higher-ranked countries such as South Korea and Singapore would graduate and take on financial obligations. With this threshold, many developing countries would be expected to graduate, since Ukraine's index value is considerably lower than the world index value. By contrast, with a threshold equal to the average index value among all Annex I countries, only the United Arab Emirates (UAE) would graduate from our sample; few non-Annex I countries would graduate since even countries with index values greater than Japan and the EU would not necessarily graduate.[54] Finally, with a threshold equal to the lowest index value among Annex II countries (i.e., Portugal), Singapore would graduate together with Israel, South Korea, and the oil-rich Middle Eastern countries.

In addition to capability and responsibility, mitigation potential — i.e., the economic cost at which a tonne of GHG or CO_2 emission can be avoided or mitigated — has also been highlighted as one of the factors that could be taken into account when determining a country's financial obligations.[55]

Table 3.4
Graduation Index: Per capita CO_2 * Per capita GDP

$$\text{Index} = \sqrt{\left(\frac{\text{Per capita } CO_2}{\text{World per capita } CO_2} * \frac{\text{Per capita GDP}}{\text{World per capita GDP}} \right)}$$

Country	Index
India	0.18
Thailand	0.59
Brazil	0.64
Ukraine (Lowest Annex I)	0.64
China	0.66
Mexico	0.99
World	1.00
Malaysia	1.17
Portugal (Lowest Annex II)	1.71
Russian Federation	1.81
Korea, Rep.	2.22
New Zealand	2.31
Israel	2.44
European Union	2.66
Saudi Arabia	2.74
Japan	2.93
Singapore	3.02
Annex I average	3.05
Canada	4.30
United States	4.65
Australia	4.73
United Arab Emirates	6.89

Notes: Here as well as in subsequent analysis, China includes mainland China as well as Hong Kong (consistent with the UNFCCC).
Sources: International Energy Agency, *CO_2 Emissions from Fuel Combustion: Highlights, 2010 Edition.* World Bank, *World Development Indicators 2011.*

Table 3.5 illustrates the effect of multiplying "carbon intensity", i.e., tonnes of CO_2 or GHG emission per U.S. dollar GDP (a proxy for mitigation potential) to per capita income and per capita CO_2 emissions with equal

Table 3.5
Graduation Index: Per capita CO_2 * Per capita GDP * CO_2/GDP

$$\text{Index} = \sqrt[3]{\left(\frac{\text{Per capita } CO_2}{\text{World per capita } CO_2} * \frac{\text{Per capita GDP}}{\text{World per capita GDP}} * \frac{CO_2/\text{GDP}}{\text{World } CO_2/\text{GDP}} \right)}$$

Country	Index
India	0.43
Brazil	0.57
Thailand	0.84
Latvia	0.86
Mexico	0.91
World	1.00
China	1.08
Portugal	1.08
Malaysia	1.33
European Union	1.46
New Zealand	1.47
Israel	1.57
Japan	1.62
Singapore	1.63
Korea, Rep.	1.77
Annex I average	1.83
Russian Federation	1.87
Saudi Arabia	2.34
Canada	2.42
United States	2.60
Australia	2.61
United Arab Emirates	3.82

Sources: International Energy Agency, *CO₂ Emissions from Fuel Combustion: Highlights, 2010 Edition*; World Bank, *World Development Indicators 2011*.

weight. Countries with carbon-intensive economies, such as Malaysia, China, South Korea, and Saudi Arabia, rank higher. Malaysia becomes a candidate for graduation in the base scenario (where the threshold equals the lowest index value among Annex II countries) while Saudi Arabia now graduates in all three scenarios regardless of the threshold chosen. Singapore and the EU, which are less carbon-intensive, improve in the rankings, though Singapore still graduates if either the lowest index value among Annex II countries or the Annex I average index value is chosen as a threshold.

It is important to note, however, that while indicators of mitigation potential can be useful in determining emission reduction targets, since it is efficient to focus mitigation activities in countries where it is cheaper to do so, the same rationale does not hold for climate change finance contributions. Relying on carbon intensity to determine graduation to financial responsibilities may well lead to an inequitable outcome if a country with low levels of responsibility and capability happens to have a highly carbon-intensive economy — which arguably could be the case with countries such as China and Malaysia.

Which countries contribute to climate change finance, and by how much, depends therefore on the graduation mechanism and the specific metric chosen. There is a range of possible graduation scenarios, based on the permutations of metrics proposed, in which a subset of non–Annex I countries "graduate" and contribute along with the Annex I countries. Economic classifications by multilateral agencies provide a mixed picture, with Singapore a candidate for graduation under some but not all of the classifications. Neither agency classifications nor quantitative metrics-based rankings take into account unique national circumstances and the dynamics of the negotiation process that, in practice, will play a key role in determining which countries contribute to climate change finance.

Determining how much individual countries should contribute is essentially a burden-sharing problem, where the goal is to allocate financial obligations across countries so as to satisfy criteria of equity and fairness. Such criteria tend to dominate discussions on burden-sharing in climate finance, even more so than with the allocation of climate change mitigation obligations since efficiency concerns are relatively unimportant here. It does not make a significant difference from a climate change mitigation and adaptation cost perspective where the finance is raised.[56]

Proposals for Allocating Obligations

Table 3.6 below summarizes some of the key burden-sharing proposals relevant to climate change finance. Mexico's proposal provides a range of possible indicators of responsibility, equity, efficiency, and payment capacity that can potentially be used to determine contributions towards climate finance. The exact indicators and the formula for determining contributions will inevitably be subject to debate and negotiation strategies adopted by key players. The EC's proposal measures a country's responsibility using its current GHG emissions and its capability using its total GDP. Expressing each variable as a share of the world total (minus LDCs, which are exempted from contributing), so as to facilitate comparison, the EC formula calculates the arithmetic mean of the two variables, which gives the country's share of total climate finance contributions.

A second category is formed by the formulas proposed by the Institute for Public Policy Research (IPPR) and the Energy Research Centre (ERC).[57] The key feature of these is the *development threshold*: a minimum level of income for each individual and an associated minimum level of emissions (also known as survival emissions) that are needed for basic development and are thus not counted towards the country's capability and responsibility. The deduction of survival emissions from calculation of a country's responsibility was also suggested by Mexico, though they do not extend such deductions to income.

In the IPPR proposal (known as the Greenhouse Development Rights, or GDRS framework), the indicators chosen are the country's total income (excluding income earned below the threshold) and the cumulative CO_2 emissions since 1990 (excluding emissions below the threshold). The country's contribution share is calculated in a similar way to EC's formula, by expressing each indicator as a share of the total value of the indicator for the contributing group of countries, and then taking the arithmetic mean.

ERC's formula, on the other hand, adjusts GDP per capita first by excluding income below the poverty line and then by taking the Human Development Index (HDI) of the country into account, reflecting the view that a country's ability to contribute should be assessed using not just its income but also other factors reflecting its development status such as education and health. Cumulative emissions (minus survival emissions) are measured starting from any year between 1850 and 1990. The method for calculating contribution shares of individual countries is also different,

Table 3.6

Proposals for Allocating Financial Obligations

Organization	Contributing countries	Indicators	Formula
Mexico – World Climate Change Fund (2008)	All countries (developing countries are net receivers)	Responsibility: Current emissions, cumulative emissions or historical contribution to rising temperatures Capability: GDP per capita + relative size of country's economy Equity: Per-capita emissions Efficiency: Emissions intensity	Final indicators, as well as formula, to be reached through consensus
European Commission (2009)	All countries except LDCs	Responsibility: Current emissions Capability: GDP	Country's share = Weighted average of country's shares of GDP and current emissions in the contributing group
G-77 and China (2008)	Annex I countries	Capability: GNP	Annual contribution = 0.5–1% of GNP
Greenhouse Development Rights (GDRS) proposal- –Baer et al. (2008), IPPR (2009)	Flexible, depending on negotiations	Capability: C = Sum of all individual incomes excluding income below a *development threshold* Responsibility: R = Cumulative CO_2 emissions since 1990, excluding emissions below a *development threshold*	Country's contribution share = Weighted average of country's shares of C and R in the contributing group

continued on next page

Table 3.6 — cont'd

Organization	Contributing countries	Indicators	Formula
IMF (2010)	Developed countries; may extend to developing countries over time	Capability: GDP (Y) Others: Openness (O), Variability (V), reserves (R), compression factor (k)	IMF calculated quota share = (0.5*Y + 0.3*O + 0.15*V + 0.05*R)^k. All variables except k expressed as shares of world total, where country's share = IMF calculated quota share / Total quota share of contributing countries
University of Cape Town– Energy Research Centre (2009)	Annex I countries	Capability: C = 2005 GDP per capita, excluding income of proportion of population below poverty line, adjusted by taking HDI into account. Responsibility: R = Cumulative emissions since any year between 1850-1990 to 2005, divided by 2005 population, with survival emissions excluded	Country's contribution share = [(R^0.6 * C^0.4) * Country's population] / Annex I population

Notes: (1) IPPR, the Institute for Public Policy Research, is a UK-based think tank researching on a variety of policy areas, including issues relating to climate change and environmental sustainability. (2) The Energy Research Centre at the University of Cape Town in South Africa is a multidisciplinary research centre focusing on a variety of energy-related research areas.

Sources: Mexico, "Enhanced Action on the Provision of Financial Resources and Investment to Support Action on Mitigation and Adaptation and Technology Cooperation"; European Commission, *Stepping Up International Climate Finance: A European Blueprint for the Copenhagen Deal*; Group of 77 and China, "Financial Mechanism for Meeting Financial Commitments Under the Convention"; Paul Baer, Tom Athanasiou, Sivan Kartha, and Eric Kemp-Benedict, *The Greenhouse Development Rights Framework: The Right to Development in a Climate-constrained World* (2008); Andrew Pendleton and Simon Retallack, *Fairness in Global Climate Finance* (2009); EcoEquity and SEI, "The Greenhouse Development Rights Calculator"; Hugh Bredenkamp and Catherine Pattlo, "Financing the Response to Climate Change" (2010); International Monetary Fund, *Reform of Quota and Voice in the International Monetary Fund – Report of the Executive Board to the Board of Governors* (28 Mar 2008); Harald Winkler, Andrew Marquard and Thapelo Letete, *Analysis of Possible Quantified Emission Reduction Commitments by Individual Annex I Parties* (Mar 2009).

with a weighted geometric average used rather than the arithmetic mean, and a slightly greater weight (60 per cent) placed on the responsibility indicator as opposed to the capability indicator (40 per cent).

The proposal by the G-77 and China in 2008 simply calculates each developed country's contribution as a fixed share (between 0.5 and 1 per cent) of its GDP, with no contributions due from the "developing" countries, essentially adopting the Kyoto Protocol Annex I definition of "developed country".[58] In the proposal by the IMF, each country's contribution share equals its actual contribution share to IMF. To derive the latter, a weighted average of a GDP variable (itself a blend with 60 per cent weight given to GDP calculated at market exchange rates and 40 per cent weight given to GDP calculated using Purchasing Power Parity, or PPP) and variables measuring the openness of the economy, variability of its income from trade and capital flows, and its official reserves, is first calculated (where each variable is expressed as a share of the world total). A "compression factor" is then applied to the average (to reduce the dispersion in relative country contributions) to give the country's contribution share. An obvious shortcoming of this proposal is that many of the variables it utilizes, such as openness to trade and official reserves, are unrelated to the dimensions of responsibility, capability, equity, and efficiency that are typically emphasized in debates about the allocation of climate finance contributions.

Generalizing across the six proposals presented in Table 3.6, the burden-sharing mechanisms for climate change finance vary depending on three key factors:

1. *Which countries contribute:* As discussed earlier in this section, there are a wide range of views on which countries should contribute to climate finance, and this is reflected in the proposals. For instance, while the G-77 and China group and the ERC in South Africa posit that only Annex I countries should contribute, Mexico, the United States and the EC argue that all countries except possibly the LDCs should contribute.

2. *Choice of indicators:* A variety of indicators for measuring both responsibility and capability have been suggested — capability can be measured using GDP or GNP, at market exchange rates or PPP, and can be adjusted based on HDI, while responsibility can be measured using current emissions, cumulative emissions (with a range of possible

start dates), and historical contribution to rising temperatures. While the EC's proposal includes no equity adjustment, the GDRS proposal and the proposal by the ERC adjust for equity by introducing the development threshold, while Mexico suggests incorporating per capita emissions to adjust for equity. Mexico also suggests incorporating indicators of efficiency into climate finance burden-sharing.

3. *Formula for calculating country contribution:* The most common formula for calculating each country's contribution is to express each indicator as a share of the total value of the indicator (among the contributing countries) and use a weighted average of the indicators to calculate the country's share of total contributions. The proposals by EC and IPPR calculate the contribution share by using the arithmetic mean of the two indicators with equal weights, whereas the ERC takes a weighted geometric average with the two indicators weighted differently. The radical alternative proposed by G-77 and China is to use the "share of GDP" formula to directly calculate the country's contributions, as opposed to calculating the country's share of total contributions first.

Comparison of Individual Country Contributions

Quite obviously, which countries contribute has a major impact on how much each country contributes. When only Annex I (or Annex II) countries contribute, their individual contributions are high; whereas with all countries or all countries except LDCs contributing, the individual contributions of Annex I countries decrease substantially. For non–Annex I countries such as China, Malaysia, and Singapore, of course, the impact of the scenario chosen can mean the difference between nil contributions and fairly substantial contributions.

Also notable is the large gap between Annex I country contributions under the G-77 plus China proposal and their contributions under the other three proposals (non–Annex I countries do not contribute under the G-77 and China proposal). The difference arises primarily because the G-77 and China proposal calculates Annex 1 country contributions directly rather than as shares of the global total, meaning that total contributions per annum are considerably higher (at around US$200–US$400 billion) than the US$100 billion figure discussed at Durban, and given the larger total contribution, individual (Annex I) country contributions are much higher as well.

The EU, Singapore, the UAE, and the United States, with relatively high emissions per capita and GDP per capita, have more stringent targets than countries such as China and Malaysia under both the EC proposal and the GDRS framework.

The GDRS formula is relatively progressive since countries that have lower per capita income or emissions will have a larger proportion of their income and/or emissions below the development threshold, which are not counted towards their contributions.

The GDRS framework factors in not just equity across countries (with higher contributions for countries with a higher graduation index), but equity within countries as well, by penalizing countries with greater inequality in income and emissions. If we take two countries with the same per capita income and emissions inequality, the country with greater inequality will have a larger proportion of its population with income and emissions below the threshold. Thus, a *smaller* proportion of its total income and emissions will be discounted from its contributions, increasing its per capita contributions relative to the country with less inequality.

The inequality effect is relatively insignificant in rich countries, as only a small proportion of their population is below the development threshold. As Table 3.7 shows, though, the inequality effect can be quite prominent for developing countries.

If we compare Brazil and China, their per capita contributions under the EC proposal are close to each other, as might be expected given that their graduation index values are roughly equal. China's per capita contribution under the GDRS proposal, however, is substantially lower than Brazil's (US$1.98 compared to US$6.51), because of greater income inequality in Brazil that is reflected in its higher Gini coefficient. Similarly, although Malaysia with a higher index score contributes more than Mexico on a per capita basis under the EC proposal, its per capita contribution under the GDRS proposal is slightly lower than Mexico's (US$12.22 versus US$12.60). Again the difference can be attributed to the higher Gini coefficient in Mexico compared to Malaysia.

In general, countries with high per capita emissions and incomes (largely developed countries) are likely to prefer formulas similar to that proposed by the EC (itself representing a significant bloc of developed countries), in which no progressive effect is introduced. Most developing countries (with relatively low per capita emissions and incomes) and NGOs emphasizing development objectives are likely to prefer formulas in which

Table 3.7
Effect of Inequality on Per Capita Annual Contributions in Selected Countries

	Graduation index	Contributions (EC proposal, US$)	Contributions (GDRS proposal, US$)	Gini coefficient
Brazil	0.64	10.32	6.51	55.0
China	0.66	11.33	1.98	41.5
Mexico	0.99	14.99	12.60	48.1
Malaysia	1.17	18.20	12.22	37.9

Sources: International Energy Agency, *CO$_2$ Emissions from Fuel Combustion: Highlights, 2010 Edition*. World Bank, *World Development Indicators 2011*; EcoEquity and SEI, "The Greenhouse Development Rights Calculator."

some form of equity adjustment is made to reduce the financing burden on countries with lower responsibility and capability levels. For Singapore, introducing progressivity into the burden-sharing mechanism increases its obligations due to its relatively high per capita emissions and income.

Adjusting for inequality within countries is not likely to be seen as a necessary criterion for allocating financial contributions among countries. Developed countries are likely to be indifferent to the issue, as the effect on their contributions is relatively insignificant. Developing countries with relatively high income and emissions inequality (such as Brazil) will likely oppose any such adjustments, whereas the opposite should be true for developing countries that have relatively low inequality.

Comparison of Existing Contributions to Multilateral Organizations

Membership dues contributed by countries to major multilateral organizations utilize burden-sharing formulas to calculate individual country membership dues. Table 3.8 below provides a summary view of how some of these organizations allocate financial obligations among their members. The burden-sharing mechanism used in the IMF is exactly the same as their suggested mechanism for allocating climate finance obligations. The World Trade Organization (WTO) bases member contributions on their share of the total trade of WTO members, with a minimum contribution rate of 0.015 per cent of the total budget from each

Table 3.8
Burden-sharing Mechanisms in Multilateral Organizations

Organization	Indicators	Formula
IMF	GDP (Y), openness (O), variability (V), reserves (R), expressed as shares of world total; k = compression factor	IMF calculated quota share = $(0.5*Y + 0.3*O + 0.15*V + 0.05*R)^k$ All variables except k expressed as shares of world total, where country's share = IMF calculated quota share / Total quota share of contributing countries
UN	GNI (at market exchange rates)	Country's share of world GNI, with downward adjustments for low income and debt and with a maximum contribution of 22%
WTO	Imports, Exports	Share of total trade of all WTO members (imports + exports), with a minimum contribution level of 0.015%
EU	GNI	Country's share of total GNI

Sources: International Monetary Fund, *Reform of Quota and Voice in the International Monetary Fund – Report of the Executive Board to the Board of Governors* (28 Mar 2008); United Nations, *Resolution Adopted by the General Assembly 64/248: Scale of Assessments for the Apportionment of the Expenses of the United Nations* (2010); World Trade Organization, *Method of Calculation of Contributions Assessed on Members of the WTO*; European Commission, *European Union: Public Finance*, 4th ed. (Belgium: European Committees, 2008).

member. Both the EU and the UN, by contrast, base member contributions largely on the GNI share of the country. The UN formula, however, makes a number of adjustments to the gross GNI share. Equity adjustments are made by incorporating a low per capita income adjustment of 80 per cent, making further downward adjustments for debt and having a maximum assessment rate for the LDCs equal to 0.01 per cent of the total UN budget. In addition, GNI is calculated at market exchange rates that are adjusted to account for excessive price fluctuations, while there is a minimum assessment rate of 0.001 per cent and a maximum assessment rate of 22 per cent for all countries.

In assessing the contributions countries can expect to make to climate change finance, it is not enough to calculate their contributions under the proposals as they stand now. Standing proposals are subject to being altered or tweaked depending on the negotiations and bargaining on climate change finance. The effect of changing indicators of responsibility and capability on assessed country contributions to adaptation finance can be examined by simulations.[59]

A greater weight on "responsibility" as measured by current emissions leads to greater contributions from developing countries and thus might be seen as inequitable.[60] The absence of clear principles is not just restricted to the question of selecting weights, but is a general feature of the debate over burden-sharing in climate finance. Deciding which countries should contribute, determining the extent to which progressivity should be incorporated into the proposal, and choosing between alternative capability and responsibility indicators in the absence of agreed overarching principles is bound to remain contentious. Negotiating positions on these are likely to be shaped by how much individual countries are required to contribute under alternative scenarios. Developed countries are likely to prefer scenarios where most countries contribute to climate finance, responsibility is measured using current rather than historical emissions, and increased weight is placed on responsibility. The opposite is likely to be true for developing countries. Indeed, current negotiating positions on financial burden-sharing are already shaped by these dynamics.

Australia favours a graduation scenario (where some non–Annex I countries contribute) to the status quo where only Annex I countries are expected to contribute. The EC favours comprehensive participation (with all countries except LDCs contributing), the use of current rather than cumulative emissions, and the absence of a progressive mechanism which places greater weight on capability indicators. NGOs such as the ERC and the IPPR favour the use of cumulative emissions and a progressive mechanism that takes inter-country as well as intra-country equity into account.

The uncertainty about the future shape of a burden-sharing mechanism is reflected in the uncertainty surrounding the projected contributions that any non–Annex 1 country (such as Singapore) might have to make to climate change finance, in the event that the set of contributing countries is expanded to include Singapore (itself a point of uncertainty). How much Singapore contributes will vary depending to a large extent on several factors, including development threshold definitions, set of contributing countries, time period chosen to measure carbon emissions (whether current or cumulative), and assignment of weights on the proxy measures for responsibility and capability indicators (such as emissions per capita and GDP per capita).

Climate Change Finance: Instruments and Sources

According to the text of the agreement reached in Cancun in 2010, climate change finance "may come from a wide variety of sources, public and private, bilateral and multilateral, including alternative sources."[61] Countries negotiating on climate change finance have sharp disagreements on issues such as whether public or private sources should be used and in what combination, the appropriate role of leveraging mechanisms, and how the "newness" of funding can be determined. One review of possible financing sources is provided by the UN Advisory Group on Climate Change Financing (AGF).[62] Its suggested funding sources are summarized in Table 3.9.

The existence of a carbon price, whether through carbon markets or some form of tax, forms the bedrock of many of the financing proposals. An emissions trading scheme allows governments to raise revenue by auctioning emissions allowances and charging a levy on offset transactions, which can then be channelled to developing countries as climate finance contributions. The purchase of offsets from developing countries by developed countries, as in the Kyoto Protocol's CDM arrangements, also directly constitutes a flow of climate finance to mitigation activity within developing countries.

Other carbon-related revenue include a direct tax on carbon, a "wires" charge (a tax on electricity generation), taxes on international aviation and shipping, the removal of fossil fuel subsidies, and redirection of fossil fuel subsidies. All of these, while effectively taxing carbon emissions and thus imposing a carbon price (whether implicitly or explicitly), can raise tax revenue or free up public funds that can be directed towards climate change finance. In the wake of the financial crisis, a "Tobin" tax on financial transactions has also been proposed as a way to raise revenue for climate finance.[63] In addition to all of these sources, governments, multilateral development banks, and private institutions can directly contribute to climate change finance.

According to the AGF report, the US$100 billion target agreed to at the Copenhagen and Cancun conferences is potentially achievable. Taking into account the fact that some of the measures may be mutually exclusive (e.g., emissions trading and carbon tax are usually considered as policy alternatives, though they do not necessarily need to be so), the amount of finance that can be raised using the maximum possible number of sources

Table 3.9
Possible Sources of Climate Change Finance

No	Sources	Type	Amount of finance generated (US$ billion) Assumed Carbon Price = US$25/tonne of CO_2	
			Net annual flows	Gross annual flows (if different from net)
1	Auctions of emissions allowances	Public	8–38	
2	Offset levies	Public	1–5	
3	Carbon market offsets	Private	8–14	38–50
4	International transport			
	International shipping taxes	Public	4–9	
	International aviation taxes	Public	2–3	
5	Other carbon-related revenue			
	Carbon tax	Public	10	
	Wires charge on electricity generation	Public	5	
	Removal of fossil fuel subsidies	Public	3–8	
	Redirection of fossil fuel royalties	Public	~10	
6	Financial transaction tax (Tobin tax)	Public	2–27	
7	Direct budget contributions	Public	Up to 200–400	
8	Development bank instruments	Public	11	30–40
9	Private finance	Private	20–24	200

Notes: Gross flows are the actual flows of finance to developing countries, while net flows discount any financial flows that eventually flow out of developing countries (e.g. as loan repayments).
Source: UN High-Level Advisory Group on Climate Change Financing, *Report of the Secretary-General's High-Level Advisory Group on Climate Change Financing* (5 Nov 2010).

(apart from direct budget contributions) lies in the US$70–US$150 billion range. The post-Copenhagen US$100 billion target can therefore be reached with a maximum of US$30 billion of direct budget contributions every year.

Should Climate Finance be Generated Primarily from Public or Private Sources?

The Cancun Agreements leave unresolved a crucial and contentious issue: the appropriate balance between public and private finance. As Table 3.10 illustrates, different countries and organizations hold quite different views on what should be the right balance. Most developing countries, as well as developmental NGOs, favour a greater role for public finance, with private finance playing only a complementary role. Most developed countries, on the other hand, emphasize private finance, with the role of public finance restricted to targeting areas that cannot be reached by private funds. Multilateral bodies and organizations, such as the UNFCCC, World Bank, and the UN AGF, and a handful of both developed and developing countries have argued that the most effective way to raise finance is to combine the use of public and private finance.

The innate attractiveness of private finance to developed countries stems from the fact that transferring large sums of public money to developing countries, many of which are rapidly emerging economies, is likely to be politically unpopular within developed countries, especially at a time when many governments of developed countries are coping with an economic recession and large budget deficits.[64] This argument, however, is primarily applicable to direct budget contributions drawn directly from existing, scarce fiscal resources and does not apply with equal force to *new*, self-sustaining sources of public and private finance such as the financial transactions tax and taxes on aviation and shipping. Moreover, private finance has potential efficiency advantages over public finance. Carbon markets allow mitigation to be carried out efficiently and at least-cost,[65] which means that private finance flows arising out of the carbon market (e.g., if offsets are purchased from developing countries) will be able to more efficiently achieve mitigation in the developing country.

Developing countries, on the other hand, harbour several concerns about private finance. Firstly, there is widespread consensus that adaptation, capacity building and some adaptation activities are unlikely to be adequately funded by profit-oriented private finance alone.[66] Adaptation

Table 3.10
Public vs Private Finance

Organization	Perspective	Private	Public
Copenhagen / Cancun	*Emphasize both*	—	—
UN AGF	*Emphasize both*	US$28–38 billion	>US$41–111 billion
World Bank, UNFCCC, AOSIS, Japan, South Africa, Ghana, Chile	*Emphasize both*		
EC	*Preference for private*	US$53 billion (43–64%)	US$30–70 billion (36–57%)
Project Catalyst	—	US$21–42 billon (23–30%)	US$70–98 billion (70–77%)
Australia, Canada, Iceland, NZ, USA	*Preference for private*	—	—
NGOs (Oxfam, Eurodad, ActionAid)	*Preference for public*	(0%)*	US$200 billion (100%)
G-77 + China, African Group, India, Indonesia, Argentina	*Preference for public*	—	—

Notes: In the estimates by the NGOs, the full climate finance requirements are to be met by public finance, and any private finance generated is effectively "surplus" finance.
Sources: Algeria, *Key Elements of LCA Negotiating Text: Final Version* (2009); Eurodad et al., *Climate Adaptation Funding: Lessons from Development Finance* (2010); European Commission, *Stepping Up International Climate Finance (2009)*; Government of India, *Climate Change Negotiations: India's Submissions to the United Nations Framework Convention on Climate Change* (Aug 2009); Group of 77 and China, "Financial Mechanism for Meeting Financial Commitments Under the Convention" (2008); Oxfam International, "Climate Finance Post-Copenhagen: The $100 bn questions" (2010); Project Catalyst, "Scaling up Climate Finance" (2009); Stewart et al., "Climate Finance: Key Concepts and Ways Forward", *Harvard Project on International Climate Agreements: Viewpoints* (2009); UN High-Level Advisory Group on Climate Change Financing, *Report of the Secretary-General's High-Level Advisory Group on Climate Change Financing* (2010); UNFCCC, *Investment and Financial Flows to Address Climate Change: An Update* (2008), pp. 74–88; World Bank, *World Development Report 2010: Development and Climate Change* (2010); World Resources Institute, *Summary of UNFCCC Submissions: 19 April 2010 to 23 November 2010*; World Resources Institute, *Summary of UNFCCC Submissions: August 2008 to 29 October 2009.*

activities are by their very nature not revenue generating, and will not attract foreign private investment. It is argued that capacity building and many mitigation projects, because of their public goods nature and long-time horizons of investment, will be underfunded if only private finance is available. This is why even supporters of private finance, such as the

EC, acknowledge that public finance will still be needed to target areas such as adaptation which are likely to be undefunded by private finance.[67] From the viewpoint of developed countries, though, mitigation tends to trump adaptation as the activity towards which finance should be directed, so that private finance is still emphasized over public finance; quite the opposite view is held by developing countries.

Secondly, public finance is perceived to provide greater stability and accountability by developing countries. Private finance flows could well be highly uncertain, subject as they are to factors such as the establishment of carbon markets throughout the world (on top of the uncertainty surrounding a global climate deal), fluctuating carbon price and the uncertainty of the investment climate in many developing countries. Developing countries are also concerned that the use of private finance can potentially lend itself to *double counting*, where the same flow of funds from a developed to a developing country is counted towards meeting both the former's financial obligations and its emission mitigation obligations. This is perceived as inequitable by developing countries (since climate finance is meant to supplement rather than replace emission targets), and developed countries generally do not support double counting either.[68]

The World Bank notes that private and public finance often play different and complementary roles; private finance can be directed at mitigation and some (individual-driven) adaptation activities, where efficiency concerns are paramount and public finance can be directed towards most adaptation activities, capacity building and some mitigation projects not targeted by private finance.[69] Combining private and public finance also allows increased scope for public–private partnerships in areas such as research and development. A more fundamental benefit of combining public and private finance is that it allows scarce public funds to be *leveraged* efficiently.

Leveraging mechanisms help to maximize the impact (e.g., quantity of emissions reduced) achieved by a given amount of financing, typically by using the funds initially raised to generate further funds.[70] There are a number of methods of leveraging finance, both public and private. Public finance can be leveraged by using the funds to incentivize further private finance flows, for instance, by providing low-interest guaranteed loans. Private finance can also be leveraged in a number of ways; e.g., intermediary carbon banks can purchase reductions in developing countries and sell them in developed country carbon markets at a higher price (taking advantage of the fact that mitigation costs are lower in developing countries), and then use the profits to purchase additional emission reductions in developing countries.

The UN AGF argues that leveraging mechanisms can be most effective only if both public and private finance are utilized. Public funds can then be used to make the initial investment and then "crowd in" much larger sums of financing from private sources through leveraging mechanisms, a process that would be difficult with private funds alone and impossible with only public finance. This can lead to much higher gross flows of climate finance, which is beneficial since net flows of finance are only sufficient to meet the *incremental* costs of mitigation and adaptation in developing countries. As already noted, initial financing requirements of mitigation and adaptation activities typically exceed the incremental costs since the latter measures factors in any potential cost-savings in the future. Indeed, current discussions on climate finance (including the AGF report) overemphasize net flows when it is gross flows of finance that will determine how much mitigation and adaptation is actually carried out in developing countries.[71]

Despite the obvious benefit to both developed and developing countries from using funds more efficiently by leveraging them, developing countries are also concerned about leveraging. One issue is simply that many of the leveraging mechanisms will result in a loss of economic rents earned by developing countries from the sale of carbon credits. The use of intermediary carbon banks, for instance, reduces the price received by developed countries for the sale of credits.[72]

A second issue concerns how leveraged funds will be counted towards developed country climate finance pledges. If both the original funds invested and the funds that are generated from them (through leveraging mechanisms) are counted, the problem of double counting again arises since it is only the leveraged funds that are directly contributing to climate change mitigation and adaptation. Possible solutions would be to count only the leveraged funds (the amount of funding that actually goes into mitigation and adaptation) or to count only the original disbursed funds. The former solution favours developed countries, which have to come up with a smaller initial contribution (which can then be leveraged up to meet the target), whereas the latter favours developing countries, which receive a flow of funds greater than promised due to leveraging.

In addition to negotiating positions and the various arguments guiding such positions, funding constraints will also play a part in determining the balance between public and private finance. As Table 3.10 shows, the maximum funds that can be realistically raised from private sources is approximately US$50 billion per year, so that a minimum of around US$50 billion of public finance will be needed. Project Catalyst estimates that public finance from direct budget contributions is unlikely to exceed US$28–US$56 billion per year.[73] Such constraints imply that it is unlikely that all or most of the required finance will be generated from one kind of source.

Is Funding "New and Additional"?

In principle, developed and developing countries both agree that the financial resources labelled as climate change finance must be "new and additional". The rationale behind the requirement of "additionality" is to prevent ODA funds from being diverted to climate change finance from other uses.[74] Similarly, newness would ensure that climate change finance pledges that were made in the past are not repackaged so as to count towards the latest climate finance pledges as well.[75]

In practice, though, "newness and additionality" is an elusive and contested concept. Questions have been raised about whether many of the fast-start finance pledges made so far can be considered new and additional. According to the World Resources Institute, for instance, Japan's US$15 billion pledge includes US$10 billion of climate finance promised in 2008 (before the Copenhagen Accord when new and additional fast-start finance was promised), while the pledges of the United States and United Kingdom include 2008 commitments to the Climate Investment Funds.[76] In addition, African countries have highlighted that some of the funding disbursed had already been pledged for foreign aid and argued that such funds do not qualify as additional.[77] The underlying cause of such debates is the fact that there is as yet no agreed baseline against which climate change finance can be judged to be "new and additional". When it comes to defining the baseline, developed and developing countries differ quite fundamentally, as Table 3.11 highlights.

Newness and Additionality of Climate Finance: Views on Possible Thresholds

Developing countries and some developed countries favour a baseline of 0.7 per cent of GNI,[78] which is designed to ensure that only once developed countries fulfil their ODA pledges of 0.7 per cent of GNI can

Table 3.11
Baseline Definitions

Baseline	Organizations in favour	Arguments for	Arguments against
No universal baseline; all climate-related ODA counts as CCF	Most developed countries (US, EU, Japan, NZ)	1. "Double-dipping": adaptation finance also fulfils ODA objectives 2. Donor flexibility	1. Lack of comparability of pledges 2. Risk of diversion of ODA
Above 0.7% of GNI	Developing countries, some developed countries (UK, Netherlands)	1. Arithmetically straightforward 2. Takes ODA pledges into account	1. Countries above threshold can divert ODA 2. Politically unacceptable to countries far below 0.7% ODA threshold (e.g., US)
Above predefined projection of ODA & past climate aid	International Institute for Environment and Development (IIED), NYU academics	1. Takes ODA pledges and past CCF pledges into account 2. Predictability of funds	1. Determination of BAU ODA and past climate aid likely to be disputed 2. Predetermined projections cannot take changing national circumstances into account
New sources only	UN High-level Advisory Group on Climate Change Financing (AGF), IIED	1. Guarantees newness 2. Additionality likely — lower chance of ODA double-counting 3. Avoids complicated issue of defining baseline	1. Restricts use of existing channels → Risk of reduced funding 2. Likely to be feasible only in the long-run

Notes: The International Institute for Environment and Development is a research institute working in the field of sustainable development. "NYU Academics" refers to Richard B. Stewart, Benedict Kingsbury, and Bryce Rudyk, from the New York University School of Law, who are the authors of a paper on climate finance entitled, "Climate Finance: Key Concepts and Ways Forward".

Sources: World Resources Institute, *Summary of UNFCCC Submissions: August 2008 to October 29, 2009*; Group of 77 and China, "Financial Mechanism for Meeting Financial Commitments Under the Convention" (2008); Government of India, *Climate Change Negotiations: India's Submissions to the United Nations Framework Convention on Climate Change* (Aug 2009); Stewart et al., "Climate Finance: Key Concepts and Ways Forward" (2009); Martin Stadelmann, J. Timmons Roberts, and Saleemul Huq, "Baseline for Trust: Defining 'New and Additional' Climate Funding", *IIED Briefing* (Jun 2010); http://pubs.iied.org/17080IIED.html; UN High-Level Advisory Group on Climate Change Financing, *Report of the Secretary-General's High-Level Advisory Group on Climate Change Financing* (2010); UNFCCC Subsidiary Body for Implementation, "Financial Resources, Technology Transfer, Vulnerability, Adaptation and Other Issues Related to the Implementation of the Convention", *Compilation and Synthesis of Fifth National Communications* (20 May 2011), p. 15.

additional financial flows be counted towards their climate change finance obligations.[79] A loophole in this baseline is that countries that already contribute more than 0.7 per cent of GNI to ODA could divert existing ODA to climate finance, but this can be rectified by having the baseline for such countries equal their existing ODA commitments.[80] Any such baseline, however, is likely to be unacceptable to most developed countries (such as the United States) which currently do not meet the 0.7 per cent threshold and would therefore have to simultaneously come up with funds to meet both their climate finance targets as well as their ODA targets.

Most developed countries (including the United States, EU, and Japan), on the other hand, appear to favour the status quo, where there is no universal definition of "new and additional" and each contributor defines its own baseline.[81] The benefit to developed countries is that this allows them maximum flexibility in deciding which funds should go towards meeting their climate change finance targets. In addition, as Norway has argued, adaptation finance simultaneously meets both development and climate objectives and therefore should be counted towards both ODA and climate finance targets.[82] The economic rationale for allowing such double-dipping is that it is rational to create greater incentives for financing activities such as adaptation that achieve multiple desirable objectives at the same time.[83] To allow such double counting, however, would require dispensing with a fixed, universal baseline. Developing countries argue that in the absence of a universal baseline, there is no guarantee that the funds disbursed will actually be "new and additional" in any real sense.

The UN AGF has suggested that to avoid the complicated issue of defining a baseline, only funding generated from completely new sources (not used to fulfil either ODA pledges or past climate finance pledges) should be used for climate finance.[84] While this guarantees newness, such a requirement would be highly restrictive (at least in the short-run), given that it would require developed countries to immediately set up new and untested funding channels rather than utilize existing sources and channels. A viable baseline in the short-term, which would allow utilization of current funding sources, would be to agree on projected business-as-usual (BAU) levels of ODA together with past climate finance pledges; climate change finance then would be counted on top of climate finance promised in the past as well as on top of the projected levels of ODA that would have been provided in the absence of any climate finance.[85] However, a baseline is difficult to agree upon, given that there is no obvious means of determining BAU ODA projections.

Given that Singapore is not a major contributor to either ODA or past climate change finance, any funds that Singapore might provide for climate finance will most likely be "new and additional" under any of the baselines discussed above. It is, however, still desirable from Singapore's perspective that some baseline is agreed upon to facilitate progress on other climate finance issues that are vital for Singapore.

Finance Allocated between Mitigation and Adaptation

As fast-start climate finance has begun flowing from developed to developing countries, issues relating to allocation and delivery of finance have become increasingly prominent in the climate finance negotiations. Of particular concern to developing countries has been the issue of allocating finance between mitigation and adaptation. There is also a convergence of views in the Transition Committee for the GCF that separate windows for different thematic areas of finance, such as mitigation and adaptation, need to be established.[86] To do so, however, will require addressing the allocation of finance between mitigation and adaptation, and while the Cancun agreement calls for a "balanced allocation between mitigation and adaptation",[87] there is no concrete definition of what a balanced allocation actually means.

Table 3.12 summarizes estimates made by different countries and organizations of the annual amounts of mitigation and adaptation finance required. To some extent, the wide variation in the estimates can be attributed to differences in views on the total amount of finance required, which can be quite substantial. The fact that the percentage of total funds allocated to mitigation and finance in the different estimates varies quite widely points, however, to more fundamental disagreements on the relative priorities different countries and organizations place on mitigation and adaptation.

From the perspective of developed countries, financing mitigation activities in developing countries presents more immediate benefits (in terms of reduced global CO_2 emissions) than financing adaptation activities, where the benefits are more long-term and indirect and hence more uncertain. Thus it should be no surprise that developed countries place a relatively high priority on mitigation finance relative to adaptation

Table 3.12
Allocation between Mitigation and Adaptation

Organization	2020		2030	
	Mitigation	Adaptation	Mitigation	Adaptation
UNFCCC			US$110 billion (62–80%)	US$28–67 billion (20–38%)
World Bank			US$140–175 billion (59–85%)	US$30–100 billion (15–41%)
African Group	US$200 billion (<74%)	> US$67 billion (>26%)		
EC	US$132 billion (80–90%)	US$14–34 billion (10–20%)		
Oxfam, ActionAid, Eurodad	US$100 billion (50%)	US$100 billion (50%)		
Project Catalyst (2015–20 estimate)	US$105–161 billion (71–89%)	US$21–42 billion (11–29%)		

Sources: UNFCCC, Investment and Financial Flows to Address Climate Change: An Update (2008); World Bank, World Development Report 2010: Development and Climate Change (2010); Algeria, Key Elements of LCA Negotiating Text: Final Version (2009); European Commission, Stepping Up International Climate Finance: Commission Staff Working Document (2009); Oxfam International, "Climate Finance Post-Copenhagen: The $100 bn questions" (2010); Eurodad et al., Climate Adaptation Funding: Lessons from Development Finance (2010); Project Catalyst, "Scaling up Climate Finance" (2009).

finance. The EC's estimates, for instance, indicate that between 80 and 90 per cent of total finance will have to be directed towards mitigation. On the other hand, development NGOs such as Oxfam and ActionAid place a relatively high emphasis on adaptation finance, stressing the urgency of financing adaptation in the poorer and more vulnerable countries, and advocate a 50–50 division of finance between mitigation and adaptation. Developing countries particularly vulnerable to climate change, such as countries in the African Group and Bolivia, have also placed a high priority on adaptation finance, with Bolivia arguing for an adaptation–mitigation finance ratio of 3:1.[88] Between these two extremes lie estimates from multilateral organizations such as UNFCCC and the World Bank and think tanks such as Project Catalyst, which argue for mitigation finance to comprise approximately 60–80 per cent of overall finance.

Table 3.13 lists the pledged contributions of fast-start finance to mitigation and adaptation. Consistent with the earlier analysis, Japan, Canada, and Norway allocate only around 6–12 per cent of finance to adaptation, reflecting the basic developed country emphasis on mitigation finance. Interestingly, though, the EU and the United States (which can be expected to contribute at least 40–60 per cent of long-term finance based on the burden-sharing formulas presented in Section 3.2) allocate between 33–34 per cent of their overall contributions to adaptation, while 52 per cent of Australia's contribution is geared towards adaptation. Developed country allocations of fast-start finance do not necessarily reflect their positions on how long-term finance should be allocated.

Which Countries Will Receive Climate Change Finance and How Much?

The current agreement on climate finance is also unclear on the question of how climate change finance should be allocated among the developing countries. The Copenhagen Accord states that "funding for adaptation will be prioritized for the most vulnerable developing countries, such as the least developed countries, small island developing states and Africa", but this merely indicates the broad criterion of vulnerability that is to be

Table 3.13
Allocation of Fast-start Finance between Mitigation, REDD+ and Adaptation

Country	Fast-start finance			
	Mitigation	REDD+	Adaptation	Others/Unspecified
Japan	91.2%	3.1%	5.7%	
Canada	72.9%	10%	11.3%	5.9%
Norway	19%	66%	12%	3%
EU	48.1%	16.4%	33.4%	2.1%
USA	45.6%	20.0%	34.4%	
Australia	24%	24%	52%	

Source: Athena Ballesteros et al., *Summary of Developed Country Fast-Start Finance Pledges* (World Resources Institute, 20 May 2011).

Table 3.14
Proposals for Allocation of Climate Finance among Countries

Organization	Recipient countries	Activities funded	Indicators
Mexico (2008) — World Climate Change Fund	All countries	Mitigation	Marginal abatement cost Total volume of emission reductions Total contribution to the fund
Switzerland (2008)	Low- and middle-income countries	Adaptation	Population size Projected GDP losses Relative vulnerability of local economy to climate change
World Bank (2010)	Developing countries	Adaptation	Central government performance Absorptive capacity Lack of social capacity Climate sensitivity Climate change exposure Population weight Poverty weight

Notes: In the Switzerland proposal, low- and middle-income countries are defined as countries with a per capita income lower than US$15,000 and countries with a per capita income of US$15,000–20,000 respectively.
Sources: Mexico, "Enhanced Action on the Provision of Financial Resources and Investment to Support Action on Mitigation and Adaptation and Technology Cooperation" (2008); Global Canopy Foundation, Little Climate Finance Book: A Guide to Financing Options for Forests and Climate Change (Oxford: Global Canopy Programme, 2009); World Bank, World Development Report 2010: Development and Climate Change (2010).

used in determining how much adaptation funding a particular country receives, without specifying precisely how the amount is to be determined. Nor does the Accord (or the subsequent agreements reached at Cancun) describe how *mitigation* finance is to be allocated.

Some proposals for allocating financial resources based on this approach are outlined in Table 3.14 above. There is a general consensus within the UNFCCC process that developing countries should be the recipients of climate finance, and this is reflected in the World Bank's proposal. Mexico's proposal, too, is consistent with this broad position. Developed countries can only use a certain fraction of their *own* contributions to the

Fund, whereas developing countries have access to the financial resources contributed by the developed countries and are thus net recipients. In contrast, Switzerland's proposal for allocating financial resources to low- and middle-income countries (rather than to developing countries as defined by the UNFCCC) may be seen to reflect the implicit position that advanced developing countries with per capita income levels approaching those of the developed countries should not be eligible to receive climate change finance.

Two types of criteria are relevant in determining how much financing an individual country should receive: equity and efficiency. Equity dictates that finance be allocated in a fair and equitable manner. Possible criteria based on equity include vulnerability (the more vulnerable a country is to climate change, the more finance it should receive), economic need (poorer countries should receive greater financial assistance), and institutional capacity to address climate change (the lower the capacity, the more the country needs outside assistance, including finance). Efficiency, on the other hand, dictates that finance be allocated to those countries that have the ability to use the finance most effectively. Efficiency-based criteria include abatement potential (the greater the abatement potential, the more finance the country should receive), abatement cost (the lower the marginal abatement cost, the more finance the country should receive), and institutional capacity to use funds effectively (the greater the capacity, the more finance the country should receive).

Key in determining the appropriate balance between these two sets of criteria is the purpose for which the fund will be used. The benefits of climate change mitigation accrue equally to all countries regardless of where mitigation is carried out, so that it does not matter for equity how mitigation finance is allocated across countries.[89] Thus, the efficiency criterion is predominant in determining which countries receive mitigation financing, as in Mexico's proposal for allocating mitigation finance.

For adaptation, on the other hand, equity issues are significant, since adaptation activities in one country will not usually lead to concrete benefits for another country. There is a case then for prioritizing the delivery of adaptation finance to countries most vulnerable to climate change and most in need of financial assistance (whether due to poverty or due to lack of institutional capacity to tackle climate change). This principle is reflected in the indicators chosen in the proposals by Switzerland and the World Bank for allocating adaptation finance.

From Singapore's perspective, the above discussion suggests that Singapore might be unlikely to receive significant inward flows of climate finance, whether for mitigation or for adaptation. For one thing, if the eligibility criterion for receiving finance is tightened from "developing country" to "low and middle-income countries" (as in Switzerland's proposal) or a comparable criterion, Singapore will not be eligible to receive any financial flows. Even if Singapore is deemed eligible to receive finance, its inward flows of either mitigation or adaptation finance are likely to be low, based on the criteria that is typically used for allocation.

The current agreement on climate finance is also unclear on the question of how climate change finance should be allocated among the developing countries. The Copenhagen Accord states that "funding for adaptation will be prioritized for the most vulnerable developing countries, such as the least developed countries, small island developing states and Africa", but this merely indicates the broad criterion of vulnerability that is to be used in determining how much adaptation funding a particular country receives, without specifying precisely how the amount is to be determined. Nor does the Accord (or the subsequent agreements reached at Cancun) describe how *mitigation* finance is to be allocated.

For mitigation finance, where low-cost mitigation potential is the major criterion, Singapore is unlikely to attract much finance due to its relatively low carbon intensity. For adaptation finance, where equity-based criteria such as economic need, vulnerability, and institutional capacity predominate, Singapore again ranks fairly well on each of those criteria and thus is unlikely to attract adaptation finance as well.

Delivery of Finance

In addition to how finance is to be allocated, there are a number of unresolved issues on how finance should be delivered to developing countries. For instance, whether climate change finance should consist mostly of grants or loans is an issue that divides developed and developing countries. As already discussed, developed countries favour the use of leveraging mechanisms which will necessarily imply the provision of much of climate change finance in the form of loans. However, developing countries (such as India, Ghana, and the members of AOSIS)[90] and NGOs such as Oxfam[91] opine that climate change finance should largely be provided as grants, since many of the adaptation and mitigation activities required are unlikely to generate the kind of returns sufficient to pay back the loans.

NGOs such as the International Institute for Environment and Development and Oxfam have also in the past expressed concerns over whether the full amount of the loans are to be counted towards climate finance, since much of the funds disbursed would eventually have to flow back to developed countries as repayments for the loans. Both the UN AGF report[92] and the Transitional Committee tasked with designing the GCF[93] suggest that only the concessionary portion of loans (such as the interest savings from taking a low-interest loan funded by climate finance) will be counted towards climate finance targets.

In addition, developing countries have expressed concerns about the accessibility of climate finance, with developing country groups such as AOSIS, the African Group, and the G-77 and China group highlighting the need for developing countries to have direct access to the funding provided.[94] For the poorest or smallest developing countries, especially, the lack of capacity to absorb sizeable amounts of incoming finance as well as the difficulty of attracting private finance have been cited as barriers to accessibility of funding.[95] Finally, developing countries have criticized the lack of predictability in the delivery of funds promised. Out of US$28.1 billion worth of fast-start finance promised so far, only US$12.6 billion of finance has as yet been committed.[96]

MRV of Financial Commitments

A critical challenge for climate finance institutions will be to monitor the funds actually delivered by developed countries, to ensure that they uphold their financial commitments, and to ensure that these funds are effectively utilized by developing countries. Accounting for financial commitments therefore requires both the *ex ante* assessment of the quantum of finance promised, as well as the *ex post* accounting for financial resources actually delivered and the environmental outcome (emission reductions, in the case of mitigation finance) achieved using the finance.[97] Many of the issues of contention highlighted in the climate finance literature such as "newness and additionality", double counting, and the definition of leverage, all revolve around principles of accounting. Agreements in MRV protocols are thus central to climate finance, as they are to actual mitigation and adaptation actions.

Developing countries which expect to be net recipients of climate change finance emphasize appropriate monitoring, reporting and verification (MRV) measures of funds promised and delivered by developed countries, to ensure greater predictability and reliability of funding. Net contributors to climate change finance, primarily the developed countries, emphasize increased MRV of implementation of nationally appropriate mitigation actions ("NAMAs") by developing countries to ensure greater accountability of how the funds are used. The use of a single channel through which all of climate change finance must flow (akin to Mexico's proposed World Climate Change Fund) would significantly simplify implementing MRV procedures for financial commitments. There is an ongoing debate within the Transitional Committee tasked with designing the GCF as to whether the Fund should absorb other multilateral climate finance sources and channels or exist in parallel to them.[98]

Given the multiplicity of *sources* of climate finance, including both public and private sources, it is unlikely that a single *channel* such as the GCF for collecting and disbursing all climate-related funds is likely to be feasible. A single channel will not necessarily be able to incorporate all private finance flows. Nor is a single fund or institutional channel even necessarily desirable. The use of multiple channels encourages decentralization, innovation, and experimentation, all desirable policy goals.[99]

Instead, the accounting framework adopted at Cancun revolves around the maintenance of a single global registry that will record both the nationally appropriate mitigation actions proposed by developing countries and the financial support (as well as technological and capacity-building support) provided by developed countries to support these actions. By meeting both the developed country demand for MRV of NAMAs and the developing country insistence on MRV of financial commitments, the registry enables financial support for mitigation to be "matched" to NAMAs in developing countries, so that funds and associated NAMAs are reported simultaneously. In addition, the Cancun agreement mediates between the two stances by increasing standards of MRV both for financial support and associated NAMAs. Developed countries agree to enhance reporting of the support they provide to developing countries (whether finance, technology transfer, or capacity building), and in return developing countries agree to enhance reporting of their NAMAs and allow "international consultation and analysis" of these actions.[100]

A key challenge to getting international agreements on MRV protocols is the issue of sovereignty. Developing countries, in particular China, have argued that they will not agree to increased MRV of their NAMAs, in particular involving international oversight and verification, that might impede on their sovereignty.[101] Developed countries, for their part, are unlikely to accept poor accounting standards of developing country NAMAs if they are to commit any funds for supporting mitigation and adaptation actions.

Governance of Climate Change Finance

At the heart of the "governance" debate in climate change finance are developing country concerns that the structure of existing climate finance institutions such as the Global Environmental Facility is dominated by developed countries and do not offer sufficient representation to developing countries.[102] A key demand of developing countries, therefore, is for the set-up of "equitable" governance structures for climate finance.

The United States supports equity as equal representation of developed countries and developing countries in governing bodies of climate finance; the EU has similarly suggested that there should be equal representation of net donors and net recipients of climate finance.[103] Developing countries (such as the countries in the G-77 and China group) have advocated "equitable and balanced representation of all countries"; since developing countries outnumber developed countries by some distance, this stance can be interpreted as representing the view that developing countries should have more than equal representation in climate finance governance structures.[104] A few developing countries such as Bangladesh and Ghana have advocated a third perspective on governance, namely that there should be balanced representation from different country groups and geographical regions; this would mean having at least some representatives from groups and regions such as Africa, the LDCs and the SIDS, all of which are particularly vulnerable to climate change and thus have a particular stake in the climate finance negotiations.[105]

There is an emerging consensus that a shift away from existing donor-dominated governance structures is required, and this is reflected in the design of the GCF that was set up during the COP16 conference in Cancun and which is expected to be the channel for a significant share of future climate finance flows. The twenty-four-member board of the fund will be composed equally of representatives from developed countries and developing countries, while the forty-member Transitional Committee that is currently designing the Fund is composed of fifteen members from developed countries and twenty-five members from developing countries. In addition, the board of the GCF will consist of representatives from both the SIDS and the LDCs, while the Transitional Committee has two representatives each from the SIDS and the LDCs.[106]

While the broad contours of the governance structure of the GCF were established at Cancun, there nevertheless remain ongoing debates about specific governance issues relating to GCF that are reflected in the proceedings of the Transitional Committee.[107] In particular, there are disagreements about how the GCF Board will be selected: whether the selection process will be controlled by the Conference of the Parties (COP), and whether developed and developing countries can separately define their own procedures for selecting their representatives on the board.

The developing country demand for a greater role in governance also underlies the debate over whether new institutions need to be established or whether existing institutions should be better utilized. Developing countries (such as India or G-77 and China), aware that existing institutions have governance structures in which they are disadvantaged, prefer the establishment of new climate finance institutions and new financing channels.[108] Developed countries, on the other hand, would prefer to utilize existing channels and institutions together with new ones, in order to take advantage of the former's expertise and experience in managing climate change finance, as well as to avoid creating parallel structures.[109]

In this regard, there has been a debate recently over the role the World Bank should play in the governance and administering of climate change finance. The Cancun agreement specified that the World Bank is to be appointed as an interim trustee of the GCF, but this has sparked opposition from developing countries and NGOs on a number of counts: the perceived "unfairness" of conditions attached by the World Bank to its loans;[110] the perceived "exclusivity" of its decision-making process and its prior support of fossil fuel projects in developing countries.[111]

A compromise offered to overcome governance issues would be for climate finance to draw on the expertise of multilateral development banks such as the World Bank in managing funds, but at the same time instituting a distinct governance structure over the fund.[112] Indeed, the Cancun agreement, by appointing the World Bank as the trustee of the

GCF while putting into place a separate process (via the Transitional Committee) for eventually appointing a governing body for the fund, effectively adopts this solution. In addition, there is a consensus within the Transition Committee designing the fund that the World Bank, as the interim trustee, will be accountable to the board of the GCF, while the selection of a permanent trustee would be through an open bidding process followed by rigorous review and selection procedures.[113] However, the exact nature of the role the World Bank will play, and how it will be received by developing countries, remains to be seen.

An international agreement on climate finance governance would require an agreed view on how centralized the decision-making process will be. A centralized decision-making structure has been proposed by the G-77 plus China group, who suggests that the COP of the UNFCCC directly appoint a board which will centrally manage the funds through which climate finance will flow.[114] A more decentralized alternative is provided by India's proposed governance structure, where the executive board appointed by the COP will have the option of devolving authority to designated national funding entities of developing countries.[115] It is unclear whether one approach is necessarily superior to the other.

Some form of decentralized decision making is likely to be more feasible because it will be difficult for a central, international body to make a large number of operational decisions on a regular basis, especially since private finance is likely to form an important component of climate change finance. The EC has argued, for instance, that multiple funding sources and bilateral or multilateral initiatives may be hampered if brought under a centralized structure, reducing the potential for raising finance compared to a decentralized structure where contributors have greater discretion and therefore a greater incentive to contribute.[116] Centralized decision-making, however, is likely to be better at ensuring that commitments (made by both developed and developing countries) are upheld, MRV standards are maintained and additionality requirements are fulfilled. Burden-sharing formulas, as well as formulas for allocating finance among developing countries, are likely to be easier to implement under a centralized structure.

A different challenge in the governance of climate finance is about how to effectively involve the private sector in the governance process, given that private finance is likely to constitute a significant portion of long-term financial flows. Neither the Transitional Committee nor the proposed board of the GCF has any members specifically representing the private sector. Because of the lack of private sector involvement, the development process of the GCF has been criticized by numerous observers,[117] including the former UN climate chief Yvo de Boer.[118] There is a consensus within the Transitional Committee that private sector engagement is needed to drive the climate finance negotiations forward, and that there needs to be active participation by observers from the private sector even if they are not members of the board; the precise role such observers will play in the governance of the fund is, however, as yet unclear.[119]

Implications for Singapore as a Possible Climate Finance Contributor

The two key questions facing policymakers in Singapore, as elsewhere, is whether national policy goals suggest that participation in any particular multilateral agreement is of net benefit to the country, and, if so, how much it might be expected to contribute under the burden-sharing mechanisms and proposals currently under discussion. On both questions, the current discourse on climate finance and trends in the negotiations point to a mixed picture. Note that Singapore is unlikely to receive significant inward flows of climate finance. Even if Singapore is not excluded from receiving finance altogether by the application of an income-based threshold, the criteria typically used for allocating mitigation finance (indicators of mitigation potential) and adaptation finance (need, vulnerability, and capacity) will most likely rule Singapore out of any significant climate finance receipts.

Whether Singapore should choose to contribute as part of a multilateral emission-reduction agreement depends on the method chosen to select the set of contributing countries. Under the status quo, where only Annex I countries are required to contribute, as well as under the economic country classifications of OECD and the UN, Singapore (like most of the non-OECD countries) is not a candidate for "graduation". If UNFCCC deliberations point towards agreements based on the economic classifications of organizations such as the World Bank and the IMF, or if it adopts a regime where all countries have to contribute to finance, Singapore will be a net contributor if it elects to participate in any multilateral agreement. Rankings based on indicators of capability and responsibility suggest that Singapore, along with other comparable high per capita income non-OECD countries, may be faced with the option of participating and taking on significant financial responsibilities. The national interest, based on a full cost-benefit assessment including distributive outcomes, can only be assessed on the basis of specific agreements and expected compliance outcomes of such agreements.

How much objective policymakers should be willing to contribute as a share of the total level of climate change funding depends on factors such as the presence or absence of progressivity in formulas adopted, the set of contributing countries, the time period chosen to measure historical responsibility, and the assignment of weights on responsibility and capability. Singapore's actual expected contribution will, in addition, be influenced by the overall global target for climate finance (currently set at US$100 billion every year). In taking principled positions on international climate change agreements, governments everywhere will try to find a balance between national reputation, real economic costs to be borne, and, most importantly, the support of its citizen constituents.

Apart from the burdens of participation, there are other issues of policy relevance that will affect the nature and form of Singapore's financial obligations, should Singapore elect to participate in any particular international agreement. The question of the appropriate baseline for determining "newness and additionality" is unlikely to matter much for Singapore. Any fund Singapore does agree to provide for climate change finance will most likely be assessed as "new and additional" under any definition of the term. There are a number of other issues, however, of relevance to Singapore as a possible future contributor to a climate finance agreement.

In general, Singapore will benefit from having greater flexibility in how it chooses to meet any financial obligations. In the public–private finance debate, for instance, Singapore would prefer to have the option to flexibly utilize both options as well as any leveraging mechanisms available to meet its obligations, so that fixed targets for either public or private finance, or restrictions on leveraging, might be counterproductive to Singapore's interests. In addition, the institutional arrangements adopted, including the mechanism for MRV and the governance of climate change finance, will determine the amount of control Singapore has over the funds it disburses and how these funds are used, as well as the amount of flexibility it has in meeting its targets. A stronger MRV regime, for instance, will mean Singapore has a greater say in ensuring that the finance it provides is being efficiently and effectively used for mitigation and adaptation, but may also mean that Singapore has less flexibility to adjust the amount of finance it provides depending on, say, macroeconomic circumstances.

Singapore's Role in the Management and Design of Climate Change Finance

As should be evident, the question of whether or not Singapore will need to contribute to climate change finance in the medium or long term remains unclear. This will depend to a large extent on the progress of future climate change negotiations. Even if Singapore does not contribute to climate change finance in the foreseeable future, it can, however, potentially play an important role both as a potential hub for climate finance as well as in designing the new financial mechanisms needed, in particular the new GCF which is meant to be a major channel for the flow of mitigation and adaptation finance. Thus, climate change finance issues will remain relevant to Singapore whether or not it needs to contribute.

Singapore can potentially set itself up as a climate finance hub, capitalizing on two distinct opportunities. Firstly, Southeast Asia is likely to see increased inward flows of climate change finance and carbon market finance, given that ASEAN countries are classed as developing countries under the UNFCCC and significant mitigation potential exists in many ASEAN countries. In particular, Indonesia is likely to receive financial support aimed at protecting its forests via the UN's Reduced Emissions from Deforestation and Forest Degradation (UN-REDD) programme. In 2010, Norway agreed to provide US$1 billion in finance to Indonesia for forest conservation and protection (beginning with a two-year moratorium on clearing implemented in June 2011).[120]

Singapore is already a regional financial hub and possesses mature capital markets that have received exposure to carbon trading. It is well equipped to set itself up as the regional hub for climate finance in carbon markets, emission mitigation projects and "Green Funds" management. As Senior Minister of State for Trade and Industry S. Iswaran pointed out in an opening speech to the Carbon Asia Forum 2009, Singapore has a number of other features in favour of it becoming an Asia-Pacific carbon hub, including the presence of companies already involved in carbon financing and trading, a strong commodities trading base that can be leveraged to support carbon trading, and incentive schemes for commodity derivatives trading and fund management that now extend to emissions derivatives as well.[121]

Singapore is also the busiest marine bunkering hub in the world[122] and one of the world's top export refining centres.[123] Thus, Singapore could play a key role in the management of any funds generated from curbing global emissions on specific sectors or industries such as shipping or global petroleum refining and petrochemical industries. In addition, Singapore is an important aviation hub as well[124] and could thus also become a regional hub for the management of funds generated from curbing emissions on aviation. Singapore's expertise in financial markets and funds management will boost its chances of becoming a hub for the management of climate finance generated from curbing international transport emissions.

A policy implication of Singapore's potential as a climate finance hub is that Singapore has a strategic interest in supporting a bigger role for private finance (in the debate over public vs private finance), thus creating a demand for the kinds of institutions and markets that, in the ASEAN region, Singapore has a comparative advantage in. Secondly, Singapore has a potentially positive role to play in the design of new financial mechanisms and institutions necessary to provide the scaled-up funding promised at Copenhagen and Cancun.

Singapore's Minister for Finance, Tharman Shanmugaratnam, was a member of the UN Secretary-General's High Level AGF which was tasked with studying potential sources of revenue for scaled-up climate funding in the lead-up to the Copenhagen summit in 2009.[125] More recently, Singapore was chosen as one of the seven countries from Asia to be represented in the forty-member Transitional Committee to design the GCF for COP17 in Durban.

The major responsibilities of the Transitional Committee include (a) determining the scope, guiding principles, and cross-cutting issues surrounding the fund; (b) determining legal and institutional arrangements for setting up the fund, in particular governance issues relating to the board that will administer and govern the fund; (c) designing operational modalities including, for example, methods to manage scaled-up funding from a wide variety of sources; and (d) setting up mechanisms for monitoring and evaluation.[126] Many of the key areas of contention covered in this chapter fall within the purview of the Transitional Committee, a body which is likely to be influential in charting the future path of climate change finance. As one of the select countries with a representative in the

Transitional Committee, Singapore therefore has an important role to play in resolving the issues of contention relating to climate change finance and in designing the GCF. In doing so, Singapore can enhance its reputation and influence in climate change negotiations.

Notes

1. This chapter draws heavily on excellent research assistance by Nahim Bin Zahur.
2. World Bank, *States and Trends of the Carbon Market 2011* (Washington, DC: World Bank, June 2011).
3. United Nations Framework Convention on Climate Change, "Report of the Conference of the Parties on its Thirteenth Session: Decisions Adopted by the Conference of the Parties [Decision 1/CP.13: Bali Action Plan]" (Bonn: UNFCCC, 14 March 2008). <http://unfccc.int/resource/docs/2007/cop13/eng/06a01.pdf>.
4. Nabojsa Nakicenovic and Rob Swart, eds., *Intergovernmental Panel on Climate Change Special Report on Emissions Scenarios* (Cambridge: Cambridge University Press, 2000).
5. Sheila M. Olmstead and Robert N. Stavins, "Three Pillars of Post-2012 International Climate Policy", *Harvard Project on International Climate Agreements: Viewpoints* (October 2009), p. 2.
6. Daniel Bodansky, "The Copenhagen Climate Change Conference: A Post-Mortem", *American Journal of International Law* 104, no. 2 (2010): 230–40.
7. "Doing the Cancun", *The Economist*, 7 December 2010 <http://www.economist.com/blogs/newsbook/2010/12/climate-change_talks>.
8. United Nations Framework Convention on Climate Change, "Report of the Conference of the Parties on its Fifteenth Session: Decisions Adopted by the Conference of the Parties [Decision 2/CP15: Copenhagen Accord]" (Bonn: UNFCCC, 30 March 2010) <http://unfccc.int/resource/docs/2009/cop15/eng/11a01.pdf>.
9. United Nations Framework Convention on Climate Change, "Report of the Conference of the Parties on its Sixteenth Session: Decisions Adopted by the Conference of the Parties [Decision 1/CP16: The Cancun Agreements]" (Bonn: UNFCCC, 15 March 2011) <http://unfccc.int/resource/docs/2010/cop16/eng/07a01.pdf#page=2>.
10. Daniel Abreu Mejia, "The Evolution of the Climate Change Regime: Beyond a North-South Divide?", *ICIP Working Paper: 2010/06* (Barcelona: Institut Català Internacional per la Pau, October 2010) <http://www20.gencat.cat/docs/icip/Continguts/Publicacions/WorkingPapers/Arxius/WP10_6_ANG.pdf>.

11. Daniel Bodansky, "The Copenhagen Climate Change Conference: A Post-Mortem", *American Journal of International Law* 104 (2010).

12. Alessandro Torello, "EU to Give Billions to Fight Climate Change", *Wall Street Journal*, 11 September 2009.

13. Richard Black, "$100bn a Year for Climate Safety", BBC News, 30 September, 2009.

14. Anna Fifield, "Investors are the Key to Meeting Carbon Emissions Targets, says Deutsche Study", *Financial Times*, 27 October 2009.

15. Ibid.

16. World Bank, *State and Trends of the Carbon Market 2009* (Washington, DC: World Bank, 26 May 2009).

17. World Bank, *World Development Report 2010: Development and Climate Change* (Washington, DC: World Bank, 2010).

18. United Nations, *United Nations Framework Convention on Climate Change* (1992) <http://unfccc.int/resource/docs/convkp/conveng.pdf>.

19. *World Development Report 2010: Development and Climate Change.*

20. Organisation for Economic Co-operation and Development, "OECD Stat Extracts" (accessed 16 September 2011) <http://www.oecd.org/LongAbstract/0,3425,en_2649_33715_39375725_119656_1_1_1,00.html>.

21. Alex Morales and Kim Chipman, "Deal-breaker for Climate-change Treaty May Be Obama's Congress", Bloomberg, 27 October 2009.

22. Fiona Harvey et al., "Climate Change Discussions Fail to Agree on Finance Pledges", *Financial Times*, 20 October 2009.

23. Ibid.

24. Jennifer Rankin, "EU to Finalize Climate Change Position", *European Voice*, 29 October 2009.

25. "EU to Give Billions to Fight Climate Change.

26. Ibid.

27. See Sheila Olmstead and Robert N. Stavins, "An Expanded Three-Part Architecture for Post-2012 International Climate Policy", Discussion Paper, Harvard Project on International Climate Agreements, September 2009.

28. United Nations Framework Convention on Climate Change, "Ideas and Proposals on the Elements Contained in Paragraph 1 of the Bali Action Plan: Submissions from Parties [FCCC/AWGLCA/2009/misc.1]" (Geneva: UNFCCC, 13 March 2009).

29. United Nations Framework Convention on Climate Change, "Ad Hoc Working Group on Long-term Cooperative Action: Fulfilment of the Bali Action Plan and Components of the Agreed Outcome [FCCC/AWGLCA/2009/4]" (New York: UNFCCC, 17 March 2009).

30. See World Resources Institute, "Summary of UNFCCC Submissions: 18 September 2009" <http://pdf.wri.org/working_papers/unfccc_submissions_summary_2009-09-18.pdf>.

31. United Nations Framework Convention on Climate Change, "Ad Hoc Working Group on Long-term Cooperative Action: Ideas and Proposals on the Elements Contained in Paragraph 1 of the Bali Action Plan [FCCC/AWGLCA/2009/MISC.4]" (Bonn: UNFCCC, 19 May 2009).

32. See Jan von der Goltz, "High Stakes in a Complex Game: A Snapshot of the Climate Change Negotiating Positions of Major Developing Country Emitters", Working Paper No. 177, Center for Global Development, 10 August 2009.

33. Emma Graham-Harrison, "China Sees Emission Trading Pilot in Next Economic Plan", Reuters, 27 September 2009.

34. Catherine Wong Mei Ling, "S'pore Well Placed to be Carbon Trading Centre", *Business Times*, 18 September 2009.

35. Nareerat Weerayapong, "Business Chiefs Call for Voluntary Carbon Cap", *Bangkok Post*, 17 September 2009.

36. Bindu Lohani, Vice President for Finance and Administration at the ADB, seminar talk at the Institute of Southeast Asian Studies, September 2009.

37. "Singapore Highlights Its Role in Expanding CDM Activities in the Region", *Government Monitor*, 26 October 2009.

38. Clifford Polycarp et al., *Summary of Developed Country "Fast-Start" Climate Finance Pledges* (World Resources Institute, 20 May 2011) <http://www.wri.org/publication/summary-of-developed-country-fast-start-climate-finance-pledges>.

39. Group of 77 and China, "Financial Mechanism for Meeting Financial Commitments Under the Convention", Submission to the Third session of the Ad Hoc Working Group on Long-term Cooperative Action under the UNFCCC (2008) <http://unfccc.int/files/kyoto_protocol/application/pdf/g77_china_financing_1.pdf>.

40. European Commission, "Stepping Up International Climate Finance: A European Blueprint for the Copenhagen Deal", 2009 <http://ec.europa.eu/clima/documentation/finance/docs/com_2009_475.pdf>.

41. UNFCCC Transitional Committee, "Workstream I: Scope, Guiding Principles, and Cross-cutting Issues", Working Paper, 29 June 2011 <http://unfccc.int/files/cancun_agreements/green_climate_fund/application/pdf/tc2_ws1_1_290611.pdf>.

42. See Article 3.1 of the Convention — United Nations, *United Nations Framework Convention on Climate Change*, 1992 <http://unfccc.int/resource/docs/convkp/conveng.pdf>.

43. See, for instance, "Financial Mechanism for Meeting Financial Commitments Under the Convention".

44. Mexico, "Enhanced Action on the Provision of Financial Resources and Investment to Support Action on Mitigation and Adaptation and Technology Cooperation", Submission to the Third Session of the Ad Hoc Working Group on Long-term Cooperative Action under the UNFCCC (13 August 2008).

45. World Resources Institute, "Summary of UNFCCC Submissions: August 2008 to October 29, 2009"; see also "Stepping Up International Climate Finance".

46. Organisation for Economic Co-operation and Development, "History of DAC Lists of Aid Recipient Countries" (accessed 16 September 2011) <http://www.oecd.org/document/55/0,3746,en_2649_34447_35832055_1_1_1_1,00.html>.

47. Ibid.

48. Asian Development Bank, "Classification and Graduation of Developing Member Countries" (11 March 2010).

49. World Bank, "How We Classify Countries" (accessed 16 September 2011) <http://data.worldbank.org/about/country-classifications>.

50. International Monetary Fund, *World Economic Outlook: April 2011* (Washington, DC: IMF, 2011), p. 169.

51. Australia, "Enhanced Action on Financial Resources and Investment", Submission to the Third Session of the Ad Hoc Working Group on Long-term Cooperative Action under the UNFCCC (2008).

52. Axel Michealowa, Sonia Butzemgeiger, and Martina Jung, "Graduation and Deepening – An Ambitious Post-2012 Climate Policy Scenario", *International Environment Agreements: Politics, Law and Economics* 5, no. 1 (2005): 25–46.

53. The soundest approach to averaging normalized variables is to use the geometric mean. Using the arithmetic mean, by contrast, is methodologically problematic because changing the benchmark used to normalize the variables can affect the relative rankings of the countries. Philip J. Fleming and John J. Wallace, "How Not to Lie with Statistics: The Correct Way to Summarize Benchmark Results", *Communications of the ACM* 29, no. 3 (1986): 218–21.

54. The average Annex I index value is derived by calculating the per capita emissions and per capita income for the Annex I countries as a group, before normalizing and taking the geometric mean.

55. See, for instance, Mexico's submission, "Enhanced Action on the Provision of Financial Resources and Investment".

56. This is not to claim that a fairness-based approach is the only or the best approach to burden sharing. The literature on cooperative game theory, for instance, would suggest allocating obligations so that no country or group of countries acting rationally has an incentive to break away from the coalition. See Carsten Helm, *Economic Theories of International Environmental Cooperation* (Cheltenham: Elgar, 2000).

57. The Energy Research Centre proposal also considers allocation of emission reduction targets, but because each country's target is calculated as a share of the total reduction target, the framework can be easily adapted to the calculation of climate finance contributions.

58. Though the G-77 and China coalition has arguably fractured in the aftermath of Copenhagen, subsequent UNFCCC submissions by its members (including

India, South Africa, Bolivia, and Ghana) still reflect the basic position that developed countries should contribute a fixed proportion of their GNP or GDP to climate change finance. See Government of India, Ministry of Environment and Forests, *Climate Change Negotiations: India's Submissions to the United Nations Framework Convention on Climate Change* (New Delhi: Ministry of Environment and Forests, August 2009); "Summary of UNFCCC Submissions: August 2008 to October 29, 2009"; and World Resources Institute, "Summary of UNFCCC Submissions: April 19, 2010 to November 23, 2010".

59. See, for instance, Rob Dellink et al., "Sharing the Burden of Financing Adaptation to Climate Change", *Global Environmental Change* 19, no. 4 (2009): 411–21.

60. "Stepping Up International Climate Finance".

61. "[Decision 1/CP16: The Cancun Agreements]".

62. UN High-Level Advisory Group on Climate Change Financing, *Report of the Secretary-General's High-Level Advisory Group on Climate Change Financing* (New York: UN, 5 November 2010) <http://www.un.org/wcm/webdav/site/climatechange/shared/Documents/AGF_reports/AGF%20Report.pdf>.

63. See, for instance, Ian Traynor, "Brown and Sarkozy Move to Fund Climate Aid with Global Banking Tax", *The Guardian*, 11 December 2009.

64. *Report of the Secretary-General's High-Level Advisory Group on Climate Change Financing*, p. 10; Stephen Minas, "Green Climate Fund: A Bad Time to Talk Finance", *Eco-Business*, 22 June 2011.

65. Robert Stavins, *Experience with Market-Based Environmental Policy Instruments, Discussion Paper 01-58* (Washington, DC: Resources for the Future, November 2001).

66. See, for instance, Alice Caravani, Neil Bird, and Liane Schalatek, "Climate Finance Fundamentals: Adaptation Finance", *Climate Finance Fundamentals Brief* 3 (Berlin: Heinrich Boll Stiftung and ODI, November 2010) <http://www.boell.de/sites/default/files/assets/boell.de/images/download_de/2011-02-adaption-finance-english.pdf>; Tim Gore, "Climate Finance Post-Copenhagen: The $100bn Questions" (Oxford: Oxfam International, May 2010); United Nations Framework Convention on Climate Change, *Investment and Financial Flows to Address Climate Change: An Update* (Bonn: UNFCCC, 26 November 2008); *World Development Report 2010: Development and Climate Change*.

67. "Stepping Up International Climate Finance".

68. J. Timmons Roberts, Martin Stadelmann and Saleemul Huq, *Copenhagen's Climate Finance Promise: Six Key Questions* (London: International Institute for Environment and Development, February 2010) <http://pubs.iied.org/17071IIED.html>; "Climate Finance Post-Copenhagen: The $100bn Questions"; "Stepping Up International Climate Finance".

69. *World Development Report 2010: Development and Climate Change*.

70. Richard B. Stewart, Benedict Kingsbury, and Bryce Rudyk, "Climate Finance: Key Concepts and Ways Forward", *Harvard Project on International Climate Agreements: Viewpoints*, 2 December 2009.

71. "Green Backing: A Preview of a Flawed Report on Climate-Change Financing", *The Economist*, 28 October 2010.

72. "Climate Finance: Key Concepts and Ways Forward".

73. Project Catalyst, "Scaling Up Climate Finance: Summary of Finance Briefing Paper, September 2009" (San Francisco: ClimateWorks Foundation, 2009).

74. Kemal Dervis and Sarah Puritz Milsom, *Responding to a Changing Climate: Challenges in Financing Climate-Resilient Development Assistance* (Washington, DC: The Brookings Institution, 2010).

75. Martin J. Stadelmann, J. Timmons Roberts, and Saleemul Huq, "Baseline for Trust: Defining 'New and Additional' Climate Funding" (London: International Institute for Environment and Development, June 2010).

76. Athena Ballesteros et al., *Summary of Developed Country Fast-Start Finance Pledges* (World Resources Institute, 20 May 2011). The World Resources Institute is a think tank based in the United States conducting policy research and analysis on global resource and environmental issues.

77. "Green Climate Fund: A Bad Time to Talk Finance".

78. "Baseline for Trust: Defining 'New and Additional' Climate Funding".

79. *Responding to a Changing Climate: Challenges in Financing Climate-Resilient Development Assistance*.

80. Eurodad and ActionAid, *Climate Adaptation Funding: Lessons from Development Finance* (2010).

81. For the EU view, see "Stepping Up International Climate Finance". For the views of the United States and Japan, see "Summary of UNFCCC Submissions: August 2008 to October 29, 2009".

82. "Summary of UNFCCC Submissions: August 2008 to October 29, 2009".

83. Richard T. Woodward, "Double Dipping in Environmental Markets", *Journal of Environmental Economics and Management* 61, no. 2 (2011): 153–54.

84. *Report of the Secretary-General's High-Level Advisory Group on Climate Change Financing*.

85. "Baseline for Trust: Defining 'New and Additional' Climate Funding".

86. "Workstream I: Scope, Guiding Principles, and Cross-cutting Issues".

87. "Decision 1/CP16: The Cancun Agreements".

88. "Summary of UNFCCC Submissions: April 19, 2010 to November 23, 2010".

89. It should be noted that constraints on CO_2 or GHG emissions are likely to also reduce local or regional pollution, and this "positive externality" effect of reducing GHG on local urban environments qualifies the statement that mitigation actions have no local environmental impacts.

90. For India's position, see *Climate Change Negotiations: India's Submissions to the United Nations Framework Convention on Climate Change*, p. 34. For AOSIS's

position, see "Summary of UNFCCC Submissions: August 2008 to October 29, 2009". For Ghana's position, see "Summary of UNFCCC Submissions: April 19, 2010 to November 23, 2010".

91. "Climate Finance Post-Copenhagen: The $100bn Questions".

92. *Report of the Secretary-General's High-Level Advisory Group on Climate Change Financing.*

93. "Workstream I: Scope, Guiding Principles, and Cross-cutting Issues".

94. For AOSIS's position, see "Summary of UNFCCC Submissions: August 2008 to October 29, 2009". The African Group's position is expressed in Algeria, *Key Elements of LCA Negotiating Text: Final Version* (Bonn: UNFCCC, 8 April 2009); while the views of the Group of 77 and China are taken from G-77 and China, *Financial Mechanism for Meeting Financial Commitments Under the Convention* (Bonn: UNFCCC, 2008).

95. "Green Climate Fund: A Bad Time to Talk Finance".

96. *Summary of Developed Country Fast-Start Finance Pledges.*

97. "Climate Finance: Key Concepts and Ways Forward".

98. "Workstream I: Scope, Guiding Principles, and Cross-cutting Issues".

99. "Climate Finance: Key Concepts and Ways Forward".

100. "[Decision 1/CP16: The Cancun Agreements]".

101. John Drexhage and Deborah Murphy, "Copenhagen: A Memorable Time for All the Wrong Reasons? — An IISD Commentary", *International Institute for Sustainable Development*, 1 February 2010 <http://www.iisd.org/publications/pub.aspx?id=1218>.

102. "Climate Finance: Key Concepts and Ways Forward".

103. "Summary of UNFCCC Submissions: April 19, 2010 to November 23, 2010".

104. *Financial Mechanism for Meeting Financial Commitments Under the Convention.*

105. "Summary of UNFCCC Submissions: April 19, 2010 to November 23, 2010".

106. "[Decision 1/CP16: The Cancun Agreements]".

107. UNFCCC Transitional Committee, "Workstream II: Governance and Institutional Arrangements — Scoping Paper", 29 June 2011 <http://unfccc.int/files/cancun_agreements/green_climate_fund/application/pdf/tc2_ws2_1_290611.pdf>.

108. For the view of G-77 and China, see *Financial Mechanism for Meeting Financial Commitments Under the Convention*. For the Indian viewpoint, see Charlie Parker et al., *Little Climate Finance Book: A Guide to Financing Options for Forests and Climate Change* (Oxford: Global Canopy Programme, 2009), p. 138.

109. See, for instance, the European Commission's view, "Stepping Up International Climate Finance".

110. For instance, Bangladesh has recently refused climate finance from Britain because it would be channelled through the World Bank — see "Dhaka Seeks Fresh UK Aid to Tackle Climate Change", *Gulf Times*, 18 July 2011.

111. Nora Honkaniemi, "Why the World Bank is Ill-fitted for Climate Finance",

Eurodad, 14 April 2010. See also Friends of the Earth International, "World Bank's Role in Fuelling Climate Chaos", press release, 11 June 2011 <http://www.globalresearch.ca/index.php?context=va&aid=25217>.

112. *Responding to a Changing Climate: Challenges in Financing Climate-Resilient Development Assistance.*

113. "Workstream II: Governance and Institutional Arrangements".

114. *Financial Mechanism for Meeting Financial Commitments under the Convention.*

115. *Little Climate Finance Book*, p. 138.

116. "Stepping Up International Climate Finance".

117. See, for instance, Mark Nicholls, "'Common Ground' Seen in Talks on UN Green Climate Fund", *Environmental Finance*, 15 September 2011; and Kenneth W. Abbott and David Gartner, *Governing the Green Climate Fund* (The Brookings Institution, 21 September 2011).

118. "Green Climate Fund: A Bad Time to Talk Finance".

119. "Workstream II: Governance and Institutional Arrangements".

120. David Fogarty, "Indonesia Forest Decree to Help CO_2 Projects", Reuters, 31 May 2011 <http://www.reuters.com/assets/print?aid=USTRE74U12R20110531>.

121. "Singapore Highlights Its Role in Expanding CDM Activities in the Region", *Government Monitor*, 26 October 2009 <http://www.thegovmonitor.com/world_news/asia/singapore-highlights-its-role-in-expanding-cdm-activities-in-the-region-12455.html>.

122. "Singapore — Asia's Energy Hub", *Energy: Factsheet 2011* (Singapore: Economic Development Board, 2011) <http://www.edb.gov.sg/content/dam/edb/en/resources/pdfs/factsheets/Energy%20Factsheet.pdf>.

123. BP, *Statistical Review of World Energy June 2009.*

124. Airports Council International, "Cargo Traffic 2008 Final", 28 July 2009.

125. UN High-Level Advisory Group on Climate Change Financing, "Membership, Secretary-General's High-Level Advisory Group on Climate Change Financing", 2010 <http://www.un.org/wcm/webdav/site/climatechange/shared/Documents/AGF%20Membership%20List%20as%20of%2008.07.pdf>.

126. UNFCCC Transitional Committee, "Co-Chairs' Summary Report on the Initial Meeting of the Transitional Committee for the Design of the Green Climate Fund [TC-1/6]", 12 May 2011 <http://unfccc.int/files/cancun_agreements/green_climate_fund/application/pdf/tc_1_6_co_chairs_summary_report.pdf>.

4

SINGAPORE'S EXTERNAL SECTOR: Impacts of Emission Mitigation Policies

The question as to whether "country competitiveness" is analogous to that of a firm's competitiveness is often assumed away, and policymakers in the United States, Europe, and Japan routinely talk of national competitiveness.[1] Among economists, however, there is no consensus on how to measure, explain, and predict international competitiveness of countries, and "perhaps none is warranted".[2] In assessing the potential impacts of emission mitigation policies on countries, the term "competitiveness" is used here in reference to firms in key internationally competing industries such as shipping, aviation, and oil refining and trading rather than to any concept of an aggregate "national competitiveness index".

Shipping, civil aviation, and oil refining and petrochemicals are three key areas of interest for Singapore, which are the subject of intense negotiations over emission reduction initiatives at the global industry or sector-specific levels. These are all industries of major significance to Singapore's role as Asia's leading transport and oil hub. Policies aimed at emissions reductions, be they local, regional, or global, will necessarily impact these key tradable goods sectors. Parallel to the post-Durban negotiations over larger strategic issues of national emission reduction targets, financing, and technology, the shipping and civil aviation industries will be subject to intense negotiations within the specialized bodies of the International Maritime Organization (IMO) and International Civil Aviation Organization (ICAO).[3] Petroleum refining and petrochemicals, as one of the major energy-intensive, heavy industries competing in global commodity markets such as steel, cement, and primary metals, is also subject to strong "level playing field" advocacy for arriving at global sectoral agreements rather than as a subject of different national emission regulations.

4.1 SHIPPING

The port of Singapore has been amongst the top five busiest ports in the world for several decades. The American Association of Port Authorities in 2009 ranked Singapore as the world's busiest container seaport on the basis of the total number of actual "twenty-foot equivalent units" (TEUs) transported through the port and second, after Shanghai, in terms of total cargo volume.[4] Singapore consistently ranks as one of the world's top competitive ports, in terms of tonnage and port efficiency.[5] The Kyoto Protocol assigned responsibility for reducing bunker greenhouse gas (GHG) emissions to the IMO, an agency of the United Nations. The IMO has focused on technical discussion around standards such as fuel efficiency, fuel quality, slow steaming, etc.[6] The debate is now deadlocked over whether any measures to reduce carbon dioxide (CO_2) emissions should be global or differentiated. Developed countries want global measures so as to avoid competitive distortion. Bunker fuel use typically represents 10–15 per cent of developed countries's transport emissions, but in some cases the figure is much higher than this, around 20–40 per cent. In the Netherlands, it is over 50 per cent.[7] Governments consequently fear political difficulties due to competitive distortions if unilateral action is taken to regulate bunker fuels.

The carbon content of bunker fuels is a target for tax or cap-and-trade. The IMO and key shipping associations will play a critical role in climate change talks. The industry is itself divided into two camps, one that supports cap-and-trade and the other that supports a carbon tax. The pro-cap-and-traders consist of the Australian Shipowners Association, the Norwegian Shipowners' Association, the Swedish Shipowners' Association, and the UK Chamber of Shipping. Those that favour a carbon tax include Denmark, the Hong Kong Shipowners' Association, and A.P. Møller-Maersk.

Singapore, Fujairah (part of the United Arab Emirates [UAE]), and the Amsterdam-Rotterdam-Antwerp (ARA) conurbation in Europe are among the more important global bunkering centres. Climate change policy will have an outsized impact on these three regions. Given its premier status in bunker market sales, shipping is a crucial issue for Singapore in climate change discussions. As one of the top four financial centres in the world and given the size of its marine operations, Singapore is well-placed to become the global centre for either bunker tax administration or for a cap-and-trade regime for shipping emission reductions. Singapore would be the preferred location for a GHG fund administrator, a centre for shipping emissions research and development (R&D), and cap-and-trade financial and price discovery centre. However, the issue of "carbon leakage" is a factor that will affect the prospects of a global agreement on shipping emissions and compliance. Essentially, ports that are not subject to emission constraints, which may be due to their location in a non–Annex 1 country, might be in a position to attract non-compliant shipping.

Singapore's Role as a Marine Bunkering Hub

Singapore is the world's largest bunkering market by far, almost double the size of the next largest bunkering centre in Fujairah. While Singapore port supplied over 42 million tonnes of bunkers to ships in 2012, Fujairah supplied 24 million tonnes in that year.[8] Its bunkering activities are a constituent part of a cluster of activities related to crude oil refining, refined oil product trade, brokerage, storage and pricing of crude oil and refined oil products, and port and shipping services.[9] Bunkering is integral to Singapore's premier role as the "East of Suez" shipping and oil refining and oil pricing hub, and it is an essential support service to one of the world's most important global maritime hubs.[10]

Marine bunkering has grown robustly over the years, and according to data from the Maritime and Port Authority of Singapore (MPA), bunker sales grew by a compound annual growth rate of 8 per cent from 2006 to 2012. Fig 4.1 below gives the data for bunker sales over the period. Bunker sales grew at an annual compound rate of 7 per cent over the

Figure 4.1
Singapore Annual Bunker Sales, million gross tonnes, 2006–12

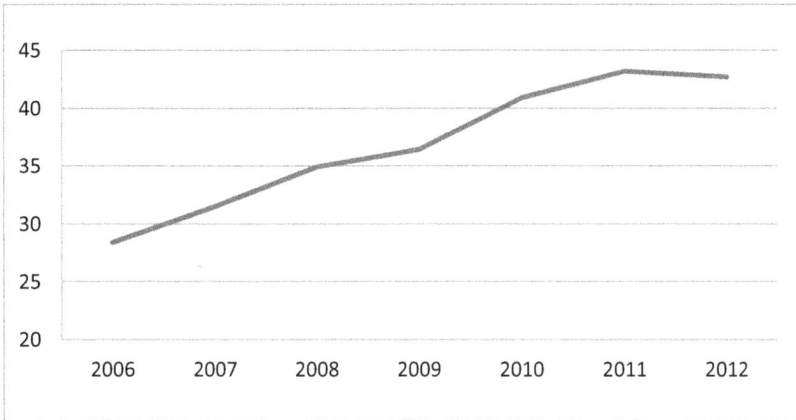

Source: Maritime and Port Authority of Singapore, "Annual Report", 2006, 2008, 2012 <http://www.mpa.gov.sg/sites/global_navigation/about_mpa/annual_reports.page>.

period, hitting a record of over 42 million tonnes in 2012. Using an average price of US$600 per tonne,[11] for example, the value of 35 million tonnes of bunkers would amount to some US$25.2 billion. This constitutes over 6 per cent of Singapore's total export value for 2013.

There are 110,000 people working in the shipping sector.[12] Supporting industries include shipping finance, marine insurance, legal services, and ship broking.[13] Official statistics from the Department of Statistics and the Ministry of Trade and Industry (MTI) give sector data by industry and services, and under the category of "transport and storage services", the contribution to gross domestic product (GDP) in 2011 was 7 per cent, as shown in Table 4.1. The statistical category under transport includes sub-sectors for road and air transport, which can then be abstracted to arrive at a better approximation of shipping and ancillary activities. The transport and storage industry accounts for 5 per cent, once air and land transport is taken out.

However, the transport category (minus road and air transport) would underestimate the contribution of a number of ancillary activities, including financial services (derivatives trade and risk management),

Table 4.1
GDP by Industry

GDP at current market prices by industry, S$ million (2011)		
Total GDP	334,093	100%
Goods producing	83,870	25%
Manufacturing	65,362	20%
Chemicals	99,403	30%
Transport		
Engineering	26,514	8%
Other*	5,322	2%
Services producing	216,629	65%
Transport and Storage	23,734	7%
Air and Land	7,882	2%
Sea	8,419	3%
Wholesale and Retail		
Trade	56,686	17%
Financial Services	37,114	11%
Fusiness Services	44,479	13%

Notes: Other* includes utilities and other goods industries; Transport figures for Air, Land and Water includes supporting services.
Source: Ministry of Trade and Industry, "Economic Survey of Singapore 2012", 2013.

brokerage, proprietary physical and derivatives trading of fuel oil by trading companies, including the trading arms of the global energy companies, and consulting and price reporting services related to Singapore's role as an oil and maritime hub. It is difficult to directly measure the GDP contribution of the constellation of activities of which bunkering plays an integral part.[14]

According to the Singapore Shipping Association (SSA), shipping contributes 7.5 per cent of Singapore's GDP.[15] According to the MPA, the maritime industry contributes 7 per cent of GDP. In its definition of "maritime industry", the MPA includes port shipping activities (the world's largest port by annual shipping tonnage), bunkering (with about eighty bunker suppliers and 130 bunker tankers operating in the port's jurisdiction), shipbuilding, repair and conversion, refining and petrochemicals (one of the world's three largest centres in refining capacity, alongside Houston and Rotterdam), and a holiday cruise centre.[16] It is not clear which year the report refers to, nor whether the GDP contribution estimate is derived from adjustments to the data provided in MTI's *Annual Economic Survey of Singapore*.

It would be necessary to drill into the system of national accounts at the necessary level of sector disaggregation to accurately assess the size of the maritime cluster of activities across the manufacturing and services sectors and its value added contribution to the Singapore economy. It is clear however that shipping, bunkering and ancillary activity have multiple linkages with the Singapore manufacturing and services sectors.

Impact of Emission Reduction Policies on Shipping

Emissions from shipping activities are not included in emission reduction targets of the Annex I countries in the Kyoto Protocol to the United Nations Framework Convention on Climate Change (UNFCCC). Article 2.2 of the Kyoto Protocol states that parties should seek ways of reducing emissions of GHG from ships, and that this must be done through the IMO.[17] Any possible agreement within the IMO requires flag states and port states to be legally compliant with emission reduction regulations will have far-reaching impacts on Singapore's role as a maritime and oil refining and trading hub. Figure 4.2 shows Singapore's CO_2 emissions, with and without marine bunkers.

Figure 4.2
Singapore CO_2 Emissions, With and Without Marine Bunkers (million tonnes)

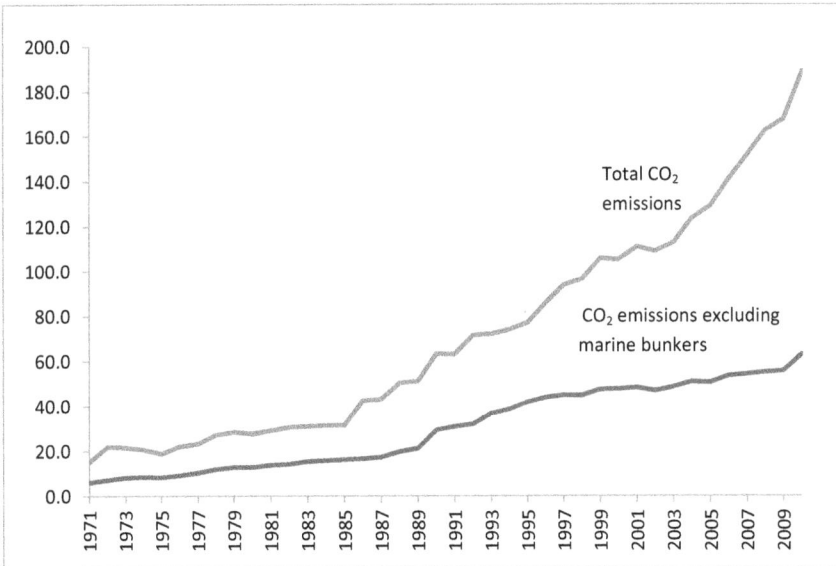

Source: IEA, "CO_2 Highlights 2012" <http://www.iea.org/media/freepublications/2012/CO2Highlights2012. xls>.

It is therefore critical to assess the key emission reduction proposals being considered at IMO deliberations for shipping and their potential impact on Singapore's competitiveness in the maritime and downstream oil industries. Given the importance of shipping and bunkering activity to Singapore's hub role, and the size of its contribution to value added in Singapore's economy, the ramifications of emission reduction regulations in global shipping will be substantive and pervasive across the entire constellation of ancillary activities.

Table 4.2 below shows the distribution of international bunker markets in terms of CO_2 content of the marine bunkers used by shipping. As the world's largest bunkering port, Singapore is also the single largest port with respect to CO_2 emissions (based on carbon content of bunkers sold).[18] The European Union (EU) as a region has the largest share, since it includes not only the key ports of London and Rotterdam,[19] but also the many second and third tier ports in the European continent. In emission terms, the UAE is at about half the size of Singapore, reflecting Fujairah's relative size as a bunkering port to Singapore. Total CO_2 emissions triple when the CO_2 content of bunkering fuels is included. Fig 4.2 above clearly shows the importance of how bunker fuels will be treated in any future emission reduction regime adopted.

Exhaust gases are the primary source of GHG emissions from ships, with CO_2 being the most important.[20] The latest IMO GHG Study found that

Table 4.2
Distribution of International Bunkers (in CO_2 terms)

	million tonnes CO_2
USA	88
Japan	19
EU-27	171
Singapore	86
Taiwan	7
UAE	41
Saudi Arabia	8
Korea	33
Brazil	11
Annex-I Total	287
Non–Annex I Total	295

Source: IEA, cited in Mark Lazarowicz, UK Prime Minister's Special Representative, "Global Carbon Trading: A Framework for reducing emissions", 2009.

emissions from international shipping accounts for 1,100 million tonnes or 2.7 per cent of global CO_2 emitted in 2007 as a result of human activity.[21] Mid-case emissions forecasts by the IMO predict that from 2007 to 2050, without emission reduction policies, ship emissions will grow by 150 per cent to 250 per cent as a result of the growth in shipping and world GDP.[22]

UNFCCC and IMO

The IMO is a specialized agency of the United Nations (UN) dealing with maritime affairs. The agency has promoted the adoption of some forty conventions and protocols and adopted well over 800 codes and recommendations concerning maritime safety, the prevention of pollution and related matters.[23] The IMO does not implement legislation; it was established to adopt legislation, while governments are responsible for implementing it. When a government accepts an IMO convention, it agrees to make it part of its own national law, and to enforce it just like any other law. The problem is that some countries lack the expertise, experience, and resources necessary to do this properly, while others perhaps put enforcement fairly low on their list of priorities.[24] This situation is disadvantageous to Singapore under any future GHG reduction agreement under the IMO.

There is no IMO register that keeps track of what member countries implement; when IMO began operations in 1959, shipping was still dominated by a relatively small number of countries, nearly all of them located in the northern hemisphere.[25] IMO tended to reflect this predominance. However, as the structure of the shipping industry began to change, so did the IMO. Today's IMO budget costs are shared between the member countries primarily in proportion to the size of each country's fleet of merchant ships. The biggest fleets in the world are currently operated by Panama and Liberia, so they pay the biggest share of IMO's budget. The top ten contributors for 2008 are displayed in Table 4.3 showing the amounts in pound sterling and as a percentage of the total budget.

The IMO is working towards the development and adoption of a regime that will regulate shipping at the global level. The IMO has implemented a package of measures, most notably an Energy Efficiency Design Index (EEDI) for new ships, and an Energy Efficiency Operational Indicator (EEOI) for all ships and guidance on best practices for the entire shipping

Table 4.3
IMO Top 10 Budget Contributors, 2012

Total	£30.52 million	
Panama	£5.40 million	17.69%
Liberia	£2.94 million	9.63%
Marshall Islands	£1.78 million	5.83%
United Kingdom	£1.36 million	4.46%
Bahamas	£1.32 million	4.33%
Singapore	£1.29 million	4.23%
Malta	£1.09 million	3.57%
Greece	£1.08 million	3.54%
China	£1.04 million	3.41%
Japan	£0.96 million	3.15%

Source: IMO, "Structure of IMO" <http://www.imo.org/About/Pages/Structure.aspx> (accessed 10 Oct 2013).

industry.[26] The EEDI for new ships has interim guidelines on the method of calculation, and voluntary verification, which is intended to stimulate innovation and technical development of all the elements influencing the energy efficiency of a ship from its design phase. The EEOI has been used to establish a common approach for voluntary CO_2 emission indexing, enabling shipowners and operators to evaluate the performance of their fleet with regard to CO_2 emissions.

As the amount of CO_2 emitted from a ship is directly related to the consumption of fuel oil, CO_2 indexing also provides useful information on a ship's performance with regard to fuel efficiency. Many of the design and operational measures are thought to be cost effective.[27] However, technical and operational measures are insufficient to reduce the desired amount of emissions from international shipping, and economic incentives/disincentives are required to meet potential emission reduction targets.[28] A recent report to the IMO finds that market-based instruments are cost-effective policy instruments with high environmental effectiveness.[29]

Members of the IMO have not reached agreement on any binding measures to control GHG emissions since it was charged by the Kyoto Protocol in 1997 to propose shipping industry emission reduction proposals at UNFCCC deliberations.[30] There is pressure from key shipping constituencies represented in the IMO to come up with specific recommendations regarding GHG emission reductions in the world shipping industry.

Submitted Positions on Emission Reductions: Cap-and-trade vs Tax

Leading shipping industry bodies and national authorities have submitted emission reduction proposals to the IMO, where they are currently under review and subject to deliberations and further submissions by members. Apart from key details and institutional features in these proposals that need scrutiny for efficiency and governance features, the most strategic general question revolves around the "tax vs cap-and-trade" debate. The two positions are articulated respectively by Denmark's April 2009 submission in favour of a tax regime, and a joint May 2009 submission by France, Germany, and Norway in favour of a trading scheme.[31] To date, the most detailed submission to the IMO describing the operating mechanism for a marine cap-and-trade scheme has been proposed by Germany.[32]

Shipping Companies

Several shipping industry bodies support efforts to cut emissions through a global cap-and-trade scheme. The Australian Shipowners Association, the Royal Belgian Shipowners' Association, the Norwegian Shipowners' Association, the Swedish Shipowners' Association, and the UK Chamber of Shipping have proposed a global emissions cap-and-trade scheme specifically for the sector.[33] This group states that it "firmly believes that the best way to achieve a real and lasting reduction in CO_2 emissions from shipping — over and beyond efficiencies in ship design and operation — is through a global and open emission trading system."[34]

Organizations that have stated their public support for the Danish tax proposal include the Hong Kong Shipowners Association and A.P. Møller-Maersk.[35] The SSA has also announced its views favourable to a tax approach to CO_2 emission reduction.[36]

The European shipping associations — constituting the world's most powerful corporate shipping interests — will play a critical role in the formation of shipping policies within their respective governments, and one would expect significant pressure on their countries' governments. In general, shipping executives support the cap-and-trade option. In a poll on Sustainable Shipping, emissions trading received 41 per cent support compared to 29 per cent of respondents who favoured a bunker tax.[37]

European Union

The EU is the single largest regional group within the IMO, and is comprised of major shipping countries such as Norway, Denmark, the Netherlands, and Greece. The EU exerts a major negotiating leverage within the IMO. The European Commission has been very clear that it would include shipping in its Emissions Trading System if the IMO does not take action on its own. EU representatives agreed that if the IMO agreement to include international maritime emissions in IMO reduction targets has not been approved by end 2011, the commission should propose that these emissions be included in the community reduction commitment.[38] The position was adopted with 610 votes in favour, 60 against and 29 abstentions.[39]

The EU Emission Trading System (ETS) is a key tool for achieving the EU's aim of reducing its land-based GHG emissions by at least 20 per cent by 2020 from 1990 levels, or by 30 per cent in the event of an international agreement.[40] The EU ETS is a cap-and-trade system: it caps the overall level of emissions allowed but, within that limit, allows participants to buy and sell allowances as they require, so as to cut emissions costs effectively. Launched in January 2005, the ETS currently covers over 10,000 installations in the energy and industrial sectors, which are collectively responsible for close to half of the EU's emissions of CO_2 and 40 per cent of its total GHG emissions.

The global carbon market continued reaching a total annual value transacted of about US$126 billion in 2008, double its 2007 value.[41] The secondary market for Certified Emission Reductions (CER), with spot, futures and options, grew to US$26 billion, a quintupling over the 2007 level. The EU ETS accounts for 80 per cent of the global market in carbon.[42] But since the severe recession of 2008–9, and the continued lack of progress in climate change negotiations at the UNFCC, prices in the EU ETS have plunged and have remained in the depressed range of about

US\$5–9 in 2013. This contrasts with US\$18 (€13) per tonne of CO_2 seen in 2010, for example.

United States

The U.S. role in the IMO and harmonization of international shipping standards is a relatively minor one, as its "hemispheric" approach to oceanic navigation has always been one that focuses on enforcing its own state and federal legislation regarding ships, both domestic and foreign flagged vessels, at the relevant jurisdictions of its major international shipping ports such as New York, Long Beach, or Houston.[43] On 30 March 2009, the U.S. Environmental Protection Agency (EPA) announced that it had asked the IMO to create an emissions control area around the U.S. and Canadian coastlines.[44] However, this relates to sulphur in bunker fuels, particulate matter emissions, and nitrogen oxide emissions, rather than to GHG emissions.

U.S. submissions to IMO deliberations have been unimportant to the debates about a global GHG emission reduction regime for shipping, and have consisted largely of general statements regarding the need for increased efficiency across the shipping fleet, further research requirements on shipping emissions, and the like.[45] However, it is more than likely that if the United States does exercise its option to join a potential IMO agreement, it would opt for a cap-and-trade scheme as well, given that its own onshore climate bills being considered in Congress are cap-and-trade schemes. A United States–EU combined position in favour of cap-and-trade, if pursued, would leave less room for the alternative bunker fuel tax proposal.

However, policy views have not crystallized, neither the EU nor the United States have fully specified formal negotiating positions on a range of issues, including the choice to tax or to establish a cap-and-trade scheme as the preferred economic mechanism to reduce carbon emissions from the shipping sector.

Shipping Emissions: Tax or Cap-and-Trade

Emissions trading works by allowing an entity that emits CO_2 to either buy (auction), or be given (allocation), a certain number of carbon allowances or credits during the compliance period to cover its emissions. At the end of the period, the emissions from the organization are compiled. If the organization has exceeded the amount covered by the allowances, more credits have to be purchased from the market. If there are allowances left over, they can be kept for future use or sold to the market. Each ship of above 400 gross tonnes would have to comply with the obligations, and the flag state has the obligation to ensure that ships flying its flag comply with the requirements. Furthermore, the port state has the right to inspect the ships flying a foreign flag entering its ports; port states would control documentation of allowances and be informed about a ship's compliance status.[46]

Under the tax proposal, all ships above 400 gross tonnes in international trade must pay a levy or tax per tonne of bunker fuel. The actual size of the initial levy or tax would essentially be a political decision, since it is not possible to determine *ex ante* the initial tax rate for any particular level of emission reduction without having a historical record of actual emission reductions for any given tax rate. Furthermore, there is no reasonable emission data on the shipping industry that would enable a robust baseline to be drawn up, from which to measure the level of emission reductions over time.[47]

It is outside the scope of this chapter to go into the details of the structure and operation of the two schemes, and what follows is a brief overview of the two alternatives.[48] A free allocation system allocates annual emissions allowances free of charge, either based on historical performance or based on a defined allocation formula reflecting ship size and type. However, allocations based on historical emissions of individual ships would be extremely complex and hugely demanding of data on many ships of different types, sizes, and vintages. The data is neither readily available nor accurate. A key weakness is that free allocation methods do not credit shipowners who have already taken action to reduce GHG emissions.

A fixed contribution in U.S. dollar per tonne, established by the GHG Compensation Fund Administrator, will be added to the price of bunker fuel as the required contribution to the fund, and recorded in the bunker delivery note. A state party to the convention must license bunker suppliers within its territory and these suppliers must be registered with the administrator. Registration will require agreement to specific monitoring, reporting, and verification (MRV) requirements as well as the collection and transfer of funds to the administrator. Flag states signatories to the convention must require ships entitled to fly their flag to purchase fuel from licensed bunker suppliers. If Singapore ratifies the new convention, and its neighbouring countries do not, Singapore's bunker trade will be adversely affected. Ships infringing these rules will be required to pay penalties, so that "leakage" does not occur or is minimized.

Implications for Singapore

Shipping is among the most important focus issues for Singapore negotiators in climate change negotiations. Unlike land-based GHG emissions, of which Singapore's contribution to global emissions would be miniscule, its role as the world's largest bunkering port by far puts the country in an altogether more critical role within IMO deliberations. It is imperative that Singapore's interests as a leading oil and maritime hub are represented clearly and forcefully.

There are key principles that command wide assent among shipowners and oil businesses which also coincide with Singapore's critical interests as an oil and maritime hub.[49] Such congruence of interests with key constituencies supports Singapore's negotiating position powerfully. All proposed measures need to be effective, equitable, and enforceable. For effectiveness, the IMO should take into account marginal abatement costs in the industry and its overall contribution to global emissions when designing the appropriate trajectory to meet emission reduction targets. For equity, proposed measures need to take special note of the potential for "leakage", whereby non-participants to any IMO agreement benefit from activity that migrates from signatory port and flag states to non-signatory states in a bid to avoid compliance costs. Maintaining a level playing field for international shipping is vital, and evasion must be minimized so that signatory port states are not competitively disadvantaged.

For enforceability, it is crucial to have clarity of methods and objectives, and to have regulatory regimes that are robust yet parsimonious as far as possible. Any emissions regime adopted for global shipping by the IMO must be transparent, rigorous, and enforceable, and deliver measurable results. Requisite legislation and MRV requirements must be at the lowest possible administrative overhead costs. Higher costs of bunkers will inevitably lead to some reduction in shipping activity, other things being equal.[50] It is important that if an IMO agreement is not universally adopted at the outset, then requisite legislation allows phased implementation leading to a global coverage of shipping emissions over time, while keeping the playing field as level as possible.

Turning now to the question of cap vs tax, it is clear that there is no consensus on the issue. A *Wall Street Journal* poll found that 54 per cent of economists favoured a carbon tax, with the rest favouring a trading scheme.[51] There are experts with good arguments on both sides as apparent in Table 4.4. In economic theory, with proper design features, the two systems can emulate characteristics that make them look similar. In general, both are market mechanisms that can get the job done at least cost.

Table 4.4
Pro Tax and Pro Cap-and-Trade Individuals and Institutions

Pro Tax
1. Jeffrey D. Sachs, Director of the Earth Institute at Columbia University
2. Baruch Fischhoff, Howard Heinz University Professor of Social and Decision Sciences and Engineering and Public Policy at Carnegie Mellon University
3. N. Gregory Mankiw, former chief economic advisor to President George W. Bush
4. ExxonMobil
5. Singapore Shipping Association
6. Denmark

Pro Cap-and-Trade
1. Barack Obama, President of the United States (2009–)
2. General Electric, Dow Chemical, Shell Oil, and Duke Energy
3. Frances Beinecke, President of the U.S. Natural Resource Defense Council
4. Fred Krupp, President of the Environmental Defense Fund
5. Robert N. Stavins, Albert Pratt Professor of Business and Government at Harvard University and the Director of the Harvard Environmental Economics Program
6. Eileen Claussen, President of the Pew Center on Global Climate Change
7. Australian Shipowners Association
8. Royal Belgium Shipowners' Association
9. Norwegian Shipowners' Association
10. Swedish Shipowners' Association
11. UK Chamber of Shipping

Sources: McKinsey, "What Matters: Tax vs. Cap Debate", <http://whatmatters.mckinseydigital. com>; Carbon Offsets Daily, <http://www.carbonoffsetsdaily.com/top-stories/is-carbon-tax-beating-cap-and-trade-exxon-ceo-favors-a-tax-3639.htm>; *Singapore Shipping Association Newsletter*, November 2007 <http://www.ssa.org.sg/library/SSA0403001/eNewsletter/07-issue9. pdf>; International Maritime Organization, "Prevention of Air Pollution from Ships, An International Fund for Greenhouse Gas Emissions from Ships", Submitted by Denmark, Marine Environment Protection Committee, 9 April 2009; Yale Environment 360, "Opinion Putting a Price on Carbon: An Emissions Cap or a Tax?", 7 May 2009 <http://e360.yale.edu/content/feature.msp?id=2148>; UK Chamber of Shipping Press Release, "Shipping Industry Supports Emissions Trading to Reduce CO_2", 24 September 2009 <http://www.british-shipping.org/News/hot_off_the_press/shipping_industry_ supports_emissions_trading_to_reduce_co2/>.

However, for Singapore, it is not the inherent features of each of the systems that provide clear arguments to favour either option. Instead, key extraneous factors clearly make it preferable for Singapore to opt for a cap-and-trade system. Firstly, the EU ETS market — despite its current depressed state reflecting the uncertainties of the post-Kyoto regime — makes it likely that the EU will come out with a common position in support of a trading scheme at the IMO. The joint position paper issued by the shipping company associations from Australia, Belgium, Norway, Sweden, and the United Kingdom and the joint submission by France, Germany, and Norway to the IMO constitutes a forceful negotiating posture likely to be adopted by the EU as a whole. The United States, though not central to IMO deliberations, will likely adopt a similar approach, as its own climate bills for onshore GHG emissions are cap-and-trade bills, if for no other reason. The likely position that the EU and the United States adopt at the IMO is, of course, no argument in favour of cap-and-trade for Singapore. It however makes it clear that the tax option will remain a less viable alternative within the key constituencies represented in the IMO, primarily the key port states and the shipping companies.

The second factor relates to Singapore's role as a global shipping and oil hub. A shipping cap-and-trade scheme makes sense for Singapore because of the positive impact that it will have on Singapore's role as a price discovery centre for carbon emission certificates. For those not familiar with the oil industry, the importance of Singapore's role in oil price discovery is often not fully understood or appreciated.[52] It is often said that Singapore's importance ranks alongside Rotterdam and Houston, but even this understates the city-state's role as an oil centre. Indeed, it would be more accurate to state that Singapore's role can be compared more appropriately to a combination of Houston and New York, or of Rotterdam and the city of London, as both New York and London are the locations for active futures markets for crude oil and refined products. Singapore combines oil refining, trading and price discovery in one location, making it a hub in multiple dimensions.[53] One only has to attend a few cocktail receptions during the Asia-Pacific Petroleum Conference and talk to oil company executives to realize the potency of such a combination in the global oil industry.[54]

Energy and GHG emissions are, of course, intimately related, and carbon pricing constitutes one element in the constellation of correlated prices in the energy sector. Important activities in organized and over-the-counter (OTC) markets include trade and risk management in price spreads between various energy products, and in related derivatives that are based on arbitrage between energy-related products, as well as arbitrage across trading regions and across spot, forward, and futures contracts. Oil storage and logistics, which play a major role in Singapore's oil ecology, are an integral part of such arbitrage activity. The establishment of Singapore as a carbon trading and pricing centre would further add to the city's centrality to the global petroleum industry. Carbon trading desks are already established in banks, brokerages, and commodity traders in Singapore to take advantage of the CDM carbon market. Singapore's role as a sophisticated financial centre will also be further enhanced by a cap-and-trade scheme for shipping emissions.

It is useful to get an idea of the importance of global commodity trade to Singapore. It is estimated that the commodities trading sector recorded a turnover from offshore trading activity of US$659 billion in 2008, a 36 per cent increase over 2007.[55] The industry has over 260 companies under the Global Trader Programme instituted by International Enterprise (IE) Singapore to encourage global players to locate their trading operations in the city. They generated S$10 billion in total business spending and a similar amount in value added in 2008, employing more than 9,500 professionals from around the world.[56]

The position of the SSA in favour of a tax scheme for bunker fuels probably reflects its members' perception that they are disadvantaged in sophisticated trading techniques and that a simple imposition of taxes will not distract shippers from their "real job" at hand. Yet, if true, these constitute poor reasons to choose any particular regime for reducing shipping emissions. The handling of risk in the purchase of bunker fuels will be a familiar issue to all shippers, regardless of size or organizational sophistication. And while potentially volatile carbon prices in a cap-and-trade regime will be an additional aspect of risk faced by shipping companies, it is likely that carbon markets are here to stay, and will remain important in the post-Kyoto world.

Disposition of Revenues Generated

In either the cap-and-trade scheme with auctioned allowances or in the tax scheme, substantial revenues will be generated. Proponents of the tax option have not specified the applicable tax rates, given that the initial tax rate imposed will be a political decision (as mentioned previously). However, in Annex 3 of Denmark's submission to the IMO in favour of a bunker fuel tax, an illustrative table lists rates at between US$7.5 to US$45 per tonne.[57] A US$10 per tonne tax rate would mean that Singapore as a port state would collect over 10 per cent of global revenues of some US$3 billion, for a global bunker fuels market of, say, 300 million tonnes. These are large sums, even at a nominal US$10 per tonne tax rate,[58] and the disposition of funds is a critical issue for Singapore as for all port states and the shipping industry as a whole.

While various parties at the IMO will have their own views on the appropriate disposition of funds collected by a legally constituted International GHG Funds Administrator, the Danish submission provides details of that country's position.[59] The Danish proposal would allocate finance to four areas: mitigation and adaptation activities in developing countries, especially least developed countries, land locked developing countries, and the small island developing states; R&D on more energy-efficient ship design and propulsion systems; technical cooperation with the existing IMO framework; and administrative expenses for the International GHG Fund operation.

With regard to concerns for equitable burden sharing, Yvo de Boer, former executive secretary of the UNFCCC, stated at the 2007 Bali meeting that the principle of "common but differentiated responsibilities" is "the cornerstone of the UNFCCC".[60] This translates into a clear policy dichotomy between the industrialized and the developing countries. The former constitute the Annex I countries which are committed to specified quantitative emission targets for the first commitment period (2008–12) and have financial and technology transfer obligations to the developing countries. The latter have neither policy obligations nor quantitative emission targets under the Kyoto Protocol. The principle of "common but differentiated responsibilities" is an area of major contention, threatening any conclusive agreement arising out of the fifteenth session of the Conference of the Parties (COP15).[61]

In the Danish submission to the IMO, it is stated that the tax scheme proposed is "embracing the UNFCCC principle of common but differentiated responsibilities and respective capabilities" while at the same time "respecting the IMO principle of 'no more favourable treatment' of ships."[62] It is obvious that there is tension between the two positions, the former favouring resource transfer to the developing countries while the latter insists on a level playing field for IMO members (along the lines of the World Trade Organization's "most favoured nation" clause).

The submission to the IMO by the Oil Companies International Marine Forum (OCIMF) asserts that the requisite legislation for controlling shipping emissions by the IMO "must use a substantial proportion of the revenue generated [50 per cent] from any market-based measure to promote and facilitate marine R&D aimed at reducing shipping GHG emissions".[63] Even more pointedly, the joint position paper of the shipping associations of Australia, Belgium, Norway, Sweden, and the United Kingdom states that

> while we recognize that the Kyoto Protocol principle of "common but differentiated responsibilities" may also need to be reflected in an emissions trading scheme for shipping, there are more sophisticated ways of meeting this principle than by simply excluding ships of a given flag. Shipping companies which choose to trade internationally should expect to comply with international legislation.[64]

It would be in Singapore's interest to support international legislation which maximizes the use of funds for shipping R&D and appropriately limits the transfer of resources to developing countries, both in quantum and in the possible uses to which developing country recipients can put such resources to. A clear distinction should be made between the functions of assisting international shipping to meet the challenges of constrained carbon emissions and official development assistance for development needs. It should be noted that Singapore as an "advanced developing country" would be expected to comply with shipping legislation as any of the developed Annex I countries, as seems to be assumed in the Lazarowicz report. Indeed, Singapore is explicitly listed along with Taiwan, UAE, Saudi Arabia, and Korea as "prime candidates for adopting absolute national targets" in the Lazarowicz study.[65]

4.2 REFINING AND PETROCHEMICALS

Singapore has long been one of the world's leading export petroleum refining centres.[66] Singapore's dominating regional role as a provider of petroleum refining, blending and storage services, exporter of petroleum and petrochemical products, port of call for bunker and jet fuels (for shipping and civil aviation), and the location of oil commodity and derivative markets remains undiminished. But as operating costs in

Singapore have escalated over the years with constraints on land and labour, competitive and lower-cost centres for refining and oil storage have begun to emerge, for instance in the neighbouring Malaysian state of Johore as well as in the nearby Indonesian islands.

Singapore intends to promote the expansion and upgrading of existing refineries and attract greenfield investments to consolidate its status as Asia's premier oil hub. By capitalizing on its capabilities and infrastructure, it is aiming to develop liquefied natural gas (LNG), biofuels, and carbon trading businesses.[67] The policy target is to increase the value added from Singapore's energy industry to S$34 billion by 2015 from S$20 billion (as of 2007), and to triple the employment in this sector from 5,700 to 15,300.[68]

With refining capacity of nearly double its rate of petroleum products consumption, Singapore has maintained its position as a global oil refining and trading centre. Akin to the shipping industry, Singapore is home to a constellation of activities such as physical oil and derivatives trading, insurance, consulting, and news and price reporting services that have been driven by its status as a refining hub. As an "oil centre", forward and backward linkages are extensive, from manufacturing, banking, and insurance to commodity trading, shipping, and risk management

Singapore is one of the world's top three export refining centres, along with the Greater Houston Area and the ARA area. Refining capacity (of crude distillation units) for Singapore's three export-oriented refineries, together with the refineries in Greater Houston and ARA, as well as a selection of other regions and countries, are shown in Table 4.5 below. Singapore and the Greater Houston area are comparable in distillation capacity, at around 1.2–1.3 million barrels per day (bpd) in 2008. Belgium and the Netherlands together (representing the ARA conurbation) have a distillation capacity of over 2 million bpd. All three areas, as mature refining centres, show little change in total distillation capacity over the past decade. We see that refinery capacity in Asia has witnessed substantial growth with China and India posting growth rates of approximately 6 per cent and 8 per cent from 1998 to 2008 respectively. However, this growth has largely been to meet rising domestic product demand. Unlike Singapore, the distillation capacities for countries such as South Korea, Taiwan, and Thailand are geared primarily for the domestic market. Houston's refineries also primarily supply the domestic market in the U.S. southern, central, and eastern seaboard regions, while the ARA refining area mainly supplies the common EU market.

Table 4.5
Refinery Capacities

Country	1998	2008	2008 over 1998	share of total (2008)
US	16,261	17,621	0.81%	19.88%
Greater Houston Area		*1,207*		*1.36%*
Belgium and Netherlands	*1,998*	*2,006*	*0.04%*	*2.26%*
Australia	810	734	−0.98%	0.83%
China	4,592	7,812	6.10%	9.50%
India	1,356	2,992	8.24%	3.38%
Singapore	*1,246*	*1,255*	*0.07%*	*1.42%*
ExxonMobil Jurong Island		605	0.00%	0.68%
SRC Jurong Island		285	0.00%	0.32%
Shell Pulau Bukom		458	0.00%	0.52%
South Korea	2,598	2,712	0.43%	3.06%
Taiwan	732	1,197	5.04%	1.35%
Thailand	890	1,187	2.92%	1.34%
EU	15,262	15,788	0.34%	17.81%
Total World	79,699	88,627	1.07%	100.00%

Source: BP, "Statistical Review of World Energy", June 2009. Data for Greater Houston Area is from US Energy Information Administration, "Refinery Capacity Report", 25 June 2009. Data on Singapore refineries is obtained from the *Oil and Gas Journal* (various issues).

Table 4.6 below shows the trade orientation of the three major ports serving the refining industry in their "catchment" areas. As can be seen, Singapore's share of total "outgoing" crude oil and refined products as a proportion of the total "incoming" is at 65 per cent, significantly higher than Houston and Rotterdam, reflecting both the small domestic market and export orientation of the country. It should be noted as well that "outgoing" volumes from Houston would also include shipment of products to other ports within the United States.

According to the Economic Development Board (EDB), besides being one of the three largest petroleum refining centres in the world, Singapore's Jurong Island is among the world's top ten petrochemical hubs, with a projected total ethylene output of 4 million tonnes per annum by the year 2012.[69] The oil industry has been integral to Singapore's economy,

Table 4.6
Petroleum Trade for Major Ports, 2008 (million tonnes)

	Incoming	Outgoing	Total	Outgoing as % of Incoming
Houston	67.3	24.0	91.3	35%
Rotterdam	136.3	22.7	159.0	16%
Singapore	130.9	110.9	241.8	62%

Source: Port of Houston Authority, "Trade Statistics", Trade Development Division, 2009 <http://www.portofhouston.com/busdev/tradedevelopment/tradestatistics.html>; Port of Rotterdam, "Port Statistics 2008", 2009 <http://www.portofrotterdam.com/mmfiles/Port_Statistics_2008_tcm26-60399.pdf>; Singapore Bunker sales (outgoing), Maritime Port Authority, "Annual Report 2008", 2009 <http://www.mpa.gov.sg/sites/pdf/mpa_annual_report_2008.pdf>; BP, "Statistical Review of World Energy", 2009; estimates for bunker trade in Singapore, excluded from the BP data, provided by FGE.

contributing approximately 5 per cent to Singapore's GDP in 2007.[70] When considered together, Singapore's energy and chemical complex contributed S\$57 billion of the manufacturing output in 2009 (28 per cent of Singapore's total manufacturing output).[71]

The oil and gas industry is not defined in the EDB source. According to the "Economic Survey of Singapore 2008", the "chemical" industrial cluster (which includes petroleum refining, petrochemicals, specialty chemicals, and others) contributed 10.2 per cent of value added to total manufacturing. Total manufacturing accounted for 20 per cent of total GDP; hence the chemical industrial cluster accounts for just over 2 per cent of total GDP. The EDB's estimate of 5 per cent for the oil sector thus probably includes estimates for other industries in addition to those included in the Economic Survey's "chemicals" industrial cluster.

In the earliest days of the oil industry growth in Singapore, since its emergence as an oil entrepôt and storage facility for the region during the early colonial era, there was probably already "an inevitable logic to Shell building a refinery on Bukom".[72] Singapore's deepwater port and geographically strategic position within the region were natural advantages, and the stable investment climate after independence in Singapore offered continuity to the oil majors' substantial capital investments in refining and petrochemical capacity in the country.

The refining and petrochemical sector directly contributes to a relative small share of GDP. However, like shipping, it is tied intimately with the services sector via oil and derivatives trading, insurance, consulting, and news and price reporting services. As an "oil centre", the complex of activities within which oil refining and petrochemical manufacturing is an integral part includes the entire gamut of downstream petroleum activity. Like shipping, the refining sector's forward and backward linkages are extensive, from banking and insurance to commodity trading, shipping and risk management. The chemical sector's value added per worker is about double that of the total manufacturing sector average. Petrochemical's value added per worker is exceeded only by the biomedical industrial cluster. The petroleum and chemicals sectors have the highest remuneration per worker across all manufacturing sectors. The total output value of the chemicals sector constitutes almost 38 per cent of total manufacturing output, and reflects the high prices of oil and chemical products (see Table 4.7).

Impact of Emission Reduction Policies on the Refining Sector

In terms of CO_2 emissions, it was already noted that power generation and petroleum refining and petrochemicals account for almost three-quarters of Singapore's carbon emissions. Power generation alone accounts for a little less than half of its total CO_2 emissions and a further quarter is accounted for by oil refining and petrochemicals. Unlike power generation which produces a non-tradable good (electricity),[73] the oil refining and petrochemicals sector produces highly fungible products which compete in international commodity markets. "A barrel of gasoline made in India is the same as a barrel of gasoline made in Indiana", as the U.S. industry group of oil refiners and petrochemicals producers puts it.[74] The U.S. refining and petrochemicals industry, like its Singapore counterpart, competes directly with other such industries around the world.

Refinery runs[75] are a function of marginal operating costs across the world, to the extent that such refineries operate in markets that are open to refined product imports without onerous tariff or non-tariff barriers. Thus, while one does not expect investments and disinvestments in capital-intensive sectors such as petroleum refining to be subject to short-term competitive pressures,[76] the actual operation or capacity utilization of such installations can fluctuate fairly rapidly, as a function of marginal operating costs. Thus, if American or Singaporean refiners are subject to binding carbon emission restraints, their consequent higher marginal operating

Table 4.7
Statistics of Singapore Manufacturing

Principal Statistics of Manufacturing by Industry Cluster, 2011

	Employment		Remuneration		Total Output		Value Added		Remuneration Per Worker	Value Added Per Worker
	S$ M	%	S$ M	%	S$ M	%	S$ M	%	S$'000	S$'000
Electronics	81,949	19.6	4,183.2	22.1	86,404.9	29.4	15,300.3	26.1	51.0	186.7
Semiconductors	43,528	10.4	2,337.2	12.3	46,736.5	15.9	8,741.5	14.9	53.7	200.8
Computer Peripherals	11,328	2.7	514.2	2.7	8,869.5	3.0	2,159.8	3.7	45.4	190.7
Data Storage	10,682	2.6	490.6	2.6	6,805.5	2.3	1,592.2	2.6	45.9	143.2
Infocomm and Consumer Electronics	9,496	2.3	569.1	3.0	22,202.9	7.5	2,423.9	4.1	59.9	255.3
Other Electronic Modules & Components	6,915	1.7	272.2	1.4	1,790.5	0.6	445.9	0.8	39.4	64.5
Chemicals	24,769	5.9	2,163.5	11.4	99,403.3	33.8	5,581.8	9.5	87.3	225.4
Petroleum	3,681	0.9	576.3	3.0	55,960.4	19.0	284.7	0.5	156.6	77.3
Petrochemicals	5,479	1.3	540.7	2.9	32,493.8	11.0	2,603.9	4.4	98.7	475.3
Specialty Chemicals	10,247	2.4	774.7	4.1	8,980.1	3.1	2,118.6	3.6	75.6	206.8
Others	5,362	1.3	271.8	1.4	1,969.0	0.7	574.5	1.0	50.7	107.1
Biomedical Manufacturing	15,378	3.7	950.6	5.0	26,530.1	9.0	13,423.6	22.9	61.8	872.9
Pharmaceuticals	5,712	1.4	541.0	2.9	22,609.8	7.7	11,731.6	20.0	94.7	2,053.9
Medical Technology	9,666	2.3	409.6	2.2	3,920.3	1.3	1,692.0	2.9	42.4	175.0
Precision Engineering	93,303	22.3	4,087.8	21.6	33,190.4	11.3	8,683.1	14.8	43.8	93.1
Machinery and Systems	41,994	10.0	2,118.3	11.2	21,806.6	7.4	5,344.3	9.1	50.4	127.3
Precision Modules and Components	51,309	12.3	1,969.5	10.4	11,383.8	3.9	3,338.9	5.7	38.4	65.1
Transport Engineering	109,119	26.1	4,349.8	22.9	26,514.2	9.0	9,071.6	15.5	39.9	83.1
Marine and Offshore Engineering	83,700	20.0	2,697.4	14.2	16,510.6	5.6	5,501.7	9.4	32.2	65.7
Aerospace	19,160	4.6	1,309.5	6.9	8,008.1	2.7	2,869.1	4.9	68.3	149.7
Land	6,259	1.5	342.9	1.8	1,995.4	0.7	700.8	1.2	54.8	112.0
General Manufacturing Industries	93,806	22.4	3,230.4	17.0	22,130.9	7.5	6,524.2	11.1	34.4	69.6
Food, Beverages and Tobacco	26,653	6.4	852.7	4.5	8,432.8	2.9	2,153.3	3.7	32.0	80.8
Printing	16,618	4.0	765.4	4.0	2,635.8	0.9	1,346.2	2.3	46.1	81.0
Miscellaneous industries	50,535	12.1	1,612.3	8.5	11,062.2	3.8	3,024.8	5.2	31.9	59.9
TOTAL MANUFACTURING	418,324	100.0	18,965.4	100.0	294,173.7	100.0	58,584.6	100.0	45.3	140.0

Notes: 1 Refers to all manufacturing establishments.
2 The industries are classified according to SSIC 2010.
3 Figures may not add up due to rounding.
Source: Economic Development Board, "Principal Statistics of Manufacturing", 2012 (Table 4.9).

costs (incorporating the cost of carbon emissions) will encourage higher capacity utilization among refiners which have lower marginal costs. For example, Singapore refiners will face competitive pressures from refineries in Thailand, and even as far away as Gujarat,[77] if Singapore were to take up binding emission constraints.

Apart from the ExxonMobil and Shell refineries in Singapore, the Singapore Refining Company is a joint venture between the Singapore Petroleum Company (SPC) and Chevron, the U.S.-based oil major. Keppel Corporation sold its entire stake in SPC to PetroChina, a China-based government-owned oil giant.[78] With the PetroChina takeover, the Singapore refining sector still remains largely an international oil majors-dominated industry with Shell, Exxon, and Chevron, with the significant exception of SRC. It is instructive to note the National Petrochemical and Refiners Association (NPRA) — which has all three companies as members — submission to the U.S. House of Representatives.[79] In the submission, the NPRA points out U.S.-specific issues affecting oil refiners and petrochemical producers such as the "overlapping and costly regulations on producers of petroleum-based products".[80] However, beyond such U.S.-centric issues, the submission raises key issues of competitiveness and energy security that apply across the board to all refiners which supply markets that are open to imports of petroleum and petrochemical products. In other words, the submission touches on economic and strategic issues that face all refiners throughout the global industry where refining is not sheltered within protected domestic markets.

Just as in shipping and aviation, the key issue of a "level playing field" or equity is emphasized in the submission. The UNFCCC's central principle of "common but differentiated responsibilities" refers to the clear policy divide between "developed" and "developing" countries regarding emission reduction constraints (under the Kyoto Protocol, the former impose it upon themselves, the latter are excused, at least in the short and medium terms, say up to 2020 or beyond). If, in the post-Kyoto world, this principle were to be imposed upon the downstream oil and gas sector, then the first issue would be whether Singapore is on one side of the divide or the other.[81]

The Australian example provides some idea of the costs involved for the refining industry to achieve emission reduction targets. Australia's four oil refining and marketing companies will need to buy more than 25 per cent of the available permits, mostly to cover emissions emitted by their customers. Caltex would be the largest purchaser of carbon permits in Australia, approaching 10 per cent of the market. Australia's oil-refining industry would therefore be threatened by high costs for carbon emissions permits under the government's proposed trading system, because Australia's four oil refiners compete against rivals in Asian nations that do not place a cost on carbon pollution.[82] In an interview, the managing director and CEO of Caltex of Australia, Des King, said: "If our competitors won't pay for permits, why should we?", and he goes on to specifically mention Singapore refineries as examples of competitors.[83]

In Europe, the debate has also focused on the international "leakage" effects of putting a price on carbon for heavy, energy-intensive industries, such as steel, cement, chemicals and plastics, primary metals, and oil refining. It is in these industries, competing in global markets, where reduced production in countries which impose emission constraints may be largely offset by increased production in other countries which do not have binding emission constraints.[84] Germany and France have pushed for an early definition of sectors exposed to carbon leakage, whereby industries relocate to parts of the world where CO_2 emissions are not regulated.[85] The oil industry in the EU has lobbied for free allocation permits (so that the initial allowances would be given free to oil refiners, and only further purchases would have to be paid for at open market prices) but free allocations would not bring an end to refiners' CO_2 emission reduction obligations. For example, in an interview the secretary general of Europia, the European oil refining industry association, said: "Today, we already have a cap that has been set by the ETS and our emissions have to be reduced over time. When we say free allocations, we mean allocations under the cap. But what is over the cap, we have to pay for, whatever happens."[86]

In the United States, domestic producers of aluminium, cement, iron and steel, pulp, paper, and certain chemicals are facing higher costs than their competitors in countries without comparable GHG constraints. The NPRA estimates that a small-sized 100,000 bpd refinery would have to spend over US$360 million annually to purchase emission allowances for the fuels it produces, assuming a modest carbon price of US$26 per tonne.[87] The American Clean Energy Security Act, which passed the U.S. House of Representatives in June 2009, attempts to address these competitiveness concerns by compensating energy-intensive, trade-exposed firms for higher costs by providing them with free allowances and through the use of border tax adjustments.[88]

In refining, it is also important to note that there is a "double whammy" aspect to international competition in the sector: not only is refining affected by the actual GHG emissions of refinery processes, but it produces refined products that are carbon-intensive in content (petroleum products are carbon-based molecules). In some scenarios, for example, OECD-based companies will be afforded import protection by tariff barriers (carbon-content import taxes) against products from countries which do not impose similar carbon-emission constraints. However, such tariff barriers on carbon-content of imports will still not "level" the playing field, since those non-OECD countries will not be subject to carbon emission restrictions on the operation of their refineries, only on the carbon-content of their exports.[89] In other words, foreign exporters of petroleum and petrochemical products will pay only for their *finished product emissions*, not the *process emissions* of their refineries abroad. According to the NPRA, foreign-based refiners would immediately gain a 10 per cent cost advantage over the U.S. refining industry as a result of this.[90]

Given the low elasticity of substitution for refined oil products,[91] users will access lowest-cost sources of those same products, making the global market for refined products extremely sensitive to competitive pressures from countries which do not have GHG emission constraints. Aggressive emission reduction programmes before sufficient technologies are available can lead to significant costs of premature transition for all users of such products, with effects reverberating throughout the economy. The effects of binding GHG emission constraints not only threaten the commercial viability of competitive refining centres such as Singapore, but also impose higher costs throughout the economy dependent on refined oil products. It threatens the energy security of countries by constricting the "supply menu" of viable and available options. In one estimate, refiners in the United States would only be able to "pass through" 50 per cent of costs on to consumers for various petroleum products.[92]

Lack of competitive alternatives in the transportation sector, for instance, are compounded by the problems that have arisen with attempts at using "sustainable" fuels such as ethanol or other biofuels. The U.S. Energy Information Administration (EIA) estimates that a 25 per cent Renewable Fuels Standard in the United States would need 66 million gallons of ethanol, an amount that would exhaust the entire American biomass supply.[93] The impact of ethanol production on rising food supply prices, and the significant GHG emissions impact in South East Asia of establishing oil palm estates for biofuels in forested areas are well documented.[94]

4.3 CIVIL AVIATION

Singapore's Changi Airport was ranked nineteenth for passenger traffic[95] and tenth for freight traffic[96] in 2008. The Singapore aviation industry in 2008 flew 1.9 million tonnes of airfreight cargo, moved over 37 million passengers, and had over 230,000 commercial aircraft movements.[97] Currently, the Civil Aviation Authority of Singapore (CAAS) and Changi Airport Group work together to further develop Singapore as a leading air hub.[98] According to the most recent data for 2014 (January to May), Singapore's airport ranked fifteenth in terms of passenger traffic, not only lower than other globally important airports such as London Heathrow, New York JFK, or Amsterdam, but also regional hubs such as Hong Kong, Dubai, and Bangkok.[99] For air cargo volumes, Singapore is behind Hong Kong, Incheon, and Tokyo Narita.

Impact of Emissions Reduction Policies on Aviation

A global agreement on aviation emissions is unlikely to be reached any time soon. The ICAO will necessarily have to align its work to develop a market-based approach in this area with the outcome of ongoing UNFCC negotiations.[100] Pressure will build on ICAO to find solutions for the aviation industry that has binding emission targets for the industry. In 2008, the EU announced that it would implement its own market-based emission regulation on the European aviation industry unless the industry manages to regulate itself.[101]

Any agreement implemented by ICAO will have consequences for international aviation hubs like Singapore and Dubai. Even though the aviation industry constitutes under 2 per cent of the GDP, the impact of higher costs and lower numbers of passengers and air cargo is likely to have significant spillover impacts on Singapore, including tourism. Fig 4.3 shows Singapore's CO_2 emissions, with and without the aviation sector. Total emissions increase by about 20 per cent if aviation is included. As for shipping, national CO_2 emissions do not include emissions from aviation, as fuel is combusted outside the country's jurisdiction, mostly in international airspace.

Figure 4.3
Singapore CO_2 Emissions, With and Without Aviation (tonnes per capita)

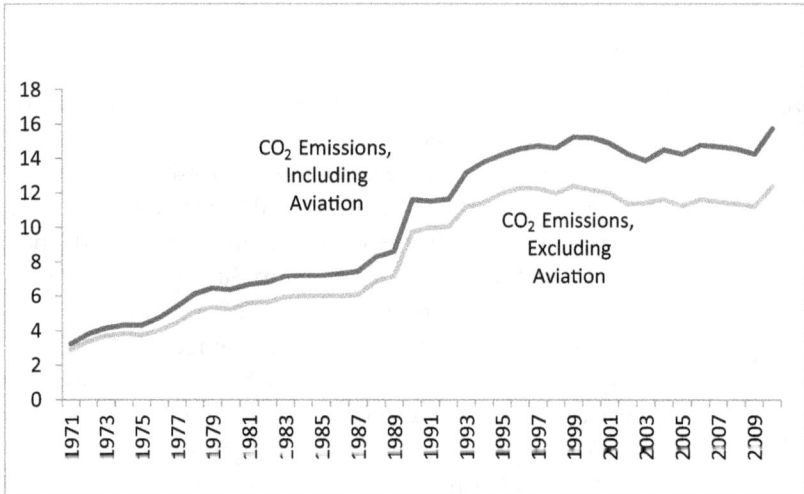

Note: Population data: World Bank, "World Population Prospects: The 2012 Revision".
Source: "IEA CO_2 Emissions from Fuel Combustion — Highlights 2012" <http://www.iea.org/media/freepublications/2012/CO2Highlights2012.xls>.

UNFCCC and ICAO

Emissions from aviation activities, like shipping, are not included in emission reduction targets of the Annex I countries in the Kyoto Protocol to the UNFCCC. Article 2.2 of the Kyoto Protocol states that parties should seek ways of reducing civil aviation emissions under the auspices of the ICAO. Since 1990, CO_2 emissions from aviation have increased by 87 per cent.[102] The global aviation industry produces about 3.5 per cent of total global carbon dioxide emissions, and the Intergovernmental Panel on Climate Change has estimated that this share will grow to 5 per cent by 2050 unless regulation on emissions is introduced.[103] Member States of the ICAO representing 93 per cent of commercial air traffic affirmed in October 2009 their commitment to address aviation emissions that contribute to climate change by working through the ICAO.[104] The ICAO is an agency of the United Nations, created in 1944 to promote safe and orderly development of international civil aviation throughout the world. It sets standards and regulations necessary for aviation safety, security, efficiency, and regularity, as well as for aviation environmental protection.[105]

In 2004, at the 35th session of its assembly, ICAO developed a template agreement for voluntary measures to reduce aviation emissions. It was used by several contracting states as a model for their emissions policy. In 2007, at the 36th session of the assembly, the focus was on developing a framework for implementing policy options to limit or reduce the environmental impact of aircraft engine emissions through technology and standards, operational measures to reduce fuel consumption, and market-based measures. However, during the 2007 assembly, consensus was not reached.

Following the 36th session, ICAO recognized the urgency and critical importance of addressing aviation emissions that contribute to global climate change and re-emphasized the need for ICAO to provide leadership in this area. Accordingly, it formed both the Committee on Aviation Environmental Protection (CAEP), and more importantly the Group on International Aviation and Climate Change (GIACC) to develop an ICAO Programme of Action on International Aviation and Climate Change. ICAO requested the GIACC to develop concrete proposals to the UNFCCC.[106] A proposal called the Programme of Action was adopted by the council of the ICAO in June 2009, and is the first global agreement to address climate impacts from this sector.[107]

In the Programme of Action agreement, GIACC recommends a global "aspirational" goal of 2 per cent annual improvement in fuel efficiency of the international civil aviation in-service fleet. This would represent a cumulative improvement of 13 per cent in the short term (2010 to 2012), 26 per cent in the medium term (2013 to 2020), and about 60 per cent in the long term (2021 to 2050), from a 2005 base level. It also considered the possibility of establishing goals of carbon neutral growth for the medium term and carbon emissions reduction for the long term. Although it did not reach consensus on these issues, the GIACC recommended that further work be undertaken by ICAO on both medium- and long-term goals.[108]

The GIACC agreed that the goals should be collectively achieved by states, without specific obligations to individual states. The different circumstances, respective capabilities, and contribution of developing and developed states will determine how each state may contribute to achieving these global aspirational goals. The GIACC also recommended a basket of measures from which states may choose to reduce international aviation emissions, covering aircraft-related technology development, improved air traffic management and infrastructure use, more efficient operations, economic/market-based measures, and regulatory measures. Each state would have the ultimate authority and responsibility to define a portfolio of measures appropriate to its circumstances, consistent with the global aspirational goals, and to develop and report to ICAO individual action plans. For developing countries, measures would be developed to facilitate their access to assistance (financial resources, technology, capacity building).

IATA

The International Air Transport Association, also known as IATA, represents approximately 230 airlines comprising about 93 per cent of scheduled international air traffic.[109] IATA is working to obtain support from various governments for the aviation industry's approach to climate change consisting of four elements: adopt industry targets to stabilize and reduce the airline industry's carbon emissions; manage civil aviation carbon emissions by treating aviation as a global industrial sector; invest in infrastructure including air traffic management; and establish fiscal and legal frameworks to promote biofuels.[110]

By pursuing the global sectoral approach, IATA proposes that governments account for aviation's emissions at a global level and as an industrial sector, rather than within national targets (similar to IMO's approach to global shipping). This would ensure similar regulations for all airlines, not matter where they are located.[111] IATA has set three goals for all commercial operations by all air carriers, with the first being an average annual improvement in fuel efficiency of 1.5 per cent from 2009 to 2020; the second, carbon-neutral growth from 2020; and the third, an absolute reduction of 50 per cent in carbon emissions by 2050, relative to 2005 levels.[112]

AEA

The Association of European Airlines (AEA) consists of thirty-three airlines, and has been representing the European airline industry for over fifty years. AEA has also called for a global sectoral approach. In their proposal, countries would be grouped into three blocks according to the maturity of their industry. There would be different targets set for the three blocks, but equal treatment of the carriers operating in the same block. For traffic between two blocks, the lower targets would apply.[113]

AGD Group

A specially formed Aviation Global Deal (AGD) Group also calls for a sectoral approach. The group of nine entities in the aviation industry suggested global emission reduction targets, with proposals from 0–20 per cent by 2020 and 50–80 per cent by 2050, with 2005 as the basis year.[114] Furthermore, the AGD Group suggested integrating the aviation sector within the overall climate framework with open access to carbon markets. A UN organization would act as an administrator for this system. All but one airline of the AGD Group are also members of IATA. The members are: Air France–KLM, British Airways, Cathay Pacific, Finnair, Qatar Airways, Virgin Atlantic, Virgin Blue Airlines Group, BAA (British Airports Authority, which was renamed Heathrow Holdings in 2012), and LOT Polish Airlines.[115]

European Union

In order to mitigate the climate impact of aviation, the EU introduced legislation to include aviation in the EU ETS under directive 2008/101/EC.[116] The EU proposed that in order to avoid distortions of competition and improve environmental effectiveness, emissions from all flights arriving at and departing from EU airports should be included from 2012, unless the industry proves it can regulate itself. Airlines would have had to pay for their emissions over the entire route, not just within EU airspace, a rule many Asian airlines flying long-haul routes to Europe said was unfair.[117]

The number of pollution permits allocated to airlines would be capped at 97 per cent of average GHGs emitted in 2004–6.[118] This cap would then be lowered to 95 per cent for the 2013–20 period, but this figure could be subject to change as part of the ongoing review of the EU's general ETS. Initially, only 15 per cent of the allowances would be auctioned. A study commissioned by the airline industry found that the current proposal would slash airlines' profits by more than €40 billion from 2011 to 2022; it asserts that the baseline on which caps are to be calculated (2004–6) is too far removed from the trading period (2011–22) and will leave seventeen years of growth unaccounted for, forcing the industry to buy massive amounts of credits even if these are given away for free in the beginning.[119]

United States

On 1 October 2009, the U.S. Senate released a draft energy and climate change bill known as the Kerry-Boxer bill. Commercial airlines would have to fly new planes that emit fewer GHG emissions. The legislation would have required the government to write standards applicable to emissions of GHGs from new aircraft and new engines used in aircraft. Accordingly, the EPA would consult with the Federal Aviation Administration in setting aircraft emissions standards.[120] The United States has made it clear that it would retaliate with trade sanctions if the EU makes any attempt to force foreign airlines to comply with its emissions trading system, whatever the timeline.[121]

Implications for Singapore

The GIACC and IATA proposals should not have any major implications for the competitiveness of Changi Airport and Singapore Airlines, since they are to be implemented on a global basis with no exemptions. As for the AEA and the AGD Group proposals, they do not seem to have any major backing outside their organizations. Furthermore, the AGD Group is relatively small, with only nine entities represented. The major concern seems to be with the EU proposal, and this section will concentrate on how the EU proposal may impact the Singapore economy.

The EU plan to include aviation in its ETS would create financial burdens on an industry which has been one of the worst affected in the current global economic recession. The plan would disproportionately affect airlines serving Europe, making it more expensive for customers to fly to or from Europe.[122] For flights between Singapore and cities in Europe, three things might happen. Firstly, some airlines might stop flying to and from European destinations because of the taxes. Secondly, because Singapore is relatively far away from Europe, airlines can start to create airport hubs outside but very near the EU, to be able to pay as little fees as possible for the last "jump" to and from EU airports. For example, an airline that has flown directly from Singapore to Italy, might begin to fly from Singapore to Turkey, and from Turkey to Italy. Passengers will prefer direct flights, but if the price difference is high enough, one can definitely see these new types of flight patterns emerging. Thirdly, since the EU region actually increases the cost of flying, one can expect the total air traffic in and out of Europe to be lower than what it would have been without the extra emission-related costs.

Changi Airport

Changi Airport handles airlines flying to more than 300 cities in 70 countries. Of these, 98 cities and 27 countries are located in Europe.[123] These are the flights that will be impacted by the new proposed regulations from the EU. The EU will tax all flights landing at EU airports, counting the *entire* distance of the flight. Table 4.8 shows the results of "CO_2 offset calculators" in terms of CO_2 emissions attributable to each passenger, and the cost of offsetting such emissions. As can be seen, the values vary widely. The price increase for a ticket from Singapore to Copenhagen, reflecting the cost of offsetting CO_2 emissions, ranges from S$26.92 to S$84.00; the calculated CO_2 emission varies from 922 kg to 1,256 kg. This variation is likely to be due to different assumptions of carbon price and technical parameters. The lack of standards for emission calculators in the aviation industry is also documented in other research.[124]

Singapore Airlines

Singapore Airlines has several large competitors with bases in the Asia-Pacific. Table 4.9 shows the annual revenue of selected Asia-Pacific airlines. Like Emirates and Cathay Pacific airlines, Singapore Airlines is fully exposed to changes in international travel due to the fact that there is no domestic market. In 2008, the Singapore Airlines Group annual revenue was almost US$8 billion, smaller than Japan Airlines, Qantas, Emirates, and Cathay Pacific.[125]

In 2008, Europe was the highest growth region for Singapore Airlines. The total number of Singapore Airlines passengers was reduced by some 830,000 compared to the year before, but the European region actually had an increase of over 220,000 passengers.[126] The European region yielded the airline a 10.5 per cent increase in revenue in 2008–9 compared to the year before, as seen in Table 4.10. The airlines' revenue

Table 4.8
Current CO_2 Offset Solutions

Current price for CO_2 offset for a round-trip flight from Singapore to Copenhagen		
	Actual CO_2 Emissions	S$
British Airways	—	$84.00
Japan Airlines	922 kg	$74.61
Scandinavian Airline Systems	1256 kg	$26.92

Sources: Various airlines websites (accessed 9 November 2009): www.flysas.com, www.britishairways.com, www.jal.com via www.ico2-zero.co.jp/JAL

Table 4.9
Asia-Pacific Airlines Revenue, 2008

Asia-Pacific Airlines by Annual Revenue, 2008, million US$	
JAL Group	$20,280
Qantas	$16,192
ANA Group	$14,077
Emirates	$12,041
Cathay Pacific	$11,164
Singapore Airlines Group	$7,964
Korean Air	$7,204
Thai Airways	$4,812
Malaysia Airlines	$4,212

Source: Centre for Asia Pacific Aviation, *Airport & Airline Asia Pacific*, no. 368, 4 August 2009.

Table 4.10
Singapore Airlines Revenue by Route Region

	2008–9, million US$	% change over previous year
East Asia	2,546.4	−10.3
Europe	2,364.3	10.5
South West Pacific	1,806.9	0.6
Americas	1,697.6	−7.8
West Asia and Africa	1,108.1	−8.6
System Wide	9,523.3	−3.1

Source: Singapore Airlines, *Annual Report 2008/2009*, 2009.

from the European region totalled S$2.4 billion, approximately 25 per cent of the global revenue.

It is difficult to discover the full ramifications of the European proposal for emission cuts in the aviation industry, due to challenges in quantifying the impact on transit passengers, tourists, lower demand in air transport and ancillary activities, etc. If ICAO implements global standards with binding emission targets for the aviation industry, Singapore, with its high degree of international exposure, will be significantly impacted. It is in Singapore's interest that the potential standards imposed are the same for all countries, in particular for those countries which have key airport hubs such as Dubai, Amsterdam, and Hong Kong. However, even if all countries would see the same standards, all flights would actually become more expensive, thus reducing global demand for aviation. In this case, Singapore would also experience reduced aviation traffic.

The real threat lies in the possibility that not all countries' aviation industries will have the same standards, thereby creating "leakage". IATA is an interest organization in the airline industry whose members represent 93 per cent of all scheduled international air traffic, and it is therefore likely to be heard in international forums. IATA calls for equal treatment of all airlines when it comes to aviation and climate change.[127] Therefore, it is quite possible that Singapore Airlines will face the same regulations as all other airlines in the industry.

GIACC, being the body charged by UNFCCC on the ultimate arrangement for the aviation industry, continues to work towards market-based solutions. GIACC has realized that there are many different national views on the matter, and will consider the outcome of the Copenhagen conference when it furthers its work in this area.[128] In its current approach to emissions reduction, GIACC does take into consideration how a country's capability and its rank as a developed or developing country may determine how any specific country can contribute to achieve the aviation industry's climate change goals. However, it is not clear whether the "common but differentiated" principle which enshrines the distinction in obligations and responsibilities of developed and developing countries in the UNFCCC will play a role in GIACC's recommendations.

4.4 SINGAPORE AS A REGIONAL AND GLOBAL HUB

Shipping and Oil Bunkering

As the world's largest bunkering port, and the single largest port state in the collection of revenues, Singapore is the natural location for the establishment of the International GHG Fund Administrator, if one were to be established under some future international climate treaty. It would be no surprise, however, that the existing International Oil Pollution Compensation Fund Administrators, based in London, makes a claim to be the appropriate location of the international GHG Fund Administrator based on precedence and historical experience as the shipping capital of the world. If a future IMO-negotiated emission mitigation programme for global shipping opts for a tax rather than a cap-and-trade programme, the role of the fund administrator will be quite straightforward as tax collector, with minimal spillover into the local economy. If, on the other hand, a cap-and-trade programme with permit auctions were to be instituted, the obvious benefits for Singapore in terms of employment of senior professionals in a private sector–led carbon market would be significant. In terms of the enhancement of the country's status as a leading global hub for the energy, maritime, and financial industries, carbon trading could be a coherent part of the strategy of eliciting private sector involvement as stakeholders in a post-Kyoto climate change regime.

On the same grounds, i.e., as the world's largest bunkering port by far, Singapore can also claim to be the natural location of an R&D centre for shipping and carbon emissions mitigation. Singapore, as the preferred location for shipping R&D, would have reasonable claim on a share of revenues collected by the fund administrator for allocation to Singapore-based R&D activity. Equitably, one could argue, the share of such revenues should reflect Singapore's size in global bunker sales. R&D funds need to be above a critical threshold for effective deployment (i.e., one cannot have too many R&D centres to be effective due to economies of scale). Hence, on efficiency grounds, Singapore again can legitimately claim to be the choice location for the establishment of *the* R&D centre for global sustainable shipping. This would have strong positive externalities for Singapore's ambitions to establish itself as a centre for "green" energy technologies.

In a post-Kyoto climate change regime, it would be incumbent on port authorities to assess the potential for "leakage" in bunkering activity to other competing ports which may not have emission regulations or have more permissive regimes. For instance, in a context where Singapore would be required to participate, but not its middle-income neighbours, nearby smaller ports such as Port Kelang and Tanjung Pelepas in Malaysia could emerge as "leakage outlets".

Oil Refining and Petrochemicals

GHG emission constraints that impact the oil refining and petrochemicals sector may be either a result of countries adopting such constraints in their national programmes, applicable to their domestic refineries; or countries agreeing to a sector-based agreement, applicable to the global refining industry, whether in the developed or the developing countries. With respect to the key criterion of a "level" playing field, the sector approach has an advantage to making such an outcome possible across all major refining centres that participate in open trading in the global oil products markets. However, if emission reductions on oil and gas downstream sectors are a function of whether a country is participating or not in a global or regional agreement, then refining centres such as Singapore will fare according to which part of the divide they fall in.

Singapore's interests as the oil and gas hub for the "East of Suez" region lie critically with maintaining the sector's ability to compete with refining centres in Asia such as India's Jamnagar refinery complex. As already mentioned in a previous section, one would expect pressure from OECD countries such as Australia, Japan, and the United States on Singapore as an "advanced developing country" to "graduate" to more stringent carbon emission reduction targets. In the petroleum refining sector specifically, regional players such as the Australian refining companies would almost certainly raise their concerns with their government officials and require that Singapore's refining industry not gain competitive advantages from carbon emission regulations that Australia may adopt.

There is the possibility that the United States, EU, or other OECD members may seek to impose carbon import tariffs on energy-intensive products imported from countries that do not impose emission reduction regulations. For an oil refining and trading hub like Singapore, it would be critical to ensure that relative cost structures stay in line with regional competitors such as India, Australia, South Korea or Thailand, as well as the large new export refineries of the Middle East.

Civil Aviation

Pressure will build on the ICAO to find solutions for the aviation industry that has binding emission targets for the industry, although the Great Recession of 2008–9 has dampened most countries's ambitions on a comprehensive post–Kyoto Protocol treaty. It is yet unclear what a possible market model for emissions reduction in the global aviation industry might look like, but one leading candidate is the cap-and-trade scheme that the EU announced for implementation on aviation in the EU. Europe's highest court recently upheld the right of the EU to impose a carbon cap-and-trade scheme on international airlines using European airports, rejecting an appeal from U.S. airlines.[129] After the expected objections from a number of countries to this proposed unilateral move by the EU — seen as a "trade war" by aviation companies in countries such as China and the United States — the now-frozen emissions scheme on foreign carriers operating at EU airports awaits a possible agreement at the ICAO's next assembly in Montreal in 2016. [130]

Singapore as a Hub

Singapore has often been described as a "hub" across a range of industries, ranging from civil aviation and shipping to banking and finance and oil refining and trading. It describes the city-state's regional and global role in these industries, offering locational and infrastructural advantages to the many firms that use its services, whether domiciled in Singapore or otherwise. The development of Singapore's roles in transport (as a major transport node, it supports civil aviation, ship bunkering, and break-bulking of seaborne cargo), finance and oil (refining, storage, and trading) can best be explained as the outcome of "economies of agglomeration", a term used in economic geography to describe the benefits that firms obtain by locating near each other ("agglomerating" or "clustering"). As more firms in related fields of business cluster together, their costs of production decline with economies of scale as clusters of competing firms attract more suppliers and customers than a single firm could attract on its own.[131] Indeed, cities form and grow to exploit economies of agglomeration.[132]

With economies of agglomeration, there is the further benefit of "network effects" where the value of a product or service is dependent on the number of others using it. As Singapore's role in oil trading became central in the "East of Suez" region, anyone wanting to participate in the business *had* to locate in Singapore where other oil trading and service companies (such as shipping, finance, storage, and brokerage firms) were already located. As Singapore began to provide the basis for establishing Asian benchmark prices ("FOB Singapore") for the region's flows of crude oil and refined oil products, firms wishing to participate in oil price discovery — a vital requirement for all firms that have to balance their own and their clients' global and regional commodity trade and finance portfolios — based their traders and portfolio managers in the city-state.

To participate effectively in the world's largest and most important market for crude oil and refined oil products supply connecting the Middle East to East Asia, traders and arbitrageurs need to be in the same agglomeration as their compatriots in the shipping, finance, oil brokerage, consulting and price reporting agencies. "FOB Singapore" price quotes for crude oil and refined products account for some 12–15 million barrels traded per day, and these are discovered only by the constant flux of information and decisions made by traders — with operational and back offices which handle shipping, insurance, finance, credit, and risk — in "informal" markets covered by brokers and price reporters. "FOB Singapore" price quotes — a "networked" product whose value is a function of the fact that everyone else uses the same price quotes for their oil trades[133] — are literally "in the air" in Singapore's Central Business District.[134] The advantages of cities were described over a century ago by Alfred Marshall thus:

> When an industry has thus chosen a locality for itself, it is likely to stay there long: so great are the advantages which people following the same skilled trade get from near neighbourhood to one another. The mysteries of the trade become no mysteries; but are as it were in the air ... if one man starts a new idea, it is taken up by others and combined with suggestions of their own; and thus it becomes the source of further new ideas. And presently, subsidiary trades grow up in the neighbourhood, supplying it with implements and materials, organizing its traffic, and in many ways conducing to the economy of its material.[135]

The city-state provided infrastructure and non-tradable intermediate inputs such as a natural deep-water harbour and, as importantly, a predictable legal environment supportive of international business transactions. One might argue that there was an element of contingency in the development of Singapore as a regional oil refining and trading centre: it happened to be the location of choice for Shell in its global competition with Standard Oil's dominance in East Asia at the turn of the twentieth century.[136] Yet, since the early establishment of Shell's first Asia-based storage tanks offshore of Singapore in 1891 and an oil refinery in 1961, it is difficult to see how Singapore's emergence as a global oil refining and trading centre could have succeeded without the government's credible commitment to the rule of law and a predictable business climate for long-lived investments in oil shipping, refining, storage, and trading facilities. The role of government — Adam Smith's famous requisites of "peace, easy taxes, and a tolerable administration of justice" — was of no less importance than the city-state's natural deep-water port strategically located at the southern end of the Strait of Malacca.[137]

Notes

1. See, for instance, Paul Krugman, "Competitiveness: A Dangerous Obsession", *Foreign Affairs*, March/April 1994.
2. See Smit, A.J. "The Competitive Advantage of Nations: Is Porter's Diamond Framework a New Theory that Explains the International Competitiveness of Countries?", *Southern African Business Review* 14, no. 1 (2010).
3. The carbon content of marine and aviation bunkers are not included in measures of the country's CO_2 emissions. Nevertheless, marine bunkering and civil aviation are industries that matter critically to Singapore's appropriate stance on international negotiations in the UNFCCC.
4. Association of Asia Pacific Airlines, "World Port Rankings", 2009 <http://aapa.files.cms-plus.com/PDFs/WORLD%20PORT%20RANKINGS%202009.pdf>.
5. Jayarethanam Sinniah Pillai, "Historical Assessment of the Port of Singapore Authority and its Progression Towards a 'High-Tech Port'", Discussion Paper 05-19 (Canberra: Asia Pacific School of Economics and Government, Australian National University, 2005).
6. This is essentially a reduction in speed by ships. The energy use of a ship per kilometre increases approximately with the square of the speed.
7. Joe Dings, ed., *Bunker Fuels and the Kyoto Protocol: How ICAO and the IMO Failed the Climate Change Test* (Brussels: European Federation for Transport and Environment: 2009).
8. While official data for Singapore is available from the Maritime and Port Authority, Fujairah data is published in press releases issued by the Port Captain; see <http://www.bunkerworld.com/community/forum/thread/fujairah-bunker-volumes-3642>.
9. For an authoritative analysis of Singapore's dominating role as an oil centre in "East of Suez" markets, see Paul Horsnell, *Oil in Asia: Markets, Trading, Refining and Deregulation* (Oxford: Oxford University Press, 1997).
10. See "A Strategic Centre for Maritime Business", Maritime and Port Authority, n.d. <http://www.mpa.gov.sg/sites/pdf/infokit4.pdf>.
11. Prices reported by Bunker World for Singapore High-Sulphur Fuel Oil (HSFO) 380 centisokes (CST) was quoted at around US$600 per tonne in May 2014. Bunker World is a price assessment and reporting service, accessed at <http://www.bunkerworld.com/markets/prices/region/sea/>.
12. *Waves*, Singapore Shipping Association Newsletter, November 2007.

13. Singapore Ministry of Transport, "Appointment of New Chief Executive at the Maritime and Port Authority of Singapore (MPA)", news release, 30 March 2009 <http://www.mpa.gov.sg/sites/global_navigation/news_center/mpa_news/mpa_news_detail.page?filename=nr090330.xml>.

14. The concept of "economies of scope", as elaborated by Alfred D. Chandler refers to how costs to an industry X are lower due to the existence of an industry Y, as opposed to "economies of scale" which refer to the example of lower per unit costs as total production volume increases. Alfred D. Chandler, Scale and Scope: The Dynamics of Industrial Capitalism (Cambridge: Harvard University Press, 1990). Also related to "economies of scope" is the analysis of "agglomeration" by Paul Krugman to explain the rise of hubs such as Silicon Valley (for the IT sector) or Detroit (for the automotive sector). See Paul Krugman, Geography and Trade (Cambridge: The MIT Press, 1991).

15. Waves.

16. See "A Strategic Centre for Maritime Business".

17. International Maritime Organization, "Climate Change: A Challenge for the IMO too!", background paper (London: IMO, 2009) <http://www.imo.org/includes/blastDataOnly.asp/data_id%3D26316/backgroundE.pdf>.

18. It should be emphasized that these carbon emissions are purely a measure of the carbon content of bunker fuel sold in Singapore. The actual combustion of these bunker fuels occurs in international waters.

19. More accurately, Rotterdam needs to be placed in the "ARA" conurbation, which includes Antwerp and Amsterdam.

20. "Climate Change: A Challenge for IMO too!"

21. IMO Marine Environment Protection Committee, "Second IMO GHG Study 2009: Prevention of Air Pollution from Ships — Update of the 2000 IMO GHG Study [MEPC 59/INF.10]" (London: IMO, 9 April 2009).

22. Ibid.

23. International Maritime Organization, "What It Is", n.d. <http://www.imo.org/About/Documents/What%20it%20is%20Oct%202013_Web.pdf>.

24. International Maritime Organization, "Frequently Asked Questions" <http://www.imo.org/About/Pages/FAQs.aspx>.

25. Ibid.

26. "What It Is".

27. "What It Is".

28. European Parliament, "EP Seals Climate Change Package", 2008 <http://www.europarl.europa.eu/sides/getDoc.do?pubRef=-//EP//TEXT+IM-PRESS+20081208BKG44004+0+DOC+XML+V0//EN>.

29. "Second IMO GHG Study".

30. Ulla Rasmussen, "It Is Time to Tackle International Transport", 13 October 2009 <http://en.cop15.dk/blogs/views/>; Ms. Rasmussen is President for the European Federation of Transport and Environment.

31. IMO Marine Environment Protection Committee, "Prevention of Air Pollution from Ships: An International Fund for Greenhouse Gas Emissions from Ships [MEPC 59/4/5]" (London: IMO, 9 April 2009) <http://www.rina.org.uk/hres/mepc%2059_4_5.pdf>; and "Prevention of Air Pollution from Ships: Cornerstones for an Outline of a Convention of a Global Emission Trading Scheme for International Shipping [MEPC 59/4/26]" (London: IMO, 8 May 2009) <http://www.amtcc.com/imosite/meetings/IMOMeeting2009/MEPC/MEPC%2059-4-26.pdf>.

32. IMO Intersessional Meeting of the Greenhouse Gas Working Group, "Maritime Emission Trading Scheme (METS): Development of Reduction Mechanisms, Including Their Implementation [GHG-WG 1/5/7]" (London: IMO, 30 May 2008) <http://www.sjofartsverket.se/pages/16278/1-5-7.pdf>.

33. See UK Chamber of Shipping, "A Global Cap-and-trade System to Reduce Carbon Emissions from International Shipping" (London: UK Chamber of Shipping, September 2009); see also Jonathan Saul, "Shippers Back Cap and Trade Scheme to Cut CO2", Reuters, 23 September 2009.

34. See "A Global Cap-and-trade System".

35. Ibid.

36. Singapore Shipping Association, "SSA Supports GHG Compensation Fund and Green Technology", press release, 24 June 2009.

37. Guy Wilson-Roberts, "Shipping and CO_2: Issues and Costs", *Bunkerworld*, July/August 2009.

38. "EP Seals Climate Change Package".

39. Ibid.

40. Ibid.

41. Karan Capoor and Philippe Ambrosi, "State and Trends of the Carbon Market 2009" (Washington, DC: World Bank, May 2009).

42. Ibid.

43. Adam Sarvana, "No Safe Harbor: The Shipping Industry's Pollution Problem Part II: A Lack of Authority", DC Bureau, 10 October 2009.

44. Environmental Defence Fund, "Protecting American Health from Global Shipping Pollution: New Report", press release, 30 March 2009 <http://www.edf.org/news/protecting-american-health-global-shipping-pollution-new-report>.

45. See, for example, "Second IMO GHG Study 2009".

46. UK Chamber of Shipping, "Shipping Industry Supports Emissions Trading to Reduce CO_2", press release, 24 September 2009.

47. See, for instance, Mark Lazarowicz, *Global Carbon Trading: A Framework for Reducing Emissions* (Norwich: The Stationery Office, 2009).

48. This overview is largely based on a recent paper submitted by the Oil Companies International Marine Forum (OCIMF) to the IMO. See IMO Marine Environment Protection Committee, "Prevention of Air Pollution from Ships:

Technical Evaluation of Market-based Instruments [MEPC/59/4/17]" (London: IMO, 7 May 2009).

49. See, for example, the report by the UK Prime Minister's Special Representative, Mark Lazarowicz (*Global Carbon Trading*). See also the submission by OCIMF to IMO ("Technical Evaluation of Market-based Instruments").

50. The author is not aware of studies of the price elasticity of demand for bunker fuels; it is reasonable to expect low values, especially in the short run, but is not likely to be zero.

51. See Matthew Hennessey, "Cap and Trade vs. Carbon Tax", *Policy Innovations*, 17 November 2007 <http://www.policyinnovations/ideas/briefings/data/cap_tax>.

52. For a definitive assessment of Singapore's price discovery role, and the ramifications of this for the city-state's status as an oil hub in "East of Suez" oil markets, see Horsnell ("Oil in Asia"). For an earlier, briefer treatment, see Tilak Doshi, *The Houston of Asia: the Singapore Petroleum Industry* (Singapore: Institute of Southeast Asian Studies, 1989).

53. In Singapore, however, active forward markets for crude oil and refined products are in informal OTC markets. There are no formal futures contracts being traded in electronic markets as in New York and London.

54. APPEC (Asia Pacific Petroleum Conference) is an established premium feature in Singapore's oil calendar, not for the conference programme, but for all the company meetings, negotiations, and cocktail receptions that occur around it. The author is aware of informal estimates of 2,000 oil men and women converging on Singapore during APPEC week.

55. See Catherine Wong Mei Ling, "S'pore Well Placed to be a Carbon Trading Centre", *Business Times*, 18 September 2009.

56. Yang Huiwen, "S'pore Set to Boost Status as an Energy Hub", *Straits Times*, 27 May 2009.

57. "An International Fund for Greenhouse Gas Emissions from Ships".

58. Current European Emission Allowances (EUA) prices of carbon in the EU ETS are in the €15 range, and estimates of what carbon prices need to be to effect a significant change in global carbon emissions range widely, up to levels of over US$100 per tonne.

59. "An International Fund for Greenhouse Gas Emissions from Ships".

60. Yvo de Boer, "Welcome to the United Nations Climate Change Conference in Bali", 2007 <http://unfccc.int/meetings/bali_dec_2007/items/4209.php>.

61. This is covered in Chapters 2 and 3.

62. "An International Fund for Greenhouse Gas Emissions from Ships", p. 3 para. 11.

63. "An International Fund for Greenhouse Gas Emissions from Ships", p. 3 para 7.3.

64. "A Global Cap-and-trade System to Reduce Carbon Emissions from International Shipping", p. 8.
65. *Global Carbon Trading*, p. 13. The ramifications of international perceptions of Singapore as an "advanced developing country" in climate change negotiations are covered in Chapters 1 and 2.
66. See *The Houston of Asia* and *Oil in Asia*.
67. Singapore introduced a concessionary tax rate of 5 per cent on LNG trading income for companies under the Global Trader Programme in May 2007. See "Energy for Growth: National Energy Policy Report" (Singapore: Ministry of Trade and Industry, 2007), p. 9 <http://www.mti.gov.sg/ResearchRoom/Documents/app.mti.gov.sg/data/pages/885/doc/NEPR%202007.pdf>.
68. "Speech by Mr Lee Yi Shyan Minister of State for Trade and Industry at the UK-Singapore Workshop on Energy Technology", 26 November 2007 <http://www.mti.gov.sg/NewsRoom/Pages/Mr%20Lee%20Yi%20Shyan%20at%20the%20UK%20-%20Singapore%20Workshop%20on%20Energy%20Technology.aspx>.
69. "Chemicals", Economic Development Board <http://www.edb.gov.sg/content/dam/edb/en/industries/Chemical%20Engineering/downloads/ChemicalsFactsheet.pdf>.
70. "Energy", Economic Development Board <http://www.edb.gov.sg/content/dam/edb/en/industries/Energy/downloads/Energy.pdf>.
71. "Careers@Singapore: Oil and Gas", Contact Singapore <http://www.contactsingapore.sg/Library/1/Pages/2189/EDB_CS_Oil_Gas_Factsheet_Sept_2011.pdf>.
72. See *Oil in Asia*, p. 139.
73. There are no regional or bilateral power grid arrangements between Singapore and its neighbouring countries.
74. Charles T. Devna and National Petrochemicals and Refiners Association (NPRA), "The American Clean Energy Security Act of 2009", 24 April 2009. This is a written submission to the Energy and Commerce Committee of the U.S. House of Representatives. Of course, the only difference between Indiana and India is location, and hence the barrel of gasoline can be traded across the global energy market depending on transportation costs.
75. "Refinery runs" refer to the utilization of various process capacities within refining plants and, as a single measure, refer usually to capacity utilization of crude distillation units.
76. Long-lived "lumpy" capital investments are subject to long-term planning horizons, and can be expected to have an impact once there is some certainty with respect to carbon emission policies in some of the key countries, including the EU and the United States.
77. The Jamnagar refinery, the world's largest single integrated and highly

sophisticated complex operated by Reliance Industries Limited, is already a major exporter of petroleum products in the "East of Suez" refined product markets, and would be a formidable competitor to Singapore-based oil refineries. Jamnagar I and II have emerged as the "Refining Hub of the World" with an aggregate refining capacity of 1.24 million barrels of oil per day (see *Oil and Gas Journal*, various issues).

78. Jessica Cheam, "Keppel to sell SPC Stake to PetroChina", *Strait Times*, 25 May 2009.

79. NPRA represents, among its more than 450 members, most of the large U.S.-based oil majors as well as Shell Petrochemical Company. Shell, of course, is a significant owner of refinery and petrochemical assets in the United States. NPRA members also include companies such as BP (the UK oil major) and Total (the French oil major). The NPRA submission to the U.S. House of Representatives dated 24 April 2009, has already been noted above.

80. This refers to various federal and state mandates that are already imposed on the sector or are being discussed at various levels of government.

81. Singapore's position vis-à-vis the developed–developing countries divide is covered in Chapter 2.

82. Angela Macdonald-Smith, "Caltex Australia Says Carbon Costs Threaten Refining Industry", Bloomberg, 23 October 2008.

83. "However, we believe international competitiveness should be fully maintained, which means 100 per cent free allocation of permits until overseas refineries such as those in Singapore which supply product to Australia bear equivalent carbon costs." in "Caltex's View — The Carbon Pollution Reduction Scheme: The Challenges Ahead", *The Star*, no. 47 (February–March 2009).

84. See, for example, Joseph Aldy et al, "Designing Climate Mitigation Policy", NBER Working Paper No. 15022, June 2009.

85. "Oil Refiners Ask for Shelter from CO_2 Trading Perils", *EurActiv*, 20 October 2008.

86. "Oil Refiners: Seeking Protection from 'Carbon Leakage'", *EurActiv*, 20 October 2008.

87. The American Clean Energy Security Act of 2009, p. 8.

88. United States Congress, "American Clean Energy and Security Act of 2009", H.R. 2454, 2009.

89. See "The American Clean Energy Security Act of 2009", p. 12.

90. See ibid., p. 13.

91. Basically, users of refined oil and petrochemical products have little choice, and hence, will face higher prices which they may or may not be able to pass through to customers. In economic terms, consumers face fairly elastic supply curves (where imports can be accessed at cheaper prices from foreign competitors which do not face binding emission constraints),

and fairly inelastic demand curves, with few choices on alternative fuels or feedstocks.

92. NERA Consulting, "Market Conditions and the Pass Through of Compliance Costs in a Carbon Emission Cap-and-Trade Program", January 2008 (quoted in "The American Clean Energy Security Act of 2009").

93. See NERA Economic Consulting Report for NPRA, dated April 2008. It is not clear whether "American" refers to the United States or the entire hemisphere, but the point remains.

94. Brittany Sauser, "Ethanol Demand Threatens Food Prices", *MIT Technology Review*, 13 February 2007 and S. Dewi et al., "Carbon Footprint of Indonesian Palm Oil Production: A Pilot Study." (Bogor: World Agroforestry Centre, ICRAF, SEA Regional Office, 2009).

95. Airports Council International, "Passenger Traffic 2008 Final", 28 July 2009.

96. Airports Council International, "Cargo Traffic 2008 Final", 28 July 2009.

97. "Air Traffic Statistics 2008/2009" in *CAAS Annual Report, 2008/2009* (Singapore: Civil Aviation Authority of Singapore, 2009).

98. Civil Aviation Authority of Singapore, "Celebrating a New Dawn in Singapore Aviation", media release, 1 July 2009 <http://appserver1.caas.gov.sg/caasmediaweb2010/opencms/Journalist/Press_Releases/2009/news_0029.html?locale=en&site=caas>.

99. As listed in Wikipedia, "World's Busiest Airport by Passenger Traffic" <http://en.wikipedia.org/wiki/World's_busiest_airports_by_passenger_traffic>.

100. Ad Hoc Working Group on Long-term Cooperative Action under the Convention (AWG-LCA) Intersessional Informal Consultations, "Update on the Continuing Progress of ICAO on International Aviation and Climate Change" (Bonn: ICAO, 10–14 August 2009) <http://unfccc.int/resource/docs/2009/smsn/igo/059.pdf>.

101. European Parliament, "Directive 2008/101/EC: Amending Directive 2003/87/EC so as to Include Aviation Activities in the Scheme for Greenhouse Gas Emission Allowance Trading within the Community", 19 November 2008 <http://eur-lex.europa.eu/legal-content/EN/TXT/?uri=CELEX:32008L0101>.

102. "Aviation and Emissions Trading", *EurActiv*, 11 October 2007.

103. Ibid.

104. Ibid.

105. International Civil Aviation Organization, "States Affirm Intent to Work through ICAO in Tackling Climate Change", press release, 9 October 2009.

106. "Update on the Continuing Progress of ICAO".

107. Ibid.

108. Ibid.

109. International Air Transport Association, "About Us" <http://www.iata.org/about/> (accessed 12 October 2009).

110. International Air Transportation Association, "Tough Targets and a Global Sectoral Approach — Aviation's Copenhagen Commitment", press release no. 42, 6 October 2009.
111. Ibid.
112. Ibid.
113. Chris Lyle, "Climate Change and Aviation: Fudge Now, Pay Later? Pressures of Time and Substance", *Centre for Aviation*, 7 September 2009.
114. Ibid.
115. Aviation Global Deal Group, "Who We Are" <http://www.agdgroup.org/> (accessed 18 November 2009).
116. "Directive 2008/101/EC".
117. David Fogarty, "Top Airlines Want Aviation Emissions in Climate Pact", Reuters, 12 February 2009.
118. "Aviation and Emissions Trading".
119. "Airlines Call for 'More Sensible' Carbon-cutting Scheme", *EurActiv*, 6 June 2007.
120. U.S. Senate, "The Clean Energy Jobs and American Power Act", 30 September 2009.
121. Elaine Fahey, "The EU Emissions Trading Scheme and the Court of Justice – The "High Politics" of Indirectly Promoting Global Standards", Amsterdam Centre for European Law and Governance Working Paper Series 2012–05, 2012.
122. Singapore Airlines, "Annual Report 2008/2009" (Singapore: Singapore Airlines, 2009).
123. Changi Airport Singapore, "Changi Connectivity", 2014 <http://www.changiairport.com/flight-info/changi-connectivity>.
124. Edgard Swinnen, "EcoBusinessLink.com Releases Surprising Results from Carbon Offset Flight Calculator Analysis", *Eco Business Links*, 2009. Swinnen surveyed thirty flight emission calculators. Of the thirty calculators tested, the CO_2 footprint results for a round trip flight from New York to Los Angeles ranged from a low of 0.84 tonnes to a high of 4.94 tonnes. Swinnen also surveyed the price of carbon at a large sample of sites, and found prices per US$/tonne CO_2 ranging from US$2.75 to US$99 <http://www.ecobusinesslinks.com/carbon_offset_wind_credits_carbon_reduction.htm>.
125. Centre for Asia Pacific Aviation, *Airport and Airline – Asia Pacific*, no. 368, 4 August 2009.
126. Singapore Airlines, "Annual Report 2008/2009".
127. International Air Transport Association, "Aviation and Climate Change: Pathway to Carbon Neutral Growth in 2020" (Quebec: IATA, 2009).
128. "Update on the Continuing Progress of ICAO on International Aviation and Climate Change".

129. "European Court Defies US Over Airline Carbon Tax", NBC News, 21 December 2011.

130. "ICAO Under Pressure to Forge a Deal for Aviation Emissions", *EurActiv*, 17 July 2014 <http://www.euractiv.com/sections/aviation/icao-under-pressure-forge-deal-aviation-emissions-303563>.

131. Economies of scale are the reduced production costs that enterprises obtain due to size, output, or scale of operation, with cost per unit of output generally decreasing as fixed costs are spread out over more units of output.

132. Paul Krugman, "Increasing Returns and Economic Geography", *Journal of Political Economy* 99, no. 3 (1991).

133. The Singapore FOB Singapore price quote ("Mean of Platts Singapore", or "MOPS") referred to is that provided by Platts, a price reporting agency and division of the McGraw Hill Group.

134. Most oil trading rooms have "squawk boxes" where bid and ask prices are quoted in real time and trades booked over the phone or instant messaging services offered by brokers and price reporting agencies.

135. Alfred Marshall, "Chapter 10: Industrial Organization Continued: The Concentration of Specialized Industries in Particular Localities", in *Book Four: The Agents of Production: Land, Labour, and Capital and Organization* (1890) <https://www.marxists.org/reference/subject/economics/marshall/bk4ch10.htm>.

136. See Section 5.1 on Singapore's early role in the downstream oil industry.

137. The straits link the Indian Ocean to the South China Sea and Pacific Ocean. Malacca is the shortest sea route between Persian Gulf oil suppliers and the large Asian markets — notably China, Japan, South Korea, and the Pacific Rim. It is the key choke point in Asia, with an estimated 15.2 million barrels per day flow in 2011, accounting for one third of the total global seaborne crude oil traded that year. See U.S. Energy Information Administration (EIA), "Global Oil Transit Chokepoints" <http://www.eia.gov/countries/regions-topics.cfm?fips=wotc&trk=p3>; Statista, "Transport Volume of Crude Oil in Global Seaborne Trade from 1999 to 2012" <http://www.statista.com/statistics/264013/transport-volume-of-crude-oil-in-seaborne-trade/>.

5

ENERGY AND EMISSIONS:
The Five Strategies

It is commonly observed that the growing complexity and strategic importance of energy policy demands a "Whole-of-Government" approach, where specialized ministries and agencies work in a coordinated way across multiple jurisdictions to implement policy. The work of integrating the different strands of Singapore's energy policy was institutionalized with the establishment of the Energy Policy Group (EPG) in March 2006.[1] Led by the Ministry of Trade and Industry (MTI), it comprises key ministries, including Environment and Water Resources (MEWR), Foreign Affairs (MFA), Transport (MOT) and Finance (MOF), and agencies like the Energy Market Authority (EMA), Economic Development Board (EDB), National Environment Agency (NEA), Land Transport Authority (LTA) and Building and Construction Authority (BCA). The EPG plays the role of formulating and coordinating Singapore's energy policies and strategies. In addition to the development of a national energy policy framework, the EPG studies a wide range of energy issues, which include power and transport sectors, energy efficiency, climate change, energy industry, energy research and development (R&D), and engaging in regional and international energy policy cooperation. Coordinating the efforts of all stakeholders will be a constant feature in Singapore's energy policy efforts in the future.

Singapore's national energy policy framework strives to achieve a balance among three objectives, namely retaining economic competitiveness, enhancing energy security, and protecting the environment.[2] In a report released in 2007, MTI identified five strategies under the country's energy policy framework: promoting competitive markets, diversifying energy sources, enhancing energy efficiency, developing the energy industry and investing in energy R&D, and stepping up international cooperation.[3]

5.1 PROMOTE COMPETITIVE MARKETS: GETTING PRICES RIGHT

Singapore has come a long way from its early role in the 1890s as a storage and trans-shipment centre for kerosene in the colonial Far East. The first bulk oil cargo destined for Asia was loaded on to the Samuel brothers' storage tanks in Pulau Bukom in 1892; the vessel Murex brought the cargo from Batum, an oil port in the Black Sea, via the Suez Canal, which was newly opened to oil traffic.[4] Shell established a strategic Far East distribution site for refined oil products with a storage facility in Pulau Bukom, an offshore island south of the main Singapore island. Interestingly, it was the opposition of the existing kerosene oil traders in Singapore that prevented the Samuel brothers from constructing their storage tanks in Pasir Panjang, their preferred location, and led them to get permission from colonial authorities based in Kuala Lumpur for purchasing the Pulau Bukom site.[5]

Despite this early example of vested interests influencing authorities in colonial Singapore, self-rule followed by independence brought in a government relatively autonomous from entrenched interests and keen to promote inward investments. Shell became the first "pioneer status" company — enjoying tax-free operations for the first five years — when they built their refinery in Pulau Bukom and commenced operations in 1961. It made sense for Shell to develop refining capacity at its Pulau Bukom site, with its existing tanks and jetties, and it seems unlikely that the tax benefits offered to pioneer status companies were the primary criterion for the final investment decision. But the credibility of the new People's Action Party (PAP) government efforts to promote a hospitable environment for large foreign investments must have mattered fundamentally in the perceptions of political risk by Shell company managers responsible for the company's long-lived investments.

By the mid-1970s, under a competitive market environment with a liberal trade regime, Singapore had already achieved its status as an oil hub for the East Asia region. Ranked alongside Houston and Rotterdam as one of the three global refining and oil trading centres, Singapore has long played a dominating regional role in crude oil and refined product trade, blending and storage, ship bunkering, and associated services ranging from banking and insurance to specialized information and pricing services and consultancies. As previously mentioned, Singapore's role in the East Asian regional oil market surpasses that of Rotterdam and Houston in their respective regional markets (Europe and the U.S. Gulf Coast). Singapore not only developed into a world-class oil refining and trading centre, but also hosts the growth of an over-the-counter (OTC) derivatives market for the East Asian time zone. This has made Singapore's regional role comparable to Houston *combined* with the city of New York (where the New York Mercantile Exchange or NYMEX hosts the trading of oil futures contracts), or Rotterdam *combined* with the City of London (where the Intercontinental Exchange, or ICE, also offers oil futures contracts).

Competitive markets will remain the cornerstone of Singapore's energy policy.[6] There is open competition in its oil refining, trading, and retailing industries. Competition has been introduced into the domestic electricity and gas markets. The Energy Market Authority (EMA) was established in 2001 to regulate and promote competition in the electricity and gas industries. The National Energy Market of Singapore (NEMS) was established in 2003. It allowed prices to reflect supply and demand fundamentals. By 2006, approximately 75 per cent of Singapore's total electricity demand was open to competition. The retail, primarily household, electricity market is still non-contestable. The EMA of Singapore is looking into the development of an Electricity Vending System (EVS) to enable full retail contestability. If successful, households and other small consumers will in the future be able to choose their own electricity retailers and price plans in the same way they can do for telecommunications providers.

The Singapore experience is in contrast to a large number of countries in Asia and the Middle East that subsidize transport and cooking fuels, causing wasteful inefficiencies and burdening the public budgets in those economies. The latest estimates from the International Energy Agency (IEA) indicate that fossil fuel consumption subsidies worldwide amounted to US$544 billion in 2012.[7] The Asia-Pacific region accounts for a significant proportion of these subsidies, with ten out of the twenty-one member economies of Asia-Pacific Economic Cooperation (APEC) accounting for US$105 billion in fossil fuel subsidies in 2010. In non-OECD (Organisation for Economic Co-operation and Development) countries, the economic impact has been especially significant given that fuel subsidies amount to between 1 and 5 per cent of gross domestic product (GDP) in several Asia-Pacific economies (such as Indonesia and Malaysia) and over 5 per cent in oil-exporting economies in the Middle East and North Africa. Fossil fuel subsidies understate the real cost of energy and thus impede energy efficiency in the transportation sector.

Market-Based Instruments: To Tax or To Cap?

In terms of pricing energy products, perhaps the key policy question facing Singapore policymakers in the context of climate change negotiations is the debate over the efficacy of different regimes to price the costs of climate change if such schemes are to be adopted by international or regional treaties. No government decision seems to have been made with respect to favouring either carbon taxes or carbon markets (with quantitative caps on carbon emissions) as the preferred option when considering participation in any future regional or international agreement over mitigation and adaptation measures.

In any national emission reduction programme facing government planners, whether through voluntary unilateral schemes or through international agreements, the test of achieving emission reduction targets at least-cost is straightforward in principle. The test of economic efficiency is the same, irrespective of the choice of market-based tools, namely carbon taxes or cap-and-trade pricing for carbon allowances. To achieve economic efficiency, marginal abatement costs of each of the sectors and industries identified need to be estimated, so that the value of the last "emission-reducing dollar" invested is equivalent across sectors and industries. In a free market for greenhouse gas (GHG) abatement investments, private capital will flow to areas where risk-adjusted returns to emission-reducing investment are highest, thus fulfilling the efficiency criterion.

Quantitative "caps" or taxes on carbon emissions are the two market-based approaches that put a price on carbon and provide an industry-wide signal to encourage emission reduction, as distinct from the direct regulatory approach ("command and control") such as specified technical efficiency standards, for example. In the market-based approach, emission reduction begins efficiently with the least-cost opportunities ("low hanging fruit"), and is pursued up to the point where marginal costs equate the marginal benefits of abatement, the necessary test of economic efficiency. A summary of the pros and cons is given in Table 5.1 below.

Both correct a market failure, as GHGs constitute an unpriced externality; that is, those responsible for GHG emissions do not have to pay for the damages they impose on the global environment, and the failure to internalize these costs in their economic behaviour lead to higher levels of emissions than is socially optimal. Both instruments put a price on carbon, and by establishing this price they create market incentives to develop and invest in emission-reduction technologies. Such incentives also encourage behavioural changes in consumption and production that reduce emissions. Both use market forces to achieve least-cost solutions. Both can generate revenue. While a tax raises revenue by definition, a cap-and-trade scheme that auctions tradable emission permits can raise similar amounts of revenue. How such revenues are used is an important issue in both cases, although it is a distinct and separate matter from the choice of the instrument. Both instruments can be adapted with special tax provisions or the use of allowances to mitigate adverse impacts on specific groups (of people or industries or other constituencies). Both systems require monitoring, reporting, and verification (MRV) systems in place.

The key difference between the two instruments — one a tax on carbon content of any specific fuel or energy technology, and the other a market in the rights to pollute — is that a tax fixes the price of carbon but allows emission levels to vary, while the cap imposes a limit on emissions and lets the price of tradable carbon allowances vary. To the extent that the ultimate objective is to set an optimal path of emission reduction to reach a targeted end state of stabilized and reduced emission rate, the cap-and-trade solution is the correct one. It achieves an environmental goal, but the cost of reaching that goal is determined by market forces. In contrast, a tax provides certainty about costs of compliance (abstracting from the inter-temporal uncertainty of the tax policy itself), but the resulting reduction in GHG or carbon emissions cannot be predetermined.

The impact of price volatility is emphasized by critics of the cap-and-trade system. A tax seems easier to define and administer, and may be seen

Table 5.1

Characteristics of Cap-and-Trade and Tax Regimes for Emission Mitigation

Characteristic	Cap and trade	Tax
	Similarities	
market failure correction economic efficiency	both systems correct market failures; both systems have similar efficiency attributes	
revenue generation	can raise revenue levels similar to tax; cap-and-trade permits are auctioned	revenue generating by definition
special provisions to mitigate adverse impacts	can enact special provisions to mitigate undesirable social or economic impacts, with safety valves and price floors and other design features	can enact special provisions to mitigate undesirable social or economic impacts via tax exemptions/ surcharges
	Differences	
cost uncertainty vs environmental uncertainty	fixes emission reduction target, and allows costs to be determined by market; issue of carbon price volatility and hence cost uncertainty	fixes tax rates, and allows market to determine level of emission reduction which is uncertain *ex ante*; residual uncertainty over future tax rates also remains (depending on government fiscal regime stability)
compliance flexibility for firms	allows compliance planning via multi-year compliance periods, and provisions to bank and borrow permits	little flexibility, and needs attention in firm's annual budgeting exercise (how much to mitigate emissions by and how much tax to pay)
flexibility to handle change in market conditions	built-in fiscal stabilization (slowdown in the economy naturally lowers carbon prices)	tax law and tax administration can at best lag the needs of changing economic conditions, at worst remain unchanged and unresponsive
administrative simplicity	more complex regulatory structure in setting up competitive markets with monitoring and reporting requirements	relatively simple administration (assuming no political lobbying process involved in special tax exemptions)
political feasibility	as it involves private sector business in carbon markets, strong constituency backing can be forthcoming	taxes are "toxic" especially in the context of the aftermath of the financial crisis of 2008–9 in most developed countries
empirical data and experience to date	poor performance of European ETS market in past few years have put negative publicity on carbon markets; successful in ozone and acid rain mitigation regimes	not often used; U.S. examples often bogged down in special interest exemptions and ineffectualness

to offer a level of certainty with the important proviso that one abstracts away the uncertainty of tax shifts due to changing or unstable government fiscal policy over time. It is clear that imposing a tax on fuels does not add to price volatility, although this again abstracts from "tax volatility" if taxes are to be adjusted often to attain targeted emission reduction rates. Volatility in market-determined carbon prices, in contrast, is a key concern of firms. However, a cap-and-trade system often incorporates features such as banking, borrowing, and multi-year compliance periods, floor and ceiling prices, and other measures (such as the ability of policymakers to purchase or delete carbon allowances) which mitigates against pronounced price volatility. Deep and liquid carbon markets also dampen volatility. Indeed, episodes of pronounced price volatility can often be the result of policy uncertainty rather than market conditions or design flaws of the scheme.

It should also be noted that the issue of price volatility is an endemic feature of most commodities, including crude oil and refined products. Fuel suppliers and purchasers, for instance, deal with price volatility as an inherent feature of their business, and various solutions are practised as a matter of course, including hedging in derivative markets, either in OTC (or swap) markets or on formal commodity exchanges. Companies in the business either have risk management departments which play an integral role in fuel sales or purchases, or they utilize the services of investment banks and brokerages which offer hedging and risk management services.

Small companies are inherently disadvantaged in meeting the human resource requirements for direct hedging expertise or in paying for risk management services, but that is not an efficiency failure. It is rather an organizational feature in economies of scale. Even smaller companies in a free market have options, including joining associations that provide collective services, or in hiring boutique brokerages which can offer risk management services at competitive prices. It is not apparent that adding the price volatility of carbon markets to the underlying price volatility of energy commodities changes the risk profile by any order of magnitude.

Not often mentioned, but an important issue to economic efficiency in corporate behaviour, is the issue of flexibility for firms. For any given tax rate, a tax requires a firm each year to decide how much to reduce its emissions and how much tax to pay. Under a cap-and-trade system, provisions for borrowing and banking carbon allowances, and extended multi-year compliance periods allow firms the flexibility to make compliance planning decisions on a multi-year basis. Compliance planning under different economic conditions is also more flexible under the cap-and-trade system. Changes in economic activity, and hence in emissions, impact firms under both systems. However, under a cap-and-trade system, reduced economic growth for instance would reduce allowance prices and vice versa. Hence, this option has built-in "stabilizers". In the tax option, government authorities, not autonomous counter-cyclical market forces, would have to raise or lower the amount of tax, depending on the level of economic growth. To put it another way, the cap is a self-adjusting system; a tax needs to be set at the discretion of the fiscal authority. In principle, taxes can be adjusted frequently and as necessary to make them counter-cyclical. But in practice, this would require an unlikely level of sophistication and alacrity on the part of any government.

Taxes are inherently far simpler to administer and implement; trading regimes require a relatively elaborate set of market regulations, governance structures, and incentive-compatible design mechanisms so that cap-and-trade regimes cannot be "gamed" by sophisticated players in the marketplace. Yet, too much cannot be made of this point, as the principles for effective trading regimes in carbon gases and other pollutants are reasonably well understood by policy administrators and regulatory economists. The success of utilizing markets to regulate environmental pollutants such as sulphur dioxide or SO_2 ("acid rain") have been well noted.[8] It should also be noted that if special interest exemptions are an integral part of tax policy formulation, as they tend to be in many liberal democracies, tax legislation can rapidly becoming Byzantine in their complexity and uncertain in ultimate economic and environmental impacts.

With respect to empirical evidence and actual experience to date, cap-and-trade has become the cornerstone of the world's largest system of carbon trading in the European Union (EU) Emissions Trading Scheme (ETS). However, since the recession of 2008 in particular, Europe's ETS now is at an ebb of market activity with massive oversupply of permits amidst falling demand and carbon prices at around €6 per tonne in mid-2014. The regime has well-studied deficiencies and shortcomings, and now faces difficult circumstances unless EU governments effectively reform the scheme and address the massive oversupply of carbon allowances. The EU ETS nevertheless established the building blocks of a successful region-wide trading regime. The poor implementation and operation of the EU ETS should not be attributed to any inherent feature of carbon markets. Cap-and-trade regimes have helped achieve low-cost reductions in SO_2 emissions and in establishing a lead-free petrol market in the United States. Cap-and-trade systems are used in three regional programmes in the United States and Canada, and developing countries such as China, South Korea, and others have started several experimental carbon trading regimes at the city and provincial levels. Table 5.2 below describes some of the tradable permit systems proposed in the APEC region in the past few years.

GHG emission taxes had initially been used in Norway, Sweden, and Germany, countries which are now engaged in the cap-and-trade scheme. Carbon taxes have also been used in a few local government programmes in the United States and Canada. A carbon tax was considered by the Clinton administration in 1992, but quickly became bogged down with myriad special exemptions. It evolved from a carbon to a Btu tax to avoid burdening the politically powerful coal states, and finally was enacted as a few pennies tax on petrol.

It is apparent that in the aftermath of the global financial crisis, and with large budget deficits being the order of the day in most industrialized countries, taxes are even more "toxic" than usual in the political economy of those countries. Hence, from a political feasibility point of view in many countries, taxes suffer a serious disadvantage relative to cap-and-trade schemes. While one can argue that "not all the people can be fooled all the time", and that most voters will see the equivalence of either option with respect to the ultimate impact on household budgets, the fact remains that taxes in popular perception in many countries are an evil to be tolerated, and that new taxes need to be amply justified in layman's terms.

Command and Control vs Market-based Instruments

Command and control regulation includes instruments that rely on regulations such as permissions, prohibitions, standard setting, and enforcement as opposed to financial incentives. The potential benefit of using command and control regulation is that it is possible to prescribe desired actions in order to achieve a specific objective. This may be useful when the threat of environmental damage is very high (e.g., in the handling of radioactive waste). In some instances, command and control regulation may also be preferred as a policy approach on the grounds of administrative simplicity. For example, compliance with technology-based command and control regulations may be enforced by simply observing

Table 5.2

Proposed Tradable Permit Systems in the APEC Region

Country	Programme	Type	Description	Status
Australia	Carbon Pollution Reduction Scheme	Cap-and-trade	Covers 1,000 largest emitters and approximately 75% of total national GHG emissions.	Rejected twice by the Senate and in 2010 was shelved until at least 2013.
Canadian and U.S. states	Western Climate Initiative	Cap-and-trade	Region-wide caps on GHG emissions with participation from four Canadian provinces and seven U.S. states.	Some states with functioning carbon markets.
China	Energy intensity trading scheme	Baseline and credit	Energy intensity trading scheme in Tianjin beginning in 2010.	Pilot trades conducted in February 2010.
Japan	On carbon emissions	Cap-and-trade	Nationwide programme approved by Cabinet.	National Bill not yet passed by the Diet. Tokyo has introduced its own cap-and-trade programme.
Mexico	Domestic trans-sector	Cap-and-trade	Places cap on GHG emissions. Starts off by targeting three largest carbon emitters. May eventually be linked to carbon markets in USA and Canada.	Not active.
New Zealand	Emissions trading scheme (NZ ETS)	Cap-and-trade	For all GHG gases covering all sectors.	Forestry projects accepted from 2008. Mandatory obligations began in 2010 with some economic sectors still to join.
South Korea	Emissions trading scheme	Cap-and-trade	Covering majority of CO_2 emissions. May be linked to bigger markets such as China.	Not very active.
Taiwan	On GHG emissions	Cap-and-trade	The final stage of the GHG Reduction Programme, with a cap on GHG emissions.	Bill passed by executive but not yet by legislative body.
USA	Waxman-Markey Bill	Cap-and-trade	On nationwide GHG emissions.	Abandoned.

Source: Doshi, T., Fulan, W and Chew, E., "Developing Carbon Trading in APEC Countries", Paper prepared for APEC (Asia Pacific Economic Cooperation), Energy Studies Institute, 4 October 2011.

the installation and operation of a given technology rather than through the ongoing measurement of actual site-specific pollution levels.

Market-based instruments (MBIs) also use government regulation (e.g., to set and enforce emission targets), but in combination with market signals. The benefit of incorporating market signals into policy design is that it provides firms with greater flexibility in determining how they can best achieve the environmental objective. This flexibility provides incentives for greater pollution reductions in firms with lower abatement costs and, if it could be implemented fully, would lead to equalization of marginal abatement costs across all market participants, meaning that no further cost savings could be made while holding constant the aggregate level of pollution reduction. This would lead to the achievement of the desired level of pollution reduction at least-cost to society.

By contrast, command and control regulations that set uniform standards on technical criteria are likely to impose higher costs on the economy, since firms with high abatement costs have to make the same reduction in pollution as firms with low abatement costs. The same level of pollution reduction could be achieved at a lower cost by asking the polluters with low abatement costs to make larger cuts in emissions than polluters with high abatement costs. Of course, command and control regulation could also set standards that vary across firms in order to achieve the cost-effective solution, but this would require the regulatory agency to gain information about abatement costs for each individual polluter. As Robert Stavins points out, "such information is simply not available to government"[9] and tends to only be available at a high cost.

5.2 DIVERSIFY ENERGY SOURCES: ENERGY SECURITY, OIL AND "THE GOLDEN AGE OF GAS"

On the eve of World War I, Winston Churchill as First Lord of the Admiralty faced the question of energy security when deciding to switch the Royal Navy's fuel source from domestic coal to oil. While improving the fleet's speed and flexibility, the switch would also have meant dependence on oil supplies from Iran. In a speech to Parliament, he made an often-quoted declaration: "on no one quality, on no one process, on no one country, on no one route, and on no one field must we be dependent. Safety and certainty in oil lie in variety and variety alone".[10] Churchill's point about diversification is the fundamental principle in discourse about energy security. It is also expressed in the common adage of "not putting all your eggs in one basket". Among economists, the concept is inherent to the study of risk and the role of portfolios of choices and assets in mitigating identified sources of security risks to the economy.

Singapore's Oil Origins and Bulk Oil Storage

In the aftermath of the separation from the Federation of Malaya in 1965, national security became an indelible strategic fixture of the first generation of Singapore's political leadership. This translated into a strategic imperative to survive as a small city-state in an era of decolonization and the emergence of protectionist regimes in Asia, Africa, and Latin America. Yet, energy security — a critical dimension of national security — was of little immediate consequence, at least in the early years of independence.

As South East Asia's historical entrepôt in the "East of Suez" region, Singapore served as an oil storage and bunkering centre and was from its beginnings an integral part of the early growth of the international petroleum trade since the late nineteenth century. Singapore's association with oil dates back to 1891, when Shell, in its competition against the globally dominant Standard Oil of the United States, built facilities on an island off Singapore's naturally sheltered deep-water port to store bulk kerosene.[11] As an urbanized city-state with trade and commerce as its main calling in its early modern history, Singapore had been reliant on a narrow range of energy fuels, primarily oil-based, adequate for the needs of power supply, road transport and household cooking.

For oil-reliant economies, the most direct and obvious energy security measure would be to require some level of bulk oil storage for both crude oil and refined products in case of a hiatus in fuel supplies. This in turn could be caused by a range of political or logistical factors such as disruptive political instability in the Middle East or other important oil producing countries, acts of piracy on the high sea, and blockage of shipping-lane choke points such as the Strait of Hormuz or the Strait of Malacca due to military conflict or maritime accidents. To gain from the benefits of collective action to such immediate threats to oil supply, the IEA legally requires each member country to have oil stock levels that equate to no less than ninety days of net imports.[12] The obligation is based on net imports of oil, including crude oil and refined products. The 90-day commitment of each IEA member country is based on an average of daily net imports of the previous calendar year. This commitment can be met through stocks held exclusively for emergency purposes and stocks held for commercial or operational use, including stocks held at refineries, at port facilities, and in tankers in ports.

In the aftermath of the oil price shock of 1979, Singapore set up a short-lived regime of a national crude oil stockpile, but this was discontinued in 1983.[13] Singapore currently neither holds strategic oil stocks nor places obligations on private companies to hold a minimum volume of stocks. There is, however, a requirement by the EMA for the privatized power generation companies to maintain a 45-day backup fuel oil and diesel stockpile on site for their exclusive right of use, and an additional 45-day backup fuel stockpile off site for their first right of use.[14] These stocks can help mitigate the impact of a disruption on the power generation sector. It should be noted that this sector accounts for only about 8 per cent of Singapore's domestic oil consumption annually, so that these stockpiles are roughly equal to about 7 days of Singapore's overall oil consumption.[15]

According to a report citing the Economic Development Board (EDB) of Singapore, the country's oil storage capacity (for crude oil and products combined) is about 20 million m^3 (126 million barrels, or MMB), of which 8 million m^3 (50 MMB) is held by independent commercial terminal operators and the rest owned by the private sector oil refiners.[16] Singapore's total final domestic consumption of oil products amounted to 420,000 barrels per day in 2011, according to the energy balance for the country reported by the IEA.[17] The storage capacity available translates to a remarkable 300 days of supply, though this is not at all surprising given Singapore's large refining and petrochemical industry geared for the global export market.

From an energy security perspective, Singapore's dependence on oil for a large share of its domestic energy requirements is thus well mitigated by the huge storage capacity operated by the oil majors, large commodity trading firms and independent storage terminal operators. During states of emergency, governments typically have the statutory authority to claim the first right of access and use of strategic commodities such as stored crude oil or refined oil products. Depending on jurisdiction, this might entail adequate compensation as might be allowed under local law or under international treaty obligations. So, despite the fact that there is no strategic petroleum reserve maintained by the government in Singapore, unlike its counterparts in larger countries such as China, India, and the United States, it would seem that Singapore has a more than adequate recourse to large private sector stocks of oil products in case of national emergencies.

Nevertheless, this has not deterred the government from building an expensive underground storage facility at the Jurong Rock Caverns. It is located 130 metres below sea level, and is Southeast Asia's first such facility. While the expected cost of the project is unreported, it was announced that Phase One will be completed at a cost of S$890 million. The facility is expected to be used to store crude oil, condensate, naphtha, and gas oil, and will have a capacity of about 1.5 million m^3 (9.5 MMB) by the time it is fully completed.[18]

According to press reports, there are also plans to build a very large floating structure (VLFS) for storing oil and petrochemicals.[19] The VLFS would be designed as a collection of large floating platforms which can either be moored to land or operated as stand-alone units, according to the Jurong Town Corporation (JTC), a government agency tasked with infrastructure development on the island. Its core structure would likely be constructed from concrete, comprising two rectangular modules, each with a storage capacity of 150,000 m^3, the equivalent of a very large crude carrier.

Given the land shortage in Singapore, oil storage facilities in locations near the city-state are being built and existing sites are being expanded. Oil storage facilities already exist or are being planned in Pangerang, Tanjung Bin, and Tanjung Langsat in the state of Johor in West Malaysia, just north of Singapore, and in the Indonesian islands of Pulau Karimun and Pulau Batam to the south of Singapore. With current plans in these locations, it is expected that total oil storage capacity in the "greater Singapore oil region" will surpass the capacity of the facilities in the Amsterdam-Rotterdam-Antwerp (ARA) oil hub in Europe by 2015.[20] There have been many press reports over the years about the competition Singapore faces from oil storage and ancillary facilities being built in neighbouring Malaysia and Indonesia. However, such assessments often fail to note the complementarities that proximate storage facilities also bring to Singapore's role as an oil trading centre. Indeed, given Singapore's land constraints, it would be to its comparative advantage to focus on being the location for the major manufacturing and commodity trading companies and their highly paid human capital assets (such as trading managers and risk and compliance officers) to support banking, finance, and the host of high value-added activity related to oil refining and marketing, while some of the necessary oil storage and other logistical operations can take place outside of Singapore's jurisdiction in surrounding waters.

The "Golden Age of Gas"

In an era of high and volatile oil prices and recurring political and social instability in the Middle East and in other key oil producing countries such as Nigeria and Venezuela, energy security concerns of oil importing countries during the 1970s and 1980s focused on securing the supply of oil imports and ensuring adequate stored reserves of crude oil and refined products. Domestically, many countries also set about securing oil refining, storage, trading, and related oil infrastructure facilities against potential terrorist or military attacks. Yet, in terms of Churchill's oft-quoted statement of not being dependent on any one source of oil supply, "variety" and the risk-reducing benefits of diversification is greatly expanded by ensuring that diversification occurs *across* different fuels as well, not just across different geographical sources of any one particular fossil fuel.

In the first few decades after independence, Singapore was completely dependent on oil for electricity generation. In 1992, Singapore started importing natural gas by pipeline, with its first contract with Malaysia for 155 million cubic feet per day (mmcf/d). Since then, the share of natural gas in power generation has increased steeply over the years. By 2010, natural gas accounted for over 78 per cent of Singapore's electricity generation. The switch from fuel oil to natural gas in Singapore was in line with (even if somewhat belatedly) the global switch away from expensive oil-based power generation around the world in favour of coal and natural gas as a consequence of the oil prices shocks of the 1970s.

Through four existing pipelines, Singapore buys natural gas from Malaysia and Indonesia under five contracts indexed to heavy fuel oil prices (see Table 5.3 below). However, the energy landscape in both Malaysia and Indonesia has changed since these contracts were signed. The lack of major discoveries and gas field developments has resulted in dwindling gas supplies relative to rapid domestic demand growth. Both countries have expressed concern over declining domestic gas production and their ability to meet rapidly growing domestic demand as well as servicing

Table 5.3
Singapore Pipeline Gas Supply and Contracts

Seller	Buyer	Pipeline	Start Year	End Year	Annual Contract Quantity (BSCM)
Pertamina (Indonesia)	Sembgas	West Natuna (Indonesia) — Singapore	2001	2022	3.37
Petronas (Malaysia)	Senoko	Peninsular Malaysia — Singapore	2001	2015	1.6
Petronas (Malaysia)	Keppel	Malaysia Plentong — Singapore	2005	2023	1.189
Pertamina (Indonesia)	Gas Supply	South Sumatra (Indonesia) — Singapore	2006	2023	3.65
Conoco (Indonesia)	Island Power	South Sumatra (Indonesia) — Singapore	2009	2023	1.04

Source: U.S. Energy Information Administration <http://www.eia.gov/countries/cab.cfm?ips=SN>; International Energy Agency (2010), "Medium-Term Oil and Gas Markets 2010", Paris, p. 268; Sovacool, B., "Energy Policy and Cooperation in Southeast Asia", Energy Policy 37 (2009): 2360.

their export commitments. With the earliest contract set to expire in 2015 and the last contract in 2023, this caused considerable uncertainty over whether the existing contracts would be renewed.[21]

Within a relatively short period, liquefied natural gas (LNG) imports were seen by government officials as an alternative to the prospects of losing pipeline gas supply from Malaysia and Indonesia. In 2006, the Singapore government announced its plan to import LNG and build the nation's first LNG receiving terminal to fulfil rising demand and to diversify its sources of natural gas. The government introduced controls in August 2006 on imports of piped natural gas (PNG) to allow the build-up of demand for LNG. In May 2013, Singapore's first LNG terminal started commercial operations. The government-financed S$1.7 billion terminal has a throughput capacity of 3.5 million tonnes per annum (Mtpa) which was increased to 6 Mtpa by end 2013 when a third tank, a second jetty and additional regasification facilities were added. The terminal's capacity will rise to 11 Mtpa when the fourth tank and additional regasification facilities are constructed.[22]

According to the EMA, the government will consult the industry and review the PNG import control policy when LNG imports reaches 3 Mtpa or in year 2018, whichever is earlier.[23] Under the current LNG "procurement framework", BG Singapore Gas Management (BGSGM) was appointed in 2008 as the LNG importer with an exclusive franchise to import LNG and sell regasified LNG in Singapore for up to 3 Mtpa or 2023, whichever is earlier. This appointment was effected via a "Request For Proposal", a solicitation made by EMA to potential suppliers for submitting business proposals which best met EMA's terms and conditions for such LNG supply. As of February 2014, 2.7 Mtpa of gas sales in Singapore were contracted by BGSGM, and the EMA set about putting in place "a robust LNG import framework" for LNG imports beyond the 3 Mtpa tranche awarded to BGSGM. The objective of this framework is to access competitively priced and reliable natural gas supply that meets the needs of local buyers while ensuring the optimal use of the LNG storage and regasification terminal throughput capacity via efficient operations and usage.[24]

For Singapore's demand for LNG beyond its first 3 Mtpa tranche, up to three potential importers will be invited to participate in the second part of the two-stage regulatory process. The shortlisted importers will be required to have negotiated binding agreements with potential buyers, together with a terminal user agreement (TUA) with Singapore LNG

Corporation (SLNG), the LNG terminal operator. Each appointed importer will be awarded an exclusive franchise period of three years or until it has sold 1 Mtpa of LNG, whichever is earlier. The appointed importer(s) will be obligated to offer regasified LNG to all potential buyers in Singapore during the franchise period at a baseline gas-sales agreement (GSA) level. The baseline GSA represents the minimum offer for any buyer during the franchise period. The baseline GSA document would be mandatory to qualify for evaluation by the EMA.

Singapore's Quest to Serve as an LNG Hub for the Region

According to Singapore's policymakers, and observers such as the IEA, Singapore can play a pivotal role as an LNG trading hub for the Asia-Pacific region, similar to its position in the oil industry as a refining and trading hub.[25] The government will allow the leasing of capacity in its third tank for trading purposes. As an incentive, the government introduced a concessionary tax rate of 5 per cent on LNG trading income for companies under the Global Trader Programme (GTP) in May 2007.[26] SLNG, the terminal operator, sees a rise in small regasification and storage terminals for off-grid power generation in the region as an opportunity to develop short-haul trading opportunities in the Southeast Asian region.[27] The terminal would provide the flexibility to barge small volumes of LNG, of between 10,000 m^3 to 40,000 m^3, to remote markets intra-regionally. As floating liquefaction becomes more widespread in the region, output from smaller gas fields in the region could also be aggregated in the Singapore terminal for distribution to other markets.

Several other countries in Southeast Asia have announced plans or have already begun construction of LNG regasification terminals, including Thailand, Vietnam, and the Philippines. The demand for "small scale" LNG is poised to grow in the region as governments look to fuel smaller power plants and industrial developments in remote areas not connected to pipelines or the national grid with natural gas. This would reduce reliance on expensive diesel-fuelled power generation. Small scale LNG is also seen as a source of gas supplies for quickly ramping up electricity production, directly replacing household liquefied petroleum gas (LPG) use or for direct supply to industry in remote areas and islands. According to one study, it is estimated that by 2020, demand in eastern Indonesia, the southern Philippines, and northern Vietnam could require over 120 small

50-megawatt (MW) power plants.[28] These power plants could require up to 60 small-scale LNG carriers to supply LNG to the region.[29]

With growing demand and improvements in technology, new market segments for smaller LNG vessels, short sailing time, and small receiving terminals are becoming viable. Indonesia's state energy firm Pertamina and state power firm PLN recently announced that they plan to build eight "mini" LNG receiving terminals in eastern Indonesia, with a total capacity of 1.4 million tonnes a year.[30] As both demand and supply of LNG within the region become focused on smaller, quick start-up projects to exploit smaller stranded gas fields and to meet demand in remote or off-grid locations, intra-regional gas trade is likely to grow in the medium term. "Short haul" trade in LNG, referring to trade within 1,500 nautical miles and short sailing times of 3–4 days, covers distances from Singapore to Malaysia, Indonesia, the Philippines, Thailand, Myanmar, and Vietnam.

At the other end of the size spectrum, the Singapore LNG terminal can also receive very large Qatari "Q-max" vessels which can load up to 270,000 m^3, while most other buyers in Asia cannot handle such vessels. The terminal can thus serve as a break-bulk centre for inter-regional trade, for onward dispatch of smaller cargoes which can be handled by smaller LNG receiving ports in Japan for example (most of which can only handle LNG vessels carrying up to 150,000 m^3).

The Singapore government's initiatives in the natural gas sector have gone beyond the building of an LNG import terminal and a policy framework supportive of the city-state's potential role as an LNG trading hub in the region. Temasek, Singapore's sovereign wealth fund, set up Pavilion Energy in April 2013 after incorporating an initial capital fund of S$1 billion for the company. The company will invest globally across LNG-related businesses, including trading, exploration, storage, processing, and shipping. According to its chief executive officer, the plan "is to acquire assets across the full value chain by building strong relationships with key partners, and investing and co-investing in gas acreage, liquefaction plants, and assets for regasification".[31] Among the deals reported, the company acquired interests in Tanzanian gas acreage, manages Singapore's equity interest in the U.S. natural gas producer Chesapeake Energy, formed a joint venture with the BW Group, a leading maritime transport company to acquire, manage and charter LNG carriers, and signed a ten-year deal with French oil and gas multinational company Total S.A. to buy 0.7 Mtpa of LNG for delivery into Asia. It is also widely expected to apply for an

LNG importer role in Singapore under the EMA's Request for Proposal (RFP) process and is in "pole position" to obtain a licence.[32]

Assessing Singapore's Energy Security

In broad terms, Singapore's performance by any reasonable measure of energy security has been exemplary. Not only has the small city-state without any domestic supply of energy managed to encourage energy efficiency by strictly following the "user pays" principle and allowing market prices to ration energy use. It has also converted its strategic location and natural deep-water port into a defining advantage in ship bunkering, oil refining, and trading for the "East of Suez" region. The move away from oil into gas for its power generation sector, and from piped gas to "portfolio LNG" via an appointed LNG aggregator, have also been significant factors in moving towards enhanced energy security.

The following summary assessment of Singapore's energy security status focuses on five key concerns: the impact of oil price shocks, policy initiatives for fuel diversification into natural gas, the outlook for Singapore as a regional LNG trading hub, the establishment of Pavilion Energy as a state-backed player in the LNG industry, and the very large investments in energy infrastructure, including storage and ancillary facilities.

Oil Price Shock Impacts

Several metrics are often cited in studies on energy security. The most direct measure concerns the extent to which the economy is subject to the risks of either volatile or higher oil prices (or both) on the domestic economy.[33] Metrics associated with this perspective might suggest that the Singapore economy remains quite vulnerable to energy security challenges. Net energy imports form a relatively high proportion of Singapore's GDP compared to other Asian economies (see Fig 5.1 below), which is unsurprising given the lack of indigenous sources of energy, its affluence and its specialization in energy-intensive industries such as oil refining and petrochemicals. At 6.5 per cent, Singapore's "net energy imports to GDP" ratio is comparable to South Korea's heavily industrialized economy (7 per cent). Its ratio is more than twice that of Hong Kong's, again unsurprisingly, given the latter's predominantly service-oriented economy. Singapore's dependence on energy imports by this measure is also higher than large

Figure 5.1
Net Energy Imports to GDP, 2010

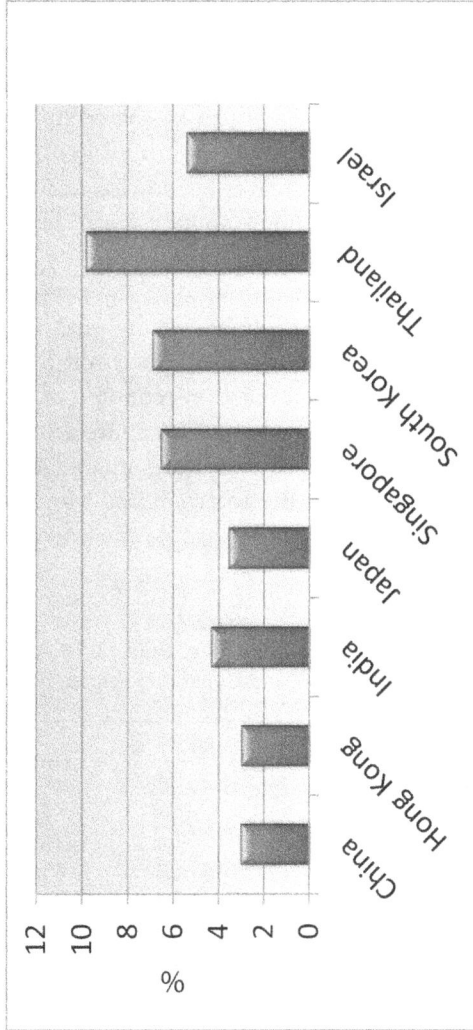

Source: ESI Economics Department calculations.

countries such as India and China as well as advanced countries such as Israel and Japan.

According to a 2004 report by the Asian Development Bank (ADB), the Singapore economy is vulnerable to disruptions in energy price and volatility, with a US$10 per barrel increase in oil prices estimated to result in a 1.7 per cent reduction in GDP, which is again high compared to other Asian economies (see Table 5.4).[34] Of the ten other Asian countries listed, only Thailand is more affected, with an estimated reduction of 2.2 per cent of GDP due to a hypothesized US$10 per barrel price shock. An oil price shock of US$10 per barrel increases consumer prices in India, Thailand, Malaysia, and Indonesia by either more or about the same as Singapore's estimated impact of 1.3 per cent.

Due to the highly open nature of Singapore's economy and its diversified economic structure, however, its energy trade balance is a relatively small proportion of its current account in its external balance of payments. So, despite the impact on economic activity and consumer prices, an upward oil price shock on Singapore is far less of an issue in terms of its ability to pay for such imports in a sustainable way (see Fig 5.2). According to data from the International Monetary Fund for 2006, the energy trade balance constitutes only some 0.15 per cent of its overall

Table 5.4
Impact of a Sustained US$10 Per Barrel Oil Price Increase
on GDP and Consumer Prices

Country	GDP (%)	Consumer Prices
China	−0.8	0.5
Hong Kong	−0.6	0.3
India	−0.8	1.7
Indonesia	0.1	1.3
Japan	−0.5	0.7
South Korea	−0.6	0.8
Malaysia	−0.9	1.4
Singapore	−1.7	1.3
Taiwan	−0.4	0.3
Thailand	−2.2	1.5

Note: ADB estimates based on the Oxford Economic Forecasting World Macroeconomic Model (2004).
Source: *Asian Development Outlook 2004* Update (staff estimates based on Oxford Economic Forecasting World Macroeconomic Model) <http://www.adb.org/sites/default/files/pub/2004/ado2004-update.pdf>.

Figure 5.2
Energy Trade Balance as a Percentage of Current Account Balance, 2006

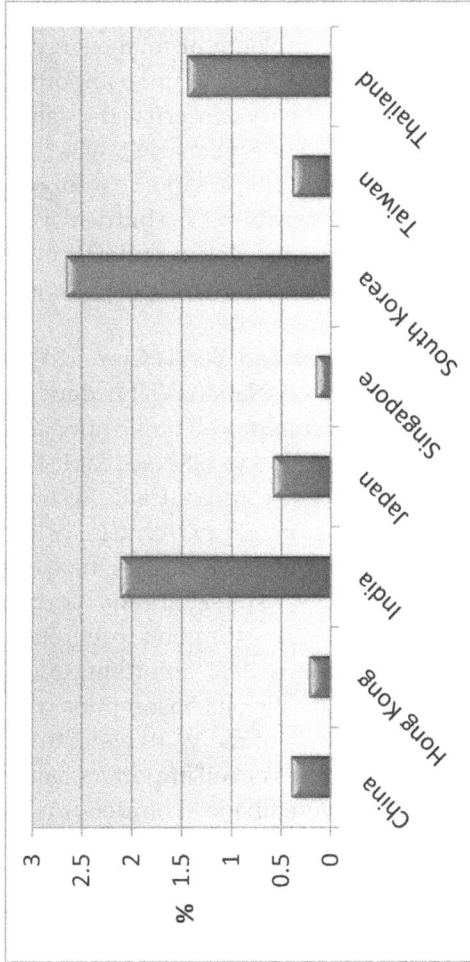

Source: ESI Energy Department calculations based on IMF Statistics.

current account balance. This ratio compares favourably to India's 2.1 per cent and South Korea's 2.7 per cent, for example.

The health and sustainability of any country's balance of payments is a function of a number of factors, including the overall rate of growth of its exports of goods and services relative to that of its imports and the terms of trade for the country.[35] For a trade-oriented economy such as Singapore's, the cost of petroleum or total energy imports per se is of little analytical interest since the bulk of these imports are destined for the export market. What is of primary concern is the value of energy imports destined for final use in the domestic market, which needs to be paid for eventually by a share of the country's export earnings. In other words, the most meaningful economic measure of the burden of energy imports is the cost, in terms of foreign exchange, of the domestic utilization of imported energy products.[36] By this measure, Singapore's "energy security" status is comfortable.

A study by the Economic and Social Commission for Asia and the Pacific (ESCAP) of the United Nations (UN) derived cost estimates of Singapore's domestic petroleum product utilization as shares of GDP and of total retained imports from 1974 to 1982 (see Table 5.5 below). As evident in the table, these costs were not insignificant. According to UN data, oil product consumption rose from 5.5 per cent in 1974 to 13.2 per cent of GDP by 1981 after the second oil price shock. Official data supports lower estimates which are, nevertheless, still significant. As a percentage of retained imports, domestic oil product consumption rose from 8.3 per cent in 1974 to a peak of over 18 per cent in 1980, according to UN data. Both series show escalating costs of domestic oil consumption, especially since 1979.

The two oil price increases of the 1970s constituted severe balance of payments shocks for the world's net oil importers, causing deterioration in their terms of trade and severe financial burdens on many of the world's large oil consuming economies. Despite the almost total dependence on oil imports for domestic energy requirements, the outward-oriented economies of East Asia withstood the effects of the two oil price shocks much better than most countries pursuing an inward-looking import-substitution industrialization strategy.[37] Singapore's real economic growth performance on average since the 1970s, for example, has outperformed that of most other countries.

The erosion of oil prices since 1981, particularly the 1986 oil price collapse, directly reduced the costs of energy use. According to one

Table 5.5
Estimated Share of Domestic Product Consumption, 1974–82
(as a % of GDP and retained imports)

	GDP		Retained Imports	
	official data	UN data	official data	UN data
1974	3.3	5.5	5.1	8.3
1975	3.6	6.8	5.8	10.9
1976	3.9	8.0	6.8	13.7
1977	4.0	8.2	7.7	15.7
1978	3.9	8.2	7.0	14.7
1979	4.6	9.5	8.0	16.3
1980	6.6	12.2	9.8	18.1
1981	7.0	13.2	9.3	17.6
1982	6.7	13.0	9.1	17.7

Source: "Energy in the ESCAP region: Policies, Issues and the Potential for regional cooperation", Development Papers No. 4, Economic and Social Commission for Asia and the Pacific (ESCAP), Bangkok, 1984.

contemporaneous report by the Development Bank of Singapore, or DBS, assuming a domestic consumption of 236,000 barrels per day and an average price of crude petroleum at US$28 per barrel in 1985 and US$15 per barrel in 1986, the cost savings resulting from the 1986 price collapse amounted to US1.12 billion (S$2.5 billions), a substantial amount compared to the total commodity trade deficit of S$8.1 billion.[38] Lower oil prices since 1981 culminating in the price collapse of 1986, had two further positive consequences for the Singapore economy. Its major trading partners enjoyed, like Singapore, lower costs of oil consumption, and higher incomes, which rebounded with higher import demand in general for Singapore's exports. Furthermore, by making energy conservation and fuel substitution less urgent, the demand prospects for refined oil products also improved the outlook for Singapore's export-oriented oil refining industry.

On the negative side, the lower oil prices, of course, had adverse impacts on net oil exporters in the region, in particular Malaysia and Indonesia, which were also major trading partners of Singapore. In 1984, for example, the two countries absorbed over a fifth of Singapore's exports. The fall in oil prices since 1981, and the collapse in 1986 in particular, also led to a sharp cutback in oil and gas exploration and development expenditures across the industry worldwide. Singapore's significant upstream and offshore oil and gas services and construction industries suffered the full impact of the downturn. There is no available assessment on the net impact of lower oil prices since 1981 on Singapore, although one observer speculated that "the negative side was felt first and is probably the more powerful."[39]

Natural Gas and Fuel Diversification

In measuring energy security from a portfolio perspective, economists typically use the Herfindahl-Hirschmann Index (HHI). For each fuel (f), the HHI is defined by $HH_f = \sum_i s_i^2$, where s_i is the percentage share of each supplier (i) in the country's fuel import portfolio. A lower HHI value indicates greater diversity of import sources either due to a greater number of sources or a more even spread across the sources.[40] The closer a market is to being a monopoly, the higher the market's concentration (and the lower its competition). If, for example, there were only one firm in an industry, that firm would have 100 per cent market share, and the HHI would equal 10,000 (i.e. 100^2), indicating a monopoly. Or, if there were thousands of firms competing, each would have nearly 0 per cent market share, and the HHI would be close to zero, indicating nearly perfect competition.

At the broadest level, i.e. across competing fuels and energy technologies, there is a significant lack of diversity in Singapore's energy economy due to its almost complete reliance on natural gas and oil. This is in contrast to other countries that have other significant sources of other energy fuels such as coal, hydroelectricity, and nuclear power. As a major export-oriented oil refining centre with complex refineries which can optimize a wide slate of different crude oils, Singapore's oil imports are well diversified, as to be expected. Constructing an HHI which ranges from 0 (perfectly diversified) to 1 (no diversification), Singapore's oil import diversification measure, based on 2009 data, is 0.17, compared to 0.5 for Israel, for example.[41]

Singapore has historically relied on the two import sources, Indonesia and Malaysia, for its pipeline natural gas imports, leading to a high HHI value for gas imports at 0.60–0.80 in recent years. The introduction of LNG imports fundamentally alters this situation, with LNG imports potentially accounting for as much as 40 per cent of Singapore's natural gas use by 2015. The chart below (Fig 5.3) provides the HHI measure of improvements

Figure 5.3
HHI for Singapore Gas Supply: Effect of Adding LNG Imports

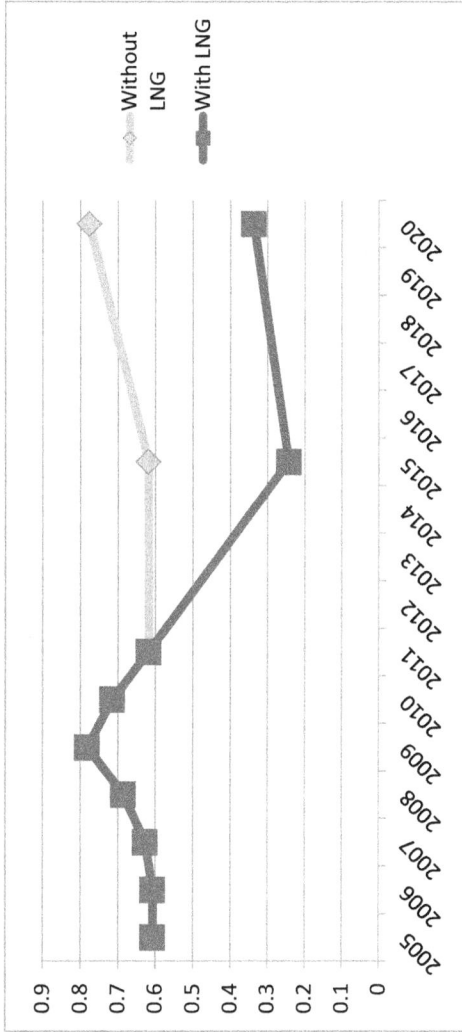

Source: Calculations by Economics Department, Energy Studies Institute, 2013.

in Singapore's security of gas supply. The chart is constructed such that the HHI ranges from a "perfectly diversified" value of zero to a "no diversification" value of 1. Because in the immediate future Singapore will import "portfolio LNG"[42] from BGSGM without relying on any specific LNG source, its LNG imports are expected to be well diversified.[43] This is enough to push Singapore's overall HHI value for power generation expected in 2015 from 0.53 (without any LNG) to 0.23 (with both pipeline and LNG imports). It indicates the lack of diversity in Singapore's pipeline gas portfolio and the improvements in energy security by importing LNG in addition to pipeline gas. By 2015, for example, with a projected 3 Mtpa of natural gas being imported via the LNG terminal, Singapore's gas supply security improves by over 2.5 times due to having the LNG supply option in addition to its pipeline imports.

The HHI can take into account country-specific geopolitical and regulatory risks of fuel supply sources by defining the HHI by $HH_{f,pol} = \sum_i (r_i * s_i^2)$, where r_i is a risk rating factor for each fuel supplying country (i). One proxy that is used to measure geopolitical risks of the fuel supplying country is the World Bank's Worldwide Governance Indicators. In the figure below, the risk rating factor r_i is defined as a composite indicator of political and regulatory risk (ranging from 1 to 3) based on the average of the "political stability and absence of violence" indicator and "regulatory quality" indicator.[44]

The chart below (Fig 5.4) exhibits the HHI for Singapore's imports of natural gas, which incorporates country-specific political and regulatory risks of the sources of natural gas imports. The HHI ranges from 0 to 3, with the value 0 defined as perfectly diversified with minimal geopolitical risk and the value 3 indicating no diversification and a maximum of political risk. The chart indicates the diversification benefits of LNG imports, even after accounting for source-specific geopolitical risks. As noted above, the sole licensed importer of LNG into Singapore, BGSGM, derives its LNG supply from a range of sources around the world, and the calculated HHI for Singapore's LNG imports reflect this.[45]

The HHI changes from 2005 to 2011 are driven by changes in the import shares of Indonesian and Malaysian piped gas into Singapore. Singapore imports more gas from Indonesia than from Malaysia, so when the import share from Indonesia increased between 2005 and 2009, the HHI also increased (because Singapore become more reliant on a single import source). After 2009, the import share of Indonesia drops so the HHI also

Figure 5.4
Adjusted HHI for Singapore Gas Supply: Effect of Adding LNG Imports

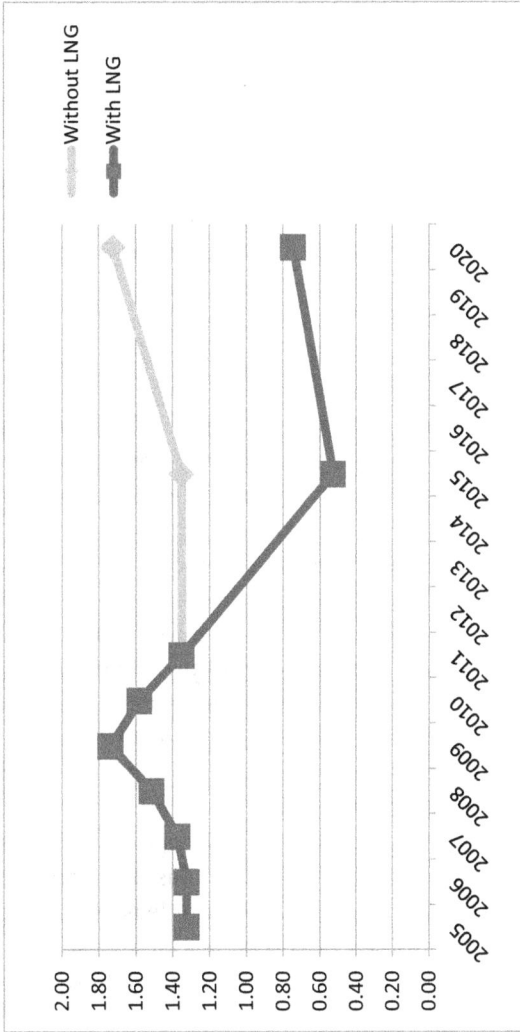

Source: Calculations by Economics Department, Energy Studies Institute, 2013.

drops. Between 2015 and 2020, one of the contracts with Malaysia expires, so again Singapore's share of piped imports coming from Indonesia goes up, which again pushes up the HHI (i.e., from a diversification perspective, importing more from the larger source is penalized). But the estimated 60 per cent improvement in the HHI in 2015 due to the exercise of the LNG import option is large.

There are limits, however, to the usefulness of measures such as the HHI. Recent reports of BGSGM's poor financial performance show that the corporate finance risk borne by the single appointed LNG importer/ aggregator is quite another matter from national energy security risks measured by the HHI. It is not clear how badly Singapore's gas supply security will be affected by BGSGM's travails, as the latter considers selling its gas assets portfolio in order to emerge from its poor state of finances.[46] The decision to appoint a further one or two exclusive LNG importers to satisfy gas demand beyond BGSGM's exclusive right to supply 3 Mtpa will help Singapore further diversify exposure. As Singapore's gas demand grows in the long term and can support several LNG importer-aggregators under the country's LNG "procurement framework" regulations, the idiosyncratic company-specific risk of all aggregators failing at the same time is much reduced.

Under the LNG procurement framework, the primary criteria set out in the RFP issued by the EMA were diversification of supply sources and price competitiveness for current and subsequent tranches (of demand); secondary criteria included flexibility of pricing formulas and contractual terms for gas supply, and ability to support the development of a trading hub in Singapore.[47] These high level qualification criteria spelt out in the RFP include a range of prerequisites on the part of bidding companies, including diversified portfolios of gas supply sources both upstream and downstream; demonstrated experience of operating in gas markets across the value chain; gas sales pricing formulas and contract terms that are flexible and can manage volatility; and not least, strong credit worthiness and financial status rating of the company's balance sheet.[48] BGSGM's recent financial travails show how even a highly rated "growth stock" company with a global reputation in the LNG industry can quickly be compromised by a series of large cost overruns, *force majeure* and asset write-downs.[49]

The policy question then naturally arises as to whether a "multi-user open-access" model for the LNG terminal operation is a better regulatory choice in terms of exposure to corporate risks of publicly listed companies.

Open access models for physical infrastructure such as ports, railways, and telecommunications networks are typically made available to clients (other than the owners) for a fee. As a regulated natural monopoly, the operator of the open access infrastructure facilities is obliged to minimize user fees consistent with the proper operation and future development of the infrastructure as needed by users. More specifically, user fees would be regulated such that the infrastructure operator would not be in a position to extract monopoly profits. In an open access model, risks are borne by individual importers and their customers or, in the case of those who import for their own supply, the risks are purely internal to their own balance sheets. The role of regulations in the case of open-access models of infrastructure use is limited to ensuring a competitive and level playing field for all users. Rules governing competitive access to the terminal and regasification facilities would need to ensure that individual companies or several players acting in collusion cannot "game" the system for their own pecuniary advantage.

The clearest theoretical advantage that the "aggregator-importer" model might have over an open access model would be that a single supplier would have the advantages of scale economies and hence, access to cheaper gas, than a multiplicity of smaller buyers contracting bilaterally with different sellers. In practice, however, a buyer of say 3 Mtpa of LNG is not likely to get a significantly cheaper price than a buyer who wants to contract only 1 Mtpa.[50] It should also be noted that an open access model is fully consistent with a pooling arrangement among buyers, so that buyers are free to coordinate with each other for collective purchases in order to get the volume discounts, if any do indeed exist, so long as the pool (or its representative agent) enters into a binding TUA as any other terminal facilities user.

Under the EMA's LNG procurement framework, buyers are allowed to enter into borrowing and lending (B&L) pool arrangements, provided that an "anchor" participant qualifies as an LNG importer and underwrites commercial and operating risks for the whole pool. According to some respondents to EMA's call for feedback on its LNG procurement framework, this requirement imposed upon the B&L pool's "anchor" participant is onerous and disadvantages the B&L arrangement relative to bids from a single aggregator.[51] The licensing procedures of EMA's procurement framework also effectively disadvantages a self-supplier, i.e., an end user that wishes to both supply LNG and consume the (regasified) natural gas in its own facilities.

Singapore's LNG Hub Ambitions

Despite the greater diversity of sources of natural gas in the future, Singapore's gas contracts, both pipeline and LNG, remain oil-indexed. Asian LNG pricing relies on long-term, oil price-indexed export contracts. There is no Asia-Pacific Basin gas price index analogous to the real-time spot price determination at the United Kingdom's National Balancing Point (NBP) and United States's Henry Hub (in Louisiana) which serve the Atlantic Basin gas markets.[52] Thus Singapore's overall energy portfolio, while more secure to source-specific risks due to the introduction of "portfolio" LNG imports, remains vulnerable to systemic disruptions in oil prices due to the lack of significant energy supplies that are not indexed to oil prices. U.S. gas prices are set by "gas-on-gas" competition within the large but hitherto isolated North American market. In Europe, there is a growing shift from oil indexation to spot-based pricing, particularly in northwest Europe, where spot gas trading hubs, such as the NBP and Title Transfer Facility (TTF) in the Netherlands, are well-established. The spot market (for non-oil indexed transactions) which accounted for about 15 per cent of European gas sales in 2005 had grown to over 35 per cent by 2010.[53] Oil indexed pricing for Russian pipeline gas exports into Europe has come under intense pressure in the aftermath of the U.S. financial crisis and the slow-down in European-wide economic growth. Gazprom reportedly has had to offer price concessions to European gas buyers such as Eni, GDF Suez, and OMV as well as linking some portion of the gas sales price to hub-based spot prices.[54]

Singapore's policymakers have pulled out all stops to encourage the development of an LNG trading hub by building the region's first multi-user LNG import, storage, and regasification terminal and putting in place the necessary regulatory framework. Success will, of course, depend on a number of factors that are not within the control of any one country or market. Among these, the availability of adequate LNG supply from a number of different sources to support the growth of a liquid spot and short-term physical market will be critical. According to the International Gas Union, global spot and short-term LNG trades since 2000 have increased by over sixfold from below 5 per cent of the LNG trade to a peak of 31 per cent of the global LNG trade or 73.5 Mtpa in 2012.[55] As important for an industry that is dependent on seaborne trade, the increasing trend of new LNG vessels being ordered for construction on "speculation" (i.e., without underlying long-term charter deals to pay for such orders) will also boost the fleet availability for spot and short-term LNG cargo trades at short notice.

Among the constraints that Singapore faces in its quest for a role as Asia's LNG hub are its relatively small domestic gas market and the lack of a regional pipeline network which would allow for flexible cross-border flows in Southeast Asia. The impacts of a small domestic market and the lack of a regional gas pipeline network are accentuated by EMA's decision to limit the quantity of LNG imported into Singapore as spot cargoes to 10 per cent of the total imported. This 10 per cent cap on spot cargoes is seen by some industry players as both unnecessary and inefficient given that this would possibly limit liquidity when long-term contracted LNG demand growth in Singapore is not expected to grow rapidly.[56] While reliance on spot cargoes may increase price volatility, this should not be of concern to regulators in the case of industrial end users whose management would presumably be responsible to their shareholders for optimizing LNG purchasing behaviour for their own corporate requirements.

According to the EMA, it is "prudential" to impose the 10 per cent cap on spot cargoes for the nascent Singapore gas market, and this cap can be reviewed as the market develops and gains experience. Views on "prudence" in the market, of course, differ among different actors. For some perspective, it is useful to note that by 2012, spot LNG deliveries to Asia constituted about a fifth of total Asian LNG supply.[57] Asia's dominant LNG importers Japan and South Korea, traditionally noted for their conservative focus on long-term supply reliability, are major buyers of spot cargoes. For some of the Japanese and Korean trading houses, spot LNG purchases can constitute up to 30 per cent of their purchase portfolios.

A regional hub for traded short-term LNG in Singapore might spur the development of an Asian gas-price index. If a significant spot and short-term trade in LNG cargoes (commonly defined as less than four years) were to develop in the region, centred on Singapore's storage terminal, Singapore could emerge as a price discovery centre. This, in turn, could have a significant impact on regional LNG sales and price-review negotiations, weakening the long-established link to an oil price index (typically, the Japan Custom-cleared Crude, or JCC, price which reflects the average price of crude oil imports into Japan).

However, Singapore's potential role as an LNG hub is far from assured, given that the vast majority of Asian trade in short-term and spot LNG cargoes are focused quite far away in Northeast Asia, where the largest

LNG importers such as Japan, South Korea, and China are located (Japan and South Korea together accounted for over half of all LNG consumed in the world in 2012). Northeast Asian LNG importers as well as other large LNG importers in the region such as India can source spot market cargoes directly from Europe, Australia, and the Middle East. Currently, the most prominent price index for Asian spot LNG cargoes is the Japan Korea Marker (JKM™), a spot price assessment by the price reporting agency Platts for cargoes Delivered Ex Ship (DES) into Japan and South Korea.[58]

The Establishment of Pavilion Energy

Resource nationalism and the first oil crisis of 1973 gave rise to the modern national oil company (NOC), a model that has become widespread in both the oil and gas sectors in the non-OECD countries. Governments, not private shareholders, already own the world's largest oil companies, and about 83 per cent of global oil reserves and production are controlled by national oil companies; privately owned multinationals now produce just 10 per cent of the world's oil and own just 3 per cent of global reserves; almost 80 per cent of future conventional oil and gas output to 2030 will come from NOCs.[59]

While the first NOCs were established in the early years of independence from the former colonial powers, primarily representing the large oil exporting countries of the Organization of the Petroleum Exporting Countries (OPEC), the NOCs of the large Asian net oil-importers are relative latecomers. More recently, however, Asian NOCs from China, Japan, Korea, India, and elsewhere have led a wave of investments for equity participation in upstream energy projects in Africa, the Middle East, Central Asia, Latin America, and Southeast Asia/Australasia. In the past decade, the Asian NOCs have become increasingly internationalized in their asset portfolios. They compete as well as form joint ventures with the international oil companies for access to oil and gas deposits around the world. With the boom in unconventional oil and gas resource development in the United States and Canada, the leading foreign investors in the sector have been the large Asian NOCs.

It is no surprise that with the steep increase in energy prices over the past decade, and with continued unrest and political instability in the Middle East, a deep sense of insecurity about the reliability of future fuel supplies has made energy security part of core national security concerns for governments across Asia. In the context of constrained or non-existent domestic production and rapidly increasing demand for hydrocarbons in the NOC's home country, the perceived need to gain "control" of larger levels of oil and gas reserves across the globe would seem high in many policymaker's strategies to enhance energy security.[60] As a consequence, the NOCs have higher risk tolerances than their private sector counterparts, investing in countries such as Myanmar, Chad, Sudan, and Venezuela. But state-directed purchases of equity in often opaque companies or direct investments in oil or gas fields, typically in countries where the rule of law is not well established, is itself a risky route to energy security, a contradiction in terms as it were. While the NOCs might have found it initially to their strategic advantage to operate in regions which had troubled relations with the Western countries, they also found that, not surprisingly, they were not protected from political and fiscal risks either.[61]

The establishment of Pavilion Energy by Temasek does not fit into the pattern of investments in the upstream oil and gas sector by the Asian NOCs described above. The government-owned Singapore Petroleum Company (SPC), founded in 1969, and until it was sold off and delisted from the Singapore Exchange in 2009, was always run as a fully commercial firm. Unlike many of its Asian NOC counterparts which were significant players in global upstream oil and gas ventures, SPC always played a relatively small role with a limited budget by oil and gas industry standards, with its major focus in downstream trading and oil refining.[62]

Like other sovereign wealth funds (SWFs) around the world, Temasek's role has been that of an equity investor in existing business enterprises across countries and various sectors. The incorporation of Pavilion Energy has been reported in the media as part of Temasek's plan to increase its exposure to the energy sector; in the year to March 2012, Temasek doubled its size of energy-related holdings to 6 per cent of its total portfolio, the latter's worth a reported S$198 billion as at March 2012.[63] More specifically, however, this represents more than just an increase in the SWF's exposure to the energy sector. Passive equity participation in existing publicly listed energy firms, for instance, carries less risk. The incorporation in Singapore of a new firm to participate in directly productive activity across the natural gas value chain is rather seen as a means to promote Singapore's national interests in the natural gas sector, in particular to encourage the full utilization of the country's publicly funded multi-user LNG terminal.

If selected to be one of the EMA-appointed LNG importers to service Singapore's post–3 Mtpa LNG demand tranches, Pavilion Energy would also be involved in LNG trade and supply of regasified natural gas to Singapore-based buyers.

Only time will tell whether Pavilion Energy succeeds in yielding reasonable returns on investment as well as in promoting Singapore as Asia's LNG hub in a cost-effective manner. It is not apparent however whether there is an *a priori* case to be made for a "state champion" in the natural gas industry to serve the national interest. The mainstream school of thought would argue that the role of government should be restricted to establishing an appropriate LNG regulatory framework as enforced by the EMA and overseeing the neutral, regulated terminal operator SLNG. SLNG, in turn, would offer its storage and terminal services not to maximize government revenues as a monopolist but at least-cost consistent with the long-term upkeep and development of the terminal and its facilities. This would ensure an operating environment that encourages the maximum feasible use of the LNG terminal facilities by Singapore's private sector natural gas customers as well as by third-party users if the terminal's role as a LNG trading hub takes off. While promoting competitive markets is one of the government's five energy policy strategies, the question is whether this market-enabling role is enough, or whether additional policy initiatives (such as incorporating and funding Pavilion Energy) are required to best pursue specific energy-sector policy targets.

The pervasive role of the Singapore government as entrepreneur, i.e., investing in directly productive activity via state-owned enterprises (SOEs), locally termed government-linked companies or GLCs, has been noted by several studies.[64] Clearly, these SOEs are intended to be run along commercial principles, with no subsidies or concealed privileges; their personnel are recruited on merit and internationally as needed; and it is government policy not to bail out failing SOEs to save jobs. The likelihood of wasting public resources on uneconomic ventures is minimized so long as SOEs are operating on commercial principles, are free to hire the best personnel available in competitive labour markets, and are allowed to fail if certain performance criteria relative to the norms of the market (such as the real return on capital employed, labour productivity, etc.) are not met within a reasonable maturation period. SOEs in many, if not most, developing countries have often been huge failures, causing a drain on public budgets and subject to all forms of economic inefficiencies, nepotism, and corruption. While the lack of publically available data makes it impossible to assess the real rate of return on investments, on average, for the many SOEs in Singapore, it is nevertheless clear that by and large, these SOEs have avoided the disasters that have befallen their counterparts in many countries and in countless cases.

Despite the general financial soundness of SOEs in Singapore, the question remains as to whether the country's policy objectives of energy security and economic competitiveness are best pursued by an SOE, in addition to the appropriate regulatory and policy environment for competitive energy markets. Potential issues of concern which have been identified include the crowding out of private enterprises in the sectors in which the SOEs dominate, the problems of coordination and control in increasingly complex bureaucracies, the avoidance of failure dominating the potential gains of success in the overly risk-averse decision-making calculus of civil servants, the tendency to hold on to existing ventures too long to avoid the consequences of failure, and the tension between the withholding of information for commercial competitive reasons and the public accountability of government-owned entities founded on taxpayers's money.[65] The extent to which these issues are handled correctly will determine not only the rate of return on Temasek's investment in Pavilion Energy, but also the latter's effectiveness in promoting Singapore's ambitions to emerge as the region's LNG trading hub.

Public Investments in Energy Infrastructure

Singapore has committed large public investments in infrastructure projects for energy security such as the underground oil storage facilities and the LNG import terminal. These investments would likely require rates of return that are lower than private sector norms. Were it not so, the private sector itself would have invested in underground caverns and floating storage structures for storing oil or in LNG storage and regasification facilities with a view to charging fees for the use of such facilities to make a profit. An economic case can be made for using lower rates of required return for public investments than that of private investments. Private investors, at the very least, have to cover their own risk-adjusted cost of capital to break even. The government, on the other hand, can apply lower interest rates in discounting future benefits relative to upfront capital costs on the rationale that, as trustee to the general public, it has a special responsibility for providing public goods such as national defence or public health. Energy security, as a subset of national defence, is a public good the consumption of which cannot be restricted to any particular individual. As profit-maximising private investment decisions do not take into account social benefits which are not privately appropriable, the level of private investment will fall short of the societal optimum in this argument.

Are Singapore officials paying too high an insurance premium in the quest for energy security? This question cannot be answered on grounds of positive economics. However, a high premium for ensuring energy security can be argued on normative grounds as described above. The policy formulation process will need to appropriately weigh the trade-off between infrastructural investments for perceived future energy security benefits at the expense of current consumption. A successful policy would be one that reflects societal preferences for the balance between energy security and economic welfare. Ultimately, the balancing of opportunity costs associated with policy actions that are adopted are the responsibility of the elected representatives of citizens.[66]

5.3 ENHANCE ENERGY EFFICIENCY: MARKET BARRIERS OR FAILURES?

Energy-efficiency programmes have been universally promoted as a means of attaining multiple policy objectives: helping net-energy importing countries in their balance-of-payments accounts, reducing costs for households and firms, enhancing national security, and improving environmental outcomes.[67] Given the widespread policy emphasis on energy efficiency, there is a clear need to assess how well such policies have fared in practice. Energy-efficiency policies include subsidies, mandatory standards, and labelling and information provisions that attempt to encourage energy-efficient investments but do not directly affect energy prices.[68]

The roots of today's widespread adoption of energy-efficiency policies date back to the 1970s. Energy security concerns arose amid the crisis environment of the oil price shocks, and stimulated major regulatory attempts to boost efficiency in several OECD countries. The United Kingdom, for instance, launched an energy saving campaign in December 1973 as a direct policy response to the 1973 crisis.[69] Automobile fuel efficiency standards were first established by the U.S. federal government in the Energy Policy and Conservation Act of 1975, and Japan established the Law Concerning the Rational Use of Energy in 1979 during the second oil crisis, a law that continues to form the cornerstone of the country's present-day energy-efficiency policies.[70] By the end of the 1970s, most developed countries had adopted a range of energy-efficiency policies, including R&D programmes, financial incentives and subsidies, energy-efficiency standards, and information and educational efforts.

Recent Trends in Energy Intensity in the Asia-Pacific

Developing countries were slower to begin implementing energy-efficiency policies, but by the 1990s most of the major economies in the Asia-Pacific region had policy frameworks in place. Before 1980, China emphasized rapid economic growth and paid little attention to energy efficiency, leading to high energy-intensity levels. From 1981 onward, though, China initiated extensive reforms to its energy policy with a much greater emphasis on energy conservation in its subsequent five-year plans.[71] In India, concerns about efficiency and conservation began to formally influence energy policy as far back as 1974, and a draft of the Energy Conservation Bill was completed in 1988, though it was only passed as an act of parliament in 2001.[72]

Over the past decade, mounting concerns over global climate change have made the emission mitigation potential of energy-efficiency investments a declared core benefit for many policymakers as well. In its latest *World Energy Outlook 2012*, the IEA predicted that if a reduction occured in global carbon dioxide (CO_2) emissions from the business-as-usual (BAU) path, it is likely to be driven largely by energy-efficiency measures.[73] In IEA projections, energy-efficiency policies account for 68 per cent and 70 per cent of the cumulative global reduction in energy use and CO_2 emissions respectively, in the "new policies scenario" relative to the "current policies scenario" by 2035. Energy efficiency policies thus have a much more significant effect than either renewables or nuclear energy in IEA's long-run outlook.[74] If energy security and dependence on imports of fossil fuels were the initiating policy concerns for energy efficiency during the 1970s and 1980s, emission mitigation and the "green growth" aspects of efficiency improvements now occupy a central place in the rationale for energy-efficiency policies across the Asia-Pacific region.

Most countries now implement a range of policy instruments targeted at improving energy efficiency across various economic sectors. A 2007 survey conducted by the World Energy Council (WEC) in seventy-six major countries (accounting for 83 per cent of the world's energy consumption) found that two-thirds of the countries have set up energy-efficiency agencies, while almost half of the countries have adopted national energy-efficiency programmes.[75] Close to half of the countries surveyed by the WEC have adopted laws with quantitative targets for energy efficiency.[76] Table 5.6 lists energy-efficiency targets adopted by major countries around the world as well as selected Asia-Pacific countries.

As of 2012, most major economies — with the notable exception of the United States — and a number of smaller countries have adopted economy-wide energy-efficiency targets. There is considerable heterogeneity in how these targets are framed. At the economy-wide level, measures of energy intensity (expressed as the amount of energy used to produce a dollar of GDP) are often the most-widely used metric to assess trends in energy use over time and across countries. Almost all the countries set targets relative to either energy intensity or aggregate energy consumption, though

Table 5.6
Energy Efficiency Targets of Selected Countries

Country	Nature of Target	Base Year	Target Date
EU	Reduce primary energy consumption by 20%	BAU 2020	2020
USA	No target	n/a	n/a
Japan	Reduce energy intensity by 30%	2003	2030
Brazil	Reduce projected power consumption by 10%	2011	2030
China	Reduce energy intensity by 16%	2011	2015
India	Improve energy efficiency by 20%	2007	2012
Thailand	Reduce energy intensity by 25%	2005	2030
Philippines	Reduce total annual energy demand of all sectors by 10%	2009	2030

Sources: IEA, *World Energy Outlook 2012*; Balachandra P., Ravindranath D., and Ravindranath N.H. (2010); "Energy Efficiency in India: Assessing the Policy Regimes and Their Impacts", *Energy Policy*, pp. 6428–38; European Commission, "Europe 2020 Targets" <http://ec.europa.eu/europe2020/targets/eu-targets/index_en.htm>; Asia Pacific Energy Research Center (APERC), "Compendium of Energy Efficiency Policies of APEC Economies", 2010; Ministry of Energy, Thailand, *Thailand 20-Year Energy Efficiency Development Plan* (Bangkok, 2011).

neither are reliable indicators of underlying energy-efficiency trends. One reason for this is simply the ease with which these measures can be computed and interpreted.[77] A more substantial reason is that from the standpoint of improving energy security and reducing GHG emissions, the relevant indicator is consumption, and it does not necessarily matter whether the target is achieved through efficiency improvements or through compositional changes in the economy towards less energy-intensive industries.

Despite the limitations of these metrics, there is evidence of aggregate achievement on reducing both energy intensity and energy consumption. According to the IEA, the annual rate of decline in global energy intensity averaged 1.2 per cent over 1980–2000 but slowed considerably to 0.5 per cent between 2000 and 2010.[78] After the onset of recession, global energy intensity actually increased in 2009 and 2010. While the global economic slowdown contracted the denominator in the energy-intensity ratio, the decline in energy consumption was evidently not as pronounced. The latest data by the IEA suggests that energy intensity improved by 0.6 per cent in 2011, getting back into alignment with the long-term trend of the past decade.

Figure 5.5 shows how energy intensity in various countries has evolved since 1980. Two broad patterns can be discerned: richer countries tend to have lower energy-intensity levels, and energy-intensity levels have fallen across the last three decades in most countries in the sample. As major natural resource producers, Canada and Australia are at higher absolute levels than the EU. The levels of the United States lie between Australia and Canada. Japan has the lowest intensity ratios among the OECD group, although given low or negligible economic growth rates over the past two decades, its rate of energy intensity improvement since the 1990s is marginal.

The picture for developing Asia is mixed. Rapidly industrializing countries such as Thailand, Malaysia, and South Korea show no improvements in trends. In contrast, the larger developing countries with lower per capita incomes, such as India and China, show dramatic improvements in energy intensity, reflecting both the rapid economic growth rates and the very low initial levels of energy efficiency as these countries began their impressive economic growth trajectories in the 1980s and 1990s. Most dramatic has been the nearly fivefold fall in energy intensity in China between 1980 and 2010, although China still remains one of the

Figure 5.5
Energy Intensities in Selected Countries, 1980–2010

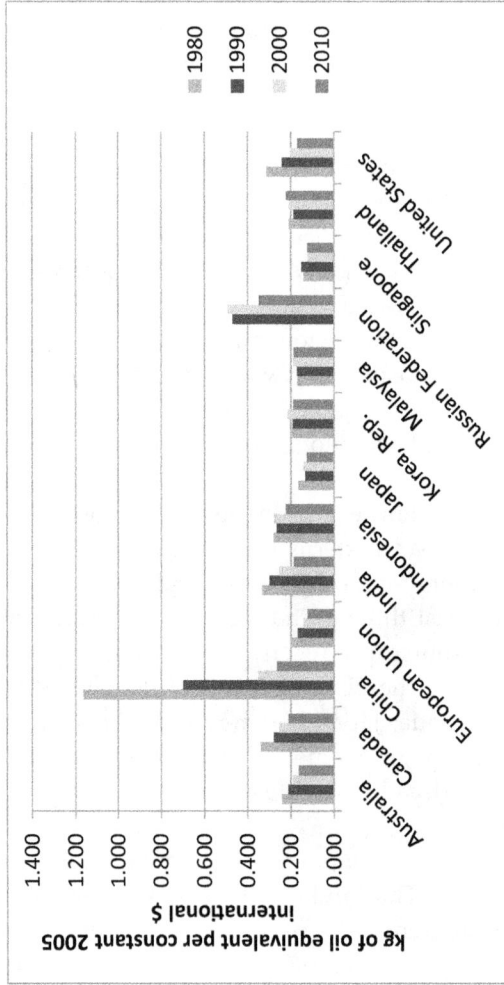

Source: Authors' calculations based on World Bank, *World Development Indicators*, 2012.

most energy-intensive major economies. While energy intensity tends to be higher in developing countries than in the OECD economies, there has been rapid convergence over the past three decades. According to the IEA, the ratio between the highest and lowest values has declined from a factor of nine in the 1980s to just below five today.[79]

An analysis of energy consumption in the Asia-Pacific presents a likewise nuanced view of energy-efficiency improvements in the region. Figure 5.6 illustrates the percentage growth of energy consumption divided by the percentage growth in GDP (measured in purchasing power parity terms) for various countries between 1980 and 2010.[80] The value is less than 0.2 in China, the EU, and the United States, implying that energy consumption grew at a rate more than five times smaller than the growth in GDP. In contrast, in middle-income rapidly industrializing countries, such as Malaysia and Thailand, energy use has grown at a faster rate than GDP.

However, using simple energy/GDP ratios to compare the energy-efficiency levels across countries is misleading. Such ratios conflate different effects, including initial resource endowments, the evolving composition of economies towards more or less energy-intensive sectors, the impact of price trajectories of various fuels and the rising incomes of households and firms in growing economies. For instance, it is to be expected that Australia, endowed with abundant energy resources, would specialize in energy-intensive extractive and industrial processing sectors, while Japan, devoid of its own energy resources, would tend to economize in its use of energy. In theory, both countries could be energy efficient relative to their factor endowments and comparative advantage, despite their divergence in energy intensities.

Energy-efficiency Policies and Measures in the Asia-Pacific

Different countries have adopted varying approaches and emphasized different targets in their national initiatives. Given the consistent and long-running policy emphasis on energy efficiency across the Asia-Pacific region, the descriptive literature on the subject is voluminous.[81] In its dedicated web page on energy efficiency, the IEA has collated among the most comprehensive databases of energy-efficiency initiatives undertaken by governments in both the OECD and non-OECD economies of the world. The IEA's energy-efficiency database lists "policies and measures"

Figure 5.6
Energy/GDP 'Elasticity', 1980–2010

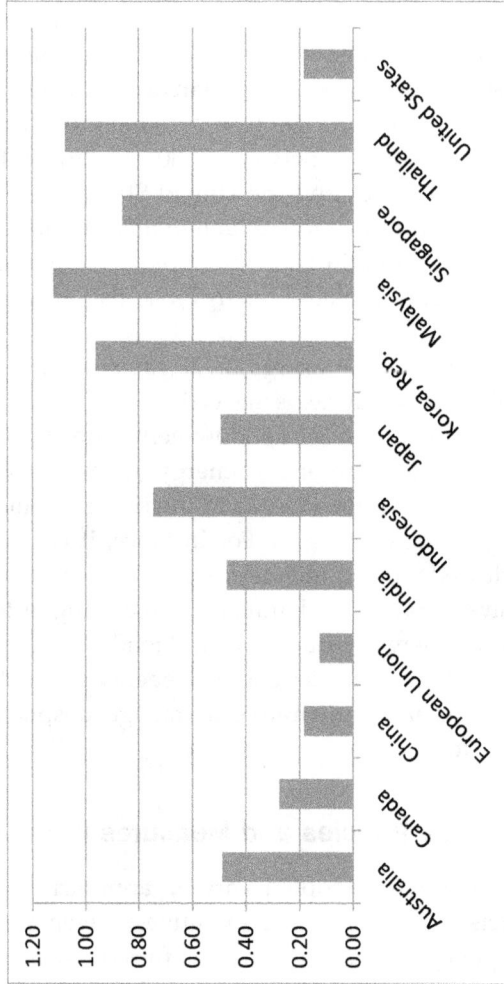

Source: Authors' calculations based on World Bank, *World Development Indicators*, 2012.

under six categories — economic instruments, policy support, regulatory instruments, information and education, voluntary approaches, and research, development, and deployment — and breaks down efforts into a range of target sectors, including buildings, commercial and industrial equipment, energy utilities, industry, lighting, residential appliances and transport.[82]

Buildings

Buildings account for a third of the world's total energy consumption.[83] Most OECD countries have mandatory codes for new and existing buildings, and such standards are being increasingly implemented in the developing countries. Direct energy-efficiency improvements in buildings, according to McKinsey's global GHG abatement cost curve, could potentially account for roughly 1.7 gigatonnes of CO_2 equivalent ($GtCO_2e$) out of a total of around 12 $GtCO_2e$ of cost-effective positive global abatement potential every year until 2030.[84] The most significant among such regulations are building energy codes, that is, energy-efficiency requirements for new buildings where it is much less costly to integrate energy-efficiency design and equipment improvements. Building energy codes can also serve as the efficiency target for refurbishments or other improvements of existing buildings.[85] By 2003, most APEC economies had implemented building energy codes, although there were significant differences in coverage (residential vs commercial buildings) and compliance mechanisms (voluntary vs mandatory codes). In addition, a range of other policies have been used to promote energy-efficiency improvements in buildings, including energy-performance labelling, financial incentives for energy management and energy audits, government "test beds" and demonstration projects, information and awareness programmes, and R&D support.

Appliances

The technical potential for energy-efficiency improvements in appliances is considerable according to engineering studies. The Lawrence Berkeley National Laboratory estimates that energy-efficient standards and labelling programmes aimed at improving the energy efficiency of equipment (including both appliances and lighting) can potentially lead to savings of 3,860 terawatt hours (TWh) of electricity and 1,041 TWh of fuel per year by 2030.[86] To put those savings in context, the world's total electricity generation in 2010 was 21,325 TWh.[87]

Efficiency improvements in appliances in industrialized economies over the past thirty years have been driven primarily by standards, labelling, and incentive purchase schemes. There has been a proliferation of energy-efficiency standards and labelling programmes around the world, rising from only twelve in 1990 (largely concentrated in industrialized economies) to more than sixty in 2005 (including many in developing economies).[88] Almost all member economies of the IEA have Minimum Energy Performance Standards (MEPS) and associated labelling programmes for appliances, and all of them have policies in place to increase energy efficiency in lighting.[89]

Transport

Transportation accounted for approximately 19 per cent of global final energy consumption in 2010.[90] The IEA notes that policies that help to improve vehicle fuel economy are among the most cost-effective measures for achieving an overall CO_2 reduction target of 50 per cent below 2005 levels by 2050 across the transport sector.[91] Most OECD countries, including the EU and Japan, have pursued improvements in fuel efficiency of internal combustion engine vehicles via high indirect taxes on petrol and diesel sales. The EU countries, in particular, have among the highest petrol taxes in the world.[92] In contrast, the United States has very low tax rates on transport fuels. There is a high degree of correlation between end-use prices and taxes on transportation fuels: whereas the highest taxes and prices tend to be in Europe, the United States has both the lowest tax and the lowest fuel price among the OECD countries. The United States has instead pursued energy-efficiency improvements primarily through mandated fleet efficiency standards on manufacturers, known as the Corporate Average Fuel Economy (CAFE) standards that were first implemented in 1975 (making the United States one of the first countries to adopt mandatory fuel economy standards).[93]

Industry

In 2010, the industrial sector (excluding energy transformation industries, such as refineries and power plants) accounted for 28 per cent of worldwide final energy consumption. However, the energy transformation sector, which converts primary energy into final energy for end-use sectors, is itself a major user of energy, accounting for 31 per cent of worldwide primary energy consumption in 2010.[94] Thus, over half of the world's primary energy supply is consumed in industry if the energy transformation sector is included.

In spite of this, the bulk of global energy-efficiency policy efforts have centred on non-industrial energy use. This is in part because of the extreme heterogeneity of the industrial sector, ranging from energy-intensive sectors such as cement and steel plants to light industries that use little energy.[95] Regulations in Japan include efficiency standards (e.g., for combustion and heating equipment) as well as obligations for industrial energy users to develop conservation plans, hire certified energy managers, and report energy-consumption levels.[96] Japan has also established tax incentives, subsidies, and low-interest loans for industrial energy-efficiency measures and adoption of energy-saving technologies. The United States has adopted standards that cover industrial equipment (e.g., induction motors), provides loan guarantees for commercial projects that adopt energy-efficient technologies, and offers technical assistance programmes to help industries identify energy conservation strategies.[97] In Europe, voluntary agreements have formed a major element of industrial energy-efficiency policy efforts, with the governments offering low-interest loans and other financial incentives in return for industries agreeing to increase their energy efficiency.[98]

Several countries have also implemented policies specifically directed towards improving power-generation efficiency. This is motivated by the fact that globally the power-generation sector alone consumes an amount of energy roughly equal to the energy consumed by the remainder of the industrial sector and greater than that consumed by the transportation sector.[99] These policies include utility demand-side management programmes that have been widely used in the United States. Under these programmes, utilities are required to operate energy-efficiency programmes, for instance by adopting time-of-use pricing to discourage peak demand or by providing cash incentives to consumers to reduce electricity demand when requested.[100] A number of countries have also implemented policies to directly enhance the efficiency of power generation by expanding the use of combined heat and power (CHP) systems, or cogeneration, through policies such as subsidies and other financial incentives for CHP (in Japan, the EU, and several U.S. states) as well as mandates requiring utilities to purchase electricity from cogenerators (in the United States).[101]

Energy Efficiency Initiatives in Singapore

Singapore considers energy efficiency as a key strategy to achieving its energy policy objectives. According to MTI's National Energy Policy Report, energy efficiency is seen as a solution across multiple objectives: "Using less energy will help reduce our dependence on imports and enhance our energy security, while at the same time cut down our CO_2 intensity, air pollution, and business costs."[102] Energy efficiency projects are thus meant to serve as a cost-effective means of contributing to the three fundamental policy objectives of economic competitiveness, energy security, and environmental sustainability. The National Environment Agency (NEA) of Singapore set up the inter-agency Energy Efficiency Programme Office (E²PO) in May 2007 to identify and implement measures to improve Singapore's energy efficiency in six priority areas, namely, power generation, industry, transport, buildings, the public sector, and households.[103]

In seeking a comprehensive energy efficiency strategy and master plan for the country, the E²PO has devised action plans that centre on the promotion of energy efficiency technologies and measures to overcome market barriers to energy efficiency, build local expertise and a knowledge base in energy management, raise the visibility of energy efficient practices in industry, and promote R&D in energy efficient technologies.[104]

Power Sector and Industry

In the power generation sector, the implementation of a competitive electricity market has improved power generation efficiency. From 2000 to 2006, the electricity generated by natural gas increased from 19 per cent to 78 per cent and the overall power generation efficiency increased from 38 per cent in 2000 to 44 per cent in 2006.[105] Cogeneration refers to the integrated production of heat and electricity, while trigeneration refers to the integrated production of electricity, heat, and chilled water. These technologies optimize the heat utilization from fuel combustion and improve overall system efficiency.

According to the E^2PO, cogeneration and trigeneration technologies should be promoted in view of the energy efficiency potential offered by these technologies. However, a challenge to the large-scale uptake of these technologies is the necessity for combined demand for electricity and heating; furthermore, space considerations come into play as cogeneration and trigeneration facilities have to be sited in close proximity to industries in need of the utilities. Nevertheless, given the vast improvements in energy efficiency that these technologies entail, the government plans to integrate such facilities into ongoing and future industrial planning.

Before industries can embark on any energy efficiency improvement path, there is a need to appraise energy usage patterns and the scope of the improvements that can be brought about. Thus, an energy appraisal is called for to identify degraded plant components that contribute to overall efficiency losses and to enable a company to take the necessary corrective actions. However, companies might be reluctant to bear the upfront cost of carrying out an energy appraisal. The Energy Efficiency Improvement Assistance Scheme (EASe) was instituted to help companies overcome this perceived barrier. It is meant to help companies which may not have the in-house energy management expertise to conduct energy appraisals. Under EASe, NEA co-funds up to 50 per cent of the cost of energy appraisals for buildings and industrial facilities. According to the NEA, each dollar spent on an energy appraisal uncovers about S$5–10 annual savings in energy costs.[106]

There are several other such schemes for the industrial sector that have been instituted to facilitate improvements in energy efficiency. The most cost-effective way of improving energy efficiency can often lie at the project conceptualization and design stage itself. With this in mind, the E^2PO introduced a Design for Efficiency Scheme to assist companies take into account energy efficiency considerations in the project design phase. The ninth furnace of the Singapore Olefins Plant (of Exxon Mobil Chemical Ltd), which was commissioned in 2007, was built under this scheme. Under another initiative, the EDB administers the Investment Allowance (IA) Scheme to promote investments in energy efficient equipment by giving a capital allowance on the cost of certain energy efficient equipment. It is awarded if energy utilization falls as a consequence of the capital expenditure. The government also launched the Energy Efficiency National Partnership (EENP) programme in 2010 to help companies put in place energy management systems and implement projects to improve energy efficiency. The government will be introducing mandatory energy management requirements for large energy users which consume more than 15 Gigawatt-hour (GWh) in the industry sector, under the Energy Conservation Act.[107]

Transportation

In the transportation sector, the Land Transport Authority (LTA) will continue its efforts of making public transportation the mode of choice. In order to make this happen, two more Mass Rapid Transit (MRT) lines will be functional by 2018, an increase in around 215 km of railway lines from its 2007 level. The goal is to have a modal split for the morning peak hours from the current 63 per cent to over 70 per cent in the next 10 to 15 years. Certificates of Entitlement (COEs) give Singaporeans the right to own a vehicle. COEs are integral to the Vehicle Quota System (VQS), a landmark scheme implemented to regulate the growth of vehicle population in Singapore. Under the VQS, vehicle annual growth rate is capped at 3 per cent, given the constrained expansion of roads and highways in Singapore's urban environment. The actual compound annual growth rate of vehicle population from 1990 to 2008 was 2.8 per cent per annum. From 2009 to 2011, the vehicle population growth rate has been capped at 1.5 per cent per annum.[108] To encourage energy efficiency in the road transportation sector, fuel economy labels are affixed to vehicles at the point of sale so as to inform the consumer of the vehicle's fuel economy in clear terms. The purchase of cleaner and more efficient vehicles such as hybrid cars and electric vehicles is being promoted via the Green Vehicle Rebate, which is a rebate of 40 per cent of the car's open market value.

Buildings

Give the urban landscape in Singapore, efficiency improvements in the building sector are important considerations. The Building and Construction Authority (BCA) of Singapore launched the BCA Green Mark Scheme in January 2005 to promote environmental awareness in the construction and real estate sectors. Buildings are awarded Certified, Gold, Gold[Plus], or Platinum rating depending on the points scored on the key criteria, including energy efficiency. New and retrofitted buildings with a gross floor area (GFA) above 5,000 m^2 that achieve a "Gold" Green Mark and above will be awarded cash incentives based on the GFA and Green Mark rating achieved. Since April 2008, all new and existing buildings undergoing major retrofitting works with a GFA above 2,000 m^2 must meet Green Mark Certified standards. The BCA Green Mark Scheme promotes adoption of green building technologies and reduces the use of electricity in the commercial sector via efficiency improvements and conservation.[109]

In 2005, the NEA and the Energy Sustainability Unit (ESU) of the National University of Singapore launched the EnergySmart Labelling Scheme to recognize energy efficient office buildings in Singapore. Buildings that perform in the top 25 per cent in terms of energy efficiency and meet good indoor air quality standards are eligible for the EnergySmart Building Label. This scheme was extended to include hotels in 2007. The EASe scheme is also applicable for the building sector so as to promote the appraisal of energy utilization of buildings in Singapore. In the case of building standards, there is some uncertainty as to how effective such standards setting will be in the long run, even if one can make relatively detailed calculations about expected energy savings from engineering measurements.

Labelling and Information Provision

As of 2006, the household sector accounted for around a fifth of Singapore's electricity consumption. Refrigeration and air conditioning were the household appliances that contributed the most to this consumption. The policy direction at reducing energy use in this sector revolves around encouraging consumers to buy energy-efficient appliances and to opt for more energy-efficient habits. The Energy Labelling Scheme requires that energy labels, which inform the consumer as to the electricity consumption of the appliance, are affixed to the appliances at the point of sale (akin to a vehicle energy labelling scheme). As of 2008, all household refrigerators and air conditioners that are sold in Singapore are energy labelled. In order to educate consumers and put them along a path to more energy efficient behaviour, the NEA has embarked on a national campaign, called the 10% Energy Challenge, that will promote electricity saving in households by advocating the complete turning off of appliances when not in use. This is purported to reduce electricity consumption by around 10 per cent.

Since January 2008, "registrable" goods have had to carry energy labels under the Environmental Protection and Management Act (EPMA).[110]

Currently, all household refrigerators, air conditioners, and clothes dryers sold in Singapore must be energy labelled. Vehicle fuel economy labels are also affixed to vehicles at the point of sale. The mandatory energy labelling scheme will improve energy efficiency and mitigate growth of energy use in residential, commercial, and transport sectors.

Assessing Energy-efficiency Policies: The "Energy-efficiency Gap"

Despite the vital role energy efficiency is envisaged to play in cutting energy demand cost effectively, it is often claimed that "only a small part of its economic potential is exploited".[111] The fact that cost-effective options to improve energy efficiency are not being adopted on a large scale has led to notions of an "energy-efficiency gap". The efficiency gap, or the difference between the level of efficiency actually achieved and the level judged to be optimal at prevailing prices, has generated considerable debate in policy circles as well as in academic literature. This paradox — the non-adoption or slow diffusion of apparently cost-effective energy-efficient technologies — has been the basis of many studies on market barriers that seem to discourage investments in such technologies.[112]

The notion of "barriers" to energy-efficiency choices, understood as market conditions that discourage energy-efficiency investments relative to an estimated optimal level, is a staple of many large-scale studies of energy efficiency. One meta-study conducted for the U.S. Department of Energy's National Energy Strategy, which reviewed U.S. energy-efficiency literature written prior to 1990, concluded that "the constraint on efficiency improvements in the short term is not primarily technical. The primary barrier is insufficient implementation of existing cost-efficient technologies."[113] In a recent well-publicized study of energy options for the United States, McKinsey and Company notes: "By 2020, the United States could reduce annual energy consumption by 23 per cent from BAU baseline projections by deploying an array of NPV-positive [net present value-positive] efficiency measures.... This potential exists because significant barriers impede the deployment of energy-efficient practices and technologies."[114] Similarly, in its recent in-depth assessment of energy efficiency, the IEA observes "the existence of a number of barriers that discourage decision makers, such as households and firms, from making the best economic choices."[115]

Subsidies and Financial Incentives

Credit unavailability is often cited as a market barrier to energy-efficiency investments.[116] The lack of access to credit might force some purchasers to choose less energy-efficient products resulting in underinvestment in energy efficiency. In a similar vein, high initial costs of energy-efficient technologies are often identified as a market barrier. This has provided a rationale to governments to offer financial incentives as a means of alleviating credit constraints or the high initial costs of investments. However, it is not clear as to why credit constraints should affect investments specifically in energy efficiency. Households or firms that are precluded from energy-efficient investments, due to budget constraints, are similarly precluded from all profitable investments that cost the same amount of money; the constraining factor is that incomes or budgets are too low, not that credit is not forthcoming or that initial costs are too high.

One rationale for government subsidies and financial incentives for encouraging energy-efficiency investments relates to the claim that consumers typically put too little weight on future energy savings and too much on upfront costs when buying appliances. For example, a much-cited early study of consumer purchases of air conditioners found "implicit discount rates" of about 20 per cent, much higher than market interest rates.[117] The empirical evidence, however, is mixed: in an econometric study of used cars, for example, the authors estimated the rate of interest implicit in a consumer's valuation of the discounted costs of the vehicle's lifetime operating costs and found that it was in the 11–17 per cent range, consistent with prevailing market interest rates for car loans.[118] Uncertainty over future energy savings, hidden costs such as the cognitive costs of searching for new products or reductions in other desirable product characteristics, the irreversibility of investments, and the associated option value of waiting are some of the reasons offered by economists to explain high discount rates. Indeed, for some economists, the so-called myopic behaviour of consumers who underrate future energy savings is consistent with standard rationality assumptions of economic decision-making.[119]

Engineering studies of energy efficiency calculate the net present value (NPV) of the particular appliance or machinery chosen based on assumptions of capital costs, current and future fuel prices, average duration and frequency of use, and discount rates. However, engineering estimates by their very nature omit relevant variables that drive actual purchase or investment decisions and cannot capture the heterogeneity of preferences across households and firms. In many cases, energy efficiency is only one among many attributes considered in the decision to invest or buy any particular energy-using equipment or durable good.

A typical example of the variance between *ex ante* engineering analysis and *ex post* studies that take into account observed consumer responses is a Mexican government subsidy programme to replace older refrigerators and air conditioners with more efficient ones. The subsidies were projected to save energy by 30 per cent; however, a follow-up analysis of the programme estimated energy savings of only 7 per cent once actual consumer responses were observed.[120] Buyers chose larger refrigerators with newer energy-using features, while many lowered their thermostat temperatures or installed more air-conditioning units in their homes as a result of the subsidy. The "rebound effect" of cheaper energy on energy demand have been widely noted, but are not captured by the estimates often provided by manufacturers and installers of various energy systems.

Another study found that realized returns from home insulation were only a fraction of the returns estimated by product engineers and manufacturers.[121] In a well-cited study of "demand-side management" conservation programmes pursued by U.S. utilities, it was found that "some of these programmes appear to be uneconomical even before correcting for biases in utility-cost accounting and in the measurement of actual electricity savings.... Furthermore, it is likely that the values for the cost per kWh [kilowatt-hour] saved that we derive from utility reports understate their true costs by a factor of two or more on average."[122]

Given the unreliability of much of the *ex ante* analysis that project energy savings from various government subsidies for efficiency programmes, it is not clear whether such subsidies have generally been cost effective. For instance, the European Court of Auditors recently reported that EU spending on programmes to spur energy savings have "gone to waste", and some of its building insulation projects were found to be "so inefficient that it would take longer than the lifetime of an improved building to recover the costs".[123]

Mandated Standards

Governments have implemented an array of standards based on technology and performance-based criteria to promote energy efficiency. Building codes, minimum energy performance standards for consumer durables, and standards for fuel efficiency in automobiles are some of the more obvious examples of government-mandated standards. These standards are usually implemented on a cost-benefit analysis (CBA) basis that purports to show the net benefits which result from restricting private choices by mandatory standards.

Perhaps one of the most debated examples of mandated standards in the literature is the regulation of CAFE for vehicles by the National Highway Traffic Safety Administration (NHTSA) in the United States. In December 2011, the NHTSA and the Environmental Protection Agency (EPA) proposed new fuel economy standards for passenger cars and light trucks for model years 2015 through 2025. The EPA and NHTSA used CBA to compute the NPV of CAFE standards utilizing key variables, including the discount rate, miles driven annually, miles driven as a response to a change in fuel costs, increases in driving due to improvements in fuel efficiency (i.e., the "rebound effect"), projections of fuel prices, the lifetime of the vehicle, and the relationship between measured and actual on-road fuel efficiency. The CBA conducted by the agencies is essentially based on the cost of the vehicle and its miles-per-gallon efficiency. However, fuel efficiency is only one attribute among many when the purchasing decision is made, along with other attributes such as safety, style, speed, and comfort. The analysis thus ignores the loss in consumer welfare if mandated fuel efficiency standards lead to changes in other desired characteristics of a car.[124]

The NHTSA estimates total cost of implementing CAFE standards at US$177 billion and total benefit at US$521 billion.[125] While environmental and energy security benefits account for US$81 billion, the remaining US$440 billion of benefits are attributed to private savings to consumers. With such large benefits accruing to car buyers, the obvious question arises as to why mandated CAFE standards are required in the first place. As the NHTSA itself concedes, the organization is "unable to reach a conclusive answer to the question of why the apparently large differences between its estimates of benefits from requiring higher fuel economy and the costs of supplying it do not result in higher average fuel economy for new cars and light trucks".[126] Put differently, why do manufacturers fail to provide higher fuel economy even in the absence of increases in CAFE standards, given the very large private benefits estimated by NHTSA's analysis?

Among the reasons offered by the NHTSA in explaining the results of its study are inadequate consumer information on the value of improved fuel economy, the low weight consumers typically place on long-term savings, the lack of salience of fuel savings in the purchasing decision, and ignorance on the part of manufacturers regarding the premiums consumers are willing to pay for improved fuel economy. To many economists, such explanations remain unconvincing in that they fail to establish the case that strict mandates are warranted rather than education campaigns that would offer consumers the basis to make better purchasing decisions.[127] Furthermore, mandated standards, unlike outright taxpayer-funded subsidies, lack explicit cost information and hence make them easier to legislate. The hidden costs of mandatory standards are, in the first instance, imposed on manufacturers and suppliers, and the ultimate cost to consumers is not transparent.

Labels and Information Programmes

Governments in the Asia-Pacific region have implemented a range of information provision and labelling programmes for buildings, appliances, and the transportation and industrial sectors. Information programmes can simply provide data (such as fuel-economy labels) or actively seek to encourage behavioural changes, such as Japan's Cool Biz programme that encourages setting air conditioners at 28°C and allowing employees to dress casually in the summer.[128] These programmes have been popular due to the relatively low costs of implementing them, but there is sparse evidence on how effective they actually are at reducing informational market failures.

Decisions made on the basis of costly or incomplete information will differ from those made with free and complete information. The appropriate question then is not whether information on energy efficiency is deficient but under what conditions do private markets fail to supply such information at optimal levels. Clearly, when information on energy efficiency has the property of a public good (i.e., when its consumption cannot be effectively excluded from use and where use by one individual does not reduce availability to others), governments can play a useful role in providing increased access to such information for firms and households.

There is another class of market failures arising from information asymmetry in which one party to a transaction has more or better information than the other party. The principal-agent or "split-incentive" problem describes a situation where the agent (for example, a builder or landlord) decides the level of energy efficiency in a building, while the principal (such as the purchaser or tenant) pays the utility bills. When the principal has incomplete information about the energy efficiency of the building, the agent may not be able to recoup the costs of energy-efficiency investments in the purchase price or rent for the building. The agent will then underinvest in energy efficiency relative to the social optimum, creating a market failure.[129] One policy solution for this sort of market failure could be the provision of credible information by a disinterested third party (possibly a government agency) about a building's energy attributes, so that buyers or renters can credibly ascertain the present value of net energy savings.

Perhaps the body of literature most influential in assessing choices in energy use at the micro-level is behavioural economics, which uses cognitive psychology and experimental disciplines to understand how individuals make decisions. Behavioural economics has drawn attention to systematic biases in decision-making that may be relevant to decisions regarding investment in energy efficiency. Behavioural failures in the context of energy-efficient investments centre on the themes of "bounded rationality" and heuristic decision-making.[130] For instance, consumers are sometimes unable to optimize their energy consumption in response to a tiered-rate structure of electricity prices[131] or a large proportion of consumers might fail to use pre-installed programmable thermostats that could help them save on their energy bills.[132] However, the empirical literature testing behavioural failures specifically in the context of energy decision-making is still very limited.[133]

In the analysis of the various behavioural attributes of individual decision making in energy technology choices, it is important to note that there may be instances where no necessary policy implications emerge. For example, in making decisions regarding the purchase of durable energy-efficient equipment, it may be rational for firms or households to wait before adopting a particular new technology or product due to uncertainty. As there is no presumption of market failure in this instance, there is no case for a policy response to those who rationally see an option value in waiting in the presence of uncertainty, consistent with standard economic theory.[134] There also may be cases where individual preferences do not match the product characteristics of new energy-efficient products.

For example, consumers may not adopt compact fluorescent lights due to a noticeable difference in the quality of light they emit.

While people might use psychological heuristics to process complex options, it does not necessarily mean that such behavioural anomalies are pervasive and of great consequence to the economy.[135] One should not overstate the policy differences brought on by the contrasts between mainstream analysis and some of the newer studies in behavioural economics. In particular, if the findings of behavioural economics are to be used to justify government regulations, the extent to which alleged behavioural anomalies affect individual choices need to be established and empirically measured in randomized trials. If private decisions look flawed to "expert" views, informational mandates providing data and guidance on points of salience to firms and households should be remedy enough. It should not be presumed that government agencies, regulators, and analysts are better equipped to make decisions which claim to "protect consumers from themselves" or "help businessmen improve business practices". Policies or regulations that mandate or subsidize energy-efficient appliances or technologies may be justifiable, if at all, when information provision — the first-best solution to alleged ignorance on the part of consumers or businessmen — is demonstrated to be ineffective.

The Cost-effectiveness of Energy-efficiency Programmes

Despite the large literature on energy-efficiency and conservation efforts, there is a lack of independent *ex post* analyses using statistical methods to measure the cost of savings actually achieved. A predominant part of the work on quantitative estimates of energy-efficiency outcomes is done by government or multilateral agencies that implement or support conservation programmes (such as the EPA and the IEA) or by interested parties such as manufacturers and suppliers of energy-efficient appliances and equipment. Accurately measuring the costs and benefits of the different efficiency and conservation programmes is difficult for several reasons. Among the first challenges faced by any CBA of government energy-efficiency regulations is defining baselines in order to assess the improvements that would have occurred in the absence of regulations. We have also noted the problem of unobserved costs and benefits in standard *ex ante* engineering analysis that make it difficult to measure the welfare impacts of various regulations. Yet another issue relates to the existence of free riders, that is, those who receive subsidies for appliances or equipment that they would have bought anyway. The presence of rebound effects further complicates outcomes and often leads to an overestimation of energy savings.

With these caveats in mind, it is not surprising to find that the evidence on the cost effectiveness of energy-efficiency and conservation programmes is mixed. Given the wide range of government programmes and measures in place to encourage energy efficiency, few general conclusions can be derived regarding their overall efficacy. Recent empirical work based on randomized trials and *ex post* analyses suggests that "on average the magnitude of profitable unexploited investment opportunities is much smaller than engineering-accounting studies suggest".[136] While inefficiencies in energy use can appear in settings where market failures are apparent, there is little rigorous evidence to suggest the vast and pervasive energy-efficiency gap that is promulgated by some of the studies cited in the literature.

Is Singapore Energy Efficient?

Singapore does not provide subsidies for energy fuels, and this has been a consistent feature of Singapore's economic growth model. The cost of imported fuels to generate electricity is passed through to end consumers, and retail transport fuels costs (after excise taxes) in Singapore are comparable to the high levels of Western Europe and Japan. As a general observation, then, there are no obvious areas where energy efficiencies in major sectors such as transport, power generation, or oil refining and petrochemicals can be improved substantially under current cost conditions.

As specialized government agencies such as the Housing Development Board (HDB), BCA, LTA, and EMA with specific mission agendas begin to formulate and implement regulations in promoting energy-efficiency initiatives, it is critical that all such new regulations meet the tests of unbiased CBA. Faulty or misconceived notions of what accrue as costs and benefits, of course, can lead to unnecessary and significant burdens being imposed on various segments of businesses and households. The guiding principle to policy interventions is that they must improve societal welfare. Accordingly, energy efficiency should not be considered a goal in itself, but as a means of achieving economically efficient resource allocation.[137]

In general, the voluminous engineering and "management science" literature on energy efficiency fails to provide strong and credible evidence of persistent investor or consumer irrationality. For instance, one recent survey of industrial practice in Singapore found "the main problem is motivating companies to embrace energy efficiency.... various studies have identified the lack of top management support as a key barrier to energy efficiency".[138] Among other "barriers" identified are the inability to conduct energy audits, the lack of capable energy service companies, the lack of financial capital to invest in technology, resistance to change and fear of disrupting production, and "an inability to show returns on investments in energy efficiency projects".[139] However, it is not explained anywhere why senior management "lacked motivation" to pursue energy efficiency initiatives. If pursuing energy efficiency also raised shareholder value, the *raison d'etre* of company management boards, then why is it that such efforts are not forthcoming?

It may well be that energy-efficiency initiatives are just not worth the cost, or the scale of benefits is just too small to justify occupying the valued time of the company's executive management. The observed lack of various capabilities and motivation in promoting energy-efficiency investments may well reflect management decisions focused on maximizing profits, and is not *prima facie* evidence of "barriers" which need surmounting by official mandates and regulations. "An inability to show returns on investment in energy efficiency projects" begs the question: with the firms's typical cost of capital, and cost of management's time and effort, do these energy-efficiency projects pay for themselves? And as importantly, are these investments of such scale that they should occupy the time and consideration of the firm's executive officers? That is, even if the *rate of return* to a particular energy-efficiency investment is high at realistic discount rates, the return may not be of such absolute size ("materiality") relative to the company's total revenues to merit the attention of senior management in the company responsible for key investment decisions.

5.4 DEVELOP ENERGY INDUSTRIES AND INVEST IN R&D: THE CASE FOR SOLAR PV?

Advocates for industry development and R&D in the energy sector have been receiving much attention in policy circles as well as the mass media. High fossil fuel prices and concerns of global climate change have motivated interest particularly in renewable energy technologies among policymakers and ordinary citizens. Proponents of renewable energy advocate strong government support for non-fossil-fuel-based electricity generation. With additional purported benefits to energy security and the creation of "green" jobs, governments around the world have legislated subsidies such as feed-in tariffs (FITs) or other policy supports such as renewable portfolio standards (RPS) to compensate renewable energy producers with guaranteed higher tariff rates. These include not only several OECD countries, but also neighbouring developing countries in Southeast Asia such as Thailand and Malaysia more recently.

Singapore's support for R&D is substantial and it has funded a number of initiatives in promoting renewable energy resources, in particular on solar PV which seems to be the most relevant to the needs of urban Singapore. The Singapore government's policy support for renewable energy technologies have in the main focused on R&D and demonstration projects. Its policy interventions have not extended to funding overt subsidies such as FITs and RPS. Given the risks of "government failure", it is important to avoid the familiar route to the creation of favoured constituencies and the waste of public resources in attempts to support particular energy technologies by outright subsidies. Assessing the success of government-funded R&D programmes to support new energy technologies is an inherently difficult exercise given the uncertain and long-run nature of R&D outcomes. In general, the weight of evidence suggests that risks and rewards from commercial deployment of new energy technologies should be left to markets to determine, and government support for technology R&D should cease well before the development stage.

Singapore's Initiatives in Industry Development and R&D

Singapore invests a substantial amount of resources in its strategy of "developing energy industries and investing in R&D", which include promising areas of research in solar energy, biofuels, and fuel cells. In the past few years, Singapore has publicly funded a range of initiatives aimed at developing the city-state into a global "clean energy" hub where technologies are developed and tested. Singapore has been positioning itself as a test bed for novel technologies — a "living laboratory".[140] For instance, the National Research Foundation (NRF) has set aside S$170 million for R&D in clean energy (Clean Energy Programme).[141] The Agency for Science, Technology, and Research (A*STAR), Singapore's premier basic-sciences research institute, has established an Energy Technology

R&D Programme, and is setting up the Singapore Initiative in New Energy Technologies (SINERGY) Centre to develop alternative energy technologies and intelligent grid management systems for distributed generation ("smart grids").[142] Several test beds have been or are being conducted in Singapore. In the transportation sector, electric vehicles (EVs) are being tested to understand the implications of adoption of this technology in the Singapore context and its potential for mitigating CO_2 emissions.

No consolidated figures for government development and R&D spending on energy are given as a category in itself. Each of the ministries report expenditure breakdowns, and the most relevant for expenditures on energy-related projects are the MTI and the Ministry of the Environment and Water Resources (MEWR). The MTI budget lists expenditure in different energy-related projects, e.g., Jurong Rock Cavern Phase I, Clean Energy Research and Testbedding Programme (CERT), Solar Capability Scheme (SCS), Grant for Energy Efficient Technologies, Launch of Pilots for Energy Efficiency Financing, Solar Testbedding on Reservoirs, and Petroleum Engineering Professorships for Capability Development. MTI, as the reporting ministry for the EMA, funds the latter's budget. EMA's expenditures on industry development and R&D include the Pulau Ubin test bed for smart grids, the Energy Emissions Statistics Surveys, and the Manpower for Energy (M4E) project. MEWR is the reporting ministry for the NEA, and under the NEA expenditure budget, programme initiatives in energy R&D include the Grant for Energy Efficient Technologies, the Environment Technology Research Programme, and the Implementation of Enhanced Grant for Energy Efficient Technologies (GREET).

Statutory agencies such as the EDB and HDB have expenditures in this category as well. The EDB set up the inter-agency Clean Energy Programme Office (CEPO) to promote the clean energy industry, especially solar. The S$50 million Clean Energy Research Programme (CERP), funded by CEPO, was launched to kick-start R&D in clean energy.[143] The inter-agency Energy Innovation Programme Office (EIPO) has allocated an additional S$195 million from NRF to promote R&D in the energy sector in the five-year period to 2015. The EDB has also launched the S$17 million CERT to test solar photovoltaic (PV) and other new technologies.[144] The HDB has been testing the viability of rooftop solar PV electricity by launching a series of solar PV test beds in HDB precincts across Singapore since 2008. In 2009, HDB announced that it would conduct a wider-scale test of 3.1 megawatt-peak (MWp) of solar PV installations over a five-year period funded from the Inter-Ministerial Committee for Sustainable Development's (IMCSD) budget of S$31 million. Various incentive schemes have been put in place to assist in financing solar installations such as the Market Development Fund (S$5 million) by EMA, the SCS (S$20 million), and the CERT platform (S$17 million) by the EDB.

Two new energy institutes have been founded in the last five years. The Solar Research Institute of Singapore (SERIS) was launched at the National University of Singapore, established in 2008 with funding of S$130 million for five years to carry out advanced research in solar technology. In 2010, the S$200m Energy Research Institute @ NTU (ERI@N) was established. Its broad-based energy research programme includes energy materials, smart grids, solar energy, sustainable buildings, wind energy, and electro-mobility. More recently, in August 2014, the Energy Research Development and Demonstration Executive Committee reported that the Singapore government will spend S$100 million to fund two initiatives in energy R&D, specifically in building energy efficiency and research on green data centres.[145]

Data on total R&D expenditures by the government cannot easily be disaggregated into energy and non-energy categories. According to A*STAR, gross public expenditure on total R&D for 2010 was S$2.5 billion, up from S$2.32 billion in 2009, while business (private) expenditure for 2010 was S$3.95 billion, up from $3.73 billion in 2009. Total R&D, public and private, therefore rose from S$6 to S$6.5 billion, an increase of over 8 per cent in one year to 2010. The government has set aside S$16 billion for R&D for the period 2011 to 2015 under its Research, Innovation and Enterprise plan, in line with the long-term goal of lifting R&D spending to 3.5 per cent of the GDP. As can be seen from Table 5.7, Singapore's long-term goal in R&D spending at 3.5 per cent of GDP will place it among the top-ranking countries, including Israel, Japan, Sweden, Finland, and South Korea.

Outlook for Solar PV: Promising ... but Wait!

A renewable energy technology that has been seen as especially relevant to Singapore's needs is solar PV which directly transforms solar radiation into electrical energy.[146] As already noted, several initiatives to test solar PV have been conducted by statutory authorities such as the HDB. Solar PV systems are seen as potentially viable sources of renewable energy for Singapore given the country's equatorial location and the lack of

Table 5.7
Top R&D Spending Countries Plus China Ranked by % of GDP
(estimates for 2011)

Country	% of GDP	Rank (size)	Expenditures on R&D (billions of US$, PPP)
Israel	4.2%	18	9.4
Japan	3.3%	3	144.1
Sweden	3.3%	16	11.9
Finland	3.1%	25	6.3
South Korea	3.0%	5	44.8
USA	2.7%	1	405.3
Austria	2.5%	19	8.3
Denmark	2.4%	28	5.1
Taiwan	2.3%	13	19.0
Germany	2.3%	4	69.5
Switzerland	2.3%	20	7.5
Iceland	2.3%	59	0.3
Singapore	2.2%	26	6.3
France	1.9%	6	42.2
Canada	1.8%	9	24.3
United Kingdom	1.7%	7	38.4
Memo:			
China	1.4%	2	153.7

Source: "2011 Global R&D Funding Forecast", published by Batelle organization, December 2010 <http://www.battelle.org/aboutus/rd/2011.pdf>.

other renewable energy resources such as hydro, geothermal, wind, or tidal energy due to meteorological, geographical or space constraints. Under current technology, nuclear power is not seen as practical for land-constrained Singapore, but will remain as a long-term option several decades away.[147]

According to a report on solar PV commissioned by the National Climate Change Secretariat (NCCS), "it is very likely that grid parity in Singapore is expected to be achieved between 2014 and 2016, and cost parity to be achieved by 2020".[148] The report defines "grid parity" as the point where the cost of renewable electricity generation is equal to or cheaper than retail electricity prices, and "cost parity" as parity with the cost of traditional electricity generation (e.g., from fossil fuels) which includes the "cost of grid operation". As argued below, while it is relatively easy to assess the confidence level of the first claim, the second seems far more problematic.

Technological progress and increased production scale have rapidly driven down solar PV module costs. From an estimated average of US$2.50 per Watt peak (Wp) for multi-crystalline silicon modules in 2010, prices have fallen dramatically since then. A manufacturer survey at end-2011 found one-fifth of retailers quoting prices below US$2.00/Wp, with the lowest retailed price quoted at around US$1.25/Wp in the United States and Asia. At these module prices and under reasonable assumptions for other relevant factors such as the typical solar intensity (at the geographical location concerned), module efficiency, annual degradation of the performance of the module, and costs of installation, solar power is already at "grid parity" relative to the 2011 Singapore retail tariff rate. According to a recent assessment of solar PV under Singapore conditions, solar power can already be supplied at the same retail price Singapore customers were paying for conventional power from the grid in 2011.[149]

To evaluate the cost of electricity generated by different technologies over their economic life, the usual approach is to construct estimates of the levelized cost of electricity (LCOE). The LCOE provides an economic assessment of the costs of generating electricity over the plant's lifetime, including initial solar module costs, installation costs, costs of operation and maintenance, cost of fuel, and the (opportunity) cost of capital. If electricity is priced equal to the LCOE over the lifetime of the generating plant, the plant would "break even", i.e., the streams of its discounted revenues and costs would be equal.

It should be noted here that the appropriate discount rate to use in deriving the LCOE depends on the purpose of analysis. For household installation decisions, the appropriate rate would be the interest rate for a personal loan. For a business investment by a (profit-maximizing) private utility company, it would be a function of the company's cost of capital and its best alternative investment opportunity. Finally, for societal benefit, the appropriate discount rate would be the "social discount" rate imputed by government policy incorporating social cost-benefit calculus. In Singapore, personal loans at an annualized interest rate of 3–6 per cent are available for households to pay for installation of solar PV systems, so a 5 per cent discount rate is a reasonable assumption. For private businesses, a 10 per cent rate or higher is probably closer to the competitive needs of private capital investment.

Figure 5.7 below gives estimates for low (optimistic), base (neutral), and high (pessimistic) cases under two discount rates, i.e., rates at which

Figure 5.7
LCOE for the Low, Base, and High Case
(@ 5 per cent and 10 per cent discount rates)

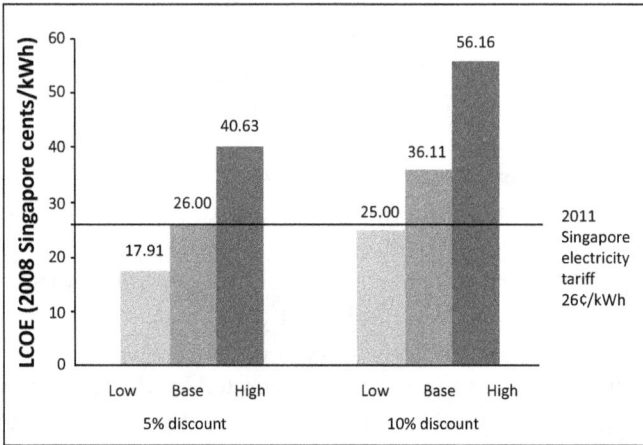

Note: Base case assumptions for calculations are 1100 kWh/kWp annual yield, 60 per cent for module cost/investment cost ratio and 0.75 per cent annual degradation rate, at a module cost of US$1.25/Wp.
Source: Doshi, T., D'Souza, N., Linh, N, Teo H.G. and Zahur, N., "The Economics of Solar PV in Singapore", op. cit.

upfront and future costs and benefits are converted to present value to make them comparable. At the 5 per cent discount rate, base case assumptions give an LCOE for solar power equal to the 2011 retail tariff of S$0.26 per kWh. So by this measure of "grid parity", under reasonable assumptions for all relevant parameters, solar PV could already pay for itself in Singapore under 2011 cost and price conditions.

However, "grid parity" — when solar power costs come down to levels which make it competitive to conventional fuels — is not a straightforward concept. In any electricity system, demand must equal supply at any given point of time in order to ensure system stability, since grid electricity cannot be economically stored. Given the need for continuous balancing of load, an electricity generating unit whose output can be controlled so as to match variations in load will be more valuable to the electricity grid than an intermittent or "non-dispatchable" electricity generating source. Intermittent sources, such as solar power, cannot dispatch power supplies into the grid when wholesale prices are high during peak usage times as they are not controlled by an operator ("dispatchable") as in a conventional electricity plant but depend on the weather, cloud cover, and daily solar cycles. As a result, intermittent sources tend to produce output that has a lower value than output from conventional sources of electricity generation, a matter which would naturally be of key concern to power generating companies. The LCOE methodology thus understates the true costs of electricity generated from intermittent sources.

The intermittency of renewable electricity technologies such as wind or solar PV makes balancing of the grid system a more complicated task. The ability to rapidly "ramp" up and down power generation is crucial when intermittent sources are connected to the system. Forecasting techniques and optimal grid distribution of intermittent sources might help alleviate the issues that arise; however, they do not eliminate them. Hence, system balancing considerations necessitate additional investment in backup generation and ramp-up and ramp-down capability. The amount of investment needed to handle the impact of intermittency on the electricity grid depends on a host of variables, including the size and configuration of the electricity system and the share of intermittent sources as a proportion of total electricity capacity (i.e., "penetration" level). According to the EMA, the Singapore grid can handle up to 350 MW of solar PV power, or about 3.5 per cent of total generating capacity; above this threshold, additional investments would be needed to stabilize the grid.[150]

While there have been a number of studies done on estimating costs of integrating intermittent sources of renewable energy, these studies are specific to the power systems studied and there are no reliable means of generalizing the results.[151] There is evidence, for example, to suggest that the link between penetration rate of intermittent power sources and balancing costs could be non-linear. In a study done for California, it was estimated that 3,000 MW of "regulation" reserves and 4,000 MW of "ramping" reserves from "fast" resources would be required if penetration rates of 33 per cent by intermittent sources were to be achieved by 2020.[152] This constitutes approximately 10 per cent of California's current installed capacity. The costs involved would have a significant impact on the state's average power tariffs if rate-payers are to foot the bill. Available data thus suggests that investment costs imposed by the need to integrate fluctuating sources of power into an electricity grid are substantial. Any full assessment of the costs of solar power needs to take these necessary investments into account.

If costs of such investments on the power grid are funded by a general electricity tariff rate increase, then this would effectively be an implicit subsidy of the intermittent power generation technology borne, in the first instance, by electricity rate-payers (prior to general equilibrium effects which would, after a time lag, distribute ultimate costs across various firms and households). If the investment costs are borne by the general government budget, the costs of this implicit subsidy would fall in the first instance on taxpayers (firms and households). To the extent that electricity bills account for a larger share of the budget of poorer households, this implicit subsidy, whether paid for by power tariffs or general taxes, would tend to have a regressive impact on household incomes unless the progressivity of tax incidence is increased to compensate such households.

Solar Power for Carbon Emission Reduction

Government policy may incorporate social measures of costs and benefits that differ from market valuations due to the presence of externalities or other market failures. Sensitivity of the LCOE of various electric power generation technologies to carbon price scenarios gives measurable indicators for the social value of solar PV in reducing carbon emissions. Whether solar PV offers an effective means of carbon emission abatement relative to other power generation technologies is discussed further in the portion on LCOE comparisons across extant power generating technologies. Nevertheless, it is well established in the literature that the first-best policy option for internalizing externalities is to utilize MBIs such as the carbon tax or cap-and-trade regimes for carbon emissions.[153] Discretionary policies such as a lower imputed interest rate for public investments or other instruments such as FITs based on technology specifications cannot approximate the efficiency characteristics of MBIs as the first-best approach to internalize environmental externalities.

When calculating LCOE, the social or environmental cost of carbon can be incorporated, as an operating cost, to assess the impact of taking economic externalities into account. Figure 5.8 below illustrates the sensitivity of the LCOE for several technologies to the carbon price at a 5 per cent discount rate. The LCOE for carbon-emission-producing electricity generating technologies such as combined cycle gas turbines (CCGTs) and diesel gensets increases as the carbon price increases.

As flat horizontal lines, the LCOE for nuclear power and solar PV are obviously invariant to the carbon price since neither give rise to carbon emissions. Diesel generation is the most expensive technology over the carbon price range.

Solar PV remains among the more expensive options in abating GHGs. As the carbon price rises to US$145 per tonne (of CO_2), the LCOE for coal-based power generation approaches the US15.73¢ per kWh level calculated for solar PV under the Singapore model base case assumptions. For solar PV to be competitive against CCGT technology, an even higher carbon price of approximately US$230 per tonne is needed. The LCOE for nuclear and coal with 90 per cent Carbon Capture and Sequestration (CCS)[154] is lower than the solar PV LCOE through the whole range of carbon prices (i.e., from US$0 to US$400 per tonne of CO_2) as shown in Figure 5.8.

These high break-even carbon prices for solar PV under Singapore conditions are consistent with other well-cited studies. For instance, in reviewing Germany's energy policies in 2007, the IEA found the

Figure 5.8
Sensitivity of the LCOE to the Carbon Price

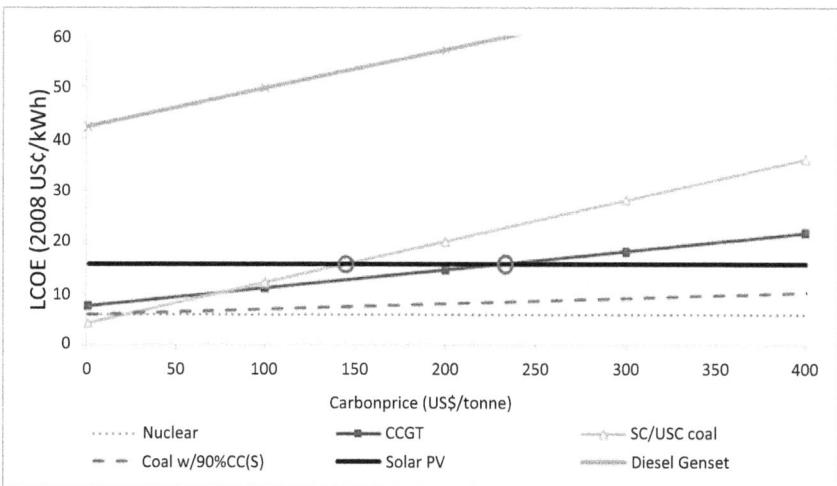

Sources: For diesel gensets and solar PV under Singapore conditions, Doshi, T., N. D'Souza, N. Linh, Teo H.G., "The Economics of Solar Power in Singapore", Discussion Paper EE/11-012011; for all other technologies, IEA, "Projected Costs of Generating Electricity", 2010.

abatement cost at around €1,000 per tonne of CO_2 abated given that solar PV displaces gas-fired power.[155] A more recent study that examines Germany's renewables policies estimates the abatement costs to be €716 per tonne of CO_2, assuming that solar PV displaces power produced from a mixture of natural gas and hard coal power plants.[156] To put this into context, the price of emission certificates in the EU ETS has never exceeded €32 per tonne of CO_2 since its inception in 2005. While solar PV module prices have come down appreciably since 2010, using intermittent technologies to reduce CO_2 emissions still remain an expensive means to abate carbon emissions.

Solar PV: Let the Market Decide

Investment decisions, such as the decision to install a solar PV system, are inherently irreversible. Given the presence of uncertainty, there is an incentive to wait before acting until the uncertainty is resolved or reduced. Thus, the option to wait has value.[157] In the case of solar installations, given the expected drop in module prices, it may be rational to delay investment as there is value to doing so and to getting cheaper modules for installations in the future, especially for countries which do not have a comparative advantage in the mass commodity manufacture of solar PV panels. If costs are expected to come down, then this can be an argument in favour of delay, not immediate action. It may make more sense to invest later, at a lower cost.

Hence, a recent report by the United Kingdom's Committee on Climate Change (CCC) recommended that it would be more prudent to defer deployment of solar PV to a later date and buy the technology from abroad as and when cost reductions were achieved.[158] In the same vein, the late Minister Mentor Lee Kuan Yew remarked that, given the scale of subsidies that China's government is devoting to solar PV panel production, it would make eminent sense for Singapore to buy cheaper panels from China when they become economical.[159] In a context where prices are expected to fall, and there is significant uncertainty as to how specific energy technologies will evolve, the recommendation to "buy from overseas later" may well be the optimal policy approach for those countries which do not have a comparative advantage in the mass manufacture of solar PV panels. [160]

To the extent that there are informational and "learning by doing" benefits in installing and integrating solar power systems in Singapore, there is a case for publicly financed test beds and local experiments in the adoption of an uncertain and still relatively costly technology. Positive externalities or "spill-over" effects from demonstration projects support the case for modest government support. A premature transition in power supply technologies, however, will not only be a costly option bought at the taxpayer's expense; it also means that lessons have not been learnt from the policy reversals in countries such as Germany and Spain where generous subsidies have been an unnecessary burden on public finance.

Singapore's largely market-based approach to public policy — and its strategy of promoting competition — has also meant that it has not followed the example of a number of its neighbours such as Malaysia and Thailand, which have instituted FIT policies to subsidize solar power. While avoiding the common practice of using fossil fuel subsidies to achieve social equity, Singapore has also refrained from instituting subsidy supports such as FITs or RPS to subsidize new renewable technologies.

Promoting Renewable Energy: The Problem of Government Failure

Since the energy crisis of the 1970s, the United States and other OECD economies have expended huge resources to promote "renewable energy" as desirable substitutes for conventional fossil fuels. Energy security and the crisis environment of the oil price shocks were at the root of some of the major attempts to boost the newer energy technologies, although, more recently, increasing concerns about global climate change have made the emission mitigation potential of renewable energy technologies a declared policy target in many countries as well. In Asia, Japan, South Korea, and more recently increasingly China, are leaders in renewable energy investments.

Renewable energy refers to wind, solar, biofuels, and geothermal resources, following the usual practice of excluding hydroelectricity and nuclear power.[161] As can be seen in Table 5.8 below, excluding nuclear and hydro makes the renewable energy sector an extremely small contributor to power generation, at 2 per cent in 2009. Fossil fuels account for two-thirds of the power generation supply, and nuclear and hydro together provide most of the other third of electricity generation. It should be noted that international data on biofuels use also includes the traditional use of firewood and agricultural waste biomass for cooking and other household use, a practice widespread in the poorer parts of developing

Table 5.8
Share of Electricity Generation by Fuel/Technology

Fuel/Technology	Electricity generation (TWh)	Shares (%)	
	2009	2009	2035
Fossil fuels	13,444	67	56
Nuclear	2,697	13	13
Hydro	3,252	16	15
Biomass and waste	288	1	4
Wind	273	1	7
Geothermal	67	0	1
Solar	21	0	3

Source: IEA *World Energy Outlook 2011*, New Policies Scenario.

economies, causing major pollution and habitat loss. For our purposes here, biofuels for renewable energy refer to corn-based ethanol and the yet-to-be commercialized technologies utilizing cellulosic material as substitutes for refined oil products.

Unpriced negative externalities (i.e., pollution and health costs imposed on societies but not taken into account by those using fossil fuels) caused by the combustion of fossil fuels are among the market failures identified for justifying government support for renewable or new energy technologies. Subsidies for renewable energy technologies to correct for externalities require that incremental net benefits are derived from the reduced pollution relative to the status quo. For an efficient outcome, these subsidies are justified up to the point where its equals the difference between the existing price of fossil fuels (including existing taxes) and the total social cost including an estimate of the environmental pollution costs incurred by the combustion of fossil fuels. However, it does not necessarily follow that unpriced negative externalities of fossil fuel use justify subsidies for renewable technologies as there are more direct and efficient means of reducing environmental costs. Governments can impose the full environmental costs directly on fossil fuels by a carbon tax or an emission permit trading regime. The latter option, of pricing externalities on the source of pollution via market-based instruments such as a tax or cap-and-trade programme for CO_2 or GHG emissions, yield far cheaper means of abating GHG emissions then subsidizing particular technologies.[162]

The cost of renewable energy technologies such as wind turbines and solar PVs have come down over the years and have sharply reduced the differentials to costs of power derived from fossil fuels. However, these technologies are generally still not competitive with fossil fuels even after externality costs are taken into account. In the case of intermittent sources of renewable energy such as wind or solar PV, the investment cost of back-up power (usually natural gas-fired) needed to integrate fluctuating supplies of renewable energy into the grid can be substantial and need to be taken into account when comparing them to costs of fossil fuel power generation.

In some discussions, relatively low fossil fuel prices are cast as "market barriers" that need to be surmounted.[163] Quite apart from a lack of rigorous definition of "market barriers", the term itself is misused. For economists, low prices are not constraints to be overcome but data to be incorporated by decision makers in firms and households who generally seek to maximize their utility (i.e., shareholder value or consumer surplus). The only requirement for economic efficiency is that low fossil fuel prices need to be correctly priced for externalities. It should be noted that estimating the externality costs of fossil fuels is itself a complex exercise, depending on assumptions of future prices and technologies as well as the uncertain environmental damage costs that pollutants and GHG emissions can cause. In particular, the assumptions of discount rates to use for future costs and benefits can radically alter the social costs of carbon, given that climate change processes can only be assessed over very long periods of time, of the order of fifty to one hundred years and longer.[164]

Perhaps most damaging to societal welfare are the effects of government failure as opposed to market failure. For example, the U.S. experience with mandated ethanol production has been characterized by an extraordinary level of special interest influence on the regulatory regime administering the ethanol programme.[165] The problem of government intervention is that it encourages erstwhile entrepreneurs to seek regulatory and financial support from government agencies rather than to undertake new technology ventures in a competitive market. It is in the very nature of the government-funding process that creates incentives for rent-seeking by those who specialize in lobbying and influencing the regulatory process.[166]

There are several factors inherent in any regulatory process that leads to government failure.[167] The first is the inability to meaningfully measure the value of government output. Typically, government expenditures are measured as cost of input rather than as economic contribution to GDP, as there is no realistic way to measure the value added of government output. The second factor is the incentive structure typically facing government personnel and regulators. It is not uncommon that incentives facing civil servants are geared towards enforcing a "department" view of projects and regulations. For example, programme managers may be more motivated to protect existing programmes that the government agency or department is identified with rather than fund new programmes which might conflict with existing department views.

A third factor is the "soft budget constraints" facing government agencies and regulatory agencies, where there are no clear profit and loss accounts comparable to those of the private sector. Such soft budget constraints mean that there are no reliable mechanisms to terminate particular programmes or expenditures. Termination of flagship programmes may mean a loss of prestige, cuts in departmental budget and number of staff appointments, and diminution of political influence. Finally, there may often be a lack of competition in the selection of projects and research programmes, and the regulatory process may be unduly influenced by organized and vocal constituency interests in renewable energy industries.

It is critical that the regulatory process be protected from influence exerted by special interests. Regulatory autonomy is a determining factor in whether the outcomes of government intervention are positive for societal interests. While government failure can never be completely eradicated, strong and prudential institutional and regulatory frameworks can do much to minimize the costs of government failure. In the case of Singapore, government policymaking is relatively autonomous and corruption is virtually absent. The practice of "buying votes" via subsidies or other pecuniary support for favoured causes has always been consciously decried by the founding members of the PAP government as unacceptable if Singapore were to succeed as a sovereign city-state.[168]

Assessing the Value of Publicly Funded R&D

The literature on the scientific and technological mainsprings of economic growth is large and well established. One review on the economics of scientific research puts it this way:

> The foremost reason economists have for studying science is the link between science and economic growth. That such a relationship exists has long been part of the conventional wisdom, articulated first by Adam Smith.... Technology, an intermediate step from science to economic growth has been the subject of extensive study by economists. More generally, the whole issue of R&D strategies of companies has occupied a significant proportion of the profession during the past fifty years or so.[169]

The economics of R&D begins with the premise associated with the work of Nobel Laureate Kenneth Arrow that "basic science" is a "non-excludable" public good. In other words, the research results of basic science cannot be commercialized by profit-motivated private enterprise, and hence there is a tendency to underinvest from a societal point of view.[170] The call then is for government to step in to rectify this market failure and to correctly account for positive externalities spun off by basic science research; i.e., governments need to fund basic science to ensure that it receives an optimal quantum of investment resources from society's point of view. In this view, the private sector then steps in to invest sufficiently in "applied science", which both benefits from the basic science research that takes place somewhere upstream to itself and which issues forth new inventions and technological breakthroughs which, in turn, yield commercial success for the firm's shareholders. Figure 5.9 below gives a schematic view.

Yet, this bare-bones mainstream model based on the "public goods" characterization of "basic science" can be misleading. To begin with, it is not clear if the simple demarcation of scientific research into "basic" and "applied" is tenable. For instance, the Bell Labs work on solid state physics (the transistor) in the 1960s and 1970s was far in advance of what any university in the world had to offer. Indeed, there are many examples where industry leads academia in driving fundamental research.[171] Some studies suggest that academic science plays a relatively small role in technological advance. According to one 1991 survey of seventy-six major American manufacturing firms in key industries such as information processing, electrical equipment, instruments, chemicals, drugs, oil, and metals, "about 11 per cent of new products and about 9 per cent of all processes could not have been developed, without substantial delay, in the absence of recent academic research".[172] Putting it alternatively, about 90 per cent of technological advance arises from industrial R&D in business laboratories, not in academic departments.

Figure 5.9
Mainstream Scheme of R&D Economics

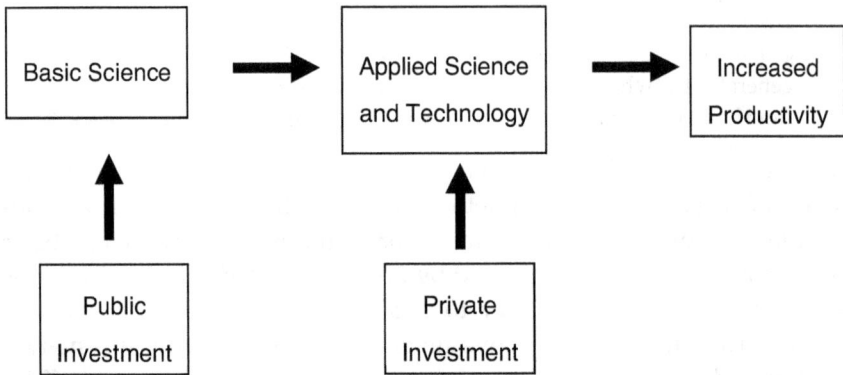

Source: Adapted from Kealey, T. *The Economic Laws of Scientific Research*, London: Macmillan, 1996.

Taking into account these complexities, we amend the schematics reflecting R&D dynamics as shown in Figure 5.10. Firstly, there is an added hatched arrow to indicate the two-way flow between "basic science" and "applied science and technology", to reflect the "cross-fertilization" between the two types of science where, as often as not, applied science leads basic science.[173] A second diagonal hatched arrow captures the direct investment flows by the private sector into "basic science", given that much of industrial R&D is done in industrial labs rather than academic departments. A comprehensive empirical study, covering 911 large U.S. companies over 1966–77, found that the more companies spent on "basic" research, the more they outperformed their competitors.[174]

It is also apparent that a significant share of public investments flow into the "applied science and technology" end of the research spectrum (the curved hatched arrow in Figure 5.10). The aim of government funding of science R&D is, ultimately, to get measurable results in increased productivity to raise the standards of living of citizens. For example, the Singapore media has recently looked into why key research directors in the Genome Institute of Singapore and the Institute of Molecular and Cell Biology left for jobs elsewhere, after being attracted to Singapore with much fanfare some years ago.[175] The news reports looked into the causes of concerns of Singapore's "whales" (i.e., top research scientists) with

Figure 5.10
Amended Scheme of R&D Economics

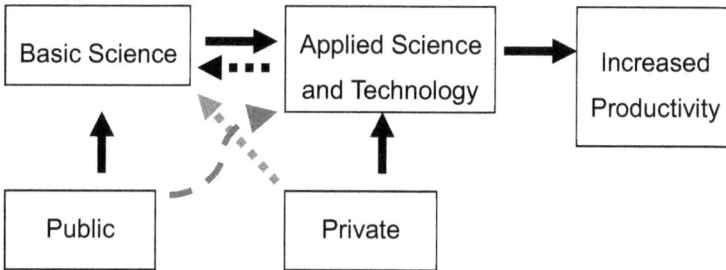

Source: Adapted from Kealey, T., op. cit.

performance metrics and the insistence of government funding agencies on "generating value for Singaporeans".[176]

R&D subsidies by government are intended to support research that the private sector will not undertake. It is not supposed to substitute for private sector R&D. However, government-funded R&D programmes can, under some circumstances, displace private-sector R&D. Thus, for instance, while companies might fund their own R&D programmes in lightly taxed countries, in higher-taxed countries, companies may devote more resources to lobbying the government to fund R&D. Government-funded R&D programmes are ultimately paid for by taxes on the private sector. This translates into an implicit view that government committees are better judges of commercial opportunities arising out of scientific research than markets; i.e., that the alternative to simply give tax credits for private sector R&D is inferior to government-directed R&D programmes. This proposition has been questioned by some studies on key rich country R&D programmes.[177]

Figure 5.11 shows that countries with a higher share of the private sector in total civilian R&D expenditure contribute a higher share of their GDP to total R&D expenditure. Taiwan lags behind somewhat, relative to the line of best fit, while Israel is an outlier with much higher total expenditures on R&D as a percentage of GDP relative to the share of private sector funding of R&D expenditures. While the correlation does not prove causality, the data is consistent with the observation that the more the government spends as a proportion of total R&D, the less that is

Figure 5.11
**Government to Business R&D Expenditure Ratio vs Total Expenditure as a
Percentage of GDP for a Sample of Countries**

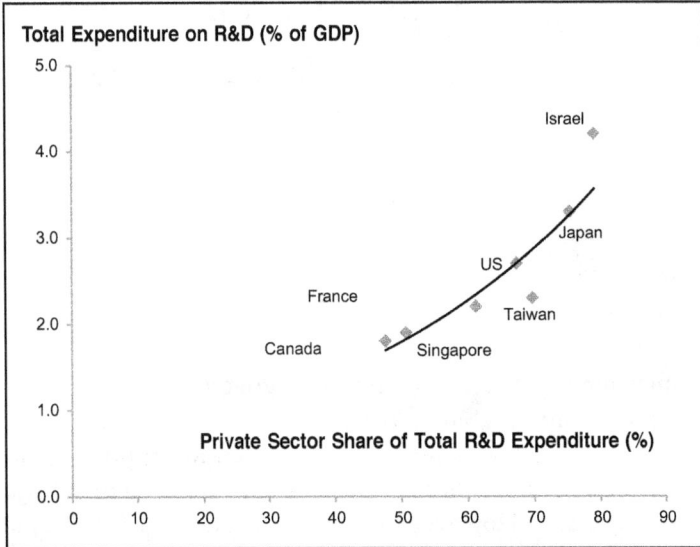

Source: OECD Main Science and Technology Indicators (MSTI) 2011/1 edition; data on R&D expenditure as % of GDP from Table 3.6.1, "2011 Global R&D Funding Forecast"; Singapore data from Ho, V., "R&D Spending Rises to S$6.5 bn in 2010: A*Star", *Business Times*, 28 December 2011.

spent in total R&D as a share of GDP. In other words, government funding might be more than proportionately displacing private sector funding, to result in lower overall R&D spending.

Perhaps the most cited example of an activist government role in "guiding" and promoting industry is the role of Japan's Ministry of International Trade and Industry (MITI, the predecessor ministry to the current Ministry of Economy, Trade and Industry, or METI) on the country's experience of successful economic growth. Contrary to popular perception regarding MITI's success, one large study of MITI policies during 1955–90 across thirteen major sectors of the economy concluded that Japan's civil servants almost invariably chose and supported poorly performing firms, and that Japan's industrial policy in the main hindered rather than advanced Japan's economic success.[178] In another study conducted by the OECD, the analysis found evidence that the impact of public sector R&D on economic growth in the OECD countries was unexpectedly negative:

The negative results for public R&D are surprising and deserve some qualification. Taken at face value, they suggest publicly-performed R&D crowds out resources that could be alternatively used by the private sector, including private R&D. There is some evidence of this effect in studies that have looked in detail at the role of different forms of R&D and the interaction between them. However, there are avenues for more complex effects that regression analysis cannot identify.[179]

Thus, despite the last qualifying sentence, the OECD data and analysis pointed to a finding consistent with the argument that it is business R&D and not government R&D that leads economic growth, and that government R&D possibly displaced business R&D at the margin.[180]

In 2008, a group of prominent economists and scientists issued a statement, after meeting in Stanford University to discuss the role of R&D in developing effective policies, for addressing the adverse potential consequences of climate change.[181] The statement pointed to the downside of R&D subsidies that tend to support favoured firms, industries, and organized interests, and advocated "agency independence" to overcome such distortions.[182] Among the set of design principles for effective R&D policies recommended by the group are: use of peer review with clear criteria for project selection; risks and rewards from commercial deployment of technologies should be left to markets to determine and government support for technology R&D should cease at the development stage; and encourage risk taking and tolerance for failure as a means of discovering valuable information by shifting the mix of R&D investments towards more "exploratory" projects characterized by greater uncertainty in the distribution of payoffs.

In order to avoid a programme of R&D subsidies becoming in effect an industrial policy of picking alleged winners in "green" technologies, modes of government funding need to be competition friendly.[183] One way of promoting competition is to exploit complementarities between private and public co-financing of research, so that if a project does not lead to commercial opportunities and leads the private sector to withdraw, the public sector should also withdraw its subsidies. "Wrong non-winners" can quickly be dropped when private entrepreneurs closest to the market make decisions, not civil servants who are invariably one step removed from the private sector.

The results of R&D are inherently uncertain. Only a portion of government-funded energy R&D is likely to achieve results in energy production or consumption profiles that can be clearly attributed to a specific R&D project or programme. Moreover, to the extent that R&D yields commercial technologies, they are likely to be measurable only years after the funded research effort is initiated. As the recent resignations by high-profile scientist-directors of research institutes in Singapore make apparent, it is not easy for governments to fund cutting-edge research while abiding by the requirements of bureaucratic accountability.

In his comments on the government's role in inculcating entrepreneurship on the eve of Malaya's independence, Dr Goh Keng Swee, often noted as Singapore's architect of economic success, wrote this: "No official selection board or public service commission can possibly spot potential captains of industry by whatever techniques of selection it may devise."[184] Analogously, it can be said that it is not likely that government-funded agencies or programmes will play a prescient role in technological and commercial developments in energy efficiency or in "green" technologies. What governments can best achieve is to create supportive environments for private sector R&D, including by means of co-funding with private sector partners. Operating conditions for R&D personnel should be particularly amenable to initiative and flexibility, where incentives for commercial success are not attenuated by bureaucratic requirements of audits and accounting. While it is clear that public financing of R&D budgets require prudent audit and control procedures, it would be naïve to expect salaried civil servants to have superior entrepreneurial instincts in promoting new energy technologies.[185]

5.5 STEP UP INTERNATIONAL AND REGIONAL COOPERATION: ASEAN, TAGP, APG, ETC.

Given its small size and reliance on energy imports, Singapore's energy policy emphasizes efforts to promote greater regional and international energy cooperation to further its energy interests.[186] To enhance energy security, Singapore will continue to be actively involved in various energy-related initiatives in major fora, including the Association of Southeast Asian Nations (ASEAN), APEC, and the East Asia Summit (EAS). Singapore will also work towards the long-term goal of promoting a regional energy market through energy projects like the ASEAN Power Grid (APG) and the Trans-ASEAN Gas Pipeline (TAGP).

Security of shipping lanes is an area that requires international cooperation. Approximately 60 per cent of China's 6.9 million barrels, 90 per cent of Japan's 5.2 million barrels, and 80 per cent of Korea's 2.2 million barrels of imported oil per day pass through the Straits of Malacca and Singapore (SOMS) from the Middle East.[187] To secure access and the freedom of navigation through SOMS, the operational agencies of Singapore are collaborating with their counterparts in Malaysia and Indonesia to improve the security of the straits.

Energy was identified as a key area for cooperation early on since the founding of ASEAN. In the aftermath of the oil crisis in 1973, the heads of ASEAN member countries formed the ASEAN Council on Petroleum (ASCOPE) in October 1975, to promote cooperation among its member countries in times of emergency due to oil shortages. Initially, cooperation was viewed as a way of enhancing energy security, although of late, climate change and the environment are also viewed as factors in support of a regional approach to the energy sector.

ASEAN Vision 2020 called for an "energy-integrated" Southeast Asia which would "establish interconnecting arrangements in the field of energy and utilities for electricity, natural gas and water within ASEAN through the ASEAN Power Grid and a Trans-ASEAN Gas Pipeline and Water Pipeline, and promote cooperation in energy efficiency and conservation, as well as the development of new and renewable energy resources".[188] The ASEAN Plan of Action for Energy Cooperation (APAEC) 2010–2015 covers the energy component of the ASEAN Economic Community Blueprint 2015 signed by ASEAN leaders in November 2007. The plan aims to "enhance energy security and sustainability for the ASEAN region including health, safety, and environment through accelerated implementation of action plans, including, but not limited to: (a) ASEAN Power Grid, (b) Trans-ASEAN Gas Pipeline, (c) Coal and Clean Coal Technology, (d) Renewable Energy, (e) Energy Efficiency and Conservation, (f) Regional Energy Policy and Planning, and (g) Civilian Nuclear Energy."

The Trans-ASEAN Gas Pipeline

The region's most ambitious mega-project, the TAGP aims to connect the gas reserves of the Andaman Sea, Gulf of Thailand, and South China Sea to the urban and industrial demand centres of Southeast Asia. Among its objectives are to ensure the reliability of gas supply to ASEAN members, encourage the use of an environmentally cleaner fuel, and to reduce dependence on oil and coal where economically substitutable.

ASEAN formed the TAGP task force in 1999, and ASEAN members signed a memorandum of understanding on the project in 2002. According to APAEC 2010–2015, the "updated ASCOPE-TAGP Masterplan 2000" involves the construction of 4,500 km of pipelines worth US$7 billion.[189] There are a range of other estimates regarding the size and cost of TAGP, with one source citing US$16 billion of investments for 5,100 km of new pipelines.[190] Potential link-ups with East and South Asia could increase investment requirements to over US$65 billion, according to another source.[191]

All large-scale multilateral infrastructure projects face critical hurdles in the financing, construction, operation, and maintenance of networks. These include the requirements of common technological specifications and standards; stable contractual arrangements to handle supply, transport, and distribution; open access arrangements to common infrastructure; and norms and legal frameworks for arbitration and dispute resolution. The TAGP mega-project is no different, facing key challenges in all these dimensions. The heterogeneity of ASEAN members with respect to income levels, stages of social and economic development, legal systems and domestic pricing regulations of natural gas has posed significant challenges to the TAGP. Given the scale of the project, it has naturally been a subject of a number of feasibility and planning studies.[192]

Currently, there are eight cross-border natural gas pipelines that are operating, with a total length of over 2,500 km. The cross-border pipelines connect Peninsula Malaysia to Singapore (delivering gas from 1992); Myanmar to Thailand from the Yadana (1999) and Yetagun (2000) fields; Indonesia to Singapore with two pipelines, one from West Natuna (2001) and the other from South Sumatra (2003); and Thailand to Malaysia from the Joint Development Area in the Gulf of Thailand (2006).[193] An estimated US$14.2 billion has already been invested in some 3,900 km of bilateral pipelines in 2008.[194]

The successful financing and construction of these cross-border pipelines have occurred on the basis of commercial consortia that involve a range of private and public sector stakeholders in the energy sector, not as part of state-led multilateral negotiations envisioned by the ASEAN proponents of the TAGP project. Finance by multilateral agencies such as the ADB has played a role in some of the pipeline projects involving the less-developed member countries of ASEAN with weak fiscal systems such as Indonesia.[195] Nonetheless, existing investments in cross-border gas pipelines in Southeast Asia are the result of successful negotiations between sovereign owners of natural gas resources in the region and the international oil and gas companies who typically provide private equity and commercial debt instruments along with the requisite technology and expertise to exploit such resources. Where commercial criteria of risk and reward simultaneously satisfied policymaker's perceptions of national interest in the exploitation of gas resources, projects reached final investment decisions; and if cross-border transport of gas helped commercialize otherwise "stranded" gas resources by reaching paying customers with long-term sales and purchase agreements, then pipelines got built.

Quite apart from the inherent challenges that all large-scale multilateral projects face, the TAGP now faces a more basic question of relevance. From when first conceived and discussed,[196] the natural gas situation in Southeast Asia has changed profoundly. If the TAGP project seemed over-ambitious when it was first mooted among ASEAN planners and diplomats in the mid-1980s, it now seems that the grand vision of a regionally interconnected grid of natural gas pipelines for ASEAN faces the threat of redundancy by fast-paced developments in the natural gas industry over the past two decades.

Southeast Asia has been among the fastest growing economic regions in the world over the past three decades. Rapid economic growth in the region has been accompanied by rising demand for energy, and in particular, electricity. Natural gas use in Southeast Asia is expected to grow rapidly in the power generation, industrial, and household sectors in the medium term. The region boasts three well-established LNG-exporting countries — Malaysia, Indonesia, and Brunei, two of which (Malaysia and Indonesia) were the world's second- and third-largest exporters respectively in 2009.[197] However, without further major discoveries and new gas field development projects, regional gas supplies are dwindling relative to the rapid growth in domestic demand. Both Malaysia and Indonesia have expressed concern over their ability to meet rapidly growing domestic demand while sustaining their LNG and pipeline export commitments.

In 2007, Indonesia switched its gas policy from an almost exclusive export-focus one to one that includes both meeting domestic demand and continuing to be a significant exporter as the country's industrial sector faced an acute shortage of natural gas. According to local media reports, the Indonesian government may no longer extend the existing LNG contracts in the future in order to meet the surge in the domestic demand.[198] While the country will continue to remain an important LNG exporter, it expects to be an importer of LNG as well. A slate of small regasification terminals are planned to come on stream at various locations in Java and Sumatra. LNG exports from Indonesia are projected to decrease consistently, to less than 5 Mtpa by 2030.

Malaysia is also set to emerge as a large Southeast Asian importer of LNG as its domestic supply is expected to drop to 1.4 billion cubic feet per day (Bcf/d) by 2025 from an estimated 2 Bcf/d in 2015.[199] The first LNG import terminal aimed at helping to ease the gas supply shortage in Peninsular Malaysia became operational in 2013. Supply to this 3.5 Mtpa terminal will be based on a combination of long-term and short-term purchase agreements from a range of sources, including the Middle East and Australia. Press reports citing Malaysian and Indonesian officials indicate that pipeline gas exports to Singapore will likely diminish going forward, due to pressing domestic needs. In one media report, Indonesia is looking at renegotiating with Singapore, to replace its pipeline gas exports with LNG from East Kalimantan or Papua, so that Sumatran gas can be used domestically in nearby Java.[200]

Given the basic supply and demand outlook for natural gas in the region's main gas producers, the outlook for extensive new pipeline development in Southeast Asia is constrained. Instead, the most notable development in the region's natural gas sector is the many announcements of new LNG regasification terminals being planned. Among those countries in the region that have announced plans or have already begun construction of LNG regasification terminals are Thailand, Vietnam, and the Philippines, apart from those planned in gas exporters Malaysia and Indonesia. It is apparent that the ability to import LNG has become a preferred option: it facilitates access to gas supply quickly. Floating LNG regasification vessels make for even quicker turnaround times to project completion.[201]

Indonesia's giant East Natuna field (formerly known as Natuna D. Alpha) in the South China Sea, the region's largest gas field by far with an estimated 46 trillion cubic feet (tcf) of recoverable gas, is seen as the lynchpin of the TAGP. Among the pipelines envisaged in the TAGP, East Natuna is expected to supply gas via pipelines to Vietnam, Malaysia, Indonesia (Java), and Thailand. Excluding the "deferred" proposed pipeline to the Philippines, the gas reserves of the East Natuna field are to support about 4,500 km of pipeline supplies to demand centres in four countries. However, given the very high CO_2 content of East Natuna's gas reserves (up to 70 per cent of total estimated reserves of over 220 tcf), exploiting the reserves will be technically and economically challenging. Reflecting the sheer scale and complexity of any project to exploit the East Natuna field, official projections for gas production from the field see first output only after 2020.[202] Given a number of large LNG projects at various stages of planning in the region, particularly in Australia, but also in newer areas such as East Africa, the development and exploitation of East Natuna is decades away if at all likely.

The ASEAN Power Grid

The APG was announced in 1997 by the ASEAN Heads of States/ Governments under the "ASEAN Vision 2020" declaration, with its declared aims to ensure regional energy security and the efficient utilization of electricity resources. It envisages development in stages: bilateral interconnections will be gradually expanded to a subregional basis and then to a totally integrated Southeast Asian power grid system. There are currently four ongoing projects, with eleven new projects planned through to 2020.[203]

ASEAN member countries vary considerably with regard to their power sector regulations, market structure, and technical characteristics, such as plant efficiency, transmission and distribution losses, HVAC/DC (high voltage alternating current/direct current) transmission lines, etc. Reflecting the heterogeneity of electric power markets among the ASEAN group, power tariffs for both industry and households differ markedly among different ASEAN member states. Key countries such as Malaysia and Indonesia have subsidized electricity, although both countries have announced their intention of slowly reducing such subsidies in favour of more targeted social welfare programmes.[204]

Brunei, Cambodia, Laos, and Myanmar have traditional vertically integrated state-owned power utilities, while Indonesia, Malaysia, Thailand, and Vietnam have state-owned utilities operating together with private independent power producers (IPPs). In ASEAN, only the Philippines and Singapore have "unbundled" power sectors, with privatized power generators and independent grid operators.

There are significant technical and economic benefits to interconnecting power grids as envisaged in the APG. System electricity-generation reserve-capacity requirements would be reduced the larger the size of the system. Load factors would improve in a larger system due to higher utilization factors. This would allow for diversification of energy supply sources. Integration efficiencies could also encourage electricity market reforms in the region, as the benefits of shared power become apparent. In the Greater Mekong Subregion (GMS), there is vast potential for exploiting hydroelectric power in Laos and Cambodia for export that is yet untapped.

There are significant technological, operational, and institutional barriers to interconnecting the different power grid systems in ASEAN. The electric power sectors in different countries have evolved separately, and standards and technologies are different. Policy preferences with respect to reliability and affordability differ across the region. As already mentioned, the market structure in power generation and distribution differ across countries in ASEAN. Some countries still have vertically integrated utilities with a monopoly over generation, transmission, distribution, and retail of electricity. In gas-exporting countries such as Brunei, Indonesia, and Malaysia, gas is offered to electricity producers at subsidized prices. IPPs and foreign investors cannot compete in an "uneven playing field", unless they are guaranteed offtake at predictable prices. International electricity grid interconnections are complex, and power purchase and pricing agreements need to be sorted out prior to the commencement of grid interconnection projects. Liabilities of various parties have to be decided upon across different legal jurisdictions.

In countries where market pricing, unbundling, and privatization have not been achieved, the financial burden often falls on already-stretched public sectors in key ASEAN countries such as Malaysia and Indonesia, not to speak of the less-developed countries such as Laos and Cambodia. Market pricing, to reflect real costs of power, can have destabilizing consequences for governments intent on subsidizing power for social welfare of its poorer citizens.

Progress in interconnecting power grids in ASEAN will likely continue on a bilateral basis, except in cases where a regional approach has strong motivation, as in the GMS. Progress will likely be slower than those laid out by government planners, as ASEAN member states are still far away from privatizing or "unbundling" electricity sectors and encouraging fully fledged energy trading. Power surplus countries such as Laos with ample hydro resources could emerge as major electricity exporters within ASEAN, supplying much needed power to rapidly growing neighbouring countries such as Thailand and Vietnam, as well as the vast energy market of China.

ASEAN Regional Cooperation

To capture economic benefits from market-based pricing in the key natural resource, infrastructure, and energy sectors, several ASEAN countries need to remove gas and power subsidies in favour of programmes that include well-targeted social safety nets. ASEAN governments, like their counterparts elsewhere in the developing world, face critical challenges to ensure popular support from key constituencies for market-oriented reforms in their energy sectors. Market-oriented reforms are needed not only to ensure fiscal health in countries which subsidize gas and power, but also to alleviate shortages of natural gas for rapidly increasing domestic demand. Governments need to maintain stable policy environments for private sector investments which require predictability and transparency.

To date, efforts at the regional integration of energy and infrastructure sectors in Southeast Asia have lagged. Indeed, in some key sectors, changes in technology and business norms have led to less need for much-discussed "integration" projects such as the ASEAN Gas Grid in favour of LNG-receiving terminals, which allow countries direct access to natural gas without dependence on cross-border pipelines. Various long-duration discussions on a host of potential regional cooperation initiatives such as common oil-storage facilities have remained fruitless. Fashioning a regional diplomatic and legal response to common regional issues has not been easy, even in areas where regional solutions are the only possible approach to cross-border problems such as the seasonal forest-fire outbreaks in the Indonesian islands of Sumatra and Borneo which often blanket large parts of Peninsular Malaysia and Singapore in thick haze and present acute health hazards.[205] Regional cooperation is key to several energy-related issues which are inherently regional in scope, such as the Indonesian forest fires and the safety and security of marine traffic, in particular the oil and gas tankers that ply the Strait of Malacca.

While much ink and speech has been devoted in ASEAN circles to various cross-border mega-projects, little has been achieved. This is not surprising because ASEAN remains primarily a forum of discussion where unanimity among all members is necessary for any common position to be adopted. Some of the cross-border mega-projects discussed in the gas and power sectors for instance do not seem likely to pass the test of economic and commercial viability. It is primarily in cases where projects make compelling sense bilaterally, between willing buyer and seller, that they have a chance of success. The existing pipelines that supply natural gas to Singapore from Malaysia and Indonesia and from Myanmar into Thailand, or the potential for large-scale hydropower supply from Laos into China and Thailand, are good examples.

Open markets and trading regimes, and the harmonization of rules, regulations, and standards are necessary in ASEAN to achieve gains from trade in natural resources and electricity, and to benefit from market-led investments and trade. A McKinsey study commissioned by ASEAN finds the region hindered by "fragmented markets, high transaction costs, and an unpredictable policy environment".[206] According to the study, if ASEAN member states are to remain competitive in the race for foreign direct investment and export market share, they will need to step up their integration efforts. The point to note is that while reducing transaction costs in intra-regional trade, investments and cross-border infrastructure development can only assist ASEAN member countries' efforts to promote economic development, that is no substitute to key energy sector reforms that the bloc's constituent members need to undertake domestically. As markets evolve, reflecting new developments in demand, supply, and technology parameters of the natural gas and power sectors in the region and globally, ASEAN planners will need to refashion some of the key "energy integration" initiatives that member states have supported. Some of the acronyms discussed in ASEAN diplomatic circles, such as the APG and the TAGP, may have already become anachronistic.

Notes

1. The necessity for some kind of central coordination in energy affairs was felt in the aftermath of the second oil price shock, and the response was the establishment in 1980 of an Energy Unit in the Ministry of Trade and Industry to act as Secretariat for the Inter-Ministry Energy Coordination Committee, which included representatives from MTI, MOF, and MFA. The erosion of oil prices after 1981, however, limited the role of the unit.

2. See Ministry of Trade and Industry Singapore (MTI), "A Changing Energy Landscape: The Energy Trillema", *MTI Insights Energy*, 13 December 2011 <http://www.mti.gov.sg/MTIInsights/Pages/Energy-.aspx>.
3. See Ministry of Trade and Industry Singapore, "National Energy Policy Report — Energy for Growth", *Research Room*, 13 November 2007. We have specifically left out a sixth strategy listed in the report ("develop whole-of-government approach") on the basis that this is not so much a "strategy" as a requirement for policy coherence when specialized ministries and agencies need to work across jurisdictions to implement energy policy initiatives. In "A Changing Energy Landscape: The Energy Trillema", MTI lists five strategies: diversify energy supplies, enhance infrastructure and systems, improve energy efficiency, strengthen the Green economy, and price energy right. This differs little from the strategies discussed in MTI's National Energy Policy Report of 2007.
4. See Paul Horsnell, *Oil in Asia: Markets, Trading, Refining and Deregulation* (Oxford: Oxford University Press, 1997), pp. 134–39.
5. Pulau Bukom was outside the purview of the port of Singapore, and the Kuala Lumpur-based colonial officials were presumably less impressed by the objections of merchant interests in Singapore. See Horsnell, *Oil in Asia*, p. 136.
6. MTI, "National Energy Policy Report — Energy for Growth".
7. International Energy Agency, *World Energy Outlook 2012* (Paris: OECD/IEA, 2012).
8. Gabriel Chan et al., *The SO_2 Allowance Trading System and the Clean Air Act Amendments of 1990: Reflections on Twenty Years of Policy Innovation* (Cambridge: Harvard Environmental Economics Program, January 2012).
9. Robert N. Stavins, "Economic Incentives for Environmental Regulation", BCSIA Discussion Paper 97-02, ENRP Discussion Paper E-97-02, Kennedy School of Government, Harvard University, June 1997 <http://live.belfercenter.org/files/Economic%20Incentives%20for%20Environmental%20Regulation%20-%20E-97-02.pdf>.
10. Cited in Daniel Yergin, *The Quest: Energy, Security, and the Remaking of the Modern World* (New York: Penguin Books, 2012).
11. The early trade of kerosene used tin cans for transport and distribution, and was called "cased oil". Bulk long distance transport via the Suez Canal constituted Shell's logistical advantage to make inroads into the Far East oil trade dominated by Standard Oil's cased oil monopoly. See Horsnell, *Oil in Asia*, p. 136.
12. See International Energy Agency, "Topic: Oil Stocks" <http://www.iea.org/topics/oil/oilstocks/>.
13. International Energy Agency, *Oil Supply Security: Emergency Response of IEA Countries* (Paris: IEA, 2007).
14. Energy Market Authority, *Review of the Long Run Marginal Cost (LRMC) Parameters for Setting the Vesting Contract Price for the Period 1 January 2013 to*

31 December 2014: Final Determination Paper (Singapore: EMA, 30 September 2012); Ministry of Trade and Industry Singapore, "2nd Minister S. Iswaran's Reply on the Impact of the Shell Oil Refinery Fire and Facilities Shut-down at Pulau Bukom on the Singapore Economy", News Room (Singapore: MTI, 20 October 2011).

15. Research and Statistics Unit, Energy Market Authority, *Singapore Energy Statistics 2012* (Singapore: EMA, 2012).

16. Sonia Kolesnikov-Jessop, "Singapore Looks to Store Oil in Caverns under the Sea", *New York Times*, 22 February 2011.

17. International Energy Agency, "Energy Balances of non-OECD Countries" (Paris: OECD/IEA, 2013).

18. Jessica Cheam. "Jurong Rock Cavern Ready by 2013", *Straits Times*, 29 October 2009.

19. Cheang Chee Yew, "Singapore Adds Infrastructure to Remain Major Asian Energy Hub", *Downstream Today*, 2 September 2013 <https://www.downstreamtoday.com/news/article.aspx?a_id=40533>.

20. Eric Yep, "Singapore Oil Hub Expands to Neighbors after Outgrowing City-State", *Wall Street Journal*, 23 January 2014.

21. For instance, see Wahyudi Soeriaatmadja, "Cut Natural Gas Exports to Singapore: Indonesian Minister", *Jakarta Globe*, 22 September 2011; Ronnie Lim, "New Taker for S'pore-bound Gas", *Business Times*, 6 July 2012.

22. See Energy Market Authority, "Overview of Gas Market: Liquefied Natural Gas" <https://www.ema.gov.sg/Gas_Market_Overview.aspx>.

23. EMA, "LNG Procurement Framework: Consultation Paper", 30 March 2012.

24. See Energy Market Authority (EMA), "Post–3 Mtpa LNG Framework: Final Determination Paper", 28 February 2014 <http://www.ema.gov.sg/cmsmedia/3Mtpa_framework_-_Final_Determination_Paper_Final_for_launch_on_28_Feb_2014.pdf>.

25. Warner ten Kate, Lászlo Varró, and Anne-Sophie Corbeau, "Developing a Natural Gas Trading Hub in Asia: Obstacles and Opportunities" (Paris: IEA, 2013).

26. Ministry of Trade and Industry Singapore, "National Energy Policy Report: LNG Trading" (Singapore: MTI, 2007), p. 61.

27. "Singapore Sets Sights on LNG Hub", *Petroleum Economist*, 22 March 2011.

28. These findings came from the Joint Industry Project, or JIP, initiated by DNV during Singapore Maritime Week in 2010, and which involved sixteen participants from the LNG industry. See Karen Boman, "Study Examines Prospects for Small Scale LNG in SE Asia", *Downstream Today*, 24 March 2011 <http://www.downstreamtoday.com/News/ArticlePrint.aspx?aid=26132&AspxAutoDetectCookieSupport=1>.

29. LNG vessels of standard size (~140,000 m³) and newer larger carriers (up to 270,000 m³) have been the mainstay of long-term LNG sales. Short haul, small LNG carriers of 10,000–30,000 m³ (or even smaller) operate in parts of Europe and Japan for short sailing times and coastal LNG transportation.

30. "Pertamina, PLN to Build 8 Mini LNG Terminals", *Business Times*, 25 March 2011.

31. Sara Stefanini, "Singapore's Pavilion Aims to Create Asian 'LNG Ecosystem'", *Natural Gas Daily*, 25 September 2013.

32. Ronnie Lim, "Temasek Brings Gas Supply under Pavilion", *Business Times*, 3 October 2013.

33. Hamilton (1983) was one of the first studies to demonstrate the negative relationship between oil prices and macroeconomic indicators; see James D. Hamilton, "Oil and the Macroeconomy since World War II", *Journal of Political Economy* 91, no. 2 (1983): 228–48. A number of subsequent studies have corroborated and further developed these findings; see, for instance, Olivier J. Blanchard and Jordi Gali, "The Macroeconomic Effects of Oil Price Shocks: Why are the 2000s So Different from the 1970s?", National Bureau of Economic Research (NBER) Working Paper No. 13368 (September 2007).

34. ADB estimates based on the Oxford Economic Forecasting World Macroeconomic Model. See Asian Development Bank, "Higher Global Oil Prices: Implications for Developing Asia in 2005", *Asian Development Outlook*, May 2004.

35. The terms of trade refer to the amount of import goods an economy can purchase per unit of export goods.

36. See Tilak Doshi, *Houston of Asia: The Singapore Petroleum Industry* (Singapore: Institute of Southeast Asian Studies, 1989), pp. 42–48.

37. For an empirical analysis of the comparative experience in economic performance of the export-oriented East Asian economies (including Singapore) and other developing countries after the 1973–74 oil price shock, see Bela Balassa, *The Newly Industrializing Countries in the World Economy* (Oxford: Pergamon Press, 1981).

38. See Doshi, *Houston of Asia: The Singapore Petroleum Industry*, p. 46.

39. Lawrence B. Krause, "Thinking about Singapore", in Lawrence B. Krause, Koh Ai Tee and Lee (Taso) Yuan, *The Singapore Economy Reconsidered* (Singapore: Institute of Southeast Asian Studies, 1987), p. 11.

40. See Nicolas Lefèvre, "Measuring the Energy Security Implications of Fossil Fuel Resource Concentration", *Energy Policy* 38, no. 4 (2010): 1635–44.

41. The calculations were conducted by Nahim Bin Zahur and Lin Fangjun, both staff members of the Economics Department at the Energy Studies Institute, National University of Singapore (personal communication).

42. In a portfolio LNG contract, the importer buys LNG from an aggregator (in

this case, BG) that sources the gas from a variety of different sources, rather than from any particular LNG project.

43. BG's long-term sources of LNG (on a contractual basis) include Australia, Trinidad and Tobago, Egypt, Equatorial Guinea, Nigeria, and the United States. See J.P. Morgan Cazenove, *Global LNG*, Global Equity Research, 13 January 2012.

44. See World Bank, "Worldwide Governance Indicators (WGI) Project" <http://info.worldbank.org/governance/wgi/index.aspx#home>.

45. The BG Group's website explains it as follows: "Our customers are supplied from our global portfolio of LNG, with multiple production sources around the world, including Egypt, Trinidad, and soon in Australia and the United States. This means our customers are not tied to the output of a single LNG plant" <http://www.bg-group.com/29/about-us/lng/>.

46. Selina Williams, "BG Group's Woes Stoke Breakup, Takeover Speculation", *Wall Street Journal*, 16 July 2014.

47. EMA, "Post–3 Mtpa LNG Framework: Final Determination Paper".

48. Ibid.

49. Alice Young, "BG Share Price Slumps as Explorer Issues 'Disappointing' 2014 Guidance", *iNVEZZ*, 27 January 2014 <http://invezz.com/news/equities/8377-bg-share-price-slumps-as-explorer-issues-disappointing-2014-guidance>.

50. I am thankful to Dr Fereidun Fesharaki for having made this point in reference to the choice of an aggregator model for arranging LNG imports.

51. See, for instance, ExxonMobil's response to the EMA's call for feedback in Annex A attached to "Post–3 Mtpa LNG Framework: Final Determination Paper".

52. The National Balancing Point, commonly referred to as the NBP, is a virtual trading location for the sale and purchase and exchange of the United Kingdom's natural gas. It is the pricing and delivery point for the ICE Futures Europe (IntercontinentalExchange) natural gas futures contract. It is the most liquid gas-trading point in Europe. Other continental European hubs include Zeebrugge and TTF. The Henry Hub is a distribution hub on the natural gas pipeline system in Louisiana. It serves as the pricing point for natural gas futures contracts traded on the New York Mercantile Exchange (NYMEX) and the OTC swaps traded on ICE.

53. Jonathan Stern and Howard Rogers, "The Transition to Hub-Based Gas Pricing in Continental Europe", Working Paper NG49 (Oxford: Oxford Institute of Energy Studies, March 2011).

54. "Gazprom Faces Tough Year in Europe", *World Gas Intelligence*, 2 May 2012, p. 5.

55. International Gas Union, *World LNG Report — 2013 Edition* (2013).

56. See "Industry Feedback", Annex A in EMA, "Post–3 Mtpa LNG Framework: Final Determination Paper".

57. This estimate is based on GIIGNL (International Group of Liquefied Natural Gas Importers) data.

58. See Platts, "Price Assessments — Natural Gas" <http://www.platts.com/price-assessments/natural-gas/jkm-japan-korea-marker>.

59. See International Energy Agency, *World Energy Outlook 2008* (Paris: OECD/IEA, 2008).

60. China's "White Paper on Energy" states that Chinese policies "will, step by step, change the current situation of relying too heavily on spot trading of crude oil, encourage the signing of long-term supply contracts, and promote the diversification of trading channels". China State Council Information Office, "China's Energy Conditions and Policies", *White Paper on Energy*, December 2007.

61. Conglin Xu, "Chinese NOCs' Expansion", *Oil and Gas Journal*, 22 April 2013.

62. It was sold to the state-owned China National Petroleum Corporation (CNPC) in January 2010 for US$2.2 billion. See U.S. Energy Information Administration, "Country Analysis: Singapore", updated 12 March 2013 <http://www.eia.gov/countries/cab.cfm?fips=sn>.

63. Chun Han Wong, "Singapore's Temasek Sets Up LNG Investment Firm Pavilion Energy", *Wall Street Journal*, 5 April 2013 <http://blogs.wsj.com/deals/2013/04/05/singapores-temasek-sets-up-lng-investment-firm-pavilion-energy/>.

64. For instance, see Linda Low, "Public Enterprise in Singapore", in *Singapore: Twenty-Five Years of Development*, edited by You Poh Seng and Lim Chong Yah (Singapore: Nan Yang Xing Zhou Lianhe Zaobao, 1984).

65. For a discussion of these issues, see Lawrence B. Krause, "The Government as an Entrepreneur", and Koh Ai Tee, "Savings, Investment and Entrepreneurship" in *The Singapore Economy Reconsidered*.

66. For one view of the government's role in savings and investments, see Tilak Doshi, "Chaining the Leviathan: A Public Choice Interpretation of Singapore's Elected Presidency", in *Managing Political Change in Singapore: The Elected Presidency*, edited by Kevin Y.L. Tan and Lam Peng Er (London: Routledge, 1997).

67. This section is largely drawn from Tilak Doshi and Nahim Bin Zahur (2013). "Energy Efficiency Policies in the Asia-Pacific: Can We Do Better?", Pacific Energy Summit: 2013 Summit Working Papers, National Bureau of Asian Research, March 2013 <http://www.nbr.org/downloads/pdfs/eta/PES_2013_summitpaper_Doshi_Zahur.pdf>.

68. Market-based instruments (MBIs) such as fuel or carbon taxes or emission

permit trading regimes ("cap-and-trade") that directly alter relative energy prices improve energy efficiency outcomes, often at lower costs. However, such policies are analytically distinct and discussed in Section 5.1. Such policies are also distinguished from conservation that is achieved by reducing the consumption of energy services at the cost of some personal comfort or satisfaction (for example, driving less or buying small capacity refrigerators).

69. Stephen Peake, *Transport in Transition: Lessons from the History of Energy Policy (RIIA)* (London: Royal Institute of International Affairs, Earthscan Publications, 1994).

70. Howard Geller et al., "Policies for Increasing Energy Efficiency: Thirty Years of Experience in OECD Countries", *Energy Policy* 34, no. 5 (2006): 556–73.

71. Lynn K. Price, Ernst Worrell, and Jonathan E. Sinton, "Industrial Energy Efficiency Policy in China" in *2001 ACEEE Summer Study on Energy Efficiency in Industry* (ACEEE, 2001).

72. P. Balachandra, Darshini Ravindranath, and N.H. Ravindranath, "Energy Efficiency in India: Assessing the Policy Regimes and Their Impacts", *Energy Policy* 38, no. 11 (2010): 6428–38.

73. *World Energy Outlook 2012*.

74. The Current Policies Scenario assumes no implementation of government policies beyond those already adopted by mid-2012, while the New Policies Scenario takes into account existing policy commitments and assumes that recently announced policies are implemented, though in a cautious manner. See *World Energy Outlook 2012*.

75. World Energy Council (WEC), *Energy Efficiency Policies around the World: Review and Evaluation* (London: WEC, 2008).

76. WEC, *Energy Efficiency Policies Around the World*.

77. Changes in energy intensity can be divided into three analytically distinct components: price-driven changes in demand, income-driven changes in demand, and "autonomous energy efficiency improvements" (AEEI). A variety of analytical techniques have been used to derive empirical estimates for AEEI, including statistical fitting of trends to historical energy/GDP data and establishing technical change parameters from estimated production functions. Forecasts for long-term AEEI derived from some early studies on global emission mitigation scenarios range from 0.5 to 1.0 per cent annually. The understanding of the AEEI remains incomplete, however, and it is important to note that minor differences in rates of change yield large differences over long time horizons.

78. The data cited in this paragraph is from *World Energy Outlook 2012*, pp. 271–72.

79. *World Energy Outlook 2012*, p. 272.

80. Note that that this average measure differs from the instantaneous energy/GDP elasticity, which is the percentage change in energy consumption associated with a minute change in GDP from a given absolute level.

81. In Asia, for instance, major studies that have summarized the region's energy-efficiency policies include M.V. Ayers and Edward L. Hillsman, eds., *Compendium of Energy Efficiency and Conservation: Policies/Programs, Regulations and Standards in the Asia Pacific Economic Cooperation (APEC) Member Economies* (APEC Secretariat, 1994); Peter Ramsey and Ted Flanigan, *Compendium: Asian Energy Efficiency Success Stories* (International Institute for Energy Conservation by Global Energy Efficiency Initiative, 1995); and *Energy Efficiency Indicators: A Study of Energy Efficiency Indicators in APEC Economies* (Tokyo: Asia Pacific Energy Research Centre (APERC) and the Institute of Energy Economics, 2001).

82. See International Energy Agency, "Energy Efficiency: Policies and Measures Databases" <http://www.iea.org/policiesandmeasures/energyefficiency>.

83. *World Energy Outlook 2012*, p. 276; and Hong Wen et al., *Building Energy Efficiency: Why Green Buildings are Key to Asia's Future* (Hong Kong: Inkstone Books, 2007).

84. See *Energy Efficiency: A Compelling Global Resource* (McKinsey and Company, 2010), p. 5.

85. International Energy Agency, *Promoting Energy Efficiency Investments, Case Studies in the Residential Sector* (Paris: OECD/IEA and AFD, 2008) <http://www.iea.org/publications/freepublications/publication/promotingee2008.pdf>.

86. Michael A. McNeil, Virginia E. Letschert, and Stephane de la Rue du Can, "Global Potential of Energy Efficiency Standards and Labeling Programs" (Lawrence Berkeley National Laboratory, November 2008).

87. *BP Statistical Review of World Energy* (London: BP, 2011).

88. McNeil et al. "Global Potential of Energy Efficiency Standards and Labeling Programs".

89. International Energy Agency, *Implementing Energy Efficiency Policies: Are IEA Members On Track?* (Paris: OECD/IEA, 2009).

90. International Energy Agency (IEA), *Energy Balances of Non-OECD Countries* (Paris: OECD/IEA, 2012).

91. Kazunori Kojima and Lisa Ryan, "Transport Energy Efficiency: Implementation of IEA Recommendations since 2009 and Next Steps", Information Paper (Paris: IEA, 2010).

92. WEC, *Energy Efficiency Policies around the World*.

93. Ibid.

94. WEC, *Energy Balances of Non-OECD Countries*.

95. Aimee McKane, Lynn Price, and Stephane de la Rue du Can, "Policies for Promoting Industrial Energy Efficiency in Developing Countries and Transition Economies", United Nations Industrial Development Organization Background Paper (Vienna: UNIDO, 2008).

96. Geller et al., "Policies for Increasing Energy Efficiency".

97. Kenneth Gillingham, Richard Newell, and Karen Palmer, "Energy Efficiency Policies: A Retrospective Examination", *Annual Review of Environment and Resources* 31 (November 2006): 161–92; and Elizabeth Doris, Jacquelin Cochran, and Martin Vorum, "Energy Efficiency Policy in the United States: Overview of Trends at Different Levels of Government", National Renewable Energy Laboratory Technical Report (Colorado: NREL, December 2009).

98. Geller et al., "Policies for Increasing Energy Efficiency". It should be noted that a major part of promoting emission mitigation efforts in the EU is incorporated in the EU ETS, a cap-and-trade system that affects energy prices directly.

99. IEA, *Energy Balances of Non-OECD Countries*.

100. Gillingham et al., "Energy Efficiency Policies: A Retrospective Examination"; Geller et al., "Policies for Increasing Energy Efficiency"; and Doris et al., "Energy Efficiency Policy in the United States."

101. Geller et al., "Policies for Increasing Energy Efficiency".

102. MTI, "National Energy Policy Report — Energy for Growth".

103. Energy Efficiency Programme Office of Singapore <http://www.e2singapore. gov.sg>.

104. See <http://www.e2singapore.gov.sg/energy-efficiency-programme-office. html>.

105. Ibid.

106. See <http://www.e2singapore.gov.sg/energy-challenge.html>.

107. Energy Efficiency Programme Office of Singapore <http://www.e2singapore. gov.sg/>.

108. Data for vehicle quota system COE quota computation, Land Transport Authority of Singapore <http://www.lta.gov.sg/corp_info/doc/VQS_worksheet. pdf>.

109. Building and Construction Authority, "About BCA Green Mark Scheme" <http://www.bca.gov.sg/greenmark/green_mark_buildings.html>.

110. Government of Singapore, "Energy Conservation Act 2012" <http://statutes. agc.gov.sg/aol/search/display/view.w3p;page=0;query=Status%3Acurinfor ce%20Type%3Aact,sl%20Content%3A%22EPMA%22;rec=0;resUrl=http%3A %2F%2Fstatutes.agc.gov.sg%2Faol%2Fsearch%2Fsummary%2Fresults.w3p% 3Bquery%3DStatus%253Acurinforce%2520Type%253Aact,sl%2520Content% 253A%2522EPMA%2522>.

111. IEA, *World Energy Outlook 2012*, p. 269.

112. See references cited in Ronald J. Sutherland, "Market Barriers to Energy Efficiency Investments", *Energy Journal* 12, no. 3 (1991): 15–34.

113. See Roger Carlsmith et al., *Energy Efficiency: How Far Can We Go?* (Oak Ridge: Oak Ridge National Laboratory, 1990).

114. See ibid, p. 5.

115. IEA, *World Energy Outlook 2012*, p. 280.

116. See, for instance, Carl Blumstein et al., "Overcoming Social and Institutional Barriers to Energy Conservation", *Energy* 5, no. 4 (1980): 355–71.

117. Jerry A. Hausman, "Individual Discount Rates and the Purchase and Utilization of Energy-Using Durables", *Bell Journal of Economics* 10, no. 1 (1979): 33–54.

118. Mark K. Dreyfus and W. Kip Viscusi, "Rates of Time Preference and Consumer Valuations of Automobile Safety and Fuel Efficiency", *Journal of Law and Economics* 38, no. 1 (1995): 79–105.

119. See, for instance, "Market Barriers to Energy Efficiency Investments".

120. See Lucas W. Davis, Alan Fuchs, and Paul J. Gertler, "Cash for Coolers", National Bureau of Economic Research (NBER) Working Paper 18044, May 2012; and Robert J. Michaels, "The Hidden Flaw of 'Energy Efficiency'", *Wall Street Journal*, 20 August 2012.

121. Gilbert E. Metcalf and Kevin A. Hassett, "Measuring the Energy Savings from Home Improvement Investments", *Review of Economics and Statistics* 81, no. 3 (1999): 516–28.

122. Paul L. Joskow and Donald B. Marron, "What Does a Negawatt Really Cost?", Massachusetts Institute of Technology (MIT) Center for Energy and Environment Policy Research, Discussion Paper MIT-CEPR 91-016WP, December 1991.

123. "EU Energy Savings Grants Used Wastefully — Auditors", Reuters, 14 January 2013.

124. See Ted Gayer and W. Kip Viscusi, "Overriding Consumer Preferences with Energy Regulations", Mercatus Center, George Mason University, Working Paper No. 12-21 (10 July 2012).

125. "Preliminary Regulatory Impact Analysis: CAFE for MY 2017–MY 2025", National Highway Traffic and Safety Administration (NHTSA), (November 2011), table 13.

126. Preliminary Regulatory Impact Analysis: CAFE for MY 2017–MY 2025", 711 as cited in "Overriding Consumer Preferences with Energy Regulations", p. 22.

127 See, for instance, "Overriding Consumer Preferences with Energy Regulations"; Hunt Alcott and Michael Greenstone, "Is There an Energy Efficiency Gap?", *Journal of Economic Perspectives* 26, no. 1 (2012): 3–28.

128. Minna Sunikka-Blank and Yumiko Iwafune, "Sustainable Building in Japan — Observations on a Market Transformation Policy", *Environmental Policy and Governance* 21 (2011): 351–63.

129. Adam B. Jaffe and Robert N. Stavins, "The Energy Paradox and the Diffusion of Conservation Technology", *Resource and Energy Economics* 16, no. 2 (1994): 91–122.

130. Bounded rationality suggests that consumers are rational but face cognitive constraints in processing information that lead to deviations from rationality

in certain contexts. See for instance Amos Tversky and Daniel Kahnemen, "The Framing of Decisions and the Psychology of Choice", *Science* 211, no. 4481 (1981): 453–58.

131. See Lee S. Friedman and Karl Hausker, "Residential Energy Consumption: Models of Consumer Behavior and Their Implications for Rate Design", *Journal of Consumer Policy* 11, no. 3 (1988): 287–313.

132. See Kenneth Gillingham and James Sweeney, "Barriers to Implementing Low Carbon Technologies", *Climate Change Economics* 3, no. 4 (2013).

133. See Kenneth Gillingham, Richard G. Newell, and Karen Palmer, "Energy Efficiency Economics and Policy", *Annual Review of Resource Economics* 1 (June 2009): 597–620.

134. The option value of waiting can be significant. See, for instance, Robert L. McDonald and Daniel Siegel, "The Value of Waiting to Invest", National Bureau of Economic Research (NBER) Working Paper No. 1019 (March 1987).

135. Gayer and Viscusi, "Overriding Consumer Preferences with Energy Regulations", p. 5.

136. Alcott and Greenstone, "Is There an Energy Efficiency Gap?", p. 1.

137. See, for instance, Adam B. Jaffe, Richard G. Newell, Robert N. Stavins, "The Economics of Energy Efficiency", in *Encyclopaedia of Energy*, edited by Cutler Cleveland (Amsterdam: Elsevier, 2004), pp. 79–90.

138. See Chai Kah Hin and Catrina Yeo, "Tapping Singapore's 'Fifth Fuel' Source", *Straits Times*, 19 August 2010.

139. Ibid.

140. Energy Market Authority Singapore, "Test-bedding of Electric Vehicles in Singapore from 2010", media release, 6 May 2009 <http://www.ema.gov.sg/media_release.aspx?news_sid=201406094xC38TUdG0QD>.

141. See Erica Tay, "S'pore Aims to be Key Player in Green Energy Push", *Straits Times*, 27 March 2007, p. 1.

142. Agency for Science, Technology and Research, "Energy @ A*STAR", 2007 <http://www.ices.a-star.edu.sg/media/9585/energy_astar.pdf>.

143. Economic Development Board, "S$8 Million Awarded to 3 Research Teams on Solar Energy under the Clean Energy Research Programme", media release, 1 July 2011 <http://www.news.gov.sg/public/sgpc/en/media_releases/agencies/edb/press_release/P-20110701-1/AttachmentPar/0/file/CERP04%20Press%20Release%20FINAL.pdf>.

144. Erica Tay, "$17m for Clean Energy Research Programme", *Straits Times*, 21 August 2007.

145. "Singapore's Energy Research and Development Sector Gets US$80m Funding Boost", *Oil & Gas News* via *Acquire Media NewsEdge*, 25 August 2014.

146. This section is largely drawn from Tilak K. Doshi et al., "The Economics of

Solar PV in Singapore", Discussion Paper EE/11-01 (Singapore: Energy Studies Institute, August 2011).

147. Elspeth Thomson, "Nuclear Power: Time for a Feasibility Study", published in the *Straits Times*, posted 4 July 2014 at <http://screentouch.edublogs.org/2014/06/04/nuclear-power-time-for-a-feasibility-study-says-dr-elspeth-thomson-energy-studies-institute/>.

148. See National Climate Change Secretariat, "Solar Energy Technology Primer: A Summary" (Singapore: NCCS and NRF, 2011), <https://www.nccs.gov.sg/sites/nccs/files/Solar%20Primer%20(revised).pdf>.

149. Tilak K. Doshi et al., "The Economics of Solar PV in Singapore", *GSTF Journal of Engineering Technology* 1, no. 2 (2013): 53–63.

150. Opening Remarks by Energy Market Authority Chief Executive Lawrence Wong at the Solar Awards Ceremony (30 November 2010), <https://www.nccs.gov.sg/news/opening-remarks-energy-market-authority-chief-executive-lawrence-wong-solar-awards-ceremony-30>.

151. International Energy Agency, *Projected Costs of Generating Electricity 2010* (Paris: OECD/IEA, 2010).

152. KEMA, "Research Evaluation of Wind and Solar Generation, Storage Impact, and Demand Response on the California Grid", prepared for the California Energy Commission, CEC-500-2010-010 (June 2010).

153. Robert N. Stavins, "Experience with Market-based Environment Policy Instruments", in *Handbook of Environmental Economics: Volume 2*, edited by Karl-Göran Mäler and Jeffrey R. Vincent (Amsterdam: Elsevier, 2005).

154. It should be noted however that CCS technology is still not commercially established in the industry generally, with capital costs being highly site-specific. Although the processes involved in CCS have been demonstrated in other industrial applications, no commercial scale projects which integrate these processes exist; the costs therefore are somewhat uncertain. Some estimates indicate that the cost of capturing and storing carbon dioxide is US$60 per tonne, corresponding to an increase in electricity prices of about US6 cents per kWh based on typical coal-fired power plant emissions; see Wikipedia <http://en.wikipedia.org/wiki/Carbon_capture_and_storage#Cost>.

155. International Energy Agency, "Energy Policies of IEA Countries: German — 2007 Review" (Paris: OECD/IEA, 2007).

156. Manuel Frondel et al., "Economic Impacts from the Promotion of Renewable Energy Technologies: The German Experience", *Ruhr Economic Papers*, No. 156 (2009).

157. Avinash K. Dixit and Robert S. Pindyck, *Investment under Uncertainty* (Princeton, NJ: Princeton University Press, 1994).

158. Committee on Climate Change, *The Renewable Energy Review: May 2011* (London: Committee on Climate Change, 2011), p. 95.

159. Rachel Chang, "Singapore to Buy Natural Gas from Qatar", *Straits Times*, 30 June 2010.

160. REC Solar began operations in Tuas, Singapore, in 2010 to produce 600 megawatts of solar panels annually. This constituted the largest single investment made by REC, valued at S$2.5 billion; see <http://www.recgroup.com/aboutREC/REC-in-Singapore/>. Nevertheless the global solar industry is dominated by the low-cost large Chinese manufacturers which have increasingly won global market share in competition with European and U.S. manufacturers; see, for example, Edgar Meza, "US, Chinese Solar EPC Companies Continue to Dominate Global PV Installations", *PV Magazine*, 6 August 2014 <http://www.pv-magazine.com/news/details/beitrag/us--chinese-solar-epc-companies-continue-to-dominate-global-pv-installations_1 00015970/#axzz3GWWRS7SP>.

161. Analysts exclude nuclear power and hydroelectricity, to reflect major environmental questions that face both technologies.

162. On the advantages of market-based instruments (MBIs) in achieving environmental goals at least cost, see Robert N. Stavins, "Environmental Economics", Resources for the Future Discussion Paper RFF DP 04-54 (23 December 2004). For a discussion of MBIs in the APEC context, see also Tilak Doshi and Wu Fulan, "Developing Carbon Trading in APEC Countries", in *Green Finance for Green Growth*, a report funded by APEC/South Korea for the APEC Finance Ministers Meeting (October 2011).

163. The adverse impact of the natural gas glut in the United States (with the unexpected success in unconventional natural gas extraction from shale rock and gas prices typically below US$3.00–4.00/mmbtu) on the economics of solar and wind technologies have been widely reported. See, for instance, Carolyn Beeler, "Energy Secretary Says Shale Boom Will Delay Grid Parity for Renewables", Bloomberg, 20 January 2012; and Steve LeVine, "The Latest Victim of Shale Gas — Clean Energy Technology", *Foreign Policy*, 23 January 2012 <http://foreignpolicy.com/2012/01/23/the-latest-victim-of-shale-gas-clean-energy-technology/>.

164. The damage on health and property caused by local pollution can be more readily measured, and alleviating local and regional pollutants such as NOx, SOx and particulate matter can be more readily targeted through policy actions at the national level. However, cross-border regional pollution can be far more difficult to handle, such as the case of the seasonal forest fires on the Indonesian islands of Sumatra and Kalimantan which affect neighbouring countries such as Malaysia and Singapore.

165. See, for instance, Jonathan Adler, "Rent Seeking behind the Green Curtain", *Regulation* 19, no. 4 (1996); Terry L. Anderson, ed., *Political Environmentalism: Going behind the Green Curtain* (Stanford: Hoover Institution Press, 2000).

166. The literature on public choice and rent-seeking is voluminous and early contributions by economists such as George Stigler, Jagdish Bhagwati, and Anne Krueger cast the foundations in this area of research during the 1970s and 1980s.

167 See, for instance, Charles Wolf, *Markets or Government: Choosing between Imperfect Alternatives* (Cambridge: MIT Press, 1991).

168. "Chaining the Leviathan: A Public Choice Interpretation of Singapore's Elected Presidency".

169. Paula E. Stephan, "The Economics of Science", *Journal of Economic Literature* 34, no. 3 (1996): 1199–1235.

170. See Kenneth J. Arrow, "Economic Welfare and the Allocation of Resources for Invention", cited in Terence Kealey, *The Economic Laws of Scientific Research* (Macmillan, 1996), p. 224.

171. According to the Bell Labs' head of transistor research in the 1940s, it was impossible to hire people "because solid state physics was not in the curriculum of the universities", cited in *The Economic Laws of Scientific Research* (London), p. 218. Indeed, Bell Labs was running a course for academic physicists (see ibid.).

172. Edwin Mansfield, "Academic Research and Industrial Innovation", *Research Policy* 20, no. 1 (1991): 1–12.

173. The term "cross fertilization" is used in *The Economic Laws of Scientific Research* to describe the dependence of academic science on technological and industrial research for continued basic science advance.

174. Zvi Griliches, "Productivity, R&D, and Basic Research at the Firm Level in the 1970s", *American Economic Review* 76, no. 1 (1986): 141–54.

175. Lim Chuan Poh, "Singapore's Biomedical Sciences Push", *Straits Times*, 27 September 2011.

176. See, for instance, Chang Ai-Lien, "Star Biomed Couple Leaving Singapore", *Straits Times*, 13 August 2011; Chang Ai-Lien, "Returns Not Always About Money, Says Star Scientist", *Straits Times*, 7 September 2011.

177. See *The Economic Laws of Scientific Research* and the references therein.

178. See Richard Beason and David E. Weinstein, "Growth, Economies of Scale and Targeting in Japan (1955–1990)", *Review of Economics and Statistics* 78, no. 2 (1996).

179. Organisation for Economic Co-operation and Development, *The Sources of Economic Growth in OECD Countries* (Paris: OECD, 2003), p. 85.

180. For this argument, see Terence Kealey, *Sex, Science and Profits* (London: Vintage Books, 2009).

181. Kenneth J. Arrow et al., "A Statement on the Appropriate Role for R&D in Climate Policy", *Economists Voice* 6, no. 1 (2009).

182. The problem of agency dependency is well recognized in the public choice

literature on the widely observed phenomenon of regulatory capture. See, for instance, George Stigler, "The Theory of Economic Regulation", *Bell Journal of Economics and Management Science* 2, no. 1 (1971): 3–21.

183. See, for instance, Philippe Aghion, "Green Innovation", transcript of audio interview of Phillipe Aghion of Harvard University, November 2010 <http://voxeu.org/index.php?q=node/5744>.

184. Goh Keng Swee, "Entrepreneurship in a Plural Economy", *Malayan Economic Review* 3, no. 1 (1958): 1–7.

185. For an example of the popular view that East Asian governments successfully "plan innovation" with Singapore as an exemplary case, see Parag Khanna and Ayesha Khanna, "What is it About Singapore?", *Straits Times*, 26 May 2012. For a devastating critique, see the review by Evgeny Morozov, "The Naked and the TED", *New Republic*, 2 August 2012.

186. This section is largely drawn from Tilak Doshi, "ASEAN Energy Integration: Interconnected Power and Gas Pipeline Grids", in *Enhancing ASEAN's Connectivity*, edited by Sanchita Basu Das (Singapore: Institute of Southeast Asian Studies, 2013), pp. 142–62.

187. International Energy Agency, *World Energy Outlook* (Paris: OECD/IEA, 2006).

188. "ASEAN Vision 2020", 15 December 1997 <http://www.asean.org/news/item/asean-vision-2020>.

189. See "ASEAN Plan of Action for Energy Cooperation (APAEC) 2010–2015" <http://aseanenergy.org/media/filemanager/2012/10/11/f/i/file_1.pdf>.

190. Benjamin K. Sovacool, "Energy Policy and Cooperation in Southeast Asia: The History, Challenges and Implications of the Trans-ASEAN Gas Pipeline (TAGP) Network", *Energy Policy* 37, no. 6 (June 2009): 2356–67.

191. Patricia Ohli, "Trans-Asian Gas Network Could Cost $66 Billion", *Pipeline and Gas Journal* 221, no. 8 (1994): 1–2.

192. In 1994, for example, ASEAN commissioned a regional "Masterplan Study on Natural Gas Development and Utilization in ASEAN" with technical assistance from the EU. See "ASEAN Plan of Action for Energy Cooperation 1999–2004" (3 July 1999) <http://www.asean.org/news/item/asean-plan-of-action-for-energy-cooperation-1999-2004>.

193. See "Natural Gas Infrastructure Development: Southeast Asia", Asia Pacific Research Centre, 2000; various press reports.

194. "ASEAN and ASCOPE Lay Foundation for Growth", *Petromin Pipeliner* (January–March 2011).

195. See, for instance, Asian Development Bank, "Loan 1357 — INO: Gas Transmission and Distribution Project" (April 2002) <http://www.adb.org/sites/default/files/project-document/71156/ino-gas-transmission.pdf>.

196. While energy cooperation in ASEAN was first mooted in the aftermath of the oil crisis in 1975 with the formation of ASCOPE, the concept of a network of

gas pipelines connecting the region was first discussed in 1986, and formally announced at an ASEAN meeting on Energy Cooperation in 1990. See "Energy Policy and Cooperation in Southeast Asia", pp. 2357–58.

197. See *BP Statistical Review of World Energy 2010* (London: BP, 2010).

198. See, for instance, "Indonesia Will No Longer Renew LNG Export Contracts", Xinhua, 18 February 2010.

199. "Malaysia LNG's New Sick Man?", *World Gas Intelligence*, 15 December 2010.

200. Alfian, "RI May Lower Gas Export to Singapore", *Jakarta Post*, 17 June 2011.

201. See International Energy Agency, *Golden Age for Natural Gas* (Paris: OECD/IEA, 2009). The report covers the outlook for small-scale LNG trade in Southeast Asia, partly based on research conducted by ESI on this topic, in collaboration with the natural gas team at the IEA.

202. In December 2010, Pertamina, the Indonesian national oil company, appointed ExxonMobil together with Petronas and Total S.A. as partners in the development of the East Natuna gas block. See Erwida Maulia, "Politicians Question ExxonMobil's Presence in East Natuna", *Jakarta Post*, 27 January 2011.

203. The Heads of ASEAN Power Utilities/Authorities (HAPUA) commissioned the ASEAN Interconnections Masterplan Study (AIMS), which was completed in 2003. See Andy Purnama Roesli, "HAPUA and the ASEAN Power Grid for Optimum Use of Energy Resources" (10–11 October 2006) <http://www.asean-sustainable-energy.net/documents/libraries/001/HAPUASecretary%20akhir%20Bangkok%206-10-06.pdf>.

204. See, for instance, "Interview: Malaysia to Revise Electricity Tariffs — Najib", Reuters, 4 February 2008 <http://uk.reuters.com/article/2008/02/04/malaysia-economy-fuel-idUKKLR4031820080204>; Reva Sasistiya, "Indonesia to Lift Subsidies Gradually", *Jakarta Globe*, 24 March 2010 <http://www.thejakartaglobe.com/business/indonesia-to-lift-electricity-subsidies-gradually/365652>.

205. See "Leaders Fiddle as Sumatra Burns", *The Economist*, 22 May 2014.

206 The McKinsey report is cited in "Report of the Eminent Persons Group on the ASEAN Charter", December 2006 <http://www.asean.org/archive/19247.pdf>.

6

CONCLUDING REMARKS:
"The Three E's"

The somewhat inelegantly termed "trilemma" — the trade-offs among the trio of policy objectives of energy security, environmental sustainability, and economic competitiveness — has given rise to much study and even more contention. The many examples of policy initiatives in various countries discussed in this book give evidence to the costly failures that can result from poorly thought out or populist solutions to energy sector issues, with unintended consequences for social welfare. In many cases, the scale of perverse effects has been such that the very purpose of energy policy is subverted. It is the contention of this book that policy objectives need clear delineation and focus, so that appropriate actions can be formulated and implemented when necessary in a manner which minimizes unintended consequences. The concluding remarks below summarize the arguments offered in earlier chapters on the "three E's" confluence of energy security, environmental sustainability, and economic competitiveness. These remarks end with an impressionistic scorecard for Singapore's performance in achieving its energy policy objectives.

ENERGY SECURITY

"Energy security" is a term that has long bedevilled energy policy debates among politicians, businessmen, and academics. Indeed, the term is evoked by players across the policy spectrum, from the more extreme "green" non-governmental organizations (NGOs) whose constant refrain is of the risks of cataclysmic climate change, to the many business groups and public or private resource owners and users with vested interests across the energy value chain. Being so contested by different political and economic constituencies, the term carries its multi-hued meanings to the point of contradiction. Hence, the call for enhanced energy security is often invoked to support conflicting policy positions. In the United States, proponents of subsidies for alternative energy and electric vehicles invoke the mantra of energy security as forcefully as the politicians who support their local coal-fuelled power stations. While both positions claim to reduce America's dependence on energy imports, their approach to climate change issues could not be more opposed.

To engage popular attention, there are attempts made every now and then to measure the many dimensions of energy security, in order to arrive at some simpler metric — somewhat akin to the Doomsday Clock signifying the distance to global (or national) disaster by the minutes remaining to midnight. One recent example is the "Index of U.S. Energy Security" compiled by the U.S. Chamber of Commerce's energy policy group.[1] In its own words, the report provides "the first quantifiable measurement of energy security based on thirty-seven individual metrics". The thirty-seven components of data are assembled under four headings — geopolitical, economic, reliability and environment. The first two categories are given 30 per cent each, and the latter two, 20 per cent each. No reasons are given as to why this particular weighting is adopted, and one can only surmise that this is the considered judgement of the report's expert authors.

These attempts at measurement often start with a smorgasbord of data — dependence on energy imports, household and business expenditures on energy use as a percentage of total operating costs, the intensity of energy inputs in economy activity, price volatility of energy commodities, political stability of energy-exporting regions, and the like. Through what are essentially ad hoc exercises of judgement, these characteristics are then arbitrarily weighted and ranked to yield a single metric measuring energy security.

Inevitably, simplistic attempts at measuring energy security come up with dubious results. Two examples suffice to make the point. The U.S. Chamber's index applies over 10 per cent weight to the crude oil price component alone, with higher oil prices bringing down the score. Yet, there is a world of difference between high oil prices caused by increasing demand for energy during prosperous times of rising incomes, and high oil prices followed by recessions caused by supply side shocks, like those of the 1970s. High oil prices on an economic upswing provide signals to encourage exploration and production efforts, spur innovation in conservation and alternative energy technologies, and generally guide markets to more efficient use of scarce resources; high oil prices during an economic downturn are usually the effect of supply-side restrictions of one sort or another.

The second example relates to the metrics employed under the "environment" heading. The U.S. Chamber's index measures variables such as carbon dioxide (CO_2) emissions per capita and per U.S. dollar gross domestic product (GDP), with higher emissions indicating a lower score for energy security. Yet, it is precisely those countries too poor to have a high carbon footprint that face the greatest challenges in providing their citizens with adequate energy at affordable prices for such basic needs as cooking and lighting. From the perspective of a developing country then, it would indeed be in its interest to score lower (i.e., more negatively) on the U.S. Chamber of Commerce index, since a higher carbon footprint is also correlated to the wealth of its citizens, other things being equal.

Energy security has been the justification for much bad policy.[2] Former U.S. President Jimmy Carter's "moral equivalent of war" energy policy with its xenophobic notion of "energy independence" is just one of the more commented upon examples of poor economic sense. The idea that energy security can be improved by ending import dependence on oil and gas from the Middle East is unrealistic and misguided. Crude oil markets are now inherently global, where arbitrage among many players establishes international trading patterns and worldwide oil prices adjusted for quality and transport differentials. A policy of simply redirecting oil trade flows established by international oil markets will almost invariably be costly and does nothing to enhance energy security.

Many large Asian national oil companies have embarked on aggressive campaigns to establish equity ownership of oil and gas fields around the world. But state-directed purchases of oil and gas stakes can endanger rather than enhance energy security. "Making oil" via exploration and production investments is not inherently superior to simply buying oil in open markets; it all depends on whether you are better at "making" oil or making other goods and services to sell in order to buy the needed oil or gas. It is well understood since the days of the eighteenth century classical economist David Ricardo that countries should specialize in their comparative advantage and use export earnings for required imports.

Willingness to pay world market prices for oil will secure all that a country needs in peacetime. While it is always possible for oil exporting countries to threaten the interests of particular net oil-importing countries for political objectives, such supply disruptions would likely hurt oil producers more than consumers; in most cases, oil producers are very dependent on oil revenues and have much fewer degrees of freedom to their oil export policies than commonly thought. In a study of oil markets since 1970, the late oil economist M.A. Adelman pronounced in 1995 that one would have to "look in vain for an example of a government that deliberately avoids a higher income".[3] Another more recent observation agrees: "for the past quarter century, the oil output decisions of Islamic Iran have been no more menacing or unpredictable than Canada's or Norway's".[4]

Ultimately, the correct policy lesson is the conventional one. Energy security is best served by efficient markets and policies which ensure that markets work, investments and technologies cross borders freely, and diverse energy commodities trade unhindered. For Singapore, without a drop of oil of its own, this lesson is a given one. Its status as one of the world's great oil refining, trading, and storage centres — with "FOB Singapore" price quotes guiding the flows of some 12–15 million barrels per day of crude oil and refined products "East of Suez" — is proof enough.

ENVIRONMENTAL SUSTAINABILITY

The much-cited Bruntland Report of 1987 defined environmental sustainability as "development that meets the needs of the present without compromising the ability of future generations to meet their own needs".[5] The perceived depletion of natural resources as known reserves of minerals and metals get exhausted and their real prices increase has been of concern to policymakers at least since the 1970s when the Club of Rome report on the "limits to growth" received wide press coverage.[6]

But fears of resource depletion seem misplaced. A World Bank study for the period 1900–86 for twenty-four major commodities show a price decline of 0.59 per cent annually; if the data is disaggregated, the fall in the price of metals is steeper, at 0.84 per cent annually.[7] Another study, covering the more extensive period of 140 years (over 1862–1999) for metals, minerals, and agricultural commodities but excluding food and fuels, found a decline of 1.3 per cent per annum.[8] A more recent analysis, based on twenty-four commodity price series and seven indices which were originally developed for the World Bank study mentioned above but which have been updated to the year 2000 in order to cover the entire century, also found "a significant deterioration in their [i.e., primary commodities] barter terms of trade over the course of the twentieth century".[9] This decline was neither continuous, nor was it distributed evenly among individual products, however. The data shows "that the far-reaching changes that the world economy underwent around 1920 and again around 1980 led to a stepwise deterioration which, over the long term, was reflected in a decline of nearly 1 per cent per year in aggregate real prices for raw materials".[10]

Reflecting the steep climb in crude oil prices in the decade to 2008 (which reached a peak of US$140 per barrel), a vociferous debate has taken place between "Peak Oil" proponents, who claim that increasing oil scarcity and the ultimate depletion of global oil reserves are already apparent, and those who hold less pessimistic views.[11] Most industry experts agree that a large portion of the easily accessed, conventional oil reserves have already been discovered, and that increased production outside of the Organization of the Petroleum Exporting Countries (OPEC) will take place in more difficult or hostile environments at higher cost and risk, such as the deep-water prospects in the Arctic. But the "oil question" (as for all natural resources) for most economists is about price, available technology, and marginal costs of production, rather than some ultimate physical "availability" in the sense of a finite amount of supply in the ground consumed at a certain rate.

To many practitioners in the industry, the limits to the supply of natural resources are not just about "below ground" issues (reserves estimates, reservoir characteristics, production engineering, etc.), but also critically a function of "above ground" matters which include regulatory and policy uncertainty, quality of local personnel and sub-contractors, security risks to personnel, lack of available infrastructure and environmental activism by non-governmental organizations. It is clear that the history of commodity prices is no guide to their future trajectory. Yet, it is also true that the long-run historical evidence is not very supportive of those who perceive increasing scarcity for minerals and metals. Thus, for instance, new technological advancements in horizontal drilling and hydraulic fracturing of shale rock have led to the remarkable surge in oil and gas production in the United States over the past few years. Far from an ever-greater dependence on oil and gas imports, the country has now emerged as a potentially large exporter of oil and natural gas. This is contrary to all expectations of expert opinion on US oil and production trends that was prevalent as recently as five years ago. The drastic drop in oil prices from the $100–120 per barrel range to S$50–60 per barrel in the second half of 2014 has only added further scepticism to proponents of increasing resource scarcity.

As concerns of depleting resources have abated since the alarmist Club of Rome report, newer concerns of rising carbon emissions and anthropogenic global warming have taken centre stage. According to the Fourth Assessment Report (AR4) by the Intergovernmental Panel on Climate Change (IPCC), best estimates for six global warming scenarios range from 1.1°C to 2.9°C for the low scenario to 2.4°C to 6.4°C for the high scenario; with a 95 per cent confidence interval, the likely range is from 1°C to 6°C.[12] Prior to the issuance of the AR4, the British government commissioned a study on the long-run potential cost of extreme climate change. The resulting "Stern Review on the Economics of Climate Change", the largest and most widely known and discussed study of its kind, was released in October 2006 by economist Lord Nicholas Stern. The then British prime minister, Tony Blair, stated that the review demonstrated that scientific evidence of global warming was "overwhelming" and its consequences "disastrous" if the world failed to act. Professor Stern's conclusions were stark and alarming: "if we don't act, the costs and risks of climate change will be equivalent to losing at least 5 per cent of GDP each year, now and forever. If a wider range of risks and impacts is taken into account, the estimates of damage could rise to 20 per cent of GDP or more".[13]

The Stern Review's findings of catastrophic economic costs differ dramatically from a number of other economic modelling studies, most prescribing relatively modest rates of greenhouse gas (GHG) emissions reduction in the short run, followed by steeper cuts in the medium and long term.[14] In order to balance the costs of action against the risks of inaction, these studies in the main call for a progressive shift in investments to more intensive emission reductions over time, beginning with relatively modest investments now, as climate change damages increase relative to global output in the long run. Ultimately, Stern's radical views on policy imperatives for steep immediate cuts in GHG emissions are a result of extreme assumptions of discount rates. Its assumption of a 0.1 per cent per annum discount rate over the long run magnifies the impact of uncertain future damages and supports deep, immediate, and hence expensive emission reductions now. It puts a very high value (over 90 per cent) on saving a life one hundred years in the future relative to saving a life now. If higher interest rates are used to discount the value of future benefits, Stern's results collapse. Some studies rate the uncertain future harm done by climate change in the twenty-second century as likely to be less costly than the certain harm done by a massive reallocation of resources now to mitigate climate change when global deaths are in the main accounted for by immediate issues of global hunger, dirty water, malaria, and indoor smoke.[15]

There are two pertinent concepts of discount rates that are typically used in the extant economic models of climate change. The first is the real return on investment which also measures the opportunity cost of capital for investment decisions. The second is often termed the "pure rate of social time preference" to reflect society's normative views on intergenerational equity. Professor William Nordhaus, of Yale University, for instance, uses a 6 per cent annual discount rate for his climate change model simulations to reflect the return to U.S. corporate capital over the four decades to 2007.[16] The IPCC's Second Assessment Report (AR2) used returns ranging from 5 per cent to 26 per cent per annum.[17]

To adopt an interest rate much lower than the general level of real returns that capital investments can achieve, one would have to substitute one's own subjective view of intergenerational equity as appropriate to justify costly investments in emission mitigation efforts. Efforts at mitigating climate change by a drastic increase in investments in energy conservation and renewable energy, for instance, can be justified by using very low discount rates, to pull investment resources away from competing uses. It can be argued that as private investment decisions do not take into account the social benefits of mitigating climate change for future generations, the level of private investment undertaken will fall short of the optimum. In this argument, the public sector should therefore make up for the shortfall by adopting an interest rate well below that of capital markets.

This line of argument essentially replaces the real cost of capital as measured in actual markets with a personal judgement as to what balance society should choose in the trade-off between the (certain) present costs of climate change mitigation measures and the (uncertain) future benefits of such measures. However, even if consumption by present and future generations is given equal weight on ethical grounds, there would still be a reason to discount future benefits. An additional unit of consumption by future generations would count for less than an additional unit of consumption today, since future generations would be richer than the current generation. Subjective views on intergenerational equity matter little to the real world of global financial and capital markets. More often than not, these markets constitute the ultimate reference points for governments responsible for protecting national interests in international climate change negotiations.

Apart from interest rates, the other most leveraging set of assumptions underlying the IPCC's global warming scenarios are the long-run economic growth projections of various countries and regions that lead to the requisite flows of energy use and GHG emissions. According to the scenarios posed in AR4, the world, on average, will be four to eighteen times richer in 2100 than today; in the extreme global warming scenario of 6°C, the average poor country income per head rises from US$1,000 today to over US$66,000 in 2100 in real terms (i.e., adjusted for inflation).[18] Any reasonable approach to deciding on the trade-off between imposing costs now to mitigate climate change and imposing costs on future generations should take the higher expected future standards of living into account. Richer countries — with their commensurately higher capacity to handle adverse environmental changes — are less vulnerable to climate change disruptions and can afford to invest more on mitigation and adaptation measures. Hence, poorer societies may well find it appropriate to focus on increasing living standards first, before taking on the challenge of alleviating climate change challenges they may have to face in the uncertain future.

ECONOMIC COMPETITIVENESS

Competitive markets help maximize the benefits of resource use across society by providing a mechanism to allocate these resources to the highest-value use. However, markets can fail to achieve this outcome due to market failures when characteristics such as public goods, externalities, or increasing returns to scale apply in specific sectors. These have provided a rationale for government to intervene in markets. However, the support for regulatory intervention often rests on the implicit assumption that government failure does not occur, and that if it does occur, then it does not outweigh the costs of the market failure to be remedied. Excessive or poorly designed regulations can negatively affect innovation, lower economic efficiency, and reduce investments, resulting in real costs to the economy.

The promotion of energy efficiency has been and is a major goal for most economies. It is rightly seen as a criterion in assuring economic competitiveness. Energy efficiency improvements may be constrained due to market failures which might call for regulatory intervention. However, these interventions require careful analysis of not only the benefits of total energy savings but also the costs. Energy efficiency regulations have often been driven by "good science", i.e., science that can be replicated and verified by a variety of accredited institutions. Yet, as we have seen in previous chapters, good science alone — without good economics — is not the basis of good policy. The existence of technical potential of particular renewable or energy saving technologies has sometimes led policymakers to institute wide-ranging programmes to promote these technologies, often at a great cost to the economy. A case in point would be the biofuels programme in the United States, which has failed to produce an economically viable alternative to liquid fossil fuels after decades of support afforded to the industry. In this case, the critical distinction between technical potential and economic viability seemed lost in the policy formulation process.

Unexploited and profitable investment options for energy efficiency and renewable energy technologies have long been held by proponents as "win-win" opportunities to help an economy save money and reduce the negative externalities associated with energy use. The fact that options to improve energy efficiency or to promote new renewable energy technologies are not being adopted on a large scale by consumers or producers despite their net private benefits has been an oft-cited "anomaly" in the literature. Mainstream economists often refer to this anomaly in informal parlance as the "$20 bill on the sidewalk" syndrome: efficient markets do not imply that there cannot be such a thing (in the very short term), only that it is not a sound investment to go looking for $20 bills on the sidewalk. It is highly likely that the cost of looking for such anomalies exceeds the benefits in most states of the world. In questioning whether such anomalies are pervasive in the energy sector, one study of energy efficiency regulations finds that "it should be a red flag that something is amiss with an analysis which assumes such perplexing consumer and firm behaviour that runs counter to the most rudimentary economic theory and our general sense that we do not live in a world in which people never make sound choices".[19]

It thus behoves analysts to assess government energy sector policies with a high degree of clarity as to what constitutes costs and benefits as perceived by private decision makers, and why they could systematically diverge from expert views of costs and benefits. Whilst market barriers might exist in specific cases, not all require a policy response. The guiding principle to policy interventions is that they must improve societal welfare. Given this perspective, energy efficiency and the support of renewable energy technologies should not be considered as a goal in itself, but as a means of achieving economically efficient and equitable outcomes.

Regulatory regimes for promoting energy efficiency, if poorly conceived, can be costly and unintentionally cause large welfare losses. Energy, like transport and telecommunications, is a key intermediate input in most sectors of the economy, and distortions in its price or reliability can have large economic and social costs. In formulating and implementing regulations to promote energy-efficiency initiatives, it is critical that new regulations meet the tests of unbiased cost-benefit analysis. Faulty or misconceived notions about costs and benefits can lead to unnecessary and significant burdens being imposed on businesses and households. Further research should utilize random controlled trials and *ex post* analysis to estimate the impact of energy-efficiency programmes in the context of heterogeneous consumers and unobserved costs and benefits. Singapore's energy efficiency initiatives described in this book could well benefit from scrutiny of carefully controlled and randomized *ex post* analysis of social costs.

Perhaps the most fundamental observation on optimal energy policy is that producers and consumers require information and price signals that reflect true social costs and who then make their own choices and adjustments. If it is claimed that households and firms are poorly informed about energy-efficiency improvements or new energy technologies that can be profitably exploited under current conditions, an information disclosure policy would seem to be the most direct and appropriate solution. Before regulatory agencies consider more intrusive forms of intervention such as awarding subsidies or imposing mandatory standards based on technology or engineering performance criteria, it should be demonstrated that private decisions are flawed and informational remedies inadequate.

The principle of consumer rationality underpins cost-benefit analysis, and in most contexts, individuals are best placed to make the market decisions that affect themselves. The heterogeneity of individuals' tastes, preferences, and financial resources suggest that analyses based on a hypothetical "average" consumer in formulating mandatory standards for energy-using durables may be deficient. If the assumption of consumer rationality is abandoned, it would lead to the presumption that the analyst or policymaker is better placed to make decisions on behalf of consumers, subverting the very basis of any analysis purporting to objectively weigh costs and benefits.

An implicit assumption underwriting popular discussions of government mandates for promoting renewable energy is that free markets are insufficient to develop new energy technologies, thus giving rise to "market barriers" which governments need to remedy. Government regulatory incentives and sanctions in support of renewable energy are thus justified by alleged market barriers, and governments need to "step in" to induce the technological developments required for the commercialization of new energy technologies. More specifically, it is often assumed that if a technology is shown to be technically feasible, then government support would make it possible for it to become commercially viable. In this argument, these potentially viable renewable energy technologies would become commercial if given government support to "scale up". But it is not clear just what it is that government can do to achieve commercialization of new technologies with greater success than the private sector. History, after all, is replete with examples of failed government enterprise.

To the extent that government agency officials are driven by specific mission objectives and key performance indicators, this naturally creates tendencies to focus on narrow criteria such as promoting energy efficiency or renewable energy. This renders other attributes less relevant. Such "mission myopia" can lead regulators to construe rational choice by consumers or investors as "misguided". The normative implication is that analysts and policymakers are better equipped to decide in the best interests of firms and households, an untenable outcome in a free market economy. Indeed, if the consumer sovereignty and profit-maximization assumptions of basic economic analysis are set aside, then the rational assessment of alternative use of resources for societal welfare becomes the province of the judgements of "experts". A natural corollary then is for governments to prefer "command-and-control" type regulations. Such regulations or mandates overrule private choice, for instance by imposing product bans or mandatory standards on technical specifications. It is well established that direct command-and-control type regulations are less cost effective than market-based instruments that "get prices right" (for instance, carbon taxes that internalize environmental externalities) and allow full choice to private decision makers.

The road ahead for energy efficiency and renewable energy policies can be positive if governments can play a constructive role in mitigating real market failures while avoiding wasteful subsidies which serve neither efficiency nor equity. While long-supported subsidies for fuels and electricity are difficult to discontinue for many governments but need to be got rid of, it is just as important to avoid the temptation to impose intrusive regulations or mandates to support renewable energy and energy efficiency objectives. As we have seen, ill-thought out mandates and regulations carry hidden costs that can lead to unnecessary burdens being imposed on firms and households. Singapore's many initiatives in promoting energy efficiency and in energy-related R&D needs to be put in a context sensitive to such potential burdens and where claimed benefits are not apparent in any objective analysis of private choice.

SINGAPORE'S SCORECARD FOR THE "3E'S" — AN IMPRESSIONISTIC SUMMARY

By any reasonable standard, Singapore has successfully achieved the broad objectives of energy security, environmental sustainability and economic growth over the decades since independence. As a free-market economy and one of Asia's leading financial, transport, and oil trading centres, Singapore has capitalized on its strategic location at the corner of the East Asian land mass between the Indian and Pacific Oceans. At the southern end of the Strait of Malacca with a natural deep-water port, the island's locational advantages were apparent to its colonial founders in the mid-nineteenth century. By the early 1980s, Singapore was already one of the world's busiest shipping and fuel bunkering ports; East Asia's hub for oil refining, petrochemicals manufacturing and trading; and an important supplier of offshore vessels, equipment, and services for the oil and gas industries in Southeast Asia and beyond.

The International Monetary Fund (IMF) lists Singapore as the country with the third highest GDP per capita (measured at purchasing power parity) in the world at almost $64,600 per annum in current international dollars in 2013, behind Qatar and Luxemburg, and ahead of Norway, Brunei and Hong Kong. Singapore's economic success has been interpreted by some observers as vindication for active government intervention and appropriate industrial policy which goes beyond the usual strictures of mainstream economic theory as inspired by Adam Smith. Indeed, it has become commonplace to argue in some influential circles that East Asian economic success in economic growth has demonstrated the fallacy of the minimalist approach to economic policy and supports the case of sophisticated government intervention in industrial policy. A positive analysis of Singapore's economic growth experience, however, suggests that the government policy did not so much "pick winners" as reduce transaction costs and risk premiums for private enterprise, particularly foreign direct investments. For Singapore to achieve rapid economic growth there was "no realistic alternative to the free enterprise system" according to Dr Goh Keng Swee, the country's founding economic architect.

Of the five strategies identified by government as integral to the country's energy policy framework — promote competitive markets, diversify energy sources, enhance energy efficiency, develop the energy industry and invest in research and development, and participate in international and regional cooperative arrangements in energy security and infrastructure initiatives — the first would seem to be the bedrock of Singapore's policy architecture. In particular, Singapore's well-established policy stance against financing subsidies outside of the social sectors such as housing, health, and education has helped the city-state avoid the pitfalls of poor energy policy. There is little reason to believe that in Singapore, where energy prices reflect real opportunity costs (including costs of traffic congestion, etc.), there is a vast "energy efficiency gap" caused by market barriers. There is even less reason to believe that such barriers need to be surmounted by some of the more intrusive government policies being pursued in many countries discussed in this book. The evidence cited for "market barriers", primarily in applied management and engineering studies, seems weak or, at best, unproven in many cases where there are no clear reasons to expect well-defined market failures.

As we have seen, there is ample evidence of the adverse unintended consequences in many countries which have liberally used a system of subsidies, taxes, and regulatory mandates to support particular technologies or fuels in the pursuit of energy policy objectives ranging from social equity to energy efficiency and "green jobs". It is often observed that the historical record of governments successfully "picking winners" is a relatively sparse one. For example, the bankruptcy of US solar manufacturer Solyndra proved to be no exception. It was just one of the more scandalous examples of renewable energy subsidies that lost taxpayers' money on a bet that governments should not take.[20]

Singapore's energy policy experience is not just one of "getting the prices right". The government has made very large public investments to build the liquefied natural gas (LNG) regasification terminal and the underground Jurong Caverns oil and petrochemicals storage infrastructure to support energy security and diversification objectives. Evidently, these investments have a public goods characteristic to them, and market values cannot measure the social cost-benefit ratio of such investments. In the provision of public goods, the government may use a lower "social rate of time discount" rather than the private sector's market-determined rate for the cost of capital. Even if the government's energy sector investments fail to yield a good return measured in terms of the opportunity costs of alternative public investments, its intangible strategic value in terms of energy security may be perceived by policymakers to be a higher-order criterion. Ultimately the success of the outcome will be measured by whether government investments in the sector can cost-effectively enhance Singapore's role as the region's premier hub for shipping and bunkering, oil refining and petrochemicals manufacture, and, looking forward, LNG trading.

Singapore is an affluent city-state with advanced capabilities of handling local environmental challenges. Since the country's inception, its leaders had envisioned the development of a "Garden City", a place where the balance between economic and environmental goals would be used as the basis for urban planning. The Parks and Recreation Department (PRD) was established in 1976 to undertake the task of "greening Singapore", and its results have been a matter of admiration for its many tourists as well as citizens. Given its space constraints, its planners have reclaimed land, resulting in the expansion of Singapore's land area to approximately 710.3 km² in 2009 from 581.5 km² in the 1960s. This amounts to a remarkable increase of over 20 per cent of the land area. Thus the country is no stranger to adapting the environment to suit its needs. Faced with the urban blight of traffic jams and gridlock, Singapore has been among the global leaders in instituting a system of congestion charges via electronic road pricing technology. The gains of an efficient road transport and mass transit systems have also had collateral benefits of reduced air pollution from road traffic.

Singapore's posture to international climate change negotiations is similarly pragmatic. As we have seen in a previous chapter, the country's leaders have clearly articulated Singapore's stand on participating in climate change mitigation and adaptation actions if a global regime on climate change policy were to be agreed. The proviso that Singapore insists on is that such agreements cannot be at the expense of the legitimate aspirations of its citizens for improving living standards. This view — that countries will be part of an agreement provided it is equitable and does not impose an inordinate constraint on its economic competitiveness and economic growth — is quite naturally shared in general by many countries. Nevertheless, "the devil is in the details", and in the context of the difficult economic recovery from the deep financial recession of 2008/9, ongoing climate change negotiations to establish a post-Kyoto global climate change regime will likely be long and tortuous.

The potential impact of adopting particular policy postures in various international climate change negotiations on Singapore's economic competitiveness is a central policy challenge. In pursuing carbon emission mitigation and adaptation actions, Singapore's policymakers, like their compatriots elsewhere, need to balance competing policy objectives. Singapore has to maintain its reputational stake in the community of nations in the post-Kyoto era while pursuing prudent policies to balance economic, social, and environmental objectives. Such objectives ultimately need to be supported in the main by its citizenry in the context of democratic values and generational changes in norms and ideals associated with a younger, more demanding electorate.

Reflecting on Singapore's extraordinary ability to marshal savings and investment resources for rapid industrial and infrastructure development, the late Nobel Laureate Franco Modigliani (in Singapore as a Lee Kuan Yew Distinguished Visitor in 1992) remarked that "Singapore is accumulating assets on a massive scale.... you wonder what is the point; do you want your kids much wealthier than you are?"[21] Singapore is one of the few countries where the IMF has questioned whether government savings might not be excessive, favouring consumption by future generations at the expense of the current one.[22] In making policy choices regarding energy security, environmental sustainability and economic welfare, the Singapore government needs to ensure a reasonable trade-off between the immediate costs incurred against the estimated future benefits of policy actions undertaken. All elected and responsible governments need to think of future generations but the challenge is in setting the right terms of bargain with the present one in policymaking and at the ballot box.

Notes

1. U.S. Chamber of Commerce, Institute for 21st Century Energy. "Index of US Energy Security", 2010 <http://www.energyxxi.org/2010-index-us-energy-security-risk-report>.
2. Tilak Doshi, "'Energy Security' has Produced Much Bad Policy", *Straits Times*, 4 January 2011 <http://www.esi.nus.edu.sg/docs/default-document-library/2011jan04-st-energy-security-has-produced-much-bad-policy.pdf>.
3. M.A. Adelman, *The Genie Out of the Bottle: World Oil Since 1970* (Cambridge, MA: MIT Press, 1995), cited in Jerry Taylor and Peter Van Doren, "The Energy Security Obsession", *Georgetown Journal of Law & Public Policy* 6, no. 2 (2008).
4. Philip E. Auerswald, "The Irrelevance of the Middle East", *American Interest* 2, no. 5 (1 May 2007): 22.
5. World Commission on Environment and Development, "Our Common Future, Report of the World Commission on Environment and Development", 1987. (Published as Annex to General Assembly document A/42/427, Development and International Co-operation: Environment, 2 August 1987.)
6. Donella H. Meadows et al., *Limits to Growth* (New York: New American Library, 1972).
7. Enzo R. Grilli and Maw Cheng Yang, "Primary Commodity Prices, Manufactured Goods Prices and the Terms of Trade of Developing Countries: What the Long Run Shows", *World Bank Economic Review*, January 1988.
8. Paul Cashin and C. John MacDermott, "The Long Run Behavior of Commodity Prices: Small Trends and Big Variability", *IMF Staff Papers*, 49, no. 2 (2002).

9. José Antonio Ocampo and María Ángela Parra, "The Terms of Trade for Commodities in the Twentieth Century", *Econ Working Papers*, 17 February 2004.

10. Ibid.

11. Matthew R. Simmons, *Twilight in the Desert: The Coming Saudi Oil Shock and the World Economy* (New Jersey: Wiley, 2005). For an early view questioning the idea of resource depletion, see Julian J. Simon, *The Ultimate Resource*, 2nd rev. ed. (New Jersey: Princeton University Press, 1998).

12. See IPCC, "Fourth Assessment Report", 2007. A "policymakers summary" of AR4 can be accessed at <http://www.ipcc.ch/pdf/assessment-report/ar4/wg2/ar4-wg2-spm.pdf>.

13. Nicholas Stern, *Stern Review on the Economics of Climate Change* (2006), p. xv <http://webarchive.nationalarchives.gov.uk/20130607054550/http://archive.excellencegateway.org.uk/141443>.

14. For references to a range of climate change models, see William D. Nordhaus, "A Review on the Stern Review of the Economics of Climate Change", *Journal of Economic Literature* 45 (September 2007): 686–702 <http://www.econ.yale.edu/~nordhaus/homepage/documents/Nordhaus_stern_jel.pdf>.

15. Matt Ridley, *The Rational Optimist: How Prosperity Evolves* (London: HarperCollins, 2010).

16. William D. Nordhaus, "A Review on the Stern Review of the Economics of Climate Change", *Journal of Economic Literature* 45 (September 2007): 695–96.

17. See K.J. Arrow et al., "Intertemporal Equity, Discounting, and Economic Efficiency", in *Climate Change 1995 — Economic and Social Dimensions of Climate Change* (Contributions of Working Group III to the Second Assessment Report of the IPCC, 1995).

18. See Matt Ridley, *The Rational Optimist: How Prosperity Evolves* (London: HarperCollins, 2010) pp. 331–32.

19. Ted Gayer and W. Kip Viscusi, "Overriding Consumer Preferences with Energy Regulations", Mercatus Center, George Mason University, Working Paper no. 12–21, 10 July 2012, p. 37.

20. According to the Wikipedia entry for Solyndra, "[it] was a manufacturer of cylindrical panels of copper indium gallium selenide (CIGS) thin-film solar cells based in Fremont, California. Although the company was once touted for its unusual technology, plummeting silicon prices led to the company's being unable to compete with conventional solar panels made of crystalline silicon. On 1 September 2011, the company ceased all business activity, filed for Chapter 11 bankruptcy, and laid off all employees, costing taxpayers over [US]$500 million". Accessed at http://en.wikipedia.org/wiki/Solyndra.

21. As quoted in Salil Tripathi, "Singapore's Savings Rate Excessive, Wages Could Be Raised", *Business Times*, 17 July 1992; cited in Tilak Doshi, "Chaining the

Leviathan: A Public Choice Interpretation of Singapore's Elected Presidency", in *Managing Political Change in Singapore: The Elected Presidency*, edited by Kevin Y.L. Tan and Lam Peng Er (London: Routledge, 1997).

22. International Monetary Fund, "Article IV Consultations 2004", cited in Henri Ghesquiere, *Singapore's Success: Engineering Economic Growth* (Singapore: Thomson Learning, 2007).

Index

ABOUT THE AUTHOR

Tilak K. Doshi is Senior Research Fellow at the King Abdullah Petroleum Studies and Research Center (KAPSARC) in Riyadh, Saudi Arabia. Prior to his current position, Dr Doshi was Chief Economist at the Energy Studies Institute of the National University of Singapore. Dr Doshi is an industry expert with over twenty-five years of international experience in leading oil and gas companies. Previously, he had been Executive Director of Energy at the Dubai Multi Commodities Centre (DMCC). Prior to joining DMCC, he worked as a Specialist Consultant for Saudi Aramco in its crude marketing and corporate planning departments. He has also held senior positions as Director of Industry Analysis at the Atlantic Richfield Company (ARCO) in Los Angeles, as Chief Asia Economist at Unocal Corporation (Los Angeles and Singapore) and as Head of Research, Louis Dreyfus Energy Asia (Singapore). He received his PhD in Economics (East-West Center/University of Hawai'i) on a scholarship provided by the U.S. government. He was a recipient of the Robert S. McNamara Research Fellowship 1984 awarded by the World Bank, Washington, DC. He is the author of *Houston of Asia: The Singapore Petroleum Industry*, a monograph published jointly by the East-West Centre (Honolulu) and the Institute of Southeast Asian Studies (1989).